e Over!
Seiyu Academy

12

Vol.12
Story & Art by
Maki Minami

Voice Over! Seiyu Academy

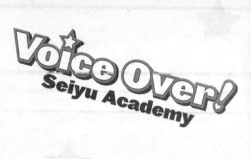

Vol.12

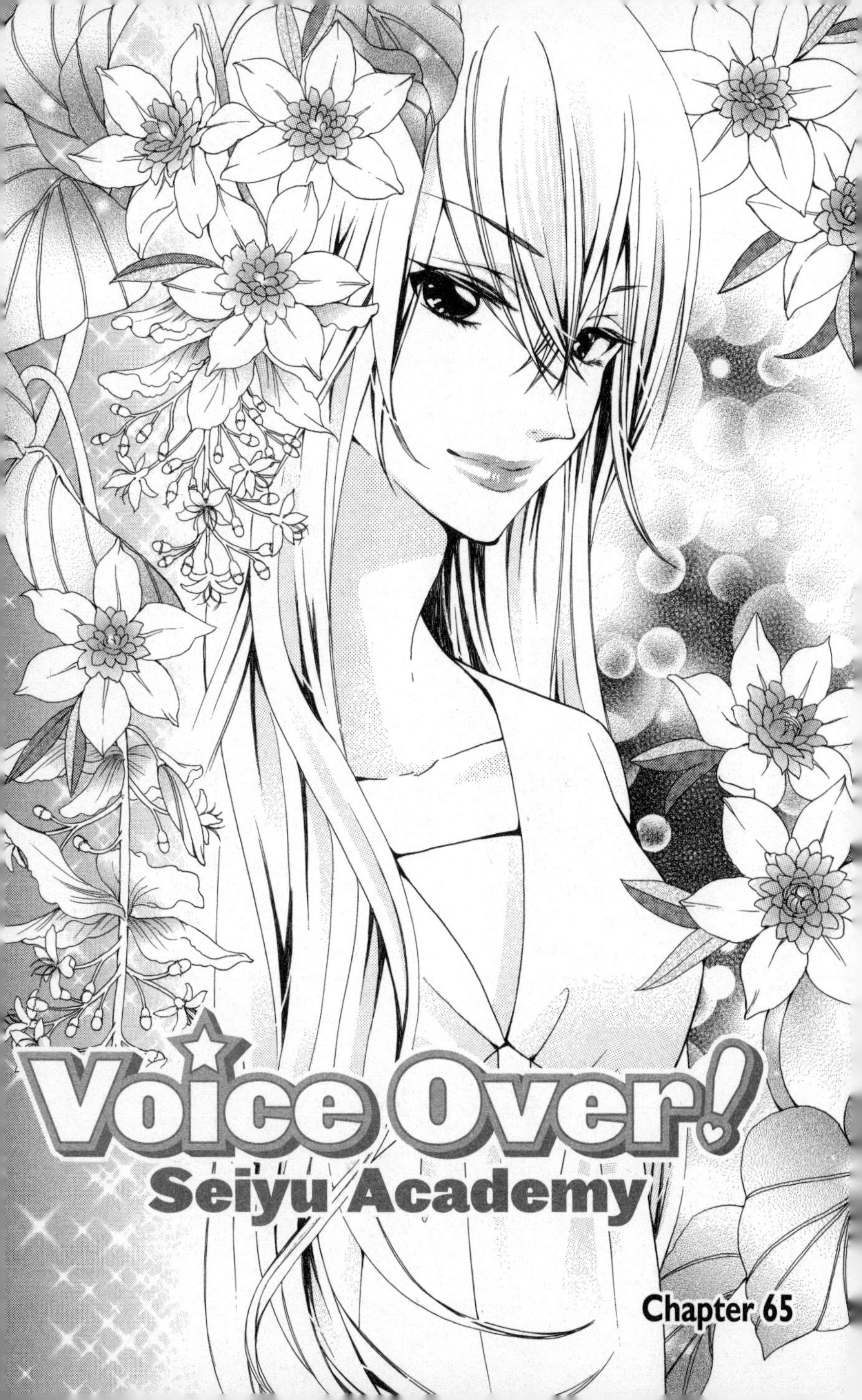
Voice Over!
Seiyu Academy
Chapter 65

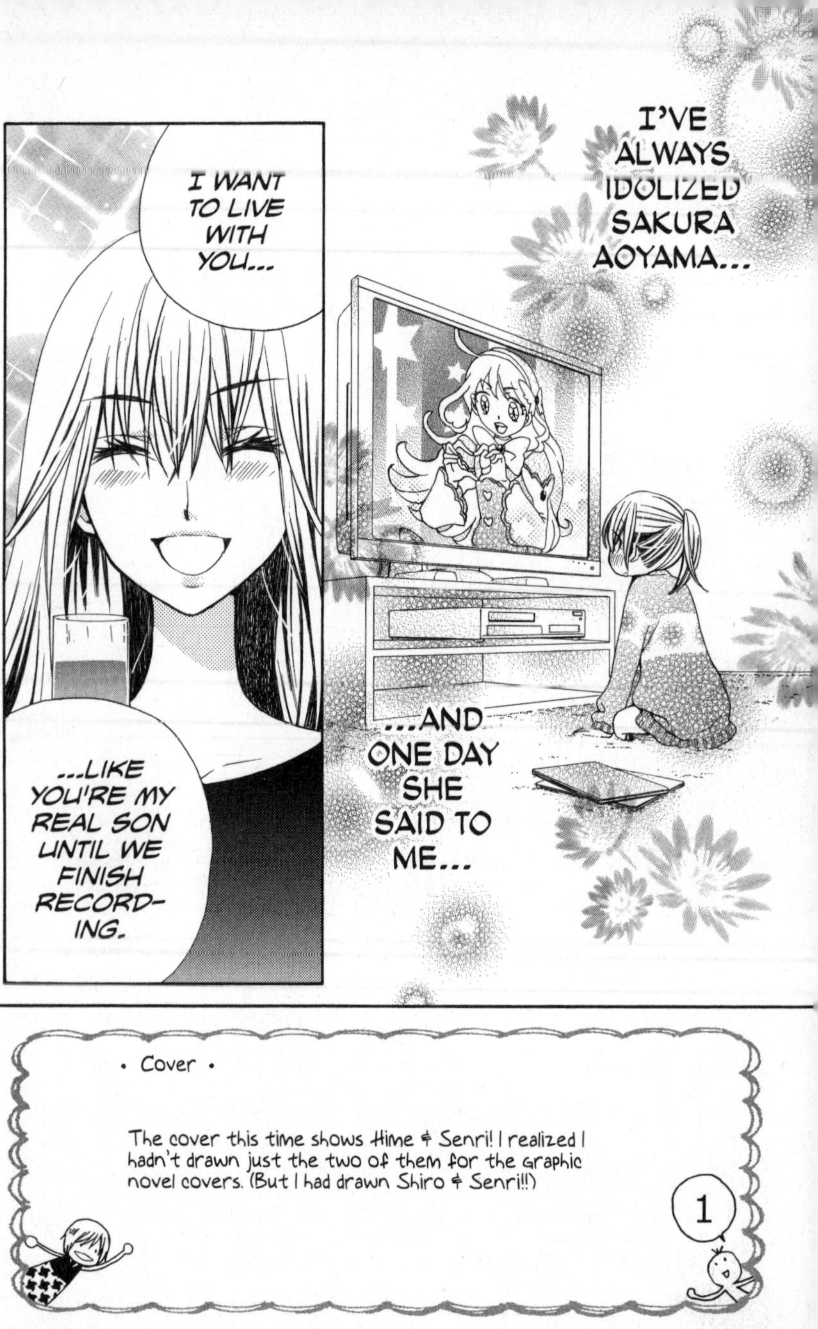
I'VE ALWAYS IDOLIZED SAKURA AOYAMA...
...AND ONE DAY SHE SAID TO ME...
I WANT TO LIVE WITH YOU...
...LIKE YOU'RE MY REAL SON UNTIL WE FINISH RECORDING.

• Cover •

The cover this time shows Hime & Senri! I realized I hadn't drawn just the two of them for the graphic novel covers. (But I had drawn Shiro & Senri!!)

1

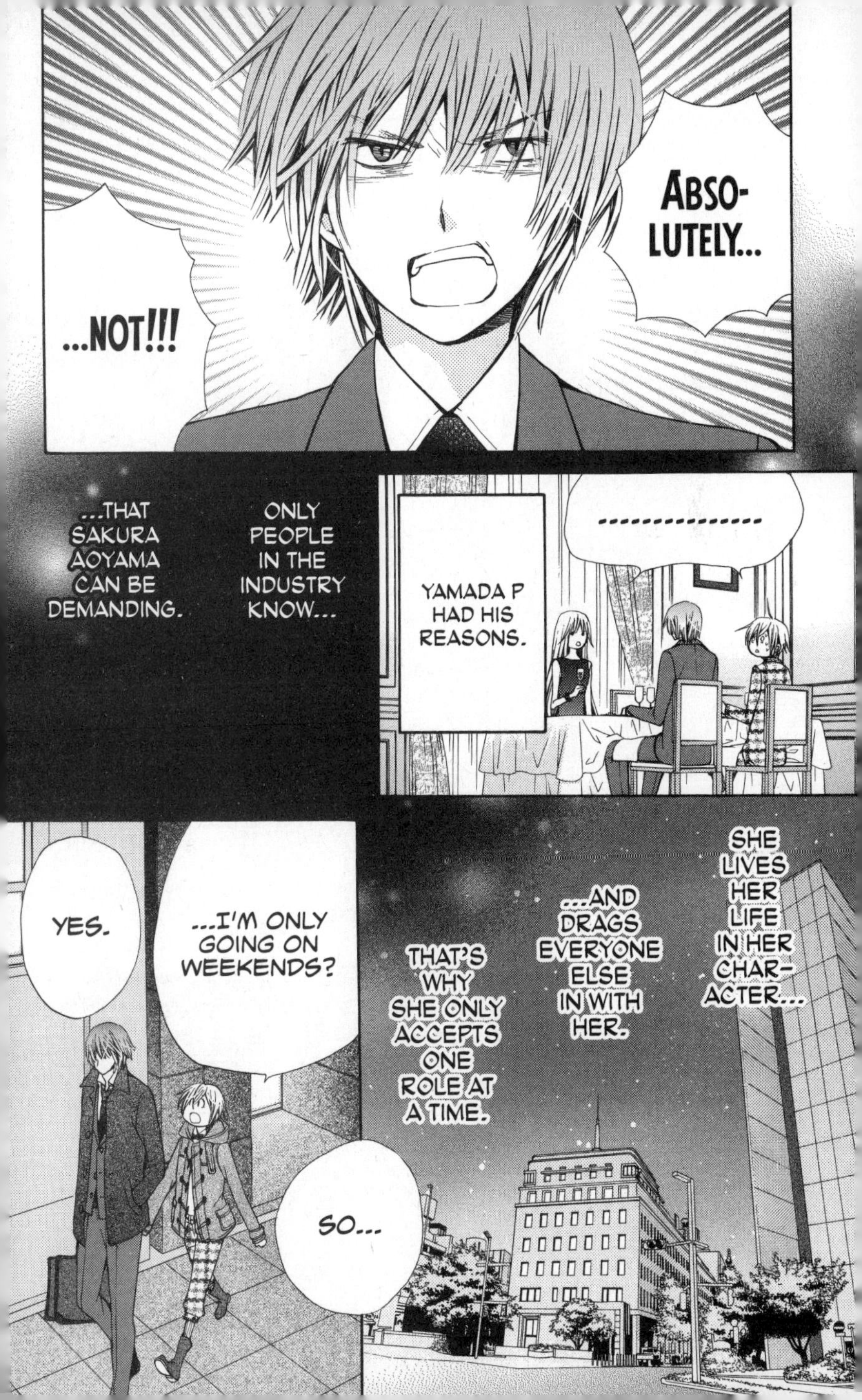
ABSO-LUTELY...
...NOT!!!
....
YAMADA P HAD HIS REASONS.
ONLY PEOPLE IN THE INDUSTRY KNOW...
...THAT SAKURA AOYAMA CAN BE DEMANDING.
SHE LIVES HER LIFE IN HER CHAR-ACTER...
...AND DRAGS EVERYONE ELSE IN WITH HER.
THAT'S WHY SHE ONLY ACCEPTS ONE ROLE AT A TIME.
SO...
...I'M ONLY GOING ON WEEKENDS?
YES.

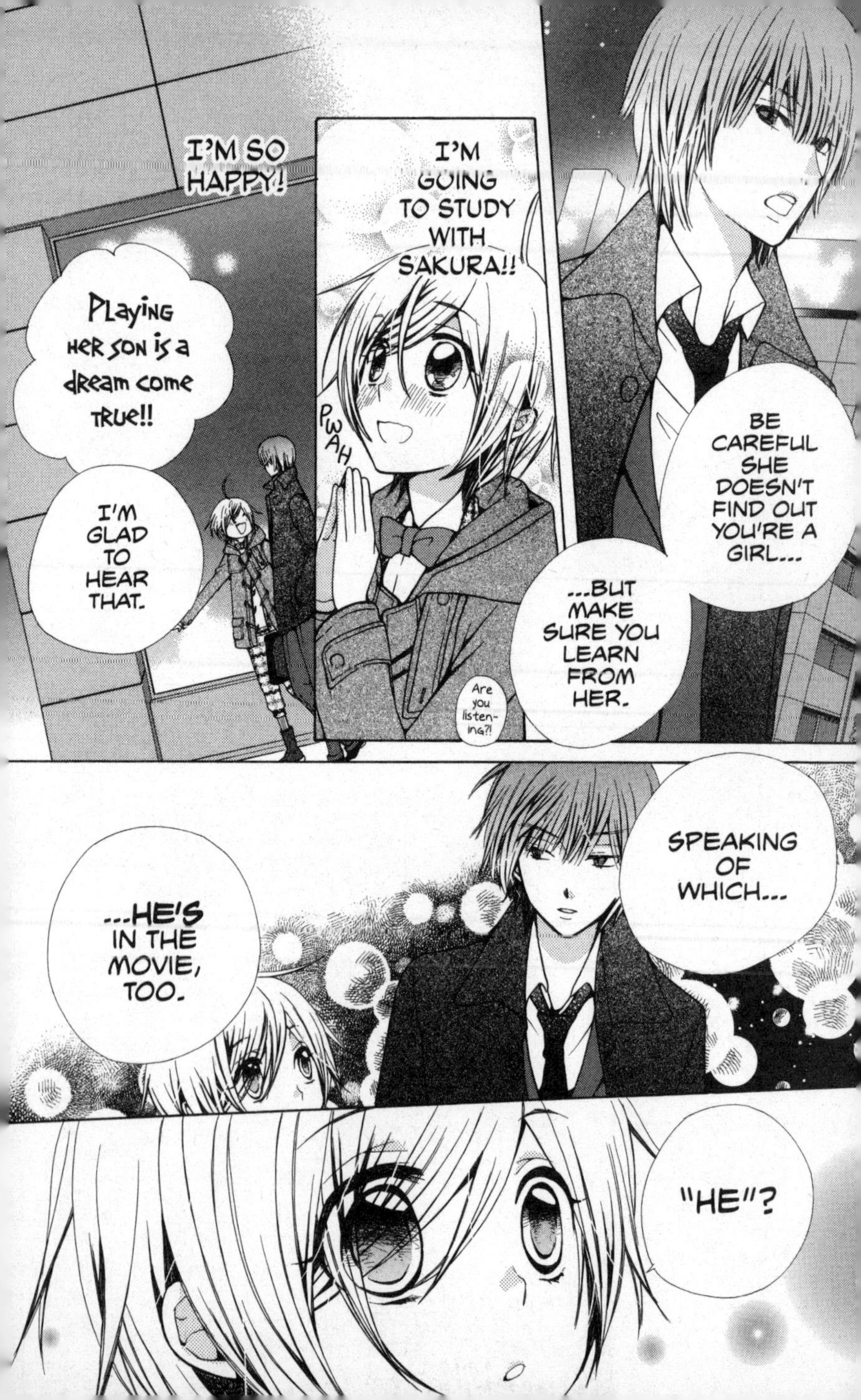
BE CAREFUL SHE DOESN'T FIND OUT YOU'RE A GIRL...
...BUT MAKE SURE YOU LEARN FROM HER.
Are you listening?!
I'M GOING TO STUDY WITH SAKURA!!
PWAH
I'M SO HAPPY!
Playing her son is a dream come true!!
I'M GLAD TO HEAR THAT.
SPEAKING OF WHICH...
...HE'S IN THE MOVIE, TOO.
"HE"?

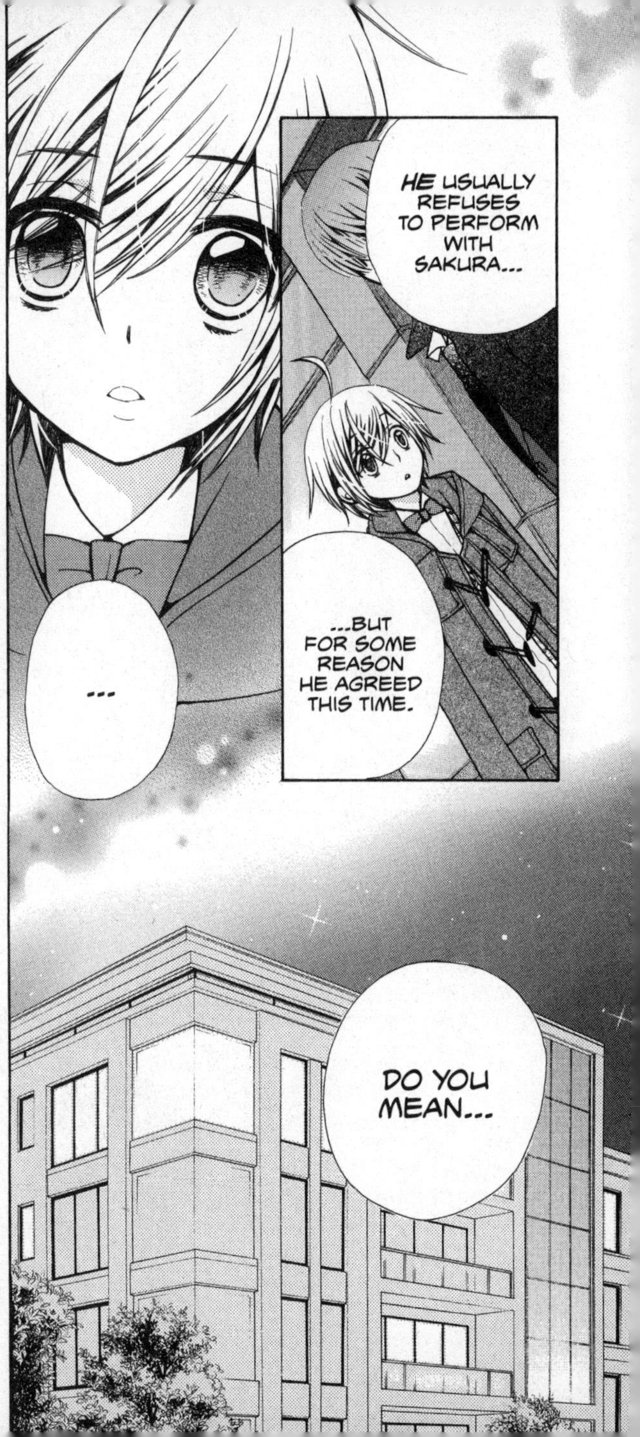
HE USUALLY REFUSES TO PERFORM WITH SAKURA...
...BUT FOR SOME REASON HE AGREED THIS TIME.
...
DO YOU MEAN...

• Greetings •

Nice to meet you & hello!!

I'm Maki Minami! Thanks for reading *Voice Over!: Seiyu Academy!* Volume 12!!

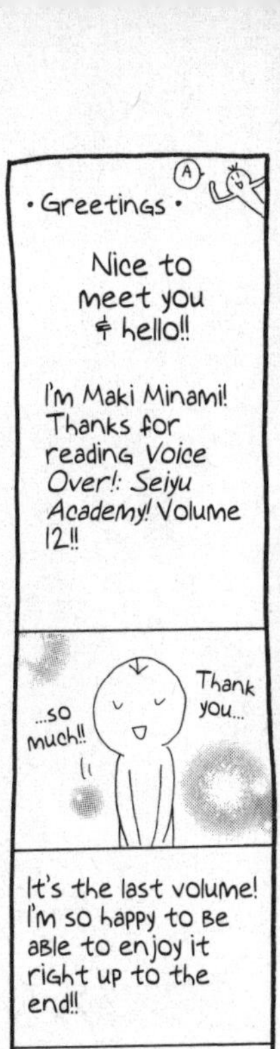
Thank you...
...so much!!

It's the last volume! I'm so happy to be able to enjoy it right up to the end!!

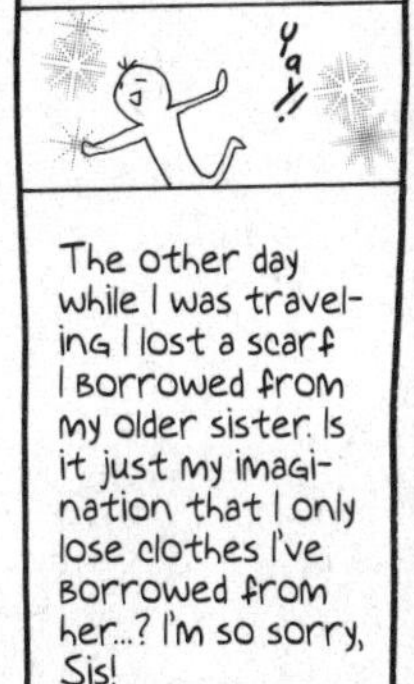
Yay!!

The other day while I was traveling I lost a scarf I borrowed from my older sister. Is it just my imagination that I only lose clothes I've borrowed from her...? I'm so sorry, Sis!

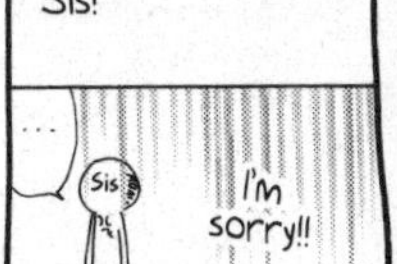
...
Sis
I'm sorry!!

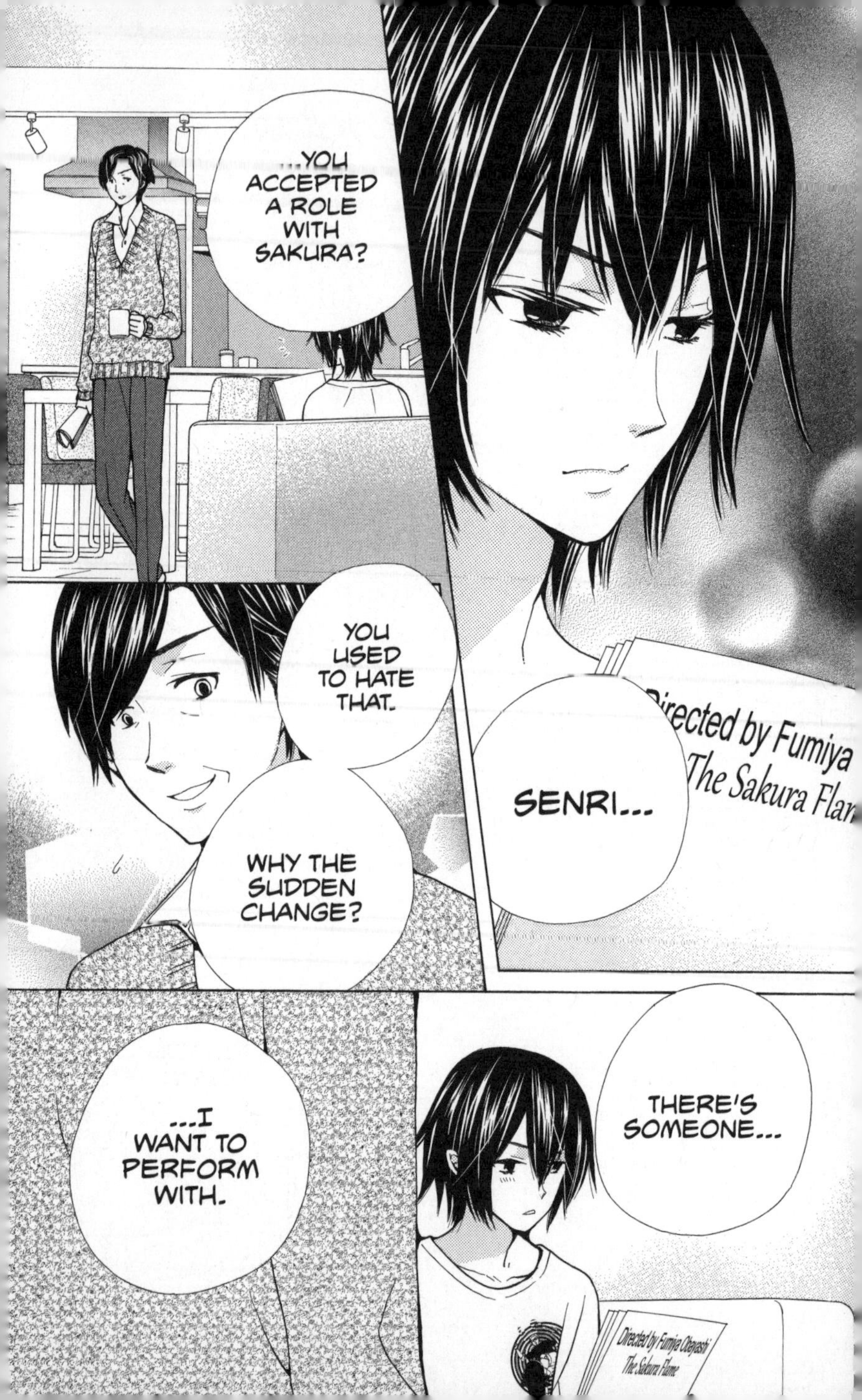
SENRI...
...YOU ACCEPTED A ROLE WITH SAKURA?
YOU USED TO HATE THAT.
WHY THE SUDDEN CHANGE?
THERE'S SOMEONE...
...I WANT TO PERFORM WITH.

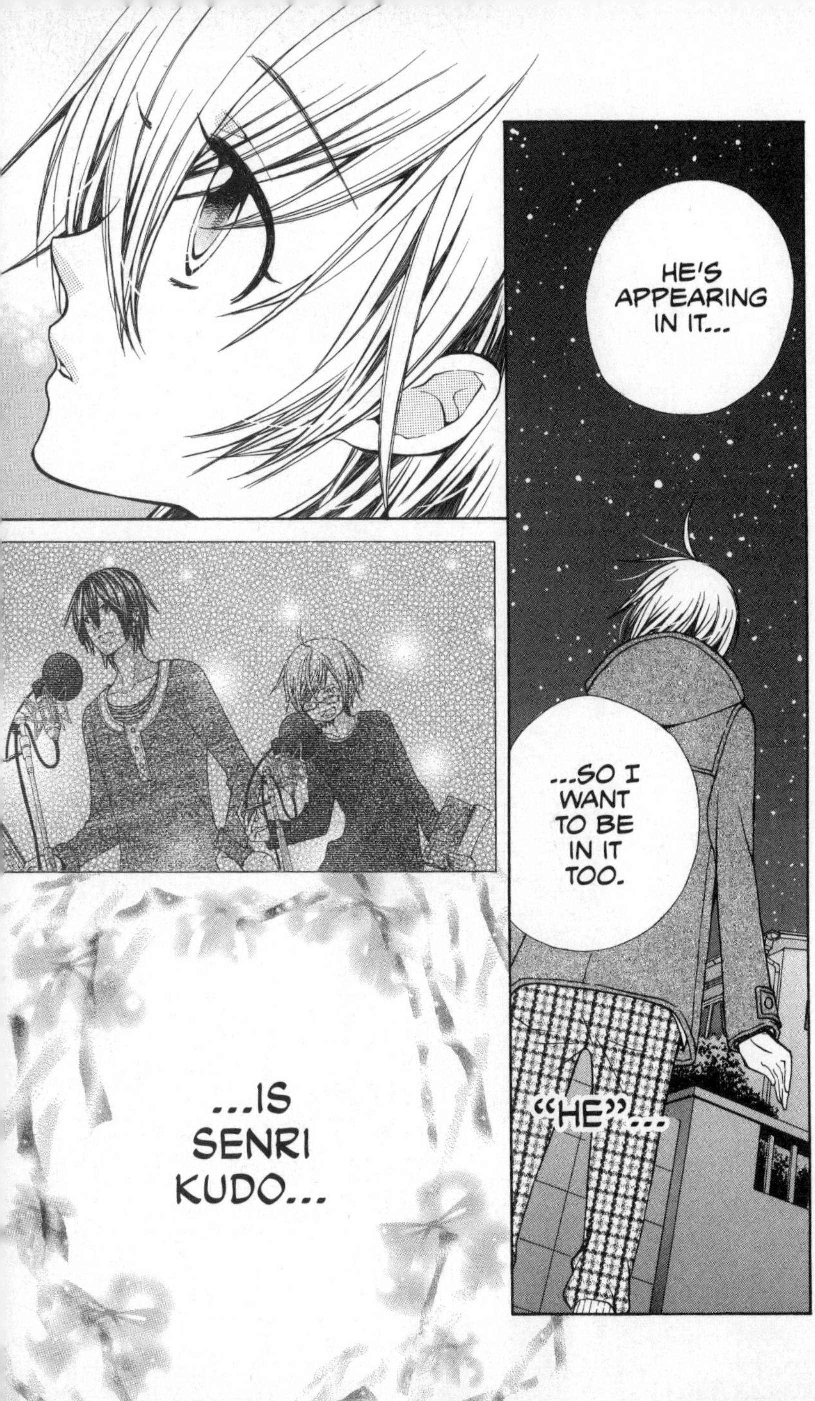
HE'S APPEARING IN IT...
...SO I WANT TO BE IN IT TOO.
"HE"...
...IS SENRI KUDO...

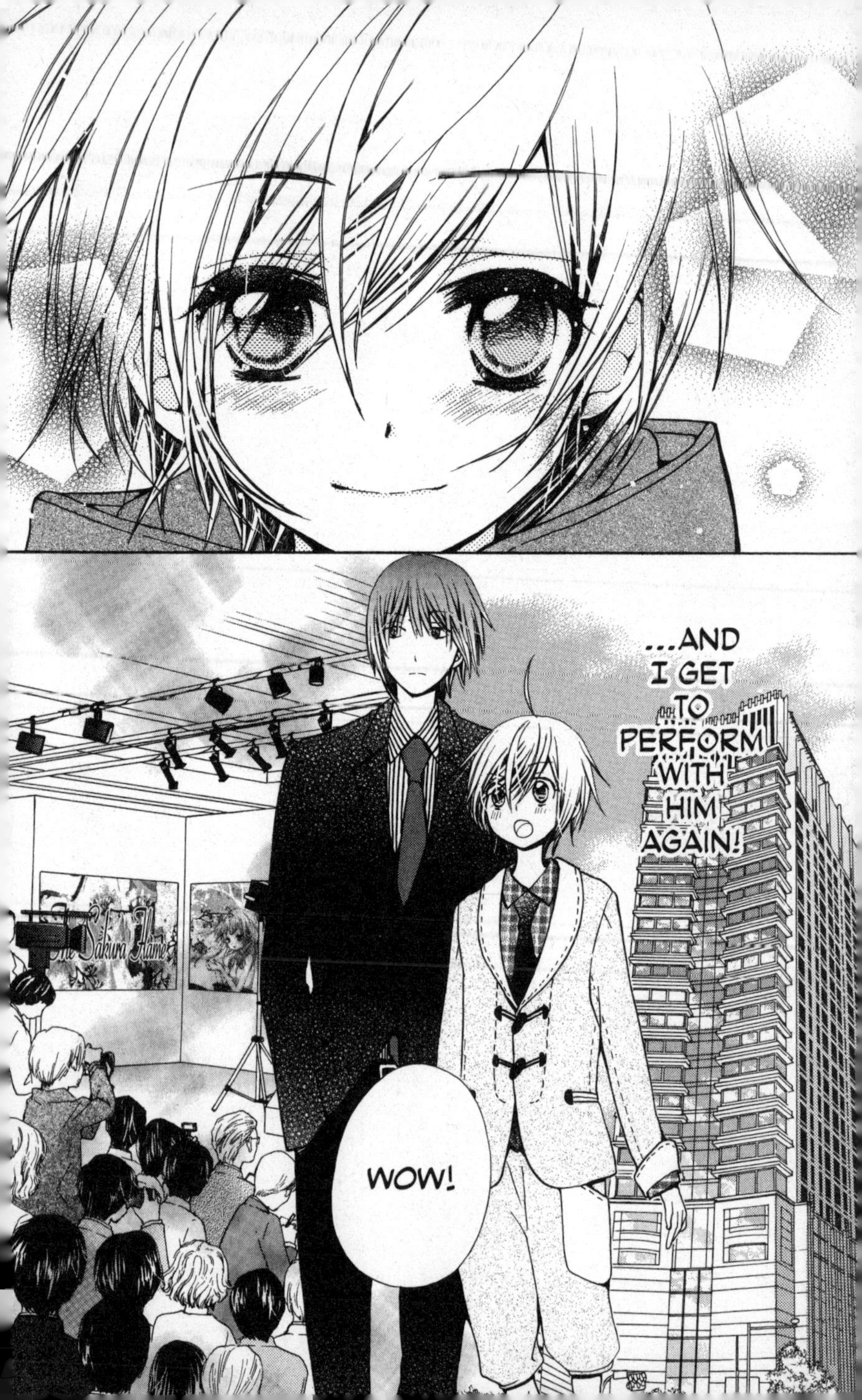
...AND I GET TO PERFORM WITH HIM AGAIN!
The Sakura Flame
WOW!

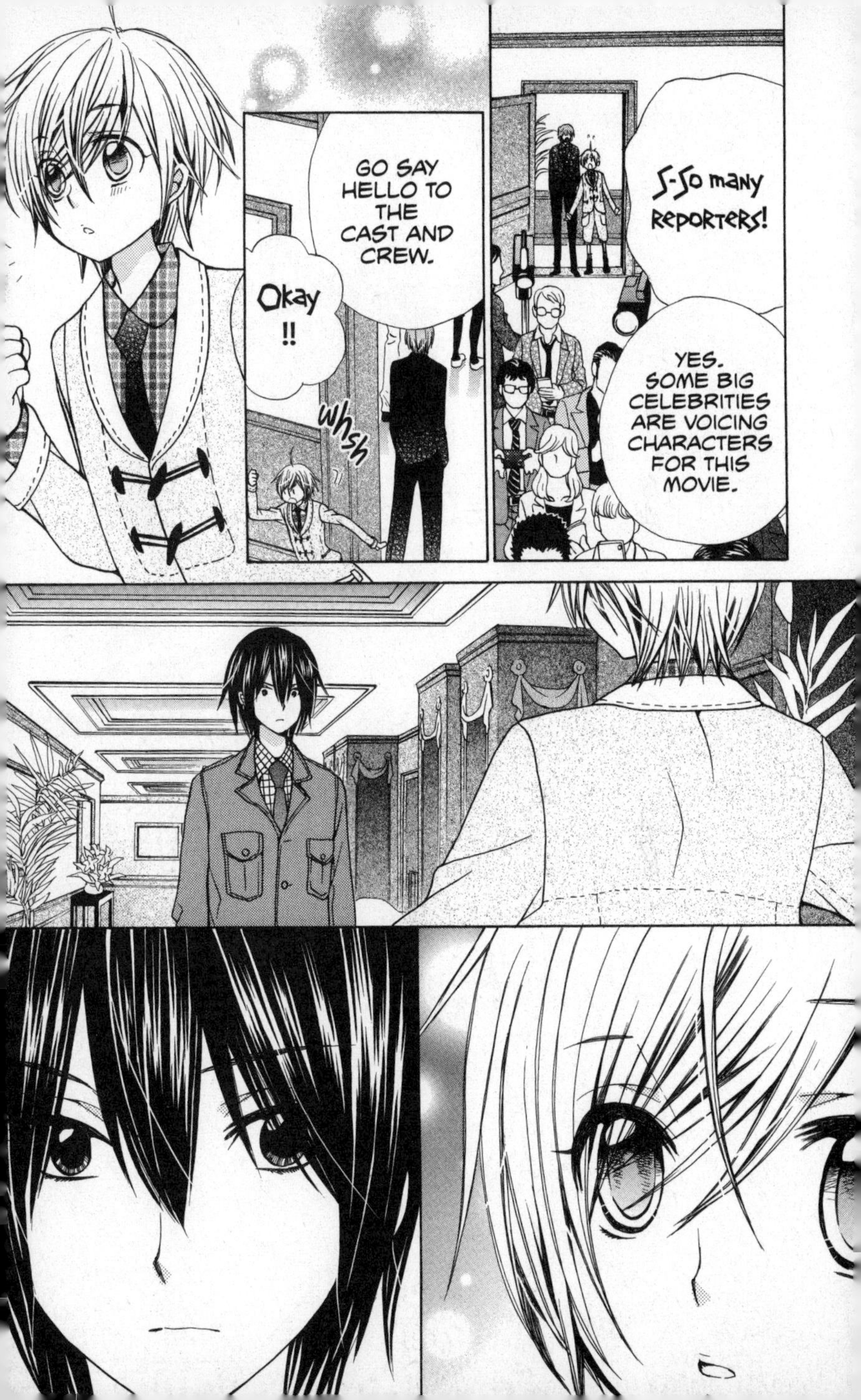
S-So many reporters!
YES. SOME BIG CELEBRITIES ARE VOICING CHARACTERS FOR THIS MOVIE.
GO SAY HELLO TO THE CAST AND CREW.
Okay !!
whsh

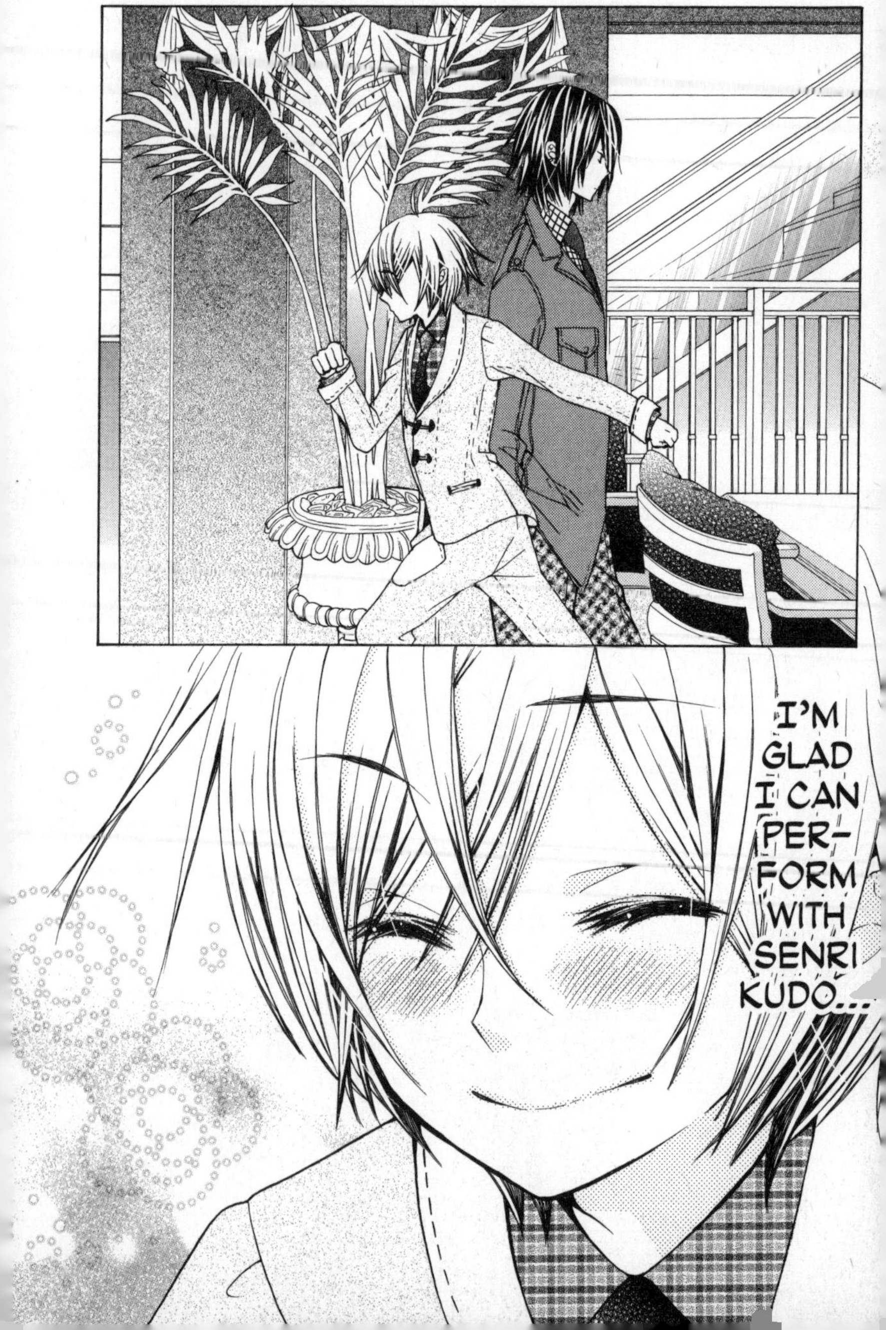
I'M GLAD I CAN PER-FORM WITH SENRI KUDO...

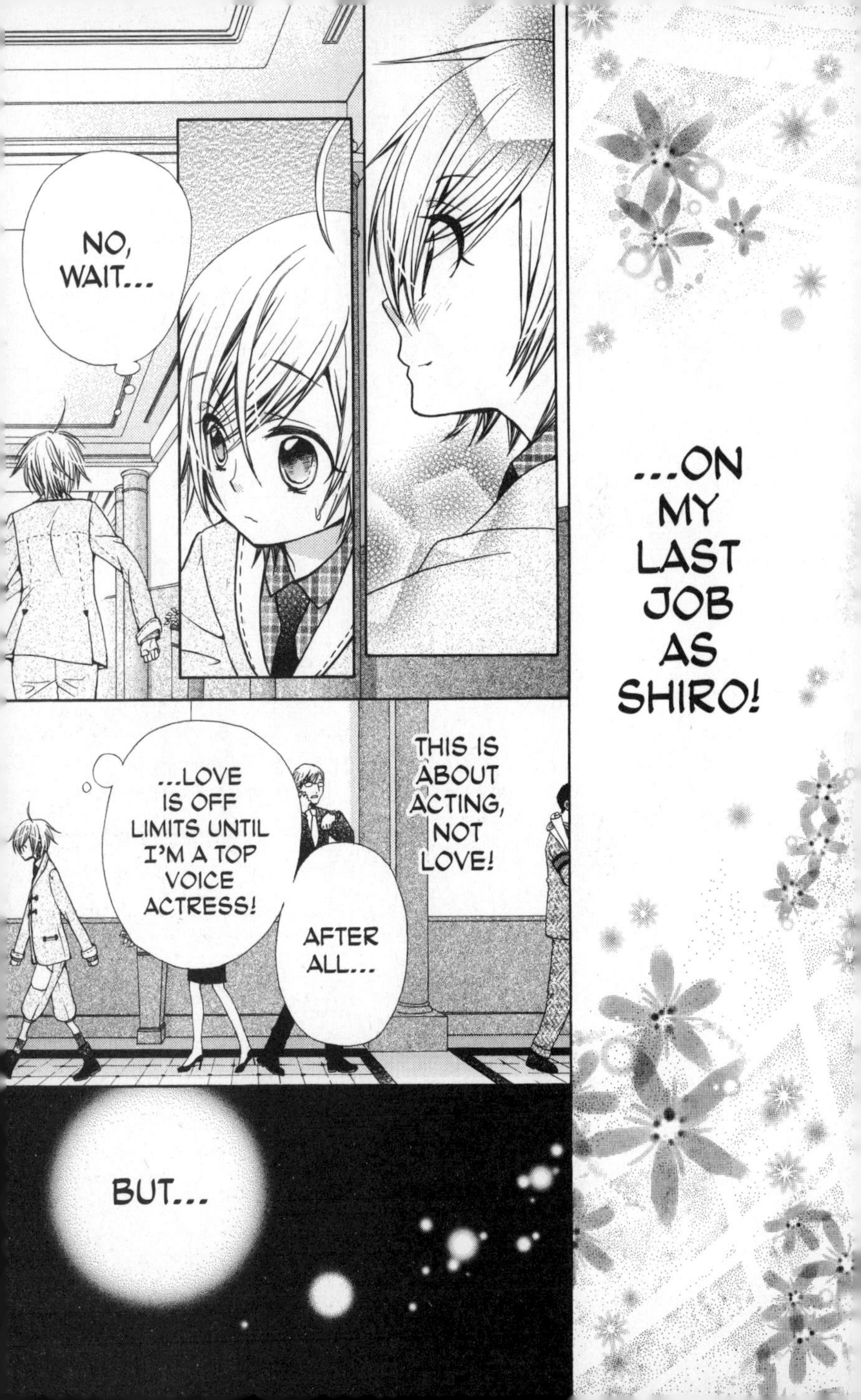
...ON MY LAST JOB AS SHIRO!
NO, WAIT...
THIS IS ABOUT ACTING, NOT LOVE!
...LOVE IS OFF LIMITS UNTIL I'M A TOP VOICE ACTRESS!
AFTER ALL...
BUT...

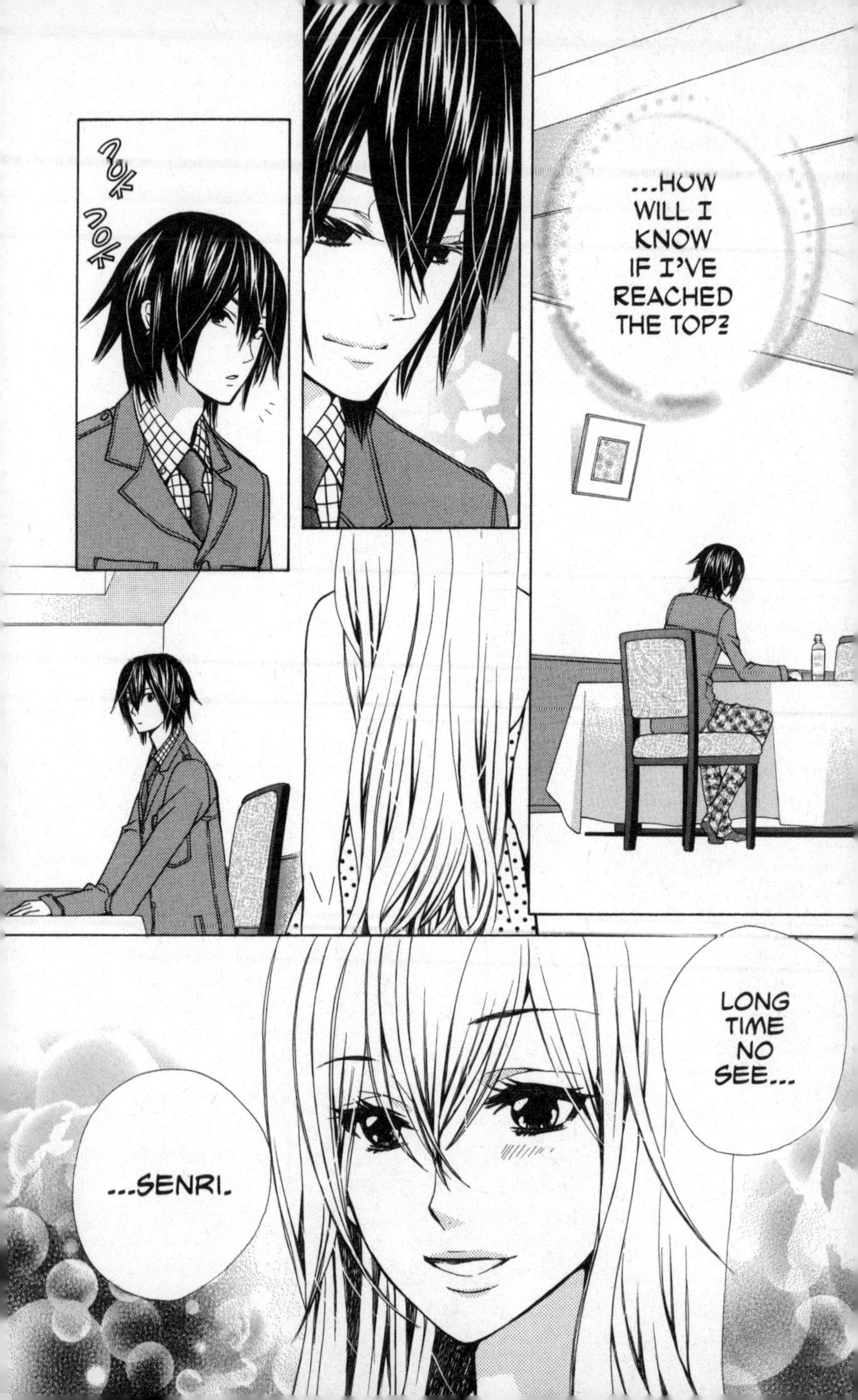

...HOW WILL I KNOW IF I'VE REACHED THE TOP?
NOD NOD
LONG TIME NO SEE...
...SENRI.

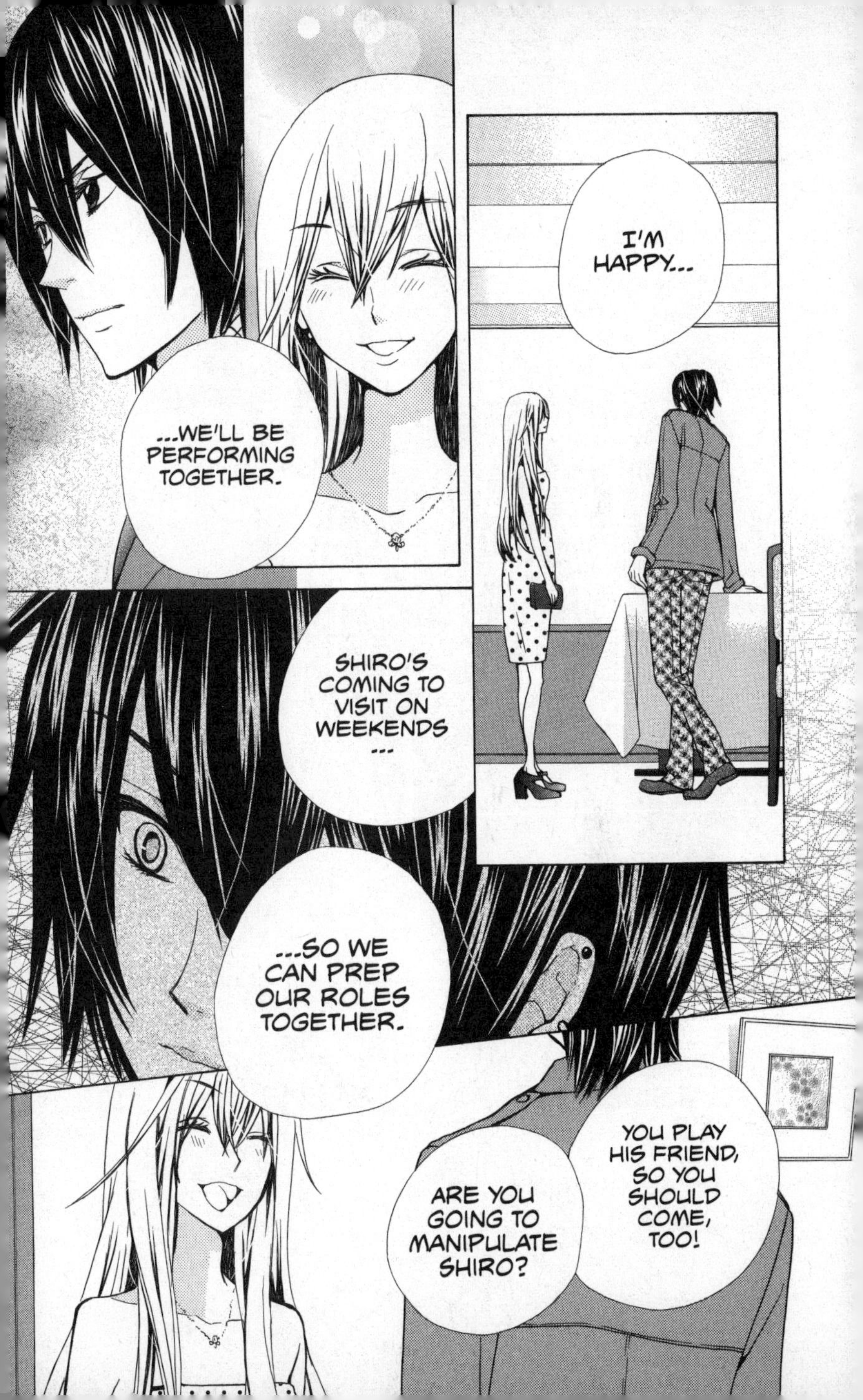
I'M HAPPY...
...WE'LL BE PERFORMING TOGETHER.
SHIRO'S COMING TO VISIT ON WEEKENDS...
...SO WE CAN PREP OUR ROLES TOGETHER.
YOU PLAY HIS FRIEND, SO YOU SHOULD COME, TOO!
ARE YOU GOING TO MANIPULATE SHIRO?

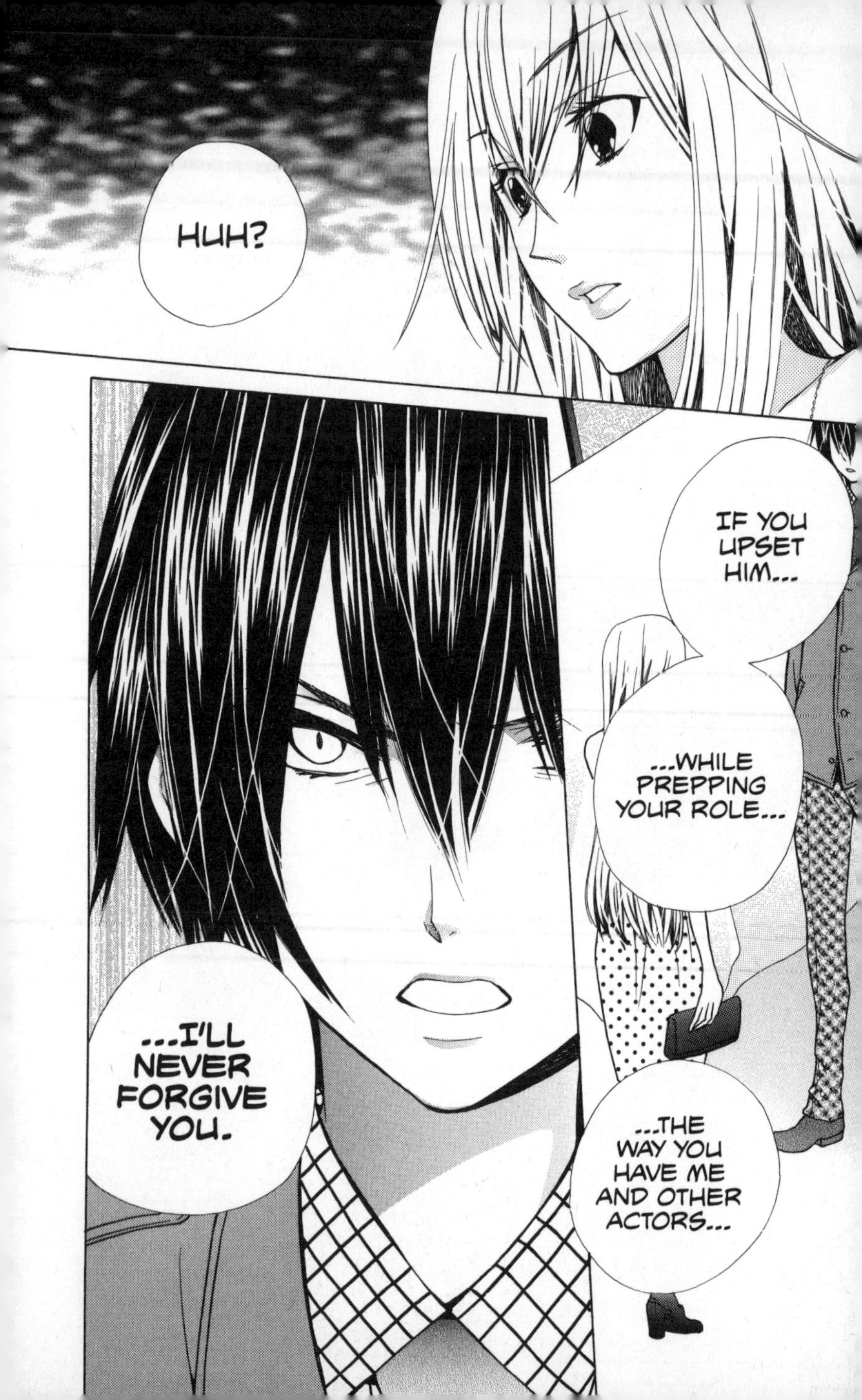
HUH?
IF YOU UPSET HIM...
...WHILE PREPPING YOUR ROLE...
...THE WAY YOU HAVE ME AND OTHER ACTORS...
...I'LL NEVER FORGIVE YOU.

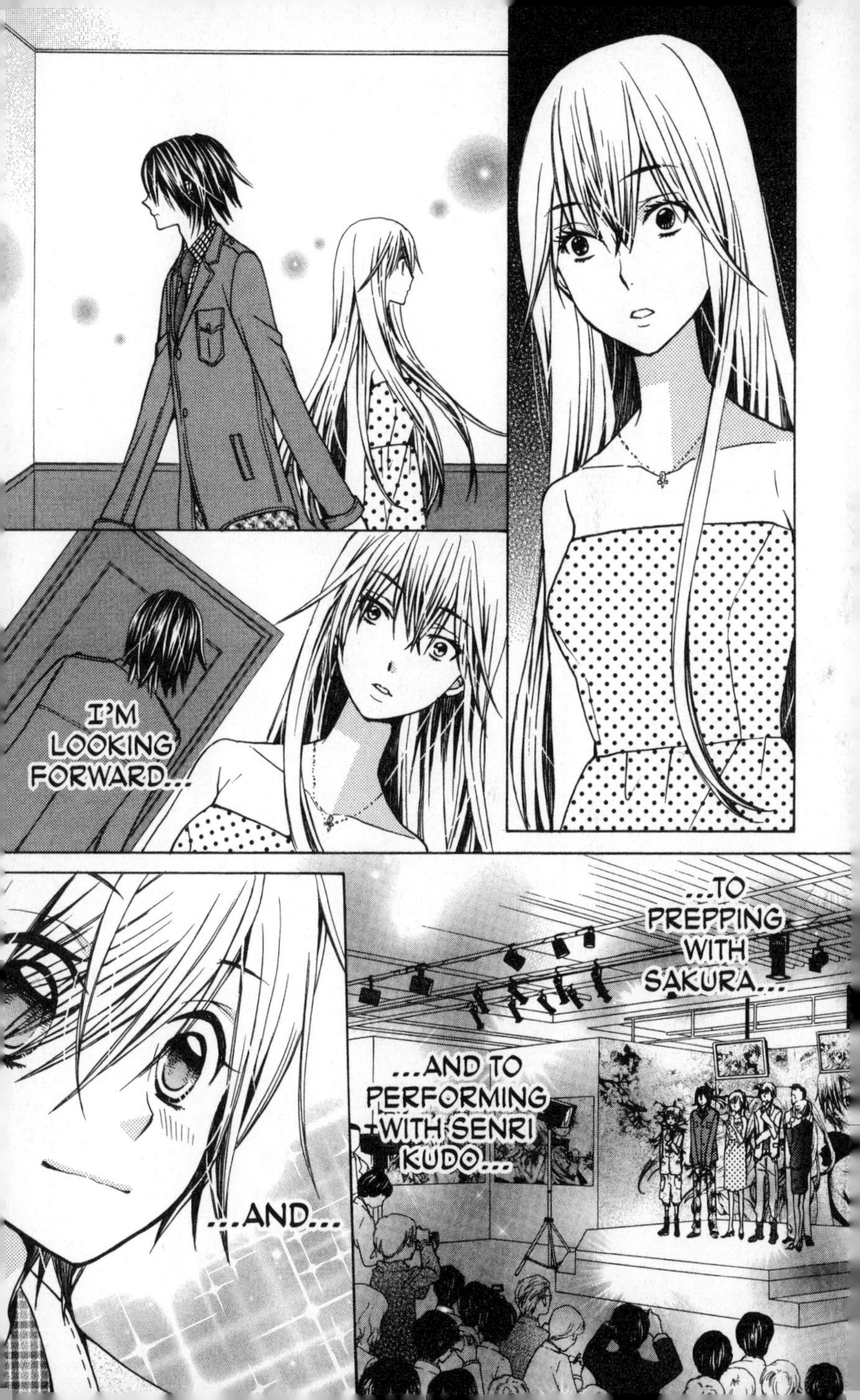
I'M LOOKING FORWARD...
...TO PREPPING WITH SAKURA...
...AND TO PERFORMING WITH SENRI KUDO...
...AND...

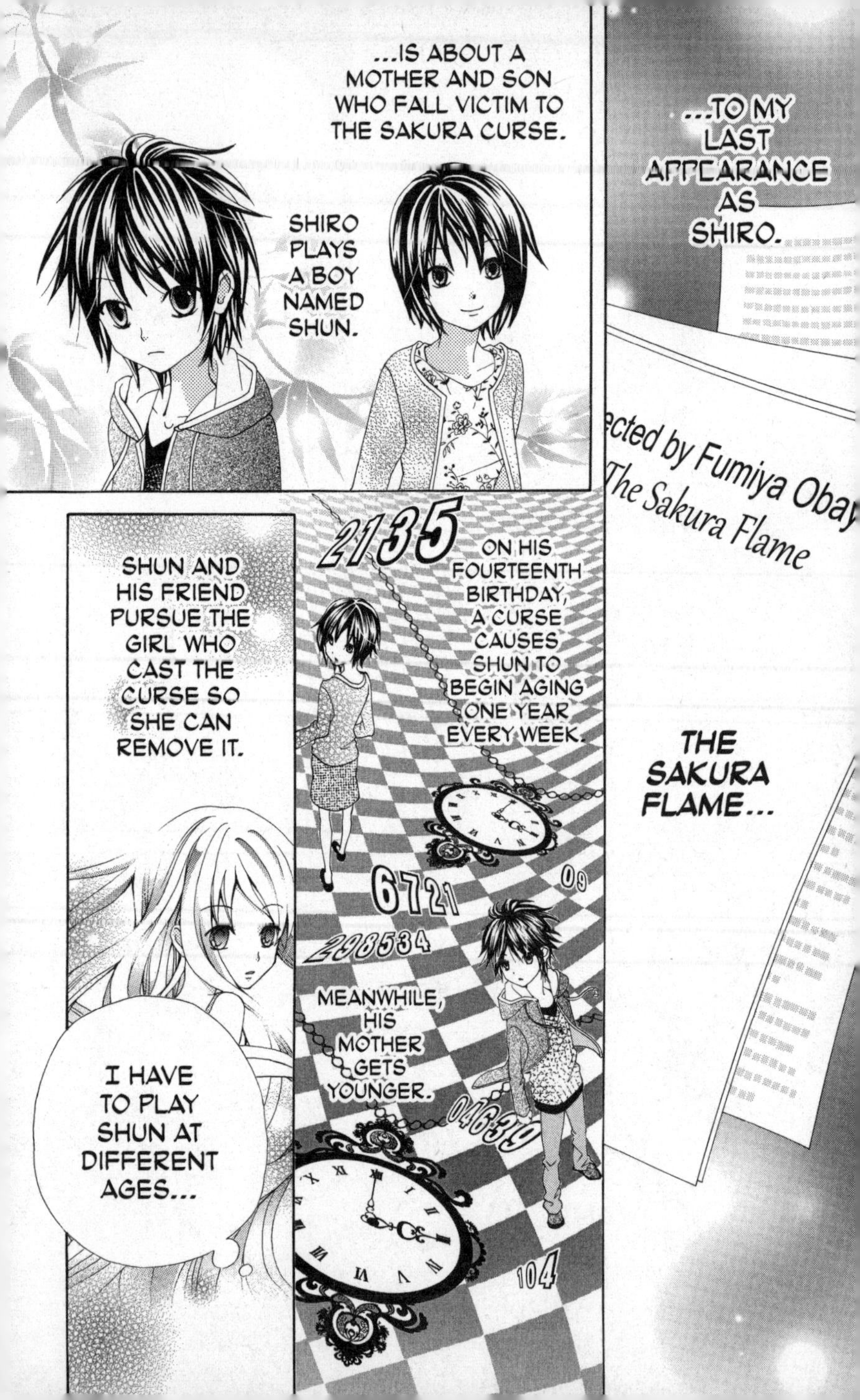
...TO MY LAST APPEARANCE AS SHIRO.
ected by Fumiya Obay
The Sakura Flame
THE SAKURA FLAME...
...IS ABOUT A MOTHER AND SON WHO FALL VICTIM TO THE SAKURA CURSE.
SHIRO PLAYS A BOY NAMED SHUN.
ON HIS FOURTEENTH BIRTHDAY, A CURSE CAUSES SHUN TO BEGIN AGING ONE YEAR EVERY WEEK.
MEANWHILE, HIS MOTHER GETS YOUNGER.
SHUN AND HIS FRIEND PURSUE THE GIRL WHO CAST THE CURSE SO SHE CAN REMOVE IT.
I HAVE TO PLAY SHUN AT DIFFERENT AGES...

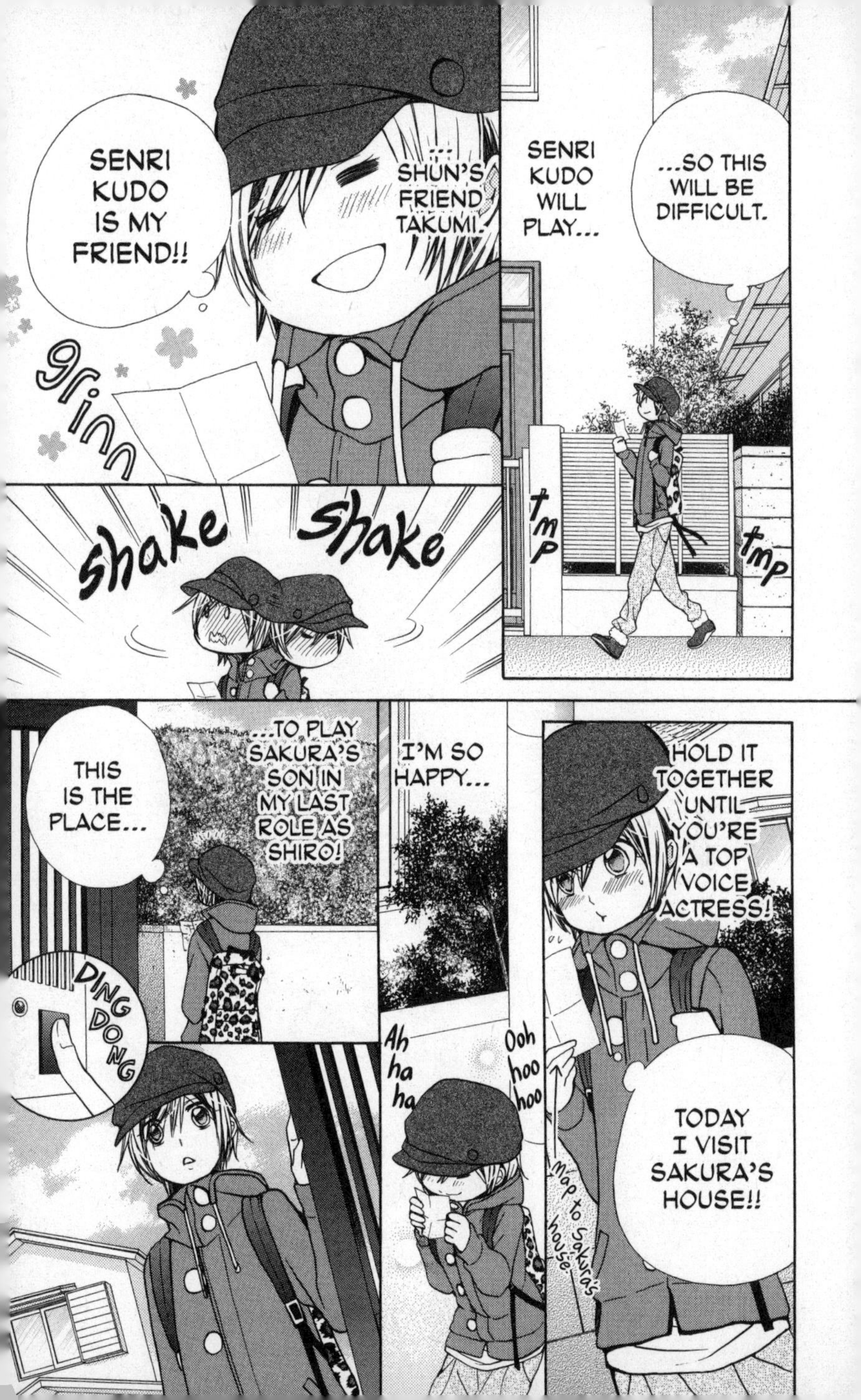
...SO THIS WILL BE DIFFICULT.
SENRI KUDO WILL PLAY...
tmp
tmp
...SHUN'S FRIEND TAKUMI...
SENRI KUDO IS MY FRIEND!!
grinn
shake
shake
HOLD IT TOGETHER UNTIL YOU'RE A TOP VOICE ACTRESS!
Map to Sakura's house
TODAY I VISIT SAKURA'S HOUSE!!
I'M SO HAPPY...
...TO PLAY SAKURA'S SON IN MY LAST ROLE AS SHIRO!
THIS IS THE PLACE...
DING DONG
Ooh hoo hoo
Ah ha ha

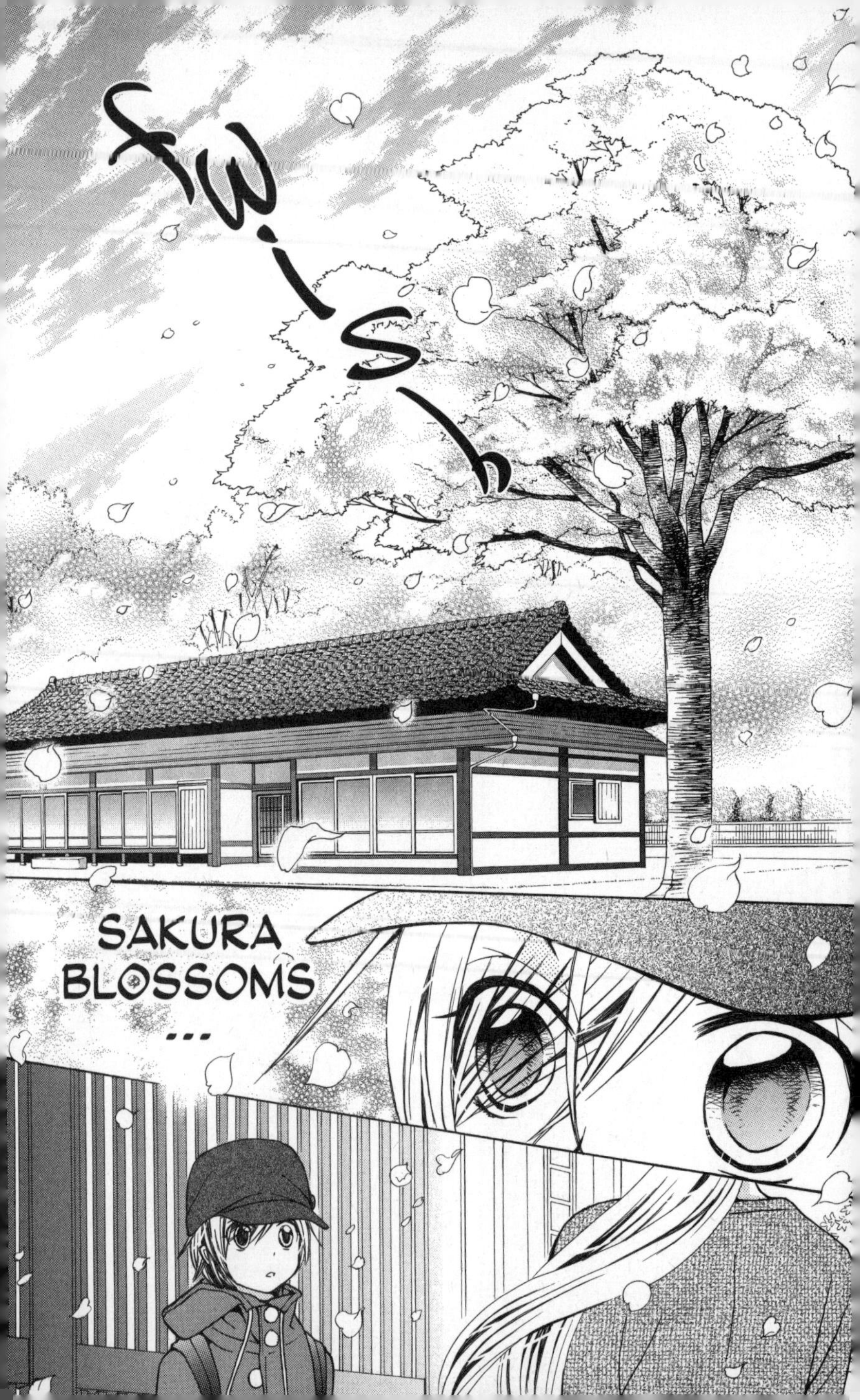
FWISH
SAKURA BLOSSOMS...

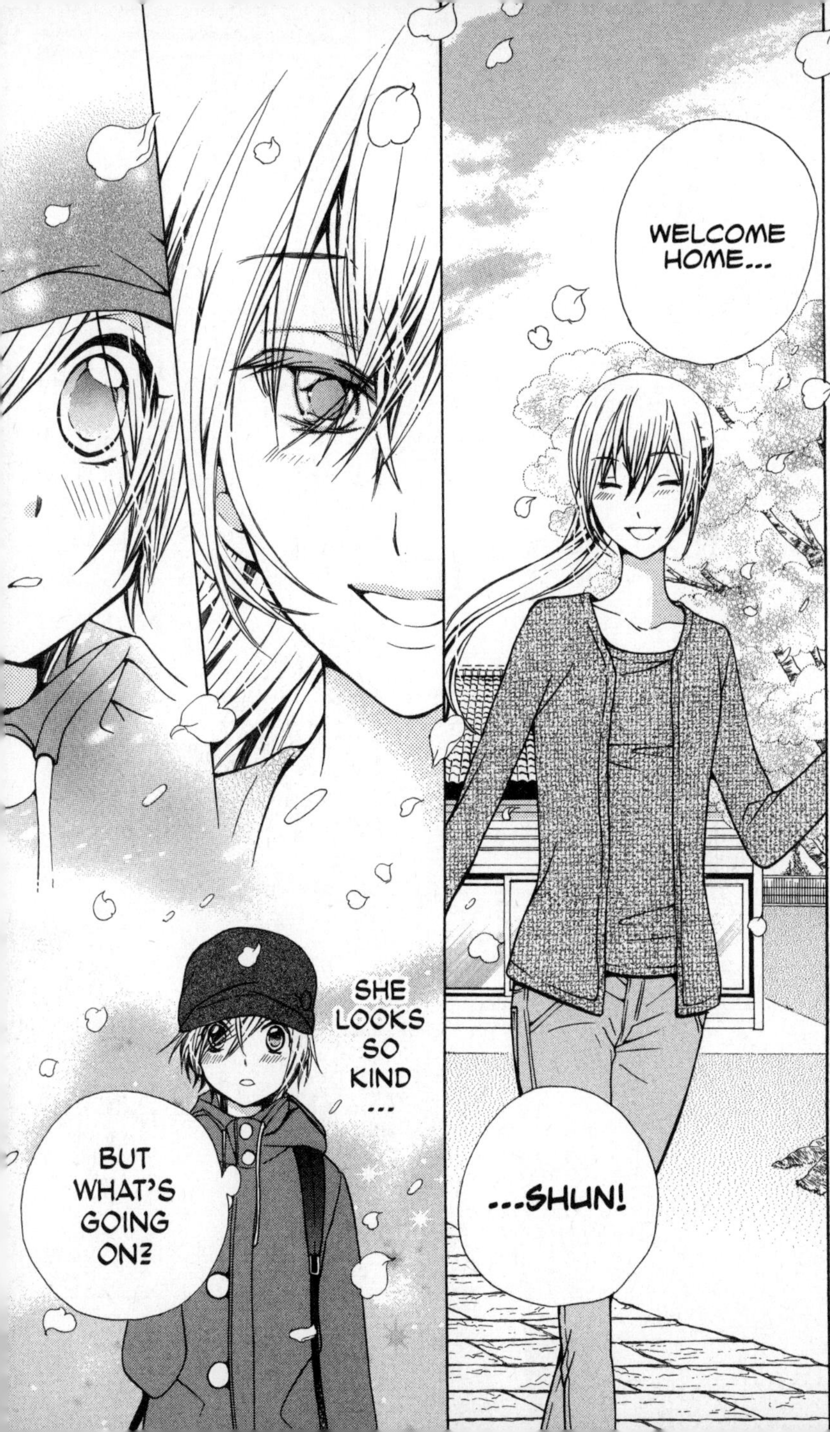
WELCOME HOME...
...SHUN!
SHE LOOKS SO KIND ...
BUT WHAT'S GOING ON?

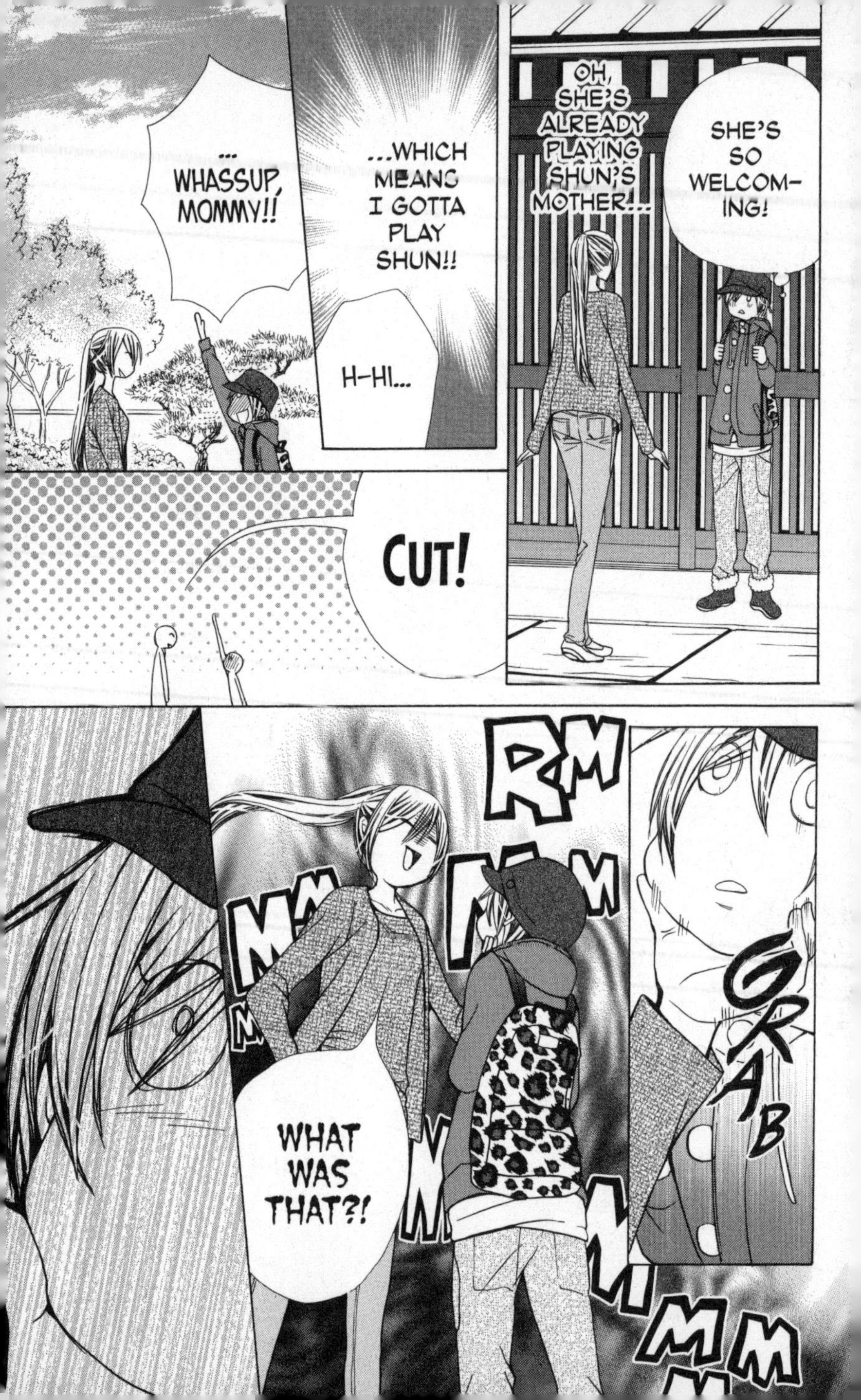
SHE'S SO WELCOM-ING!
OH, SHE'S ALREADY PLAYING SHUN'S MOTHER!...
...WHICH MEANS I GOTTA PLAY SHUN!!
H-HI...
...WHASSUP, MOMMY!!
CUT!
GRAB
RMMMM
WHAT WAS THAT?!

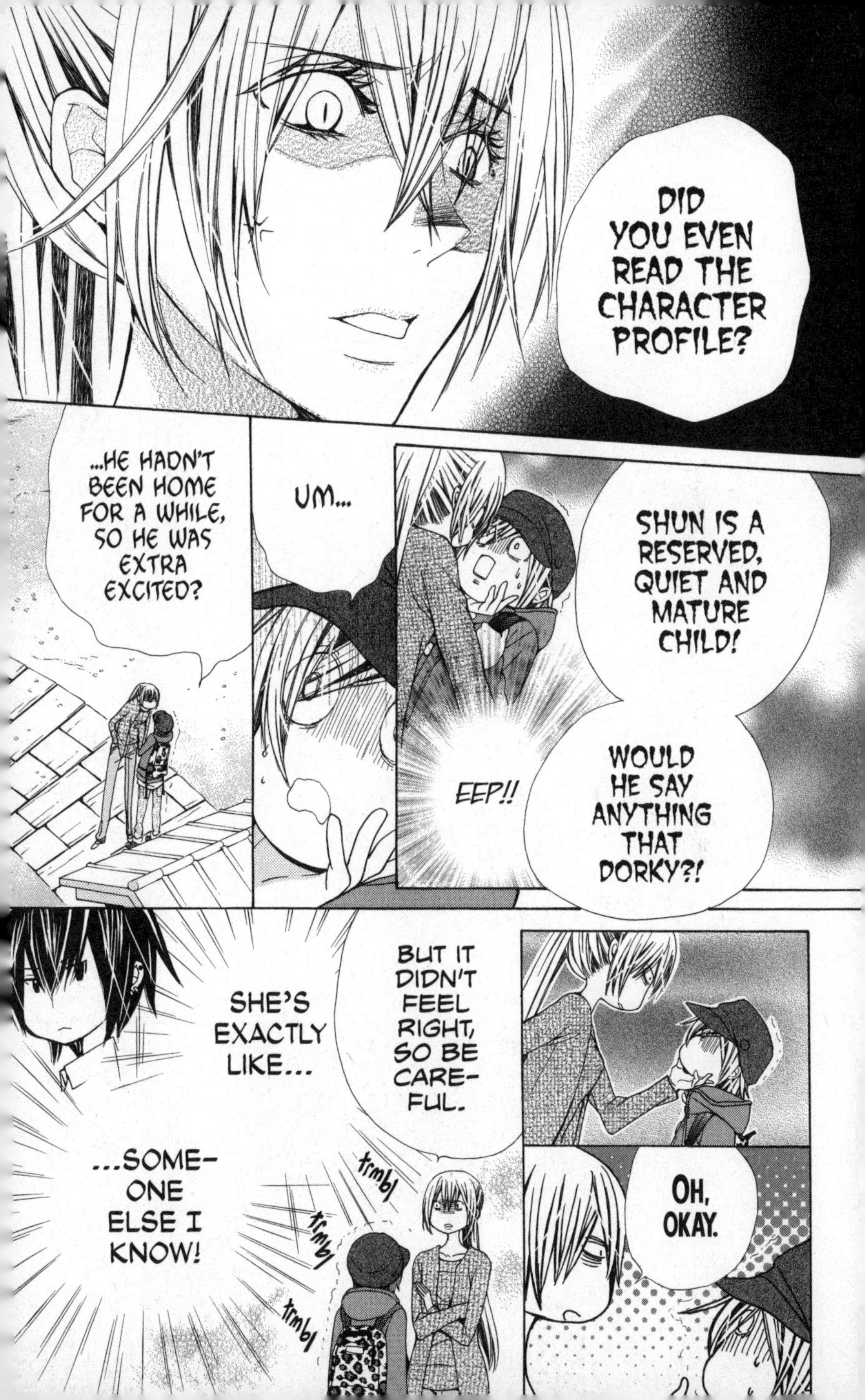
DID YOU EVEN READ THE CHARACTER PROFILE?
SHUN IS A RESERVED, QUIET AND MATURE CHILD!
WOULD HE SAY ANYTHING THAT DORKY?!
EEP!!
UM...
...HE HADN'T BEEN HOME FOR A WHILE, SO HE WAS EXTRA EXCITED?
OH, OKAY.
BUT IT DIDN'T FEEL RIGHT, SO BE CARE-FUL.
SHE'S EXACTLY LIKE...
...SOME-ONE ELSE I KNOW!
trmbl
trmbl
trmbl

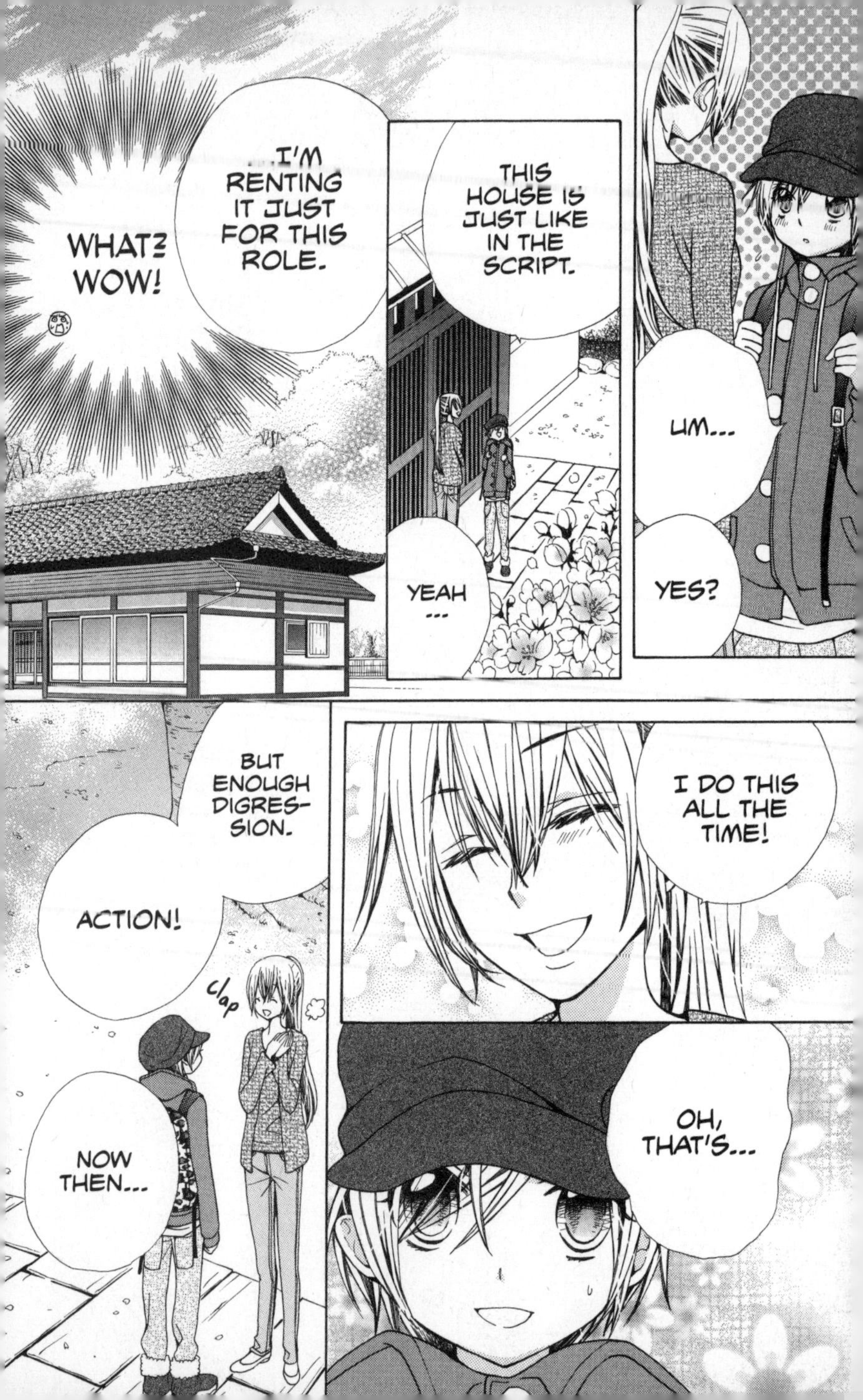
UM...
YES?
THIS HOUSE IS JUST LIKE IN THE SCRIPT.
YEAH...
I'M RENTING IT JUST FOR THIS ROLE.
WHAT? WOW!
I DO THIS ALL THE TIME!
OH, THAT'S...
BUT ENOUGH DIGRESSION.
ACTION!
clap
NOW THEN...

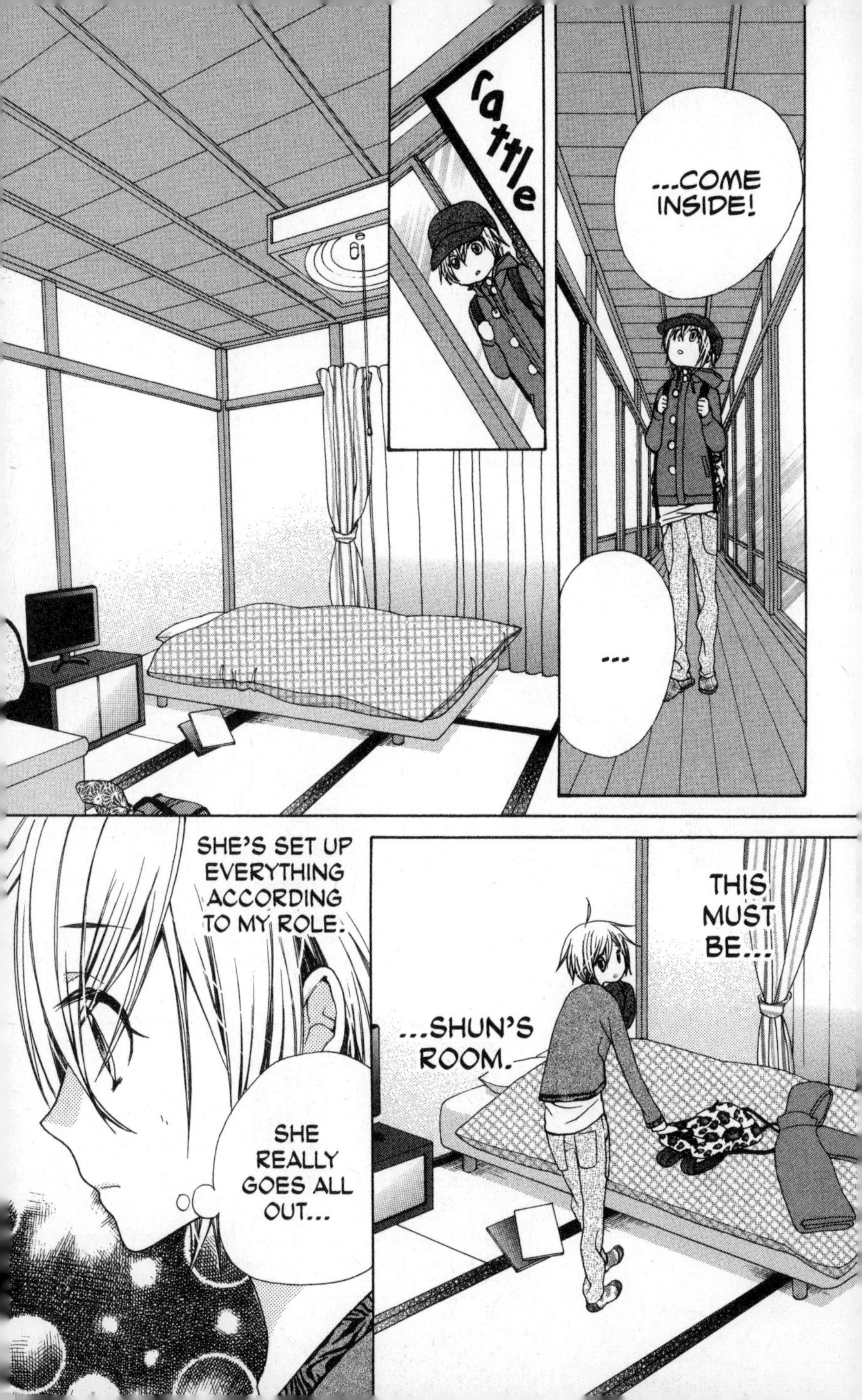
...COME INSIDE!
...
rattle
THIS MUST BE...
...SHUN'S ROOM.
SHE'S SET UP EVERYTHING ACCORDING TO MY ROLE.
SHE REALLY GOES ALL OUT...

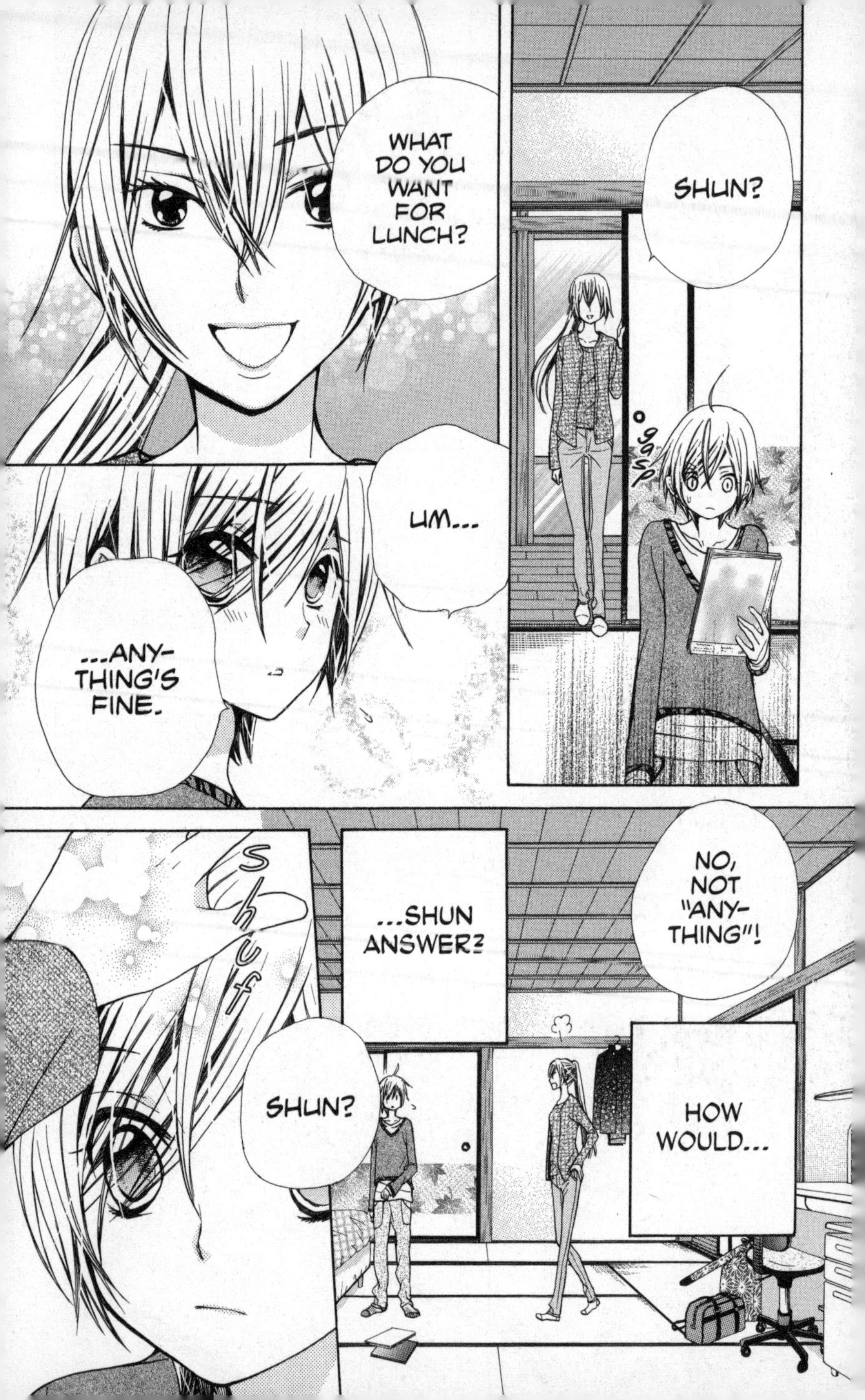
SHUN?
gasp
WHAT DO YOU WANT FOR LUNCH?
UM...
...ANY-THING'S FINE.
NO, NOT "ANY-THING"!
SHUN?
HOW WOULD...
...SHUN ANSWER?
shuf

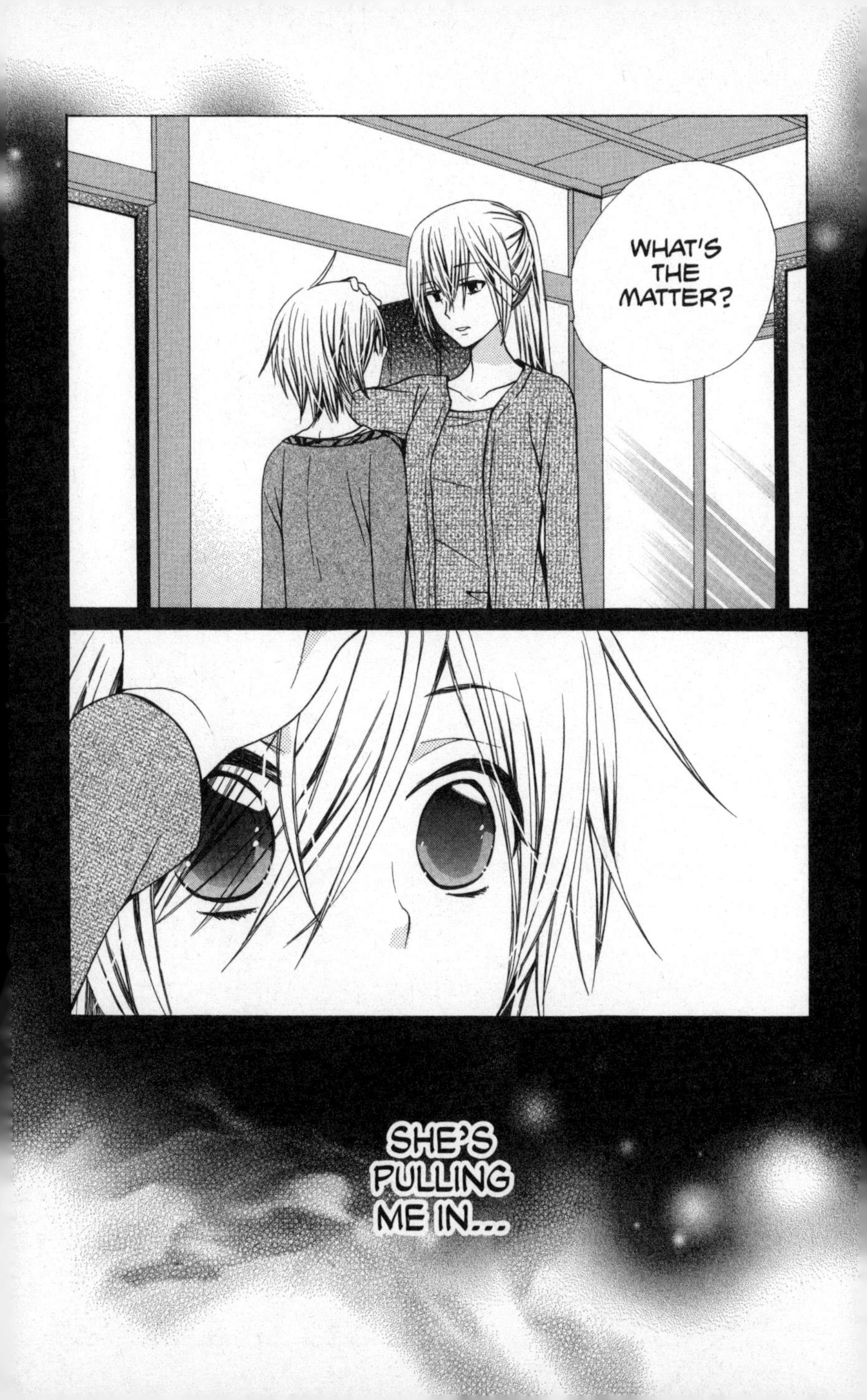
WHAT'S THE MATTER?
SHE'S PULLING ME IN...

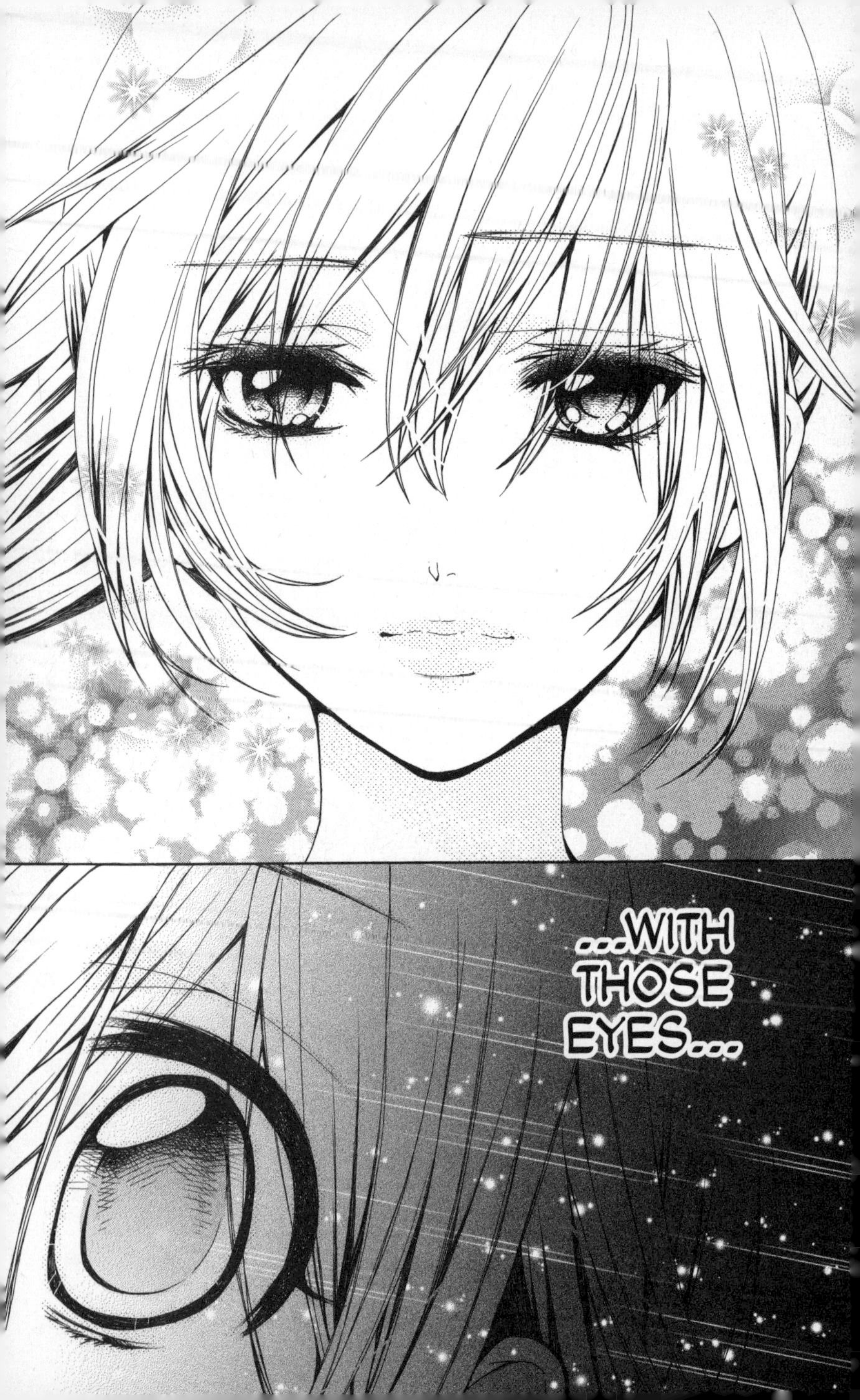
...WITH THOSE EYES...

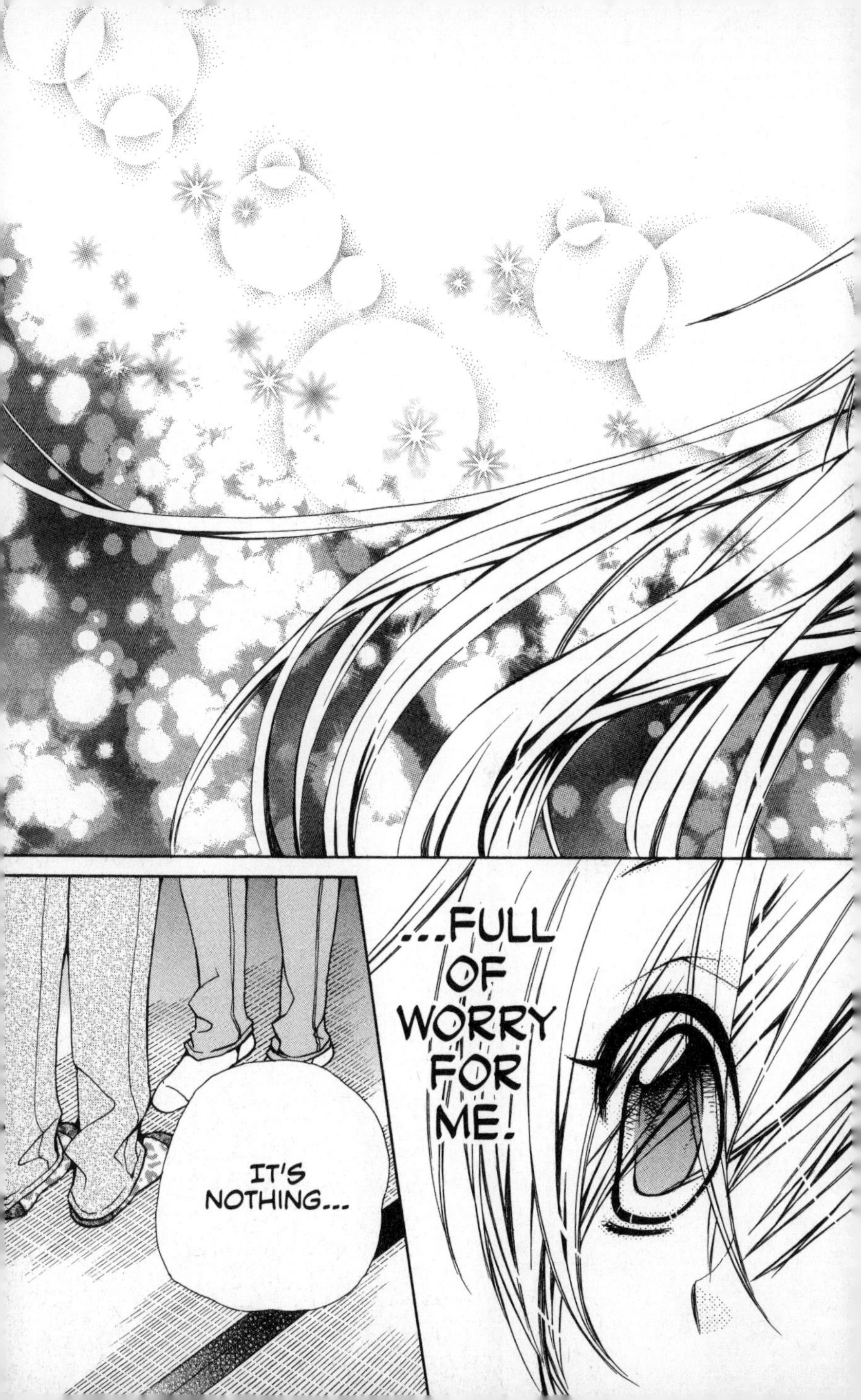
...FULL OF WORRY FOR ME.
IT'S NOTHING...

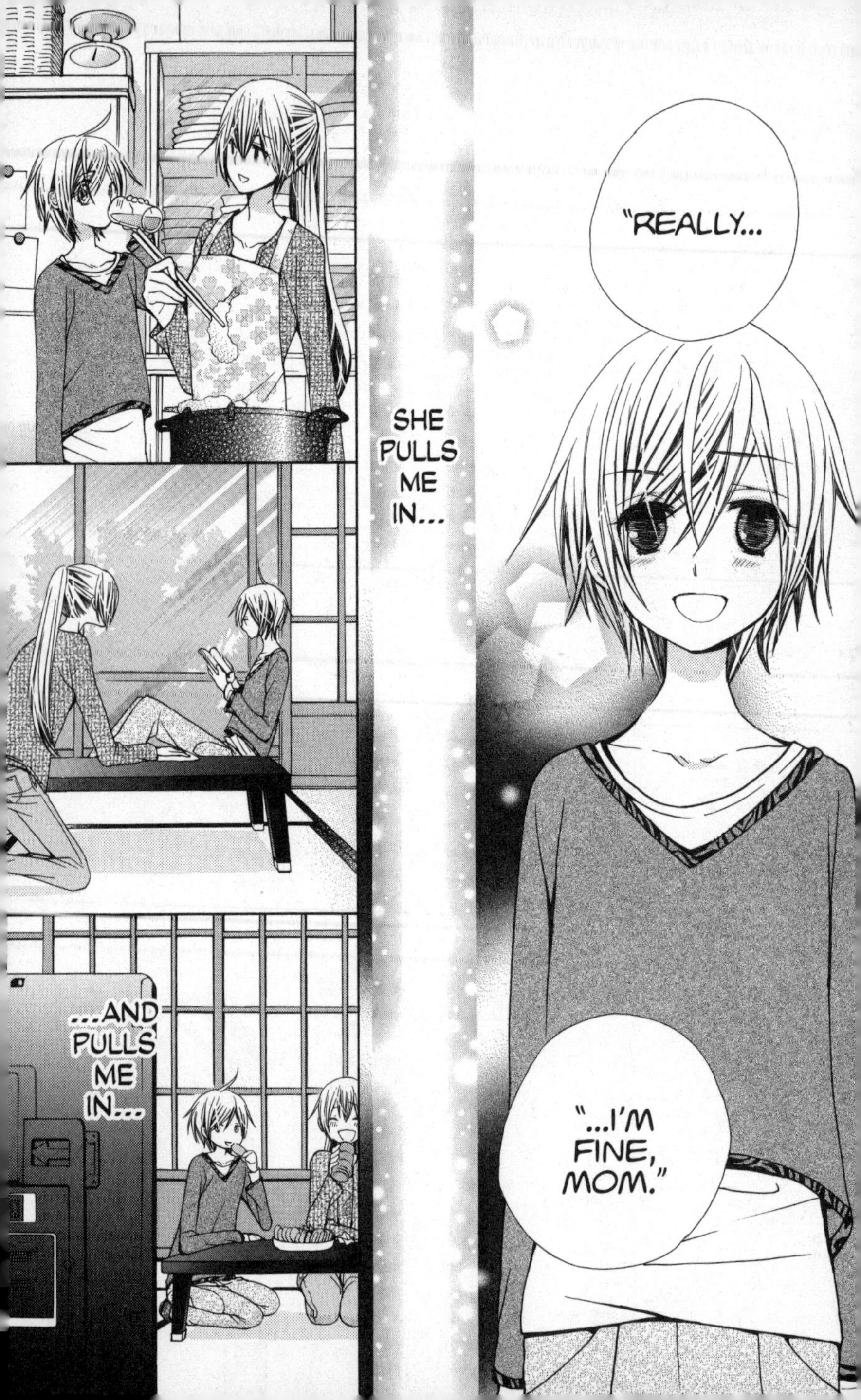
"REALLY...
"...I'M FINE, MOM."
SHE PULLS ME IN...
...AND PULLS ME IN...

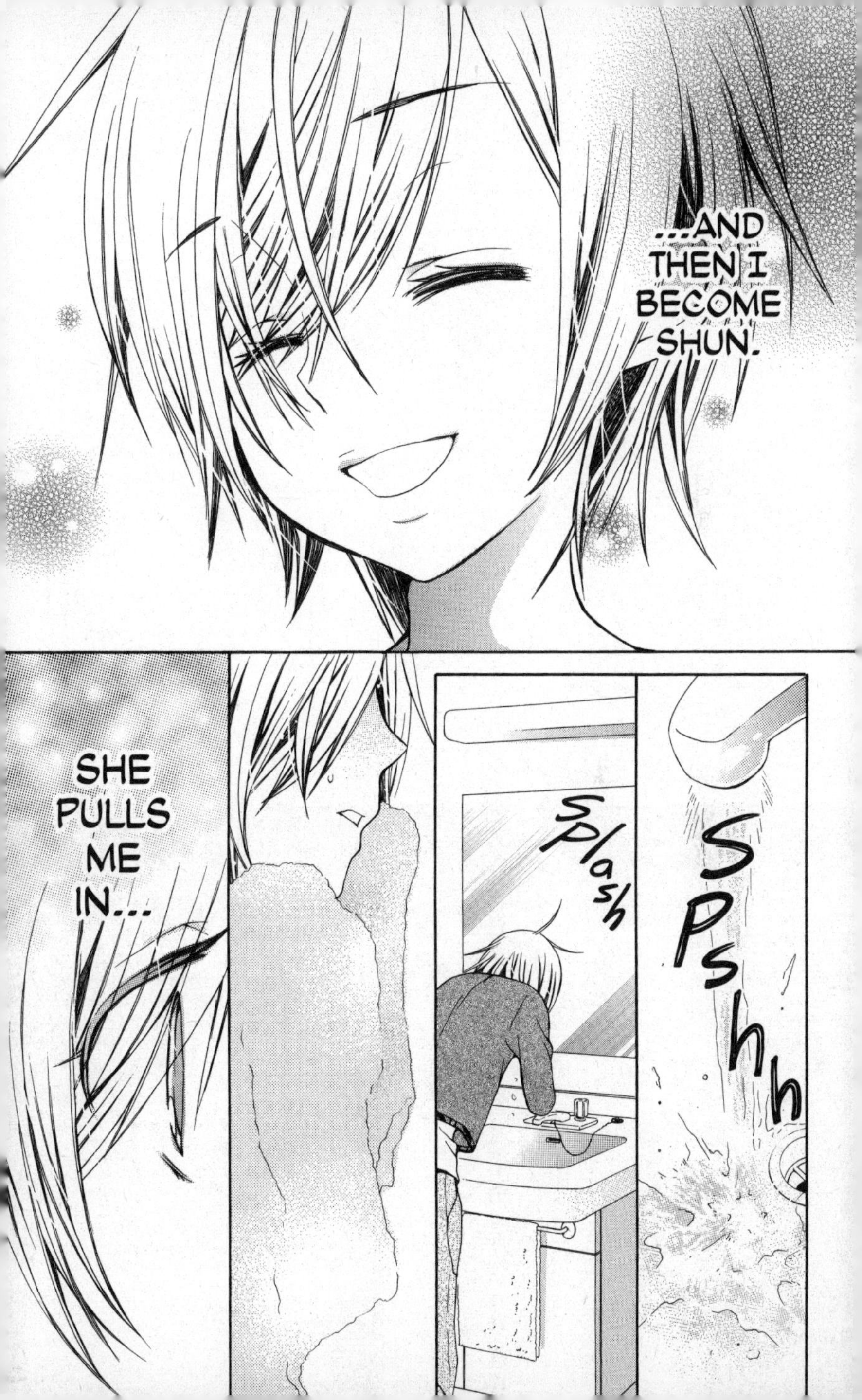
...AND THEN I BECOME SHUN.
SPshh
Splash
SHE PULLS ME IN...

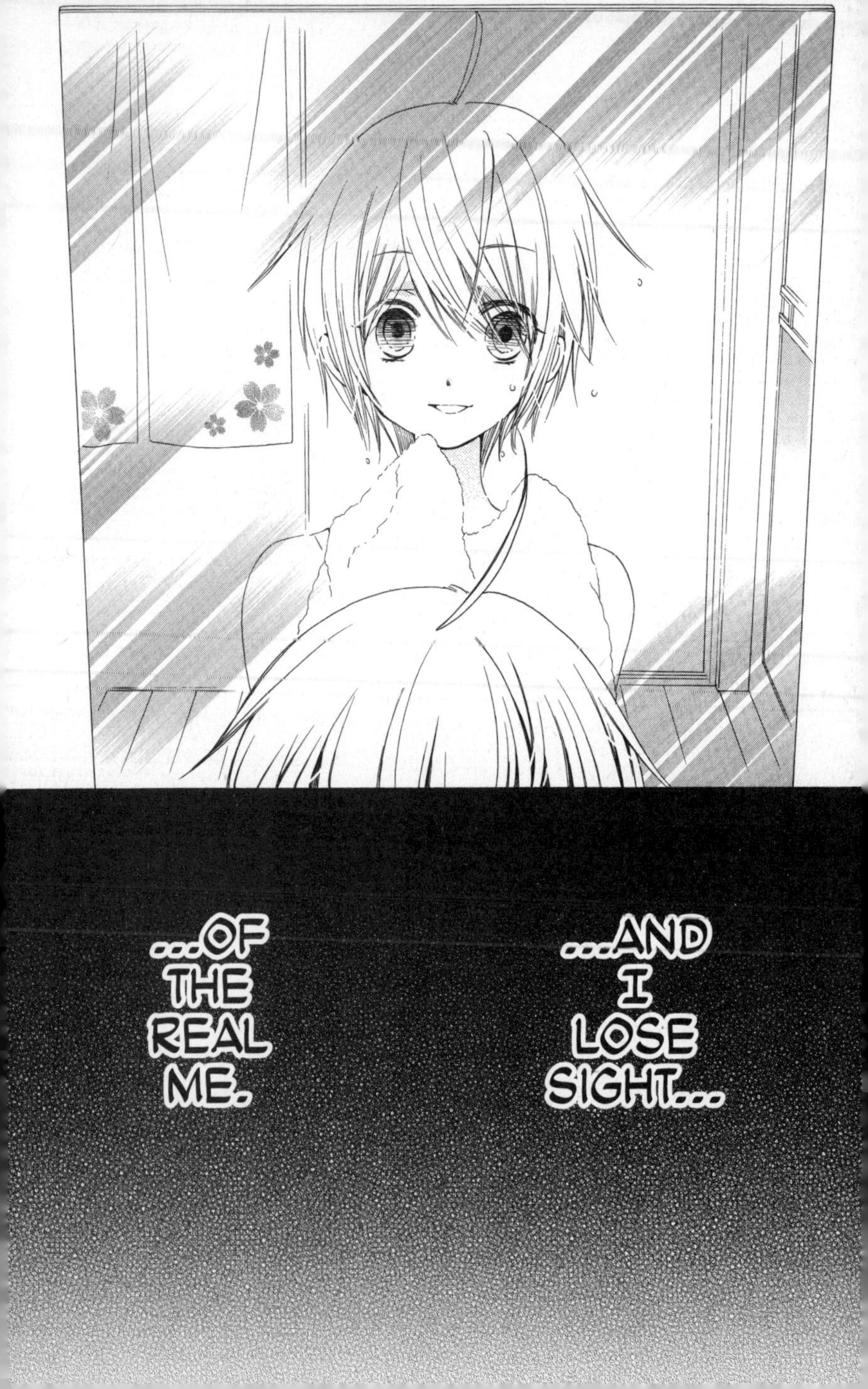
...AND I LOSE SIGHT...
...OF THE REAL ME.

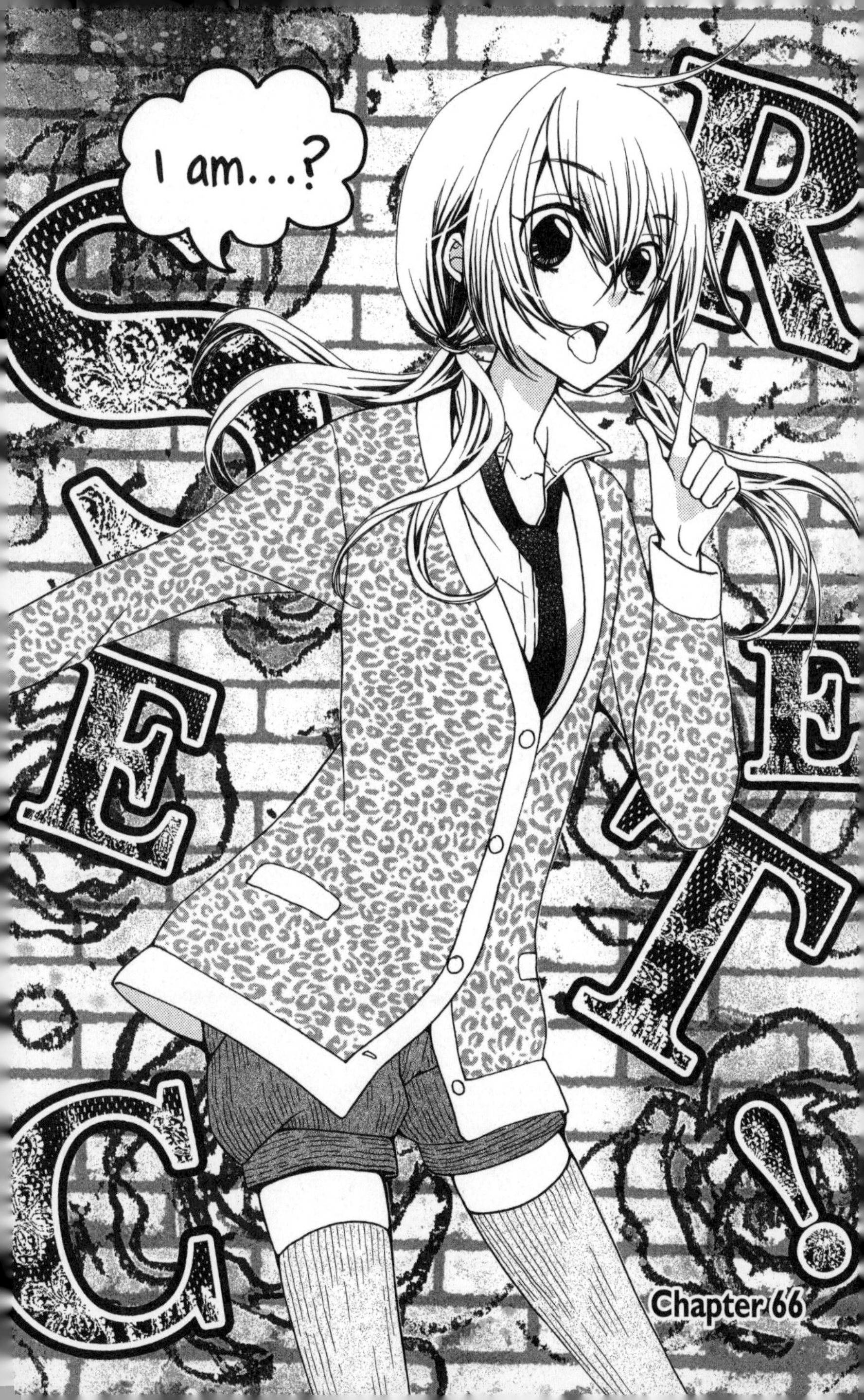
I am...?
SECRET!
Chapter 66

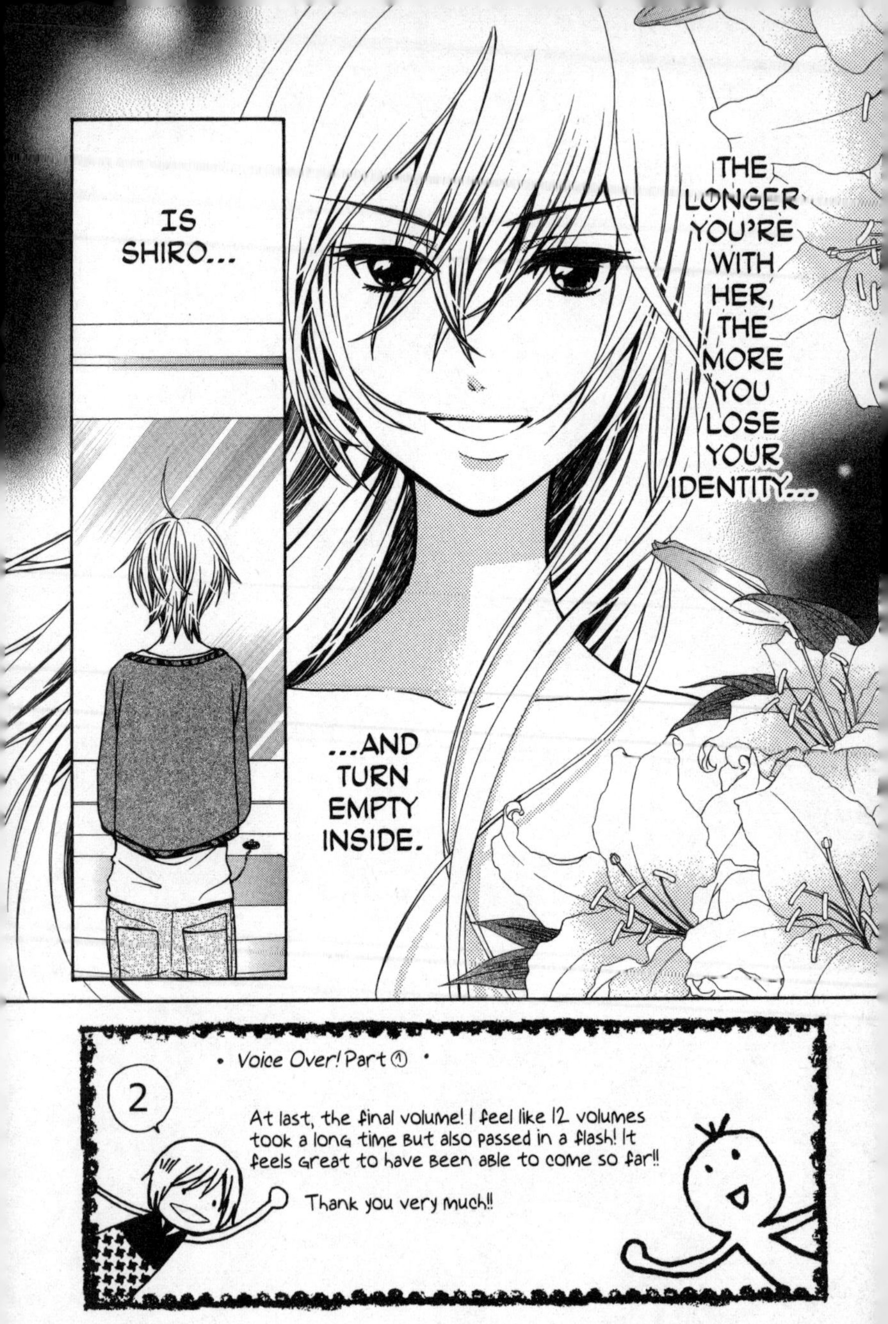
THE LONGER YOU'RE WITH HER, THE MORE YOU LOSE YOUR IDENTITY...
...AND TURN EMPTY INSIDE.
IS SHIRO...

• *Voice Over!* Part ① •

2

At last, the final volume! I feel like 12 volumes took a long time but also passed in a flash! It feels great to have been able to come so far!!

Thank you very much!!

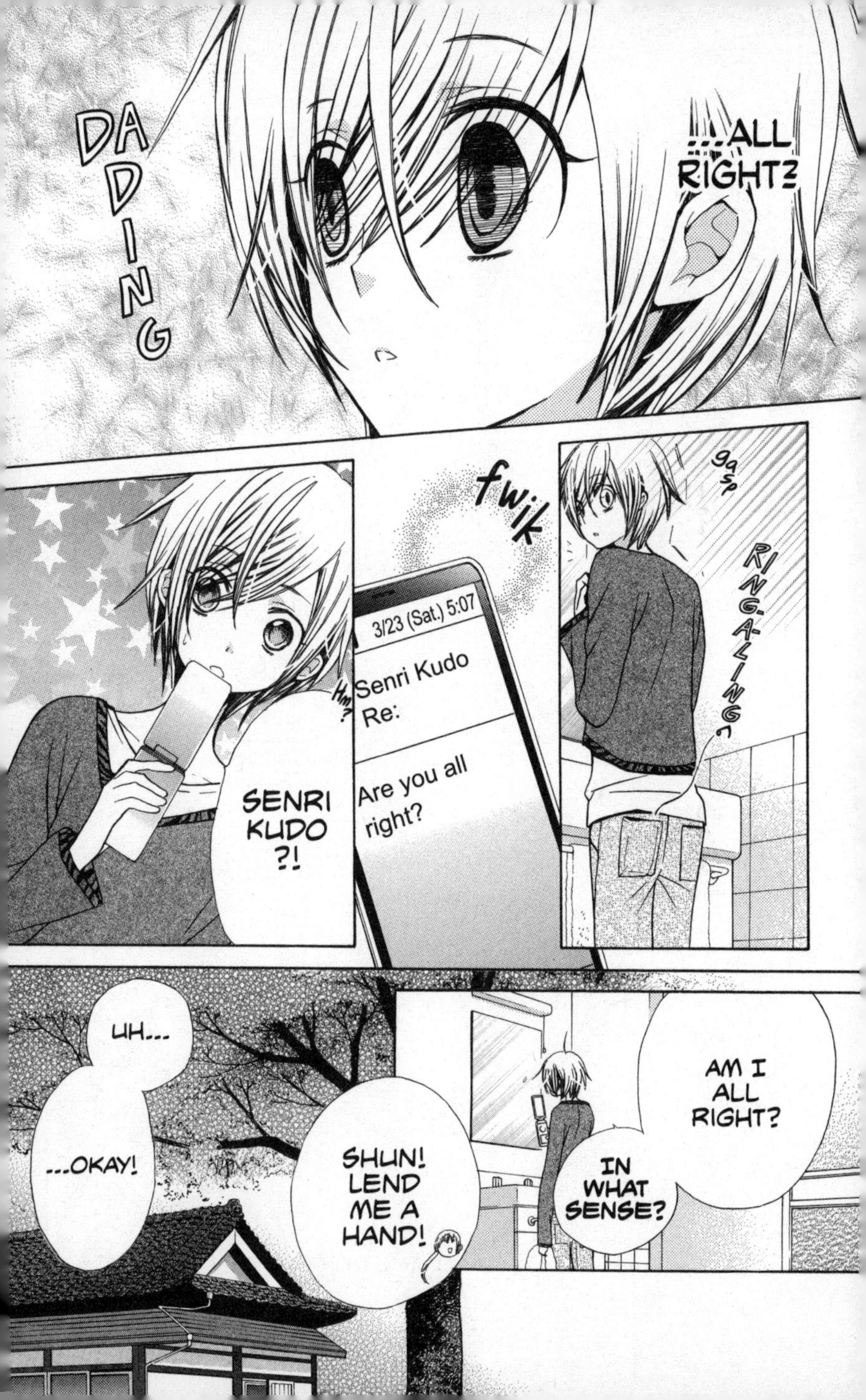
...ALL RIGHT?
DADING
gasp
RINGALING
fwik
3/23 (Sat.) 5:07
Senri Kudo
Re:
Are you all right?
Hm?
SENRI KUDO ?!
AM I ALL RIGHT?
IN WHAT SENSE?
SHUN! LEND ME A HAND!
UH...
...OKAY!

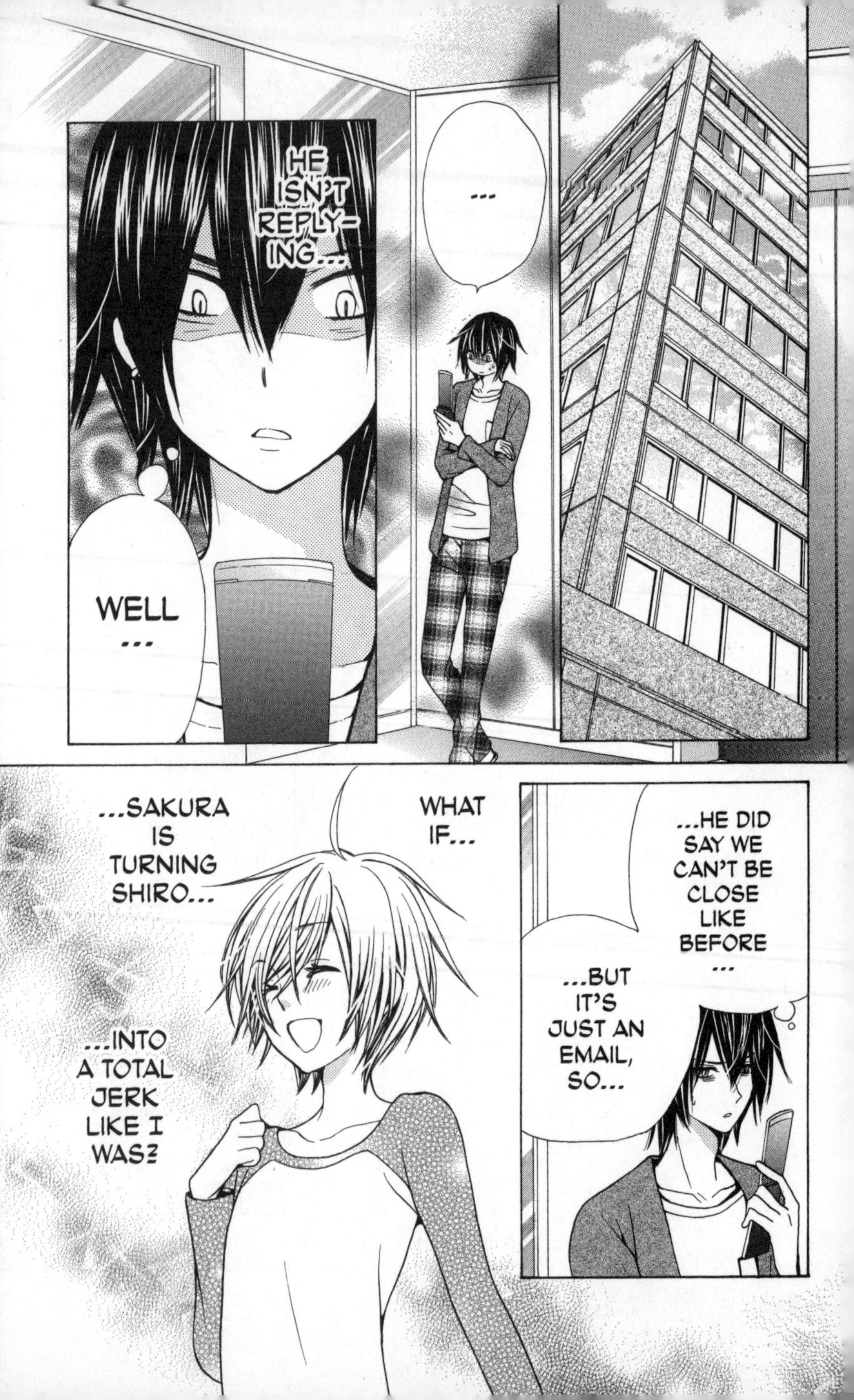
...
HE ISN'T REPLY-ING...
WELL...
...HE DID SAY WE CAN'T BE CLOSE LIKE BEFORE...
...BUT IT'S JUST AN EMAIL, SO...
WHAT IF...
...SAKURA IS TURNING SHIRO...
...INTO A TOTAL JERK LIKE I WAS?

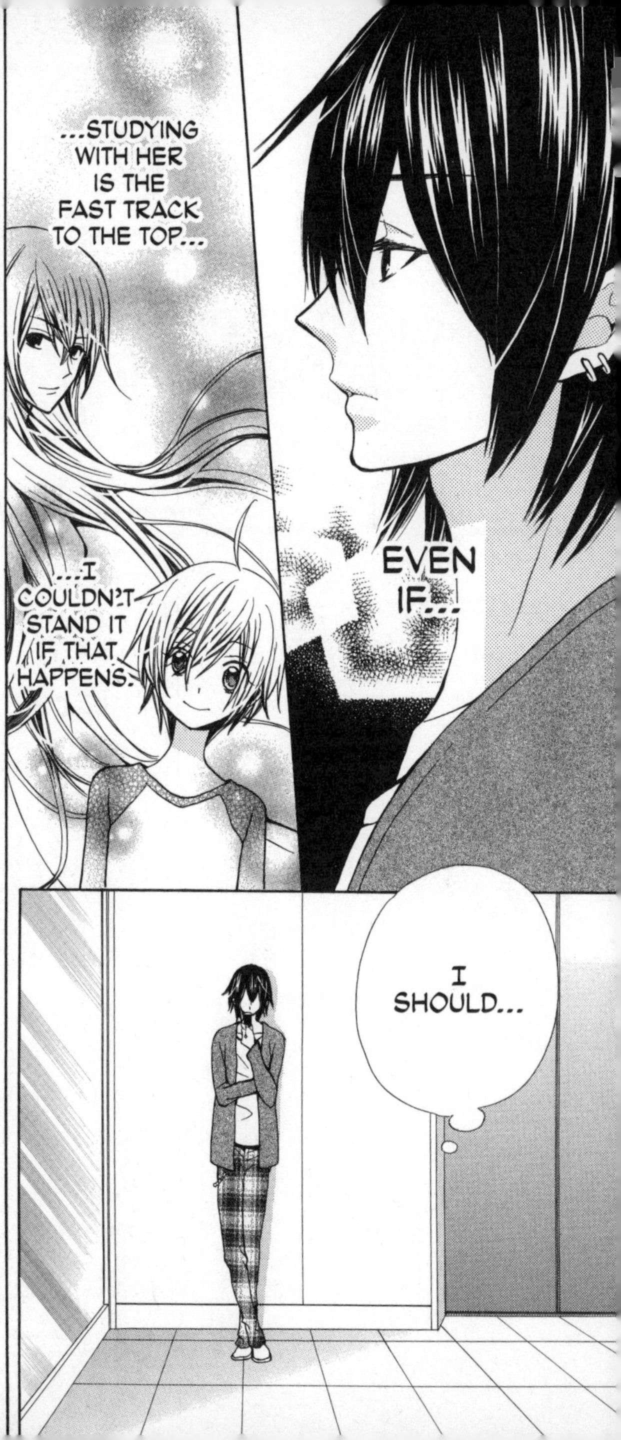
EVEN IF...
...STUDYING WITH HER IS THE FAST TRACK TO THE TOP...
...I COULDN'T STAND IT IF THAT HAPPENS.
I SHOULD...

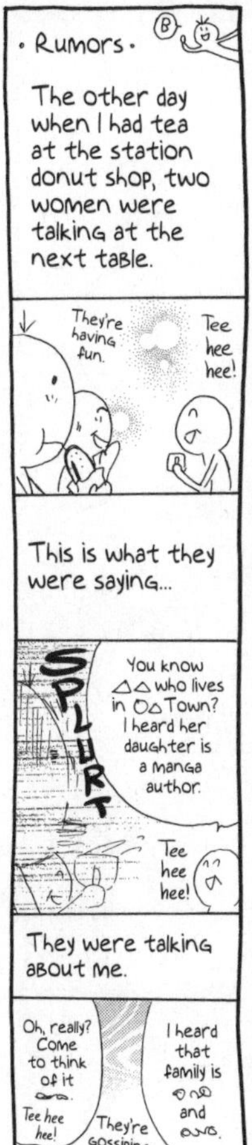
• Rumors •
The other day when I had tea at the station donut shop, two women were talking at the next table.
They're having fun.
Tee hee hee!
This is what they were saying...
SPLURT
You know △△ who lives in ○△ Town? I heard her daughter is a manga author.
Tee hee hee!
They were talking about me.
Oh, really? Come to think of it
Tee hee hee!
I heard that family is and
They're gossiping about me, but their info is wrong...
I left before it could get any worse...

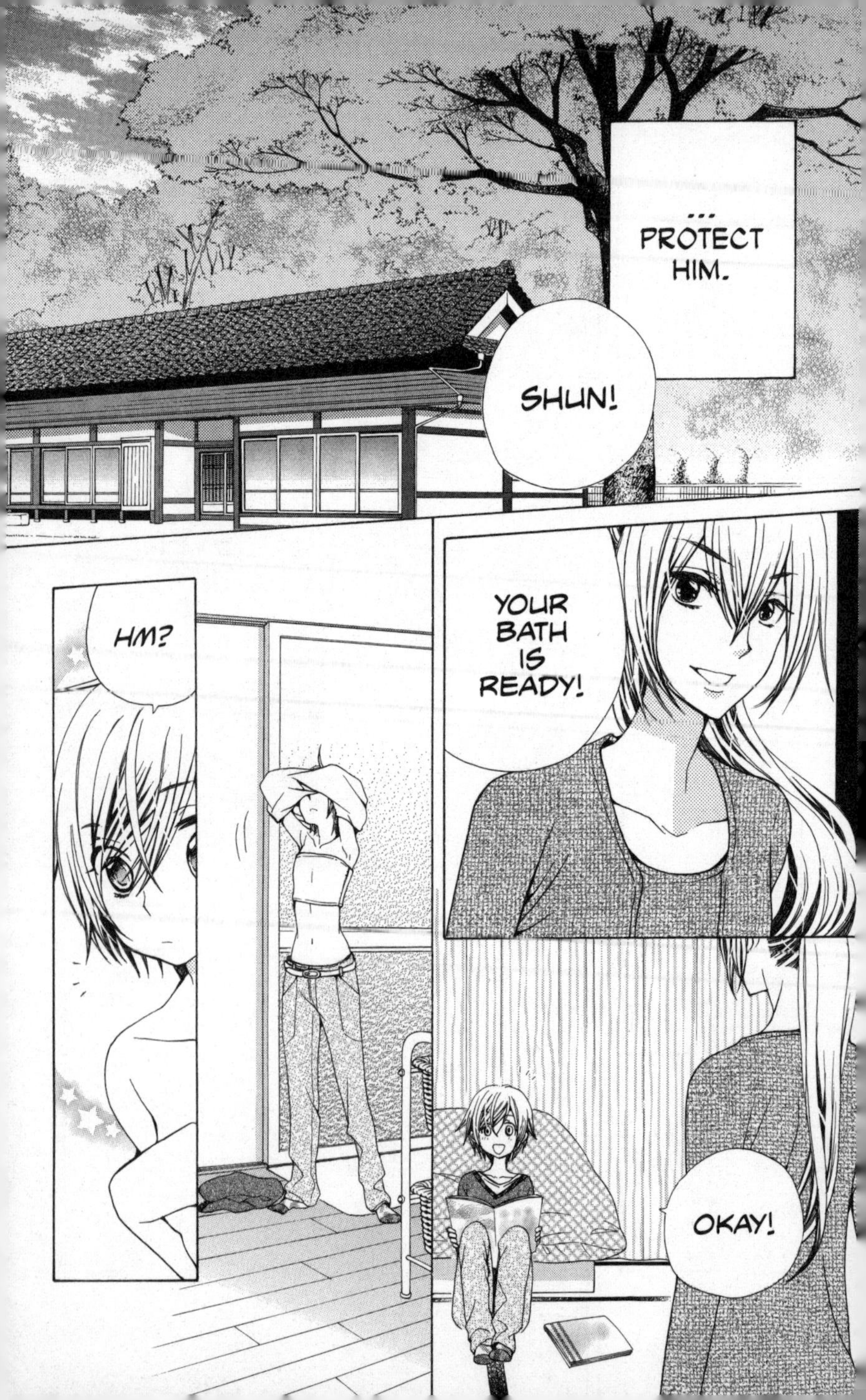
... PROTECT HIM.
SHUN!
YOUR BATH IS READY!
OKAY!
HM?

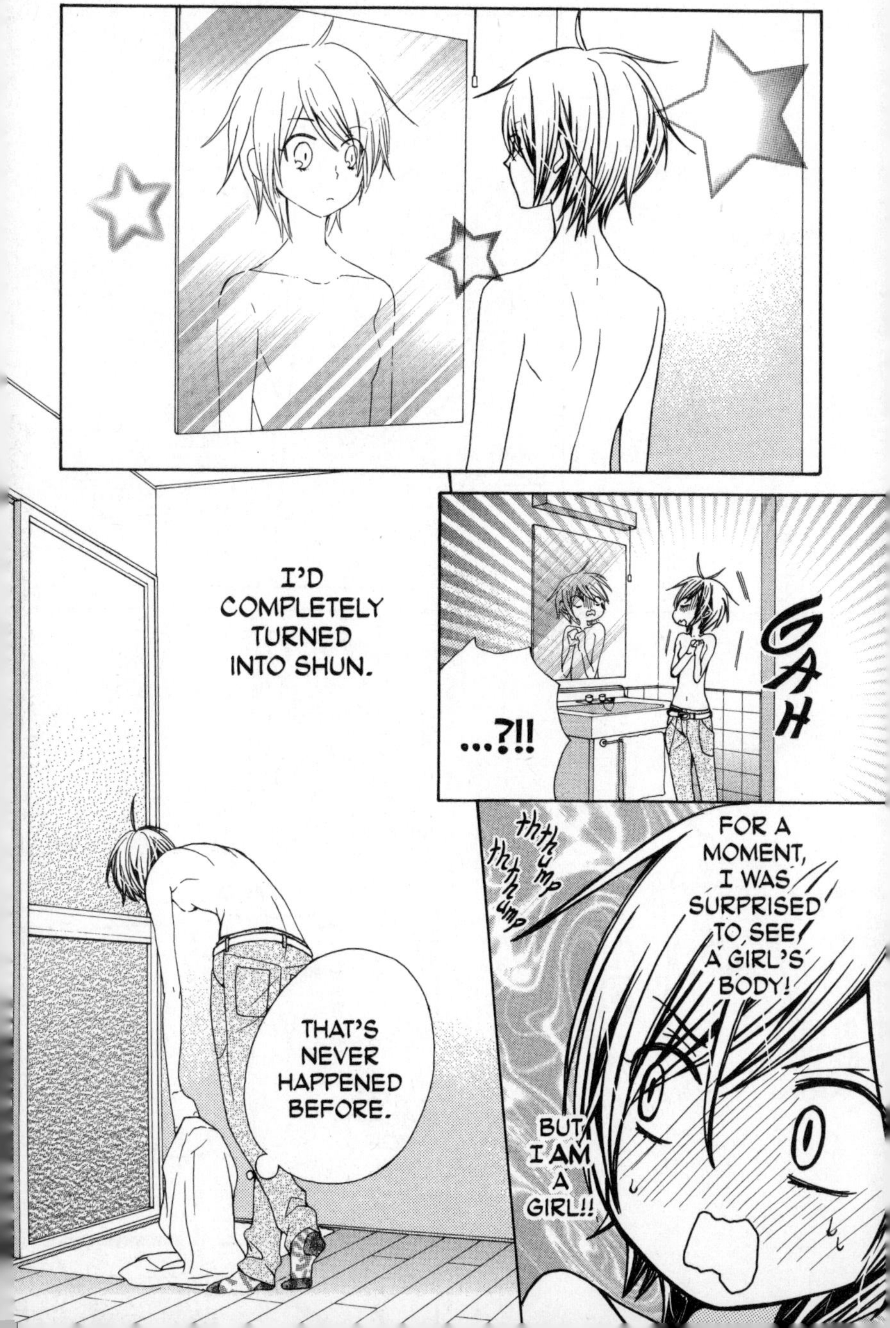
GAH
...?!!
FOR A MOMENT, I WAS SURPRISED TO SEE A GIRL'S BODY!
ththump ththump
BUT I AM A GIRL!!
I'D COMPLETELY TURNED INTO SHUN.
THAT'S NEVER HAPPENED BEFORE.

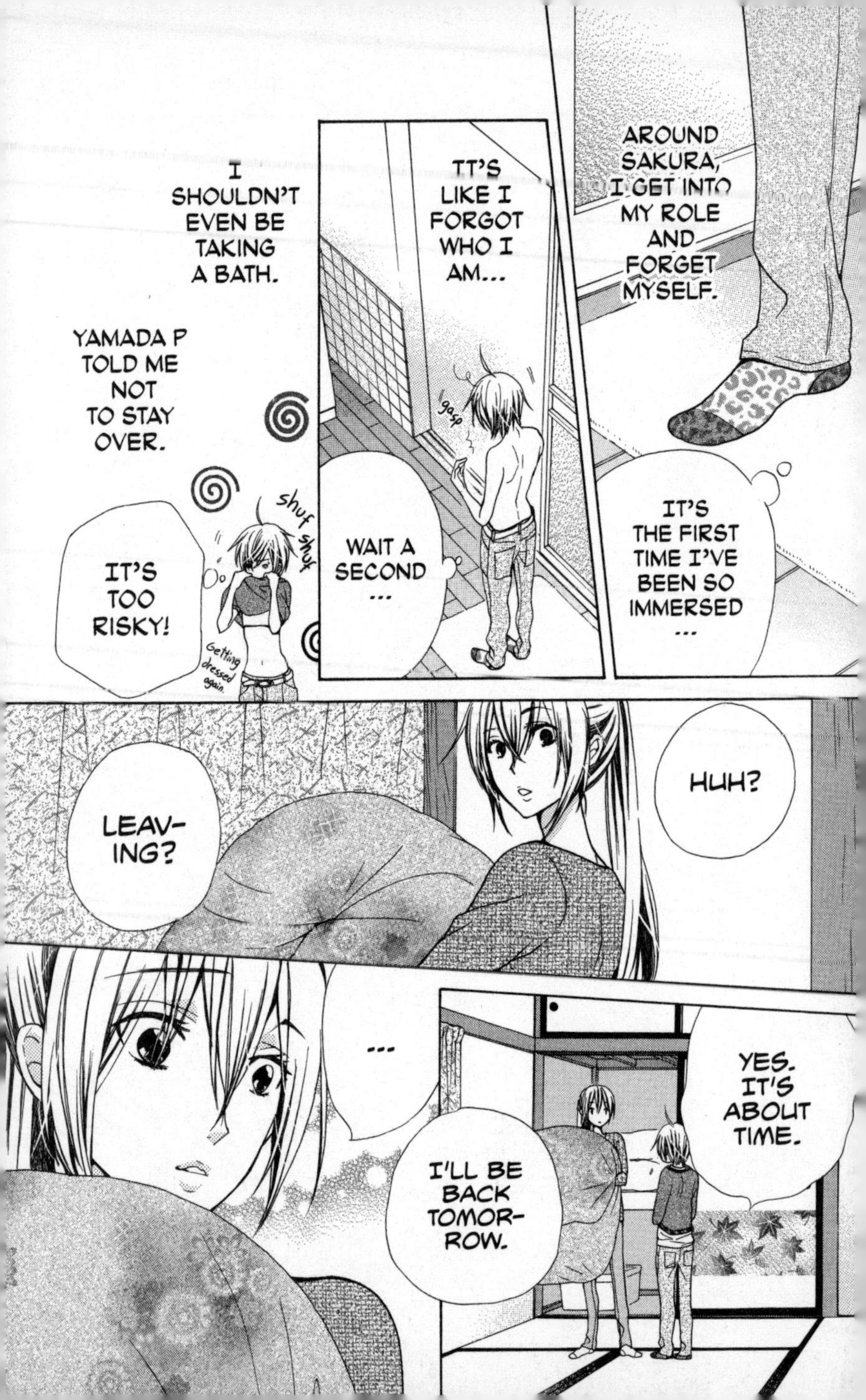
AROUND SAKURA, I GET INTO MY ROLE AND FORGET MYSELF.
IT'S THE FIRST TIME I'VE BEEN SO IMMERSED...
IT'S LIKE I FORGOT WHO I AM...
gasp
WAIT A SECOND...
I SHOULDN'T EVEN BE TAKING A BATH.
YAMADA P TOLD ME NOT TO STAY OVER.
shuf shuf
IT'S TOO RISKY!
Getting dressed again.
HUH?
LEAVING?
YES. IT'S ABOUT TIME.
I'LL BE BACK TOMOR-ROW.
...

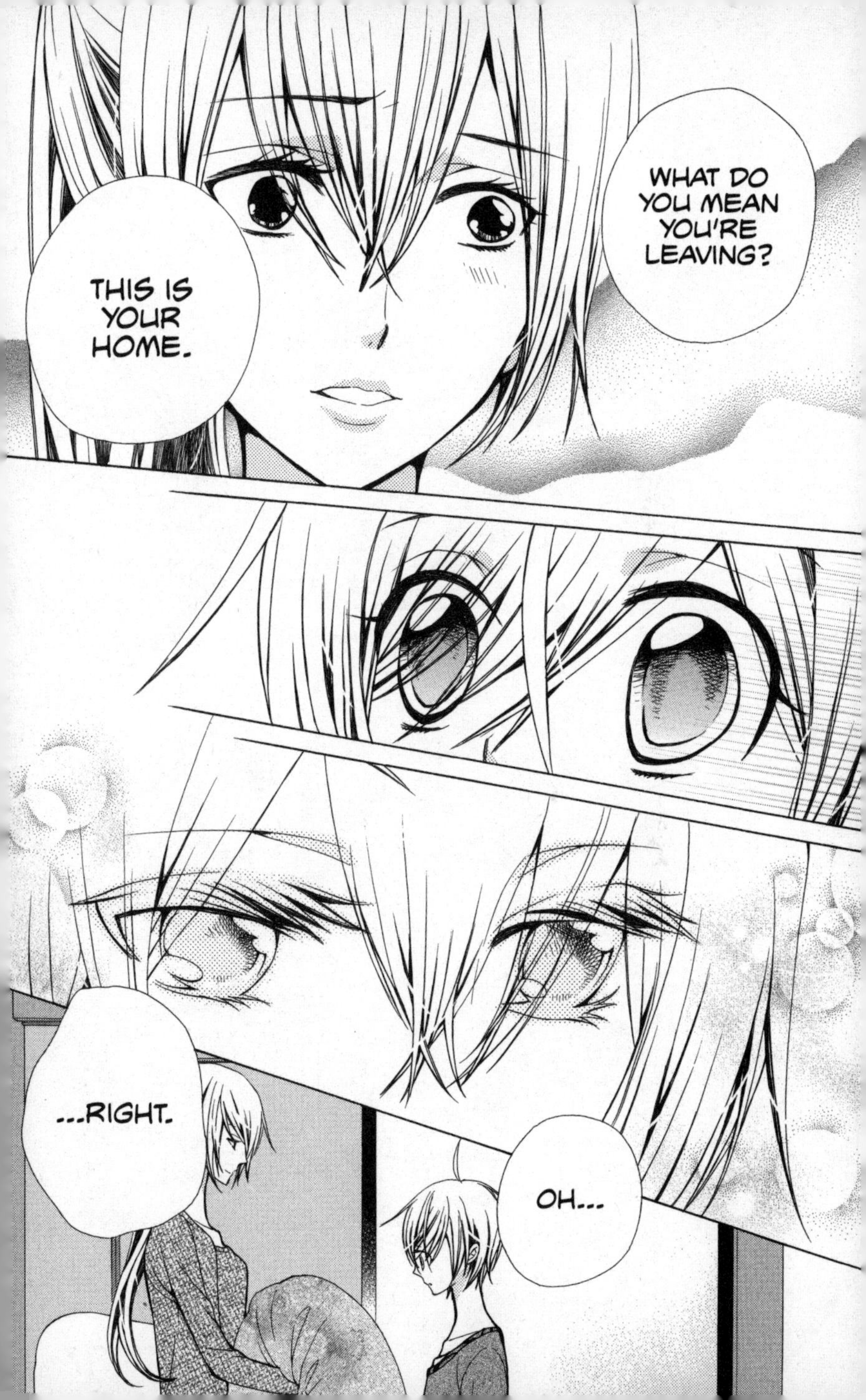
WHAT DO YOU MEAN YOU'RE LEAVING?
THIS IS YOUR HOME.
OH...
...RIGHT.

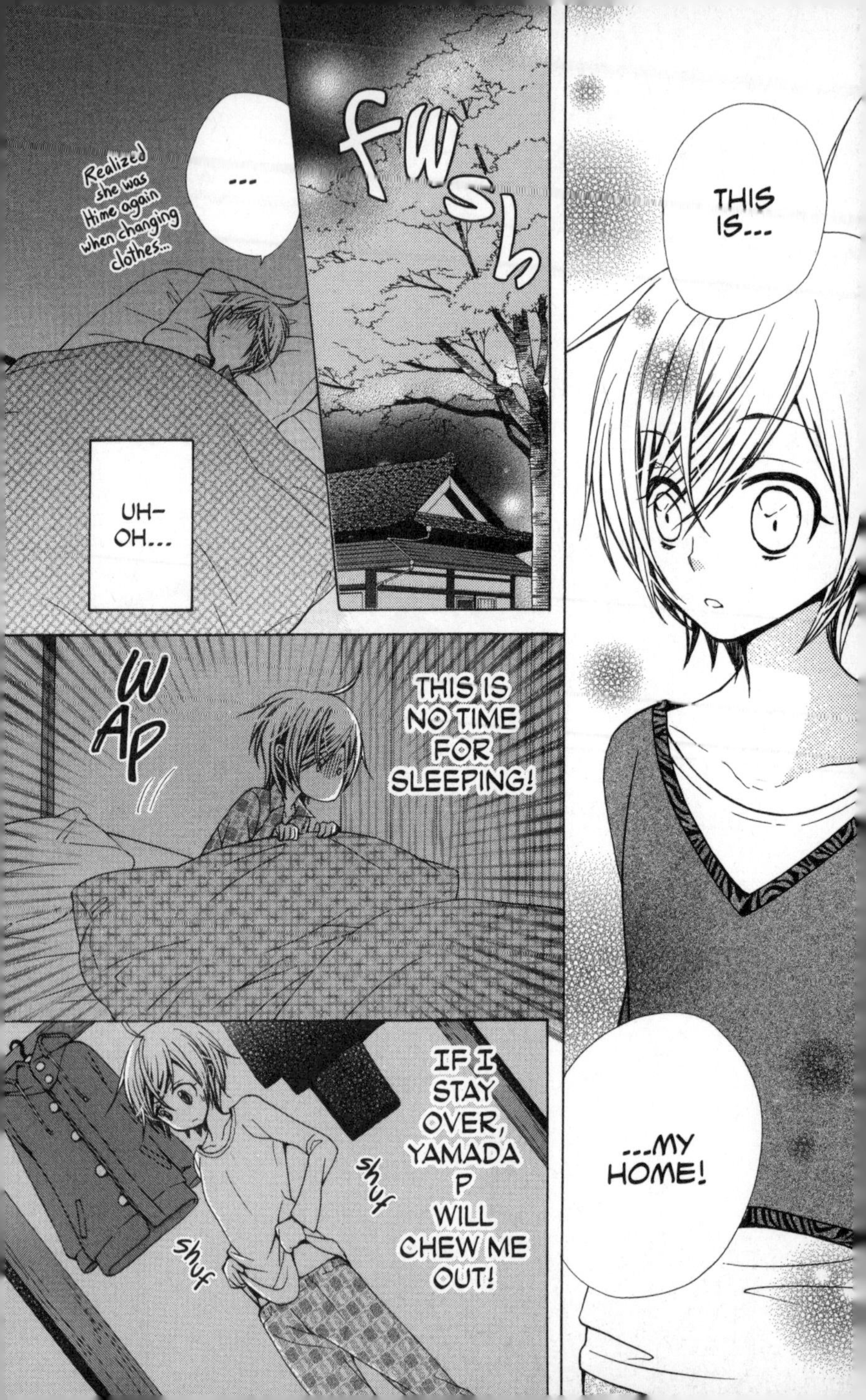
THIS IS...
...MY HOME!
fwsh
...
Realized she was Hime again when changing clothes..
UH-OH...
WAP
THIS IS NO TIME FOR SLEEPING!
IF I STAY OVER, YAMADA P WILL CHEW ME OUT!
shuf
shuf

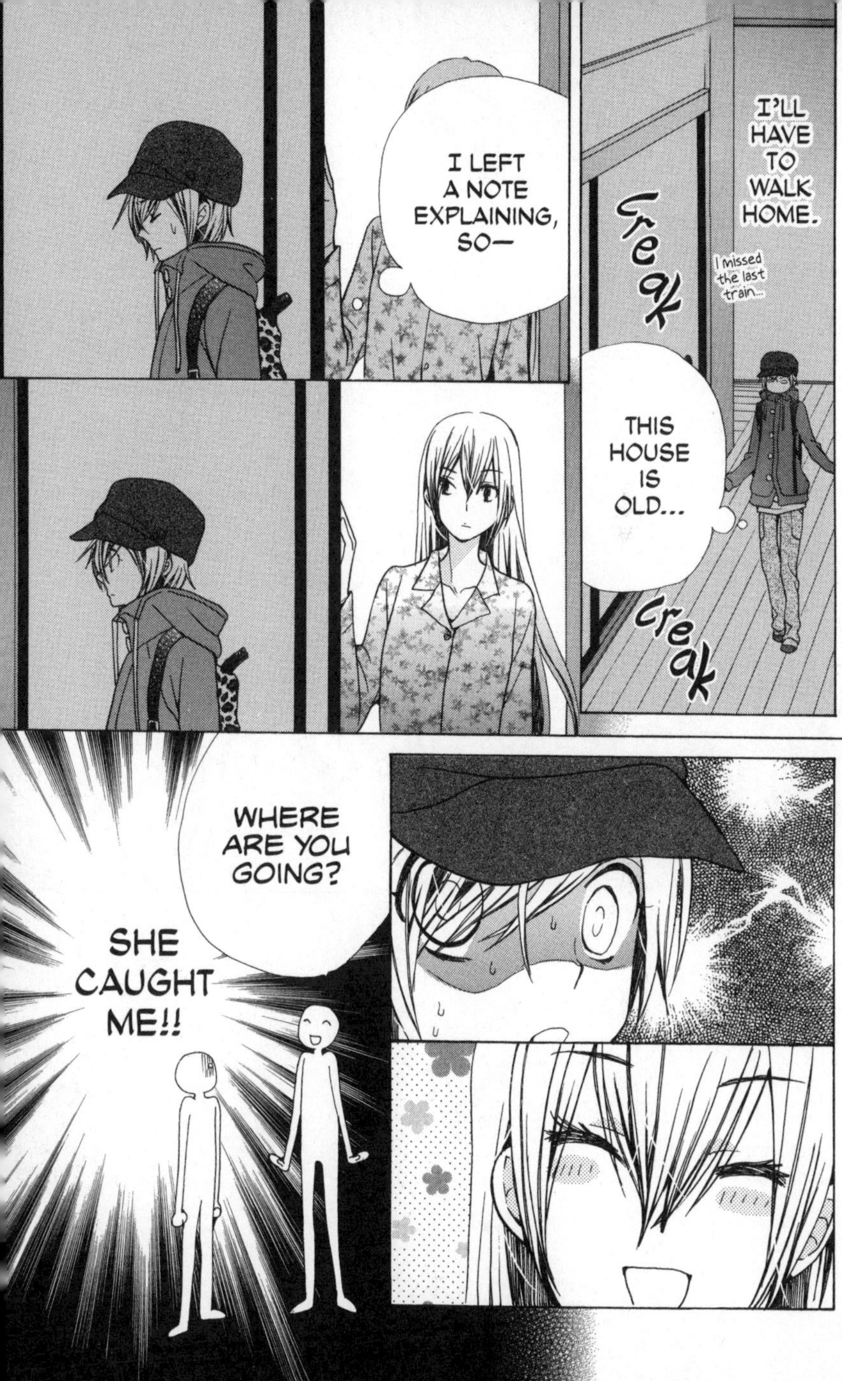
I'LL HAVE TO WALK HOME.
I missed the last train...
Creak
THIS HOUSE IS OLD...
Creak
I LEFT A NOTE EXPLAINING, SO—
WHERE ARE YOU GOING?
SHE CAUGHT ME!!

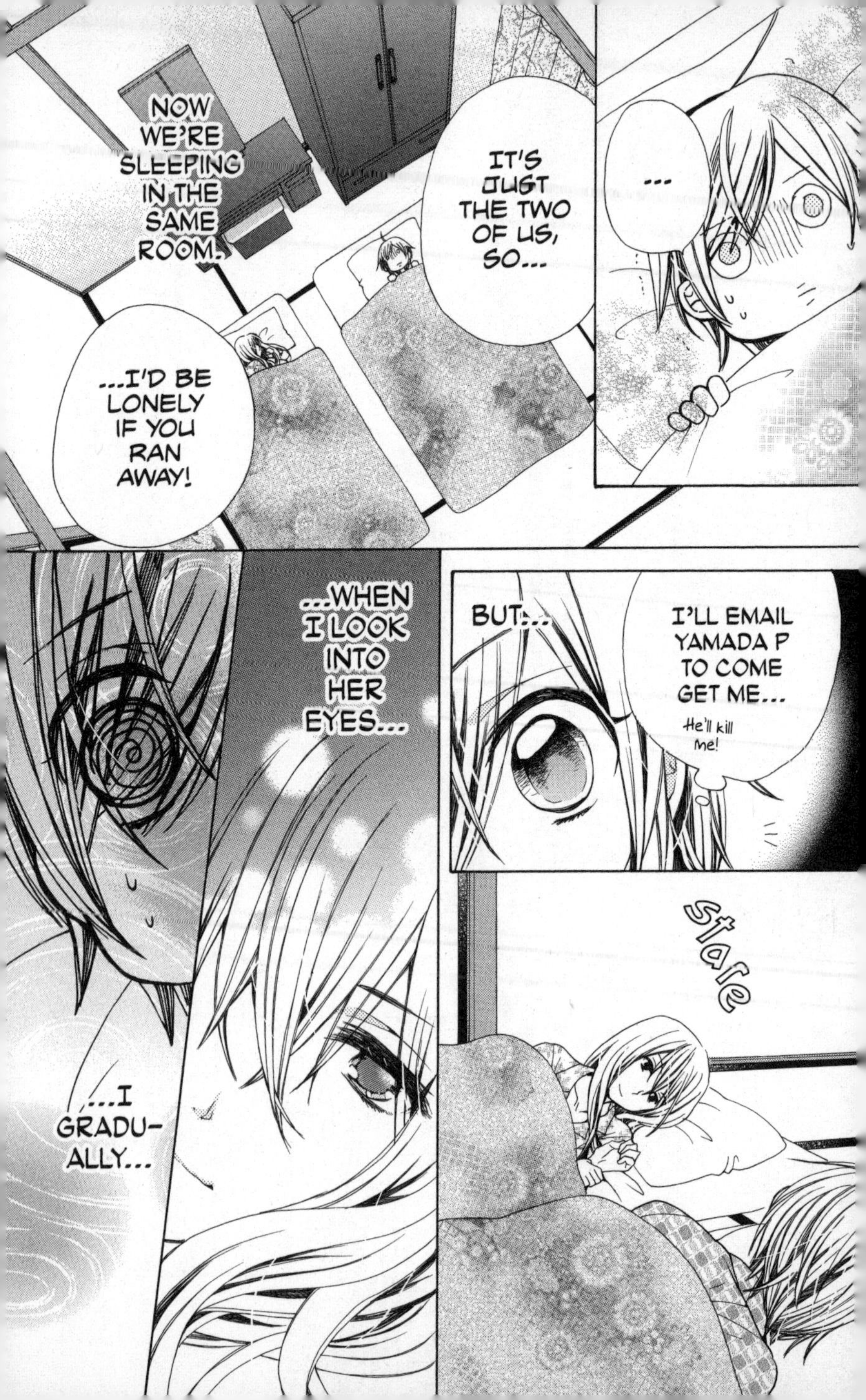
...
IT'S JUST THE TWO OF US, SO...
NOW WE'RE SLEEPING IN THE SAME ROOM.
...I'D BE LONELY IF YOU RAN AWAY!
I'LL EMAIL YAMADA P TO COME GET ME...
He'll kill me!
BUT...
Stare
...WHEN I LOOK INTO HER EYES...
...I GRADU-ALLY...

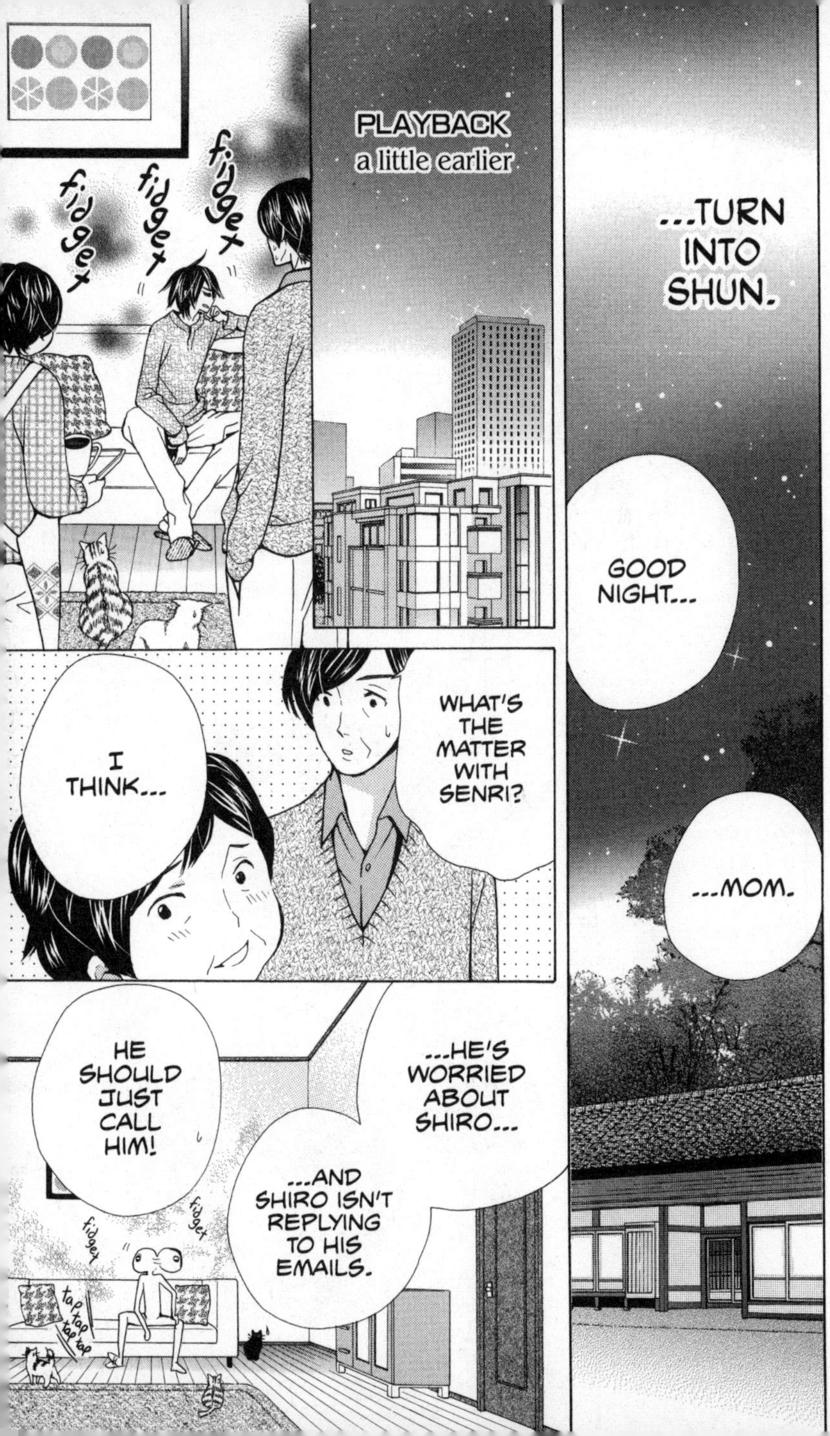
...TURN INTO SHUN.
GOOD NIGHT...
...MOM.
PLAYBACK
a little earlier
fidget
fidget
fidget
WHAT'S THE MATTER WITH SENRI?
I THINK...
...HE'S WORRIED ABOUT SHIRO...
...AND SHIRO ISN'T REPLYING TO HIS EMAILS.
HE SHOULD JUST CALL HIM!
fidget
fidget
tap tap tap tap

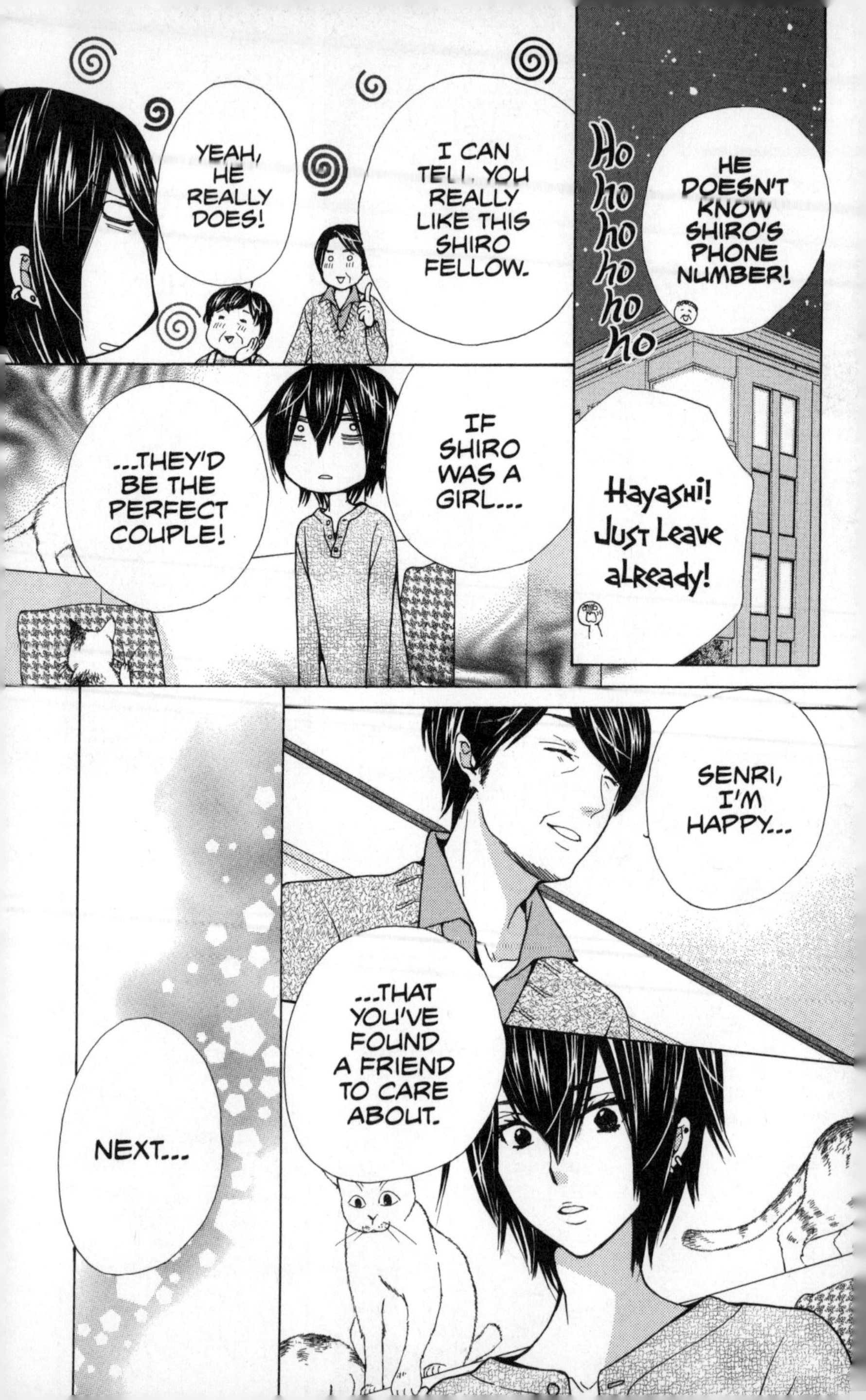
HE DOESN'T KNOW SHIRO'S PHONE NUMBER!
Ho ho ho ho ho ho ho
Hayashi! Just Leave already!
I CAN TELL YOU REALLY LIKE THIS SHIRO FELLOW.
YEAH, HE REALLY DOES!
IF SHIRO WAS A GIRL...
...THEY'D BE THE PERFECT COUPLE!
SENRI, I'M HAPPY...
...THAT YOU'VE FOUND A FRIEND TO CARE ABOUT.
NEXT...

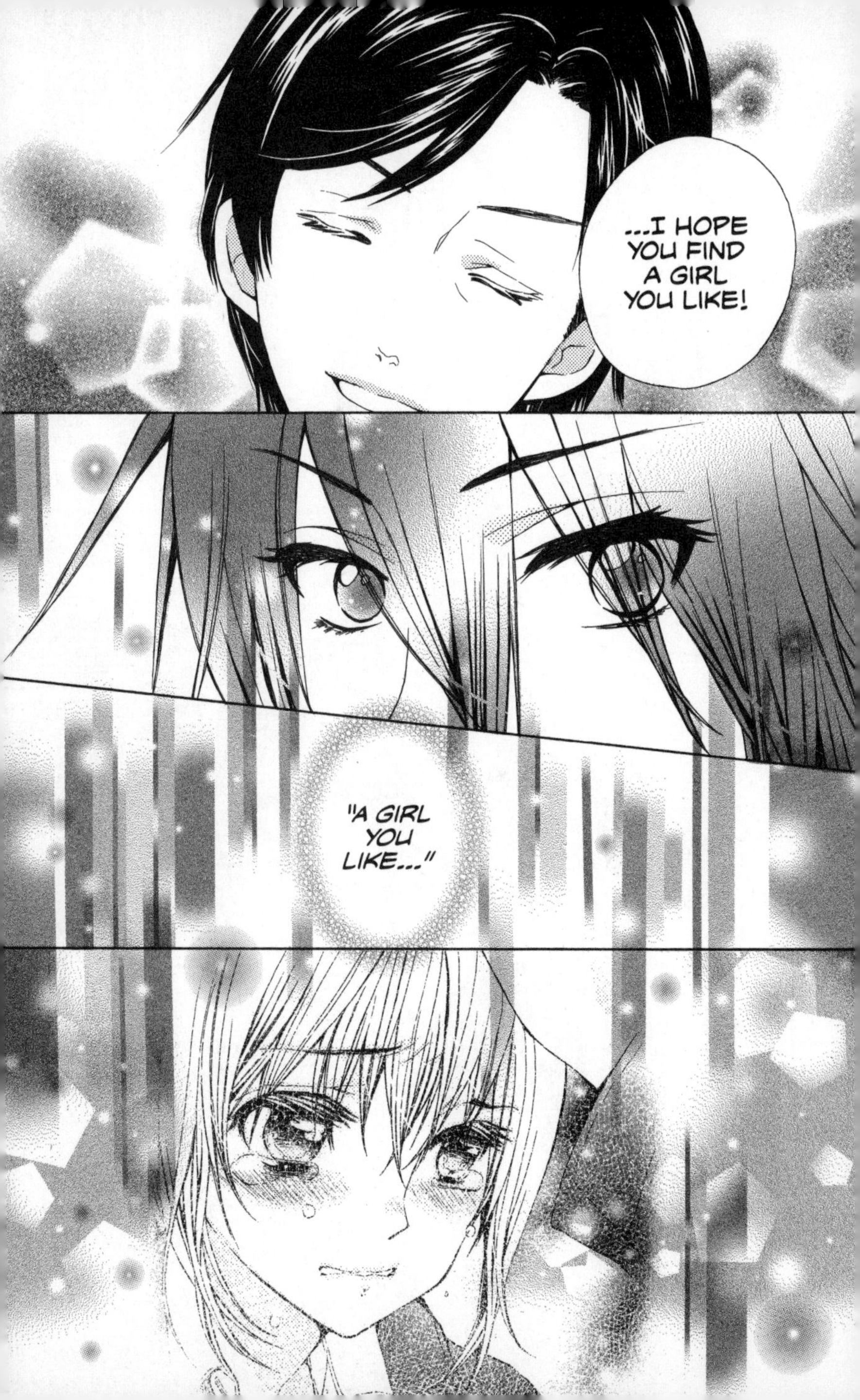
...I HOPE YOU FIND A GIRL YOU LIKE!
"A GIRL YOU LIKE..."

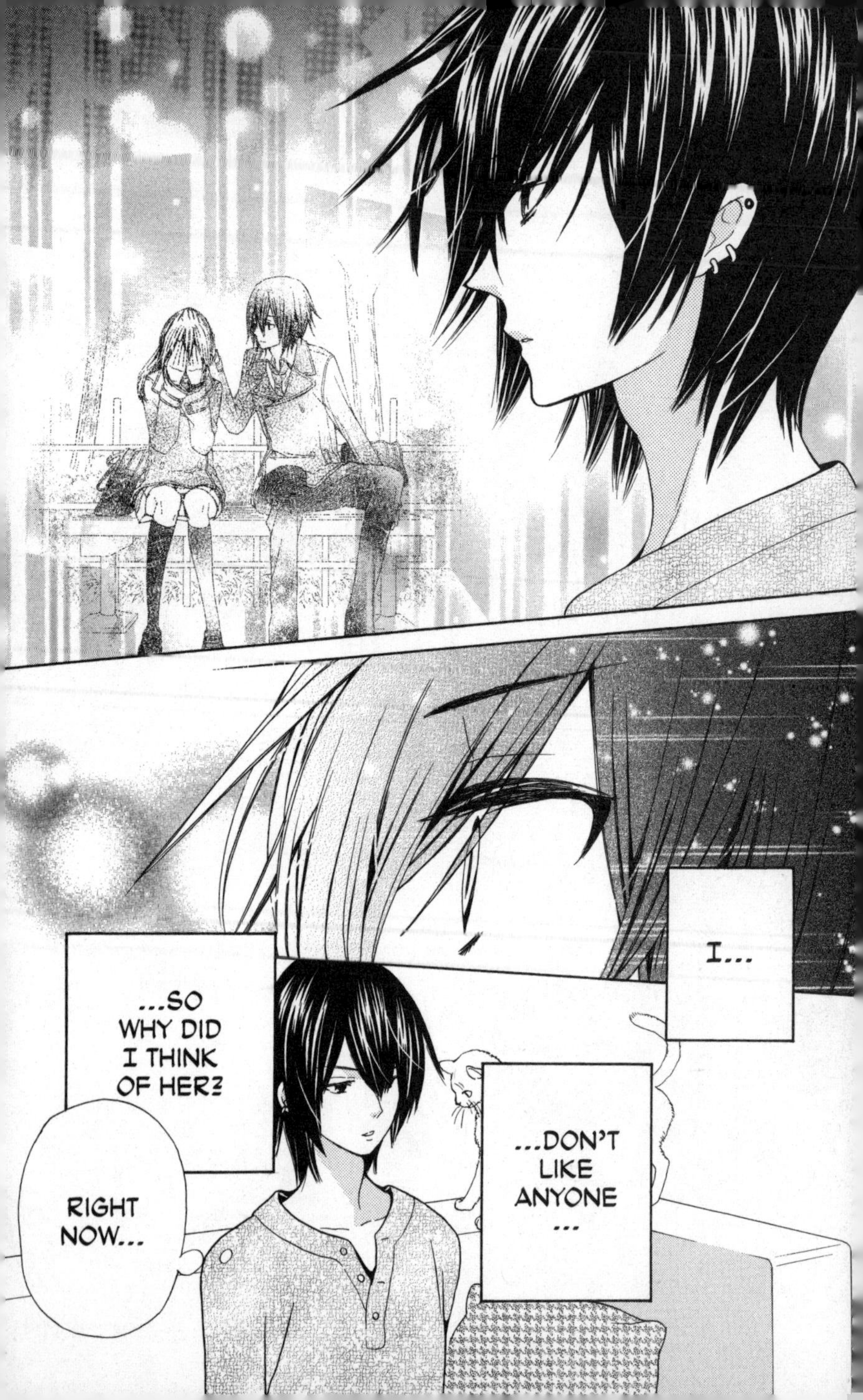
I...
...DON'T LIKE ANYONE ...
...SO WHY DID I THINK OF HER?
RIGHT NOW...

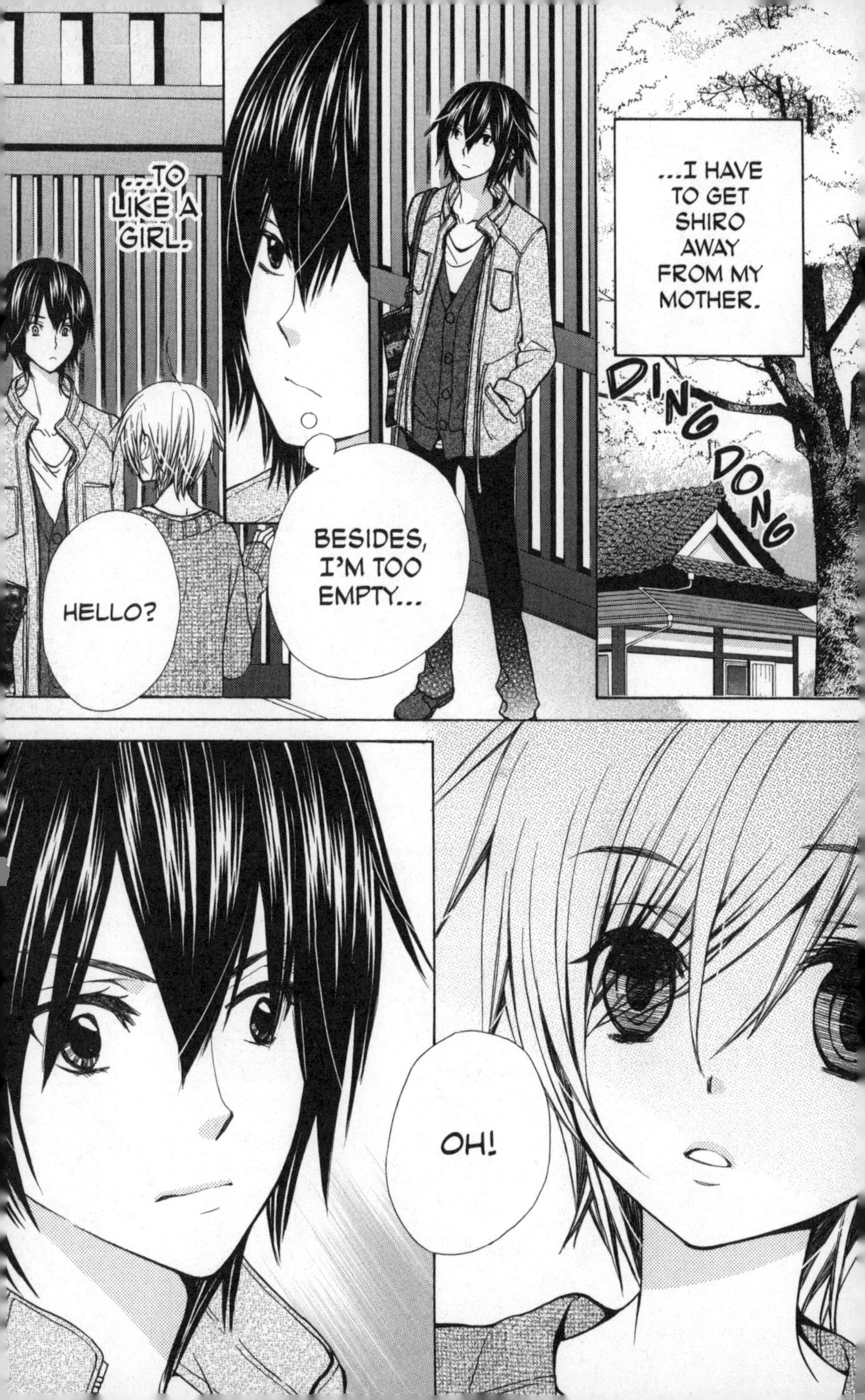
...I HAVE TO GET SHIRO AWAY FROM MY MOTHER.
DING DONG
BESIDES, I'M TOO EMPTY...
...TO LIKE A GIRL.
HELLO?
OH!

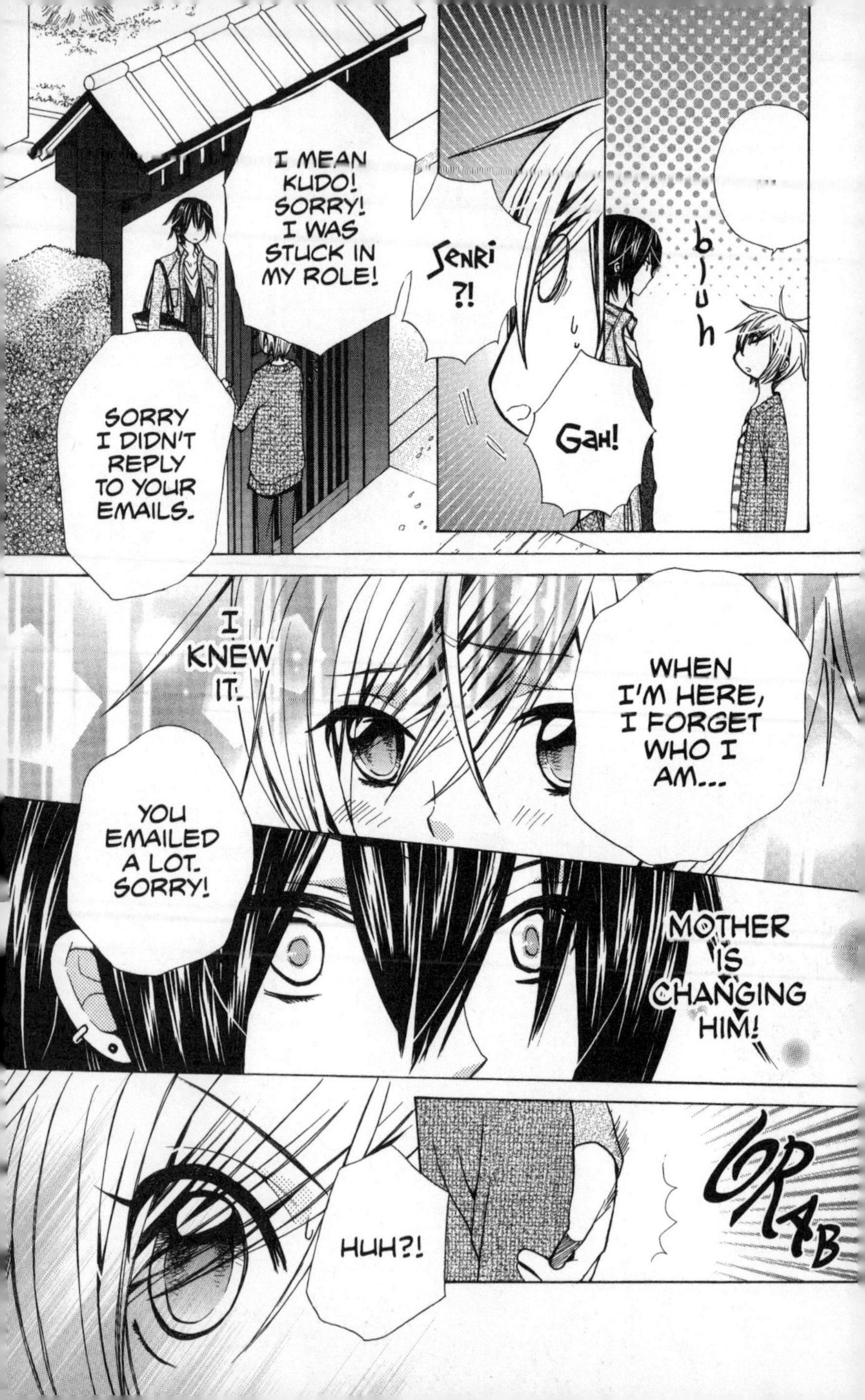
...
bluh
Senri ?!
Gah!
I MEAN KUDO! SORRY! I WAS STUCK IN MY ROLE!
SORRY I DIDN'T REPLY TO YOUR EMAILS.
WHEN I'M HERE, I FORGET WHO I AM...
I KNEW IT.
MOTHER IS CHANGING HIM!
YOU EMAILED A LOT. SORRY!
GRAB
HUH?!

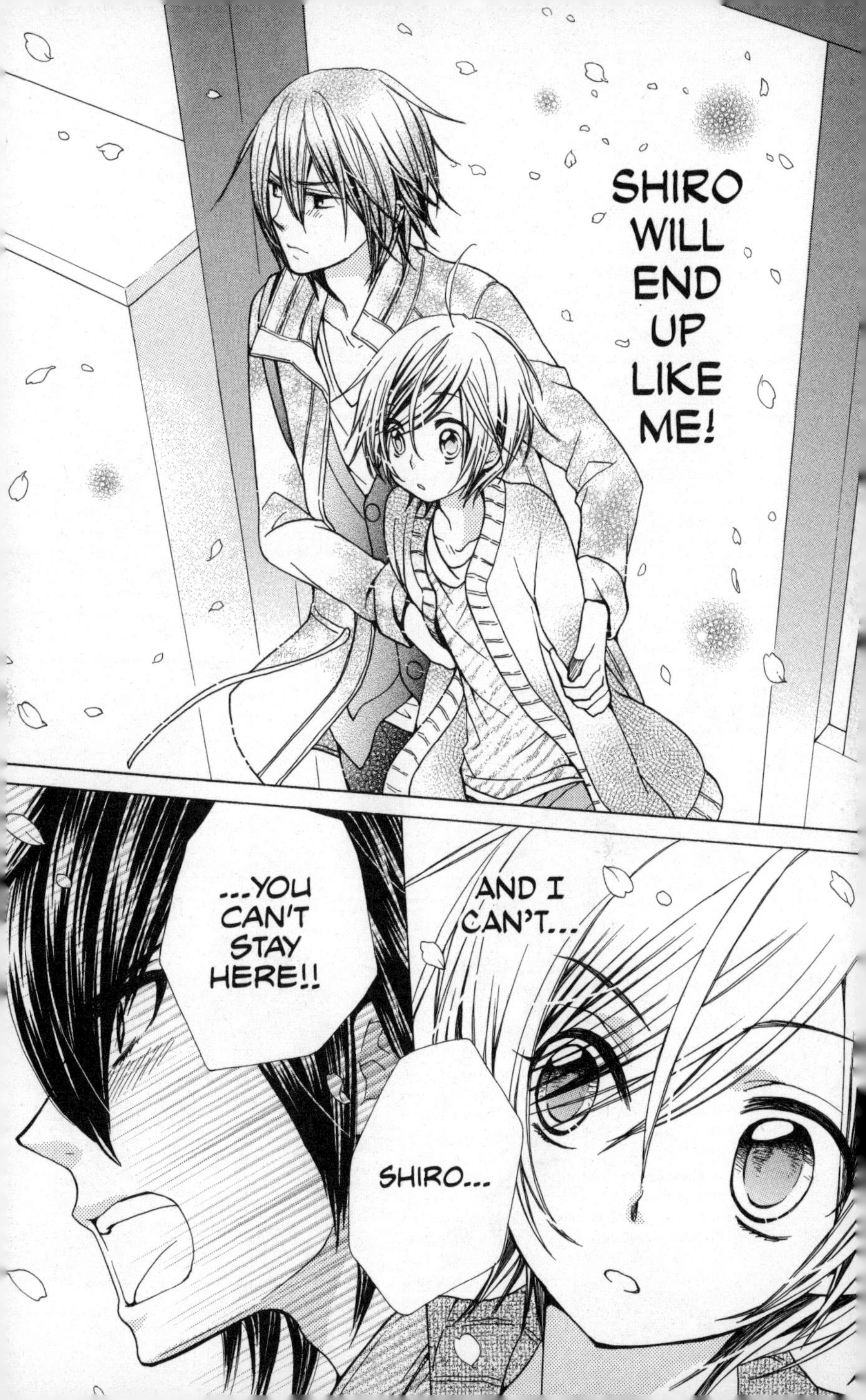
SHIRO WILL END UP LIKE ME!
AND I CAN'T...
SHIRO...
...YOU CAN'T STAY HERE!!

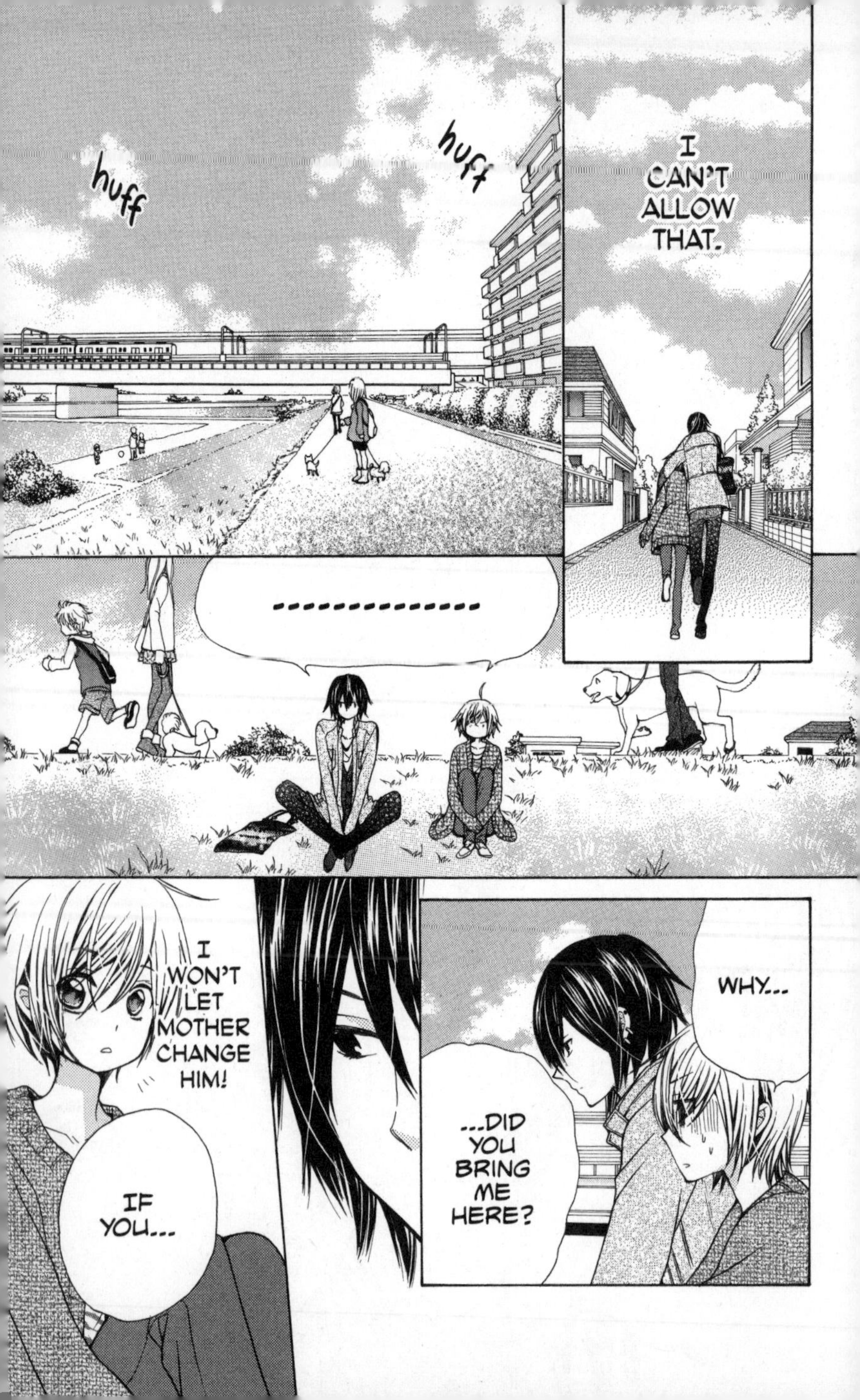
I CAN'T ALLOW THAT.
huff
huff

WHY...
...DID YOU BRING ME HERE?
I WON'T LET MOTHER CHANGE HIM!
IF YOU...

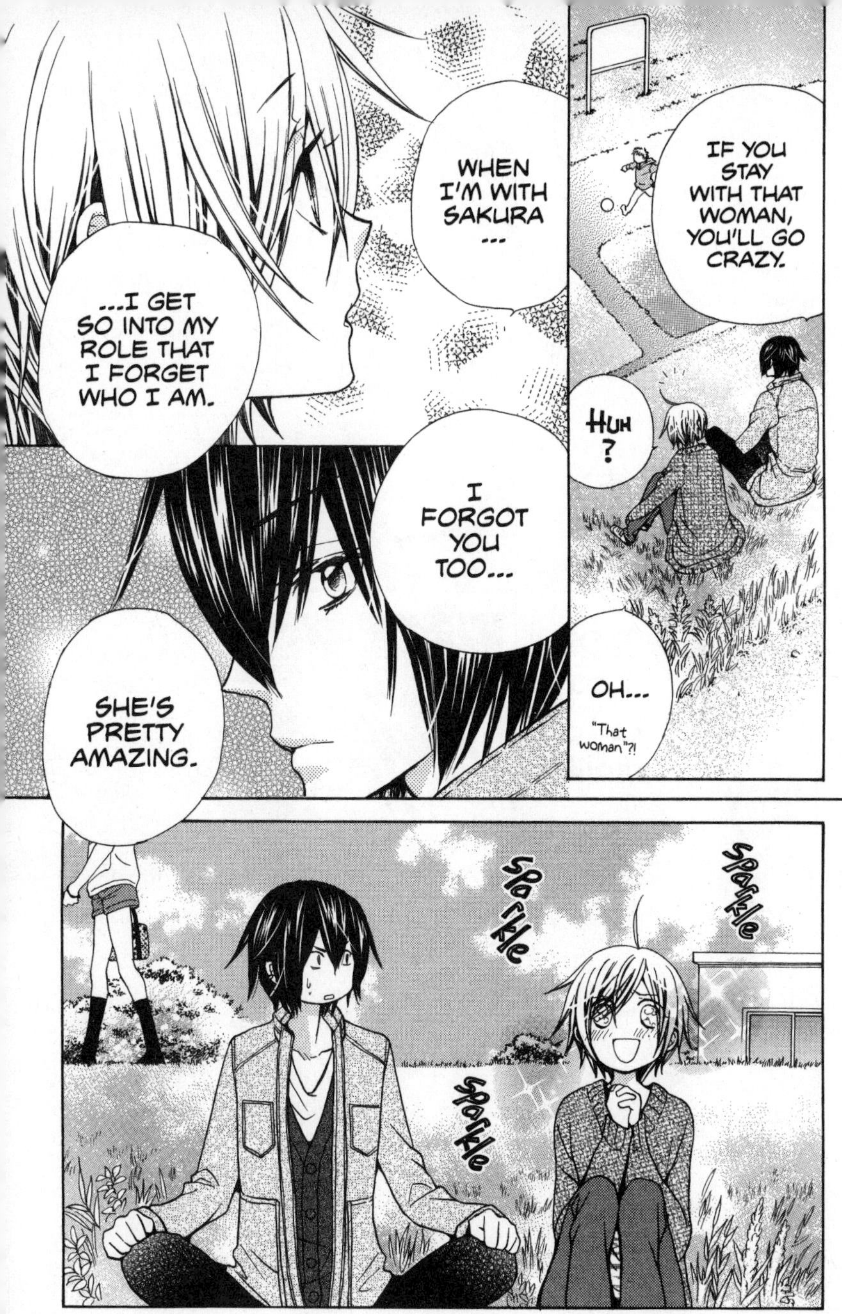
IF YOU STAY WITH THAT WOMAN, YOU'LL GO CRAZY.
HUH?
OH...
"That woman"?!
WHEN I'M WITH SAKURA...
...I GET SO INTO MY ROLE THAT I FORGET WHO I AM.
I FORGOT YOU TOO...
SHE'S PRETTY AMAZING.
SPARKLE
SPARKLE
SPARKLE

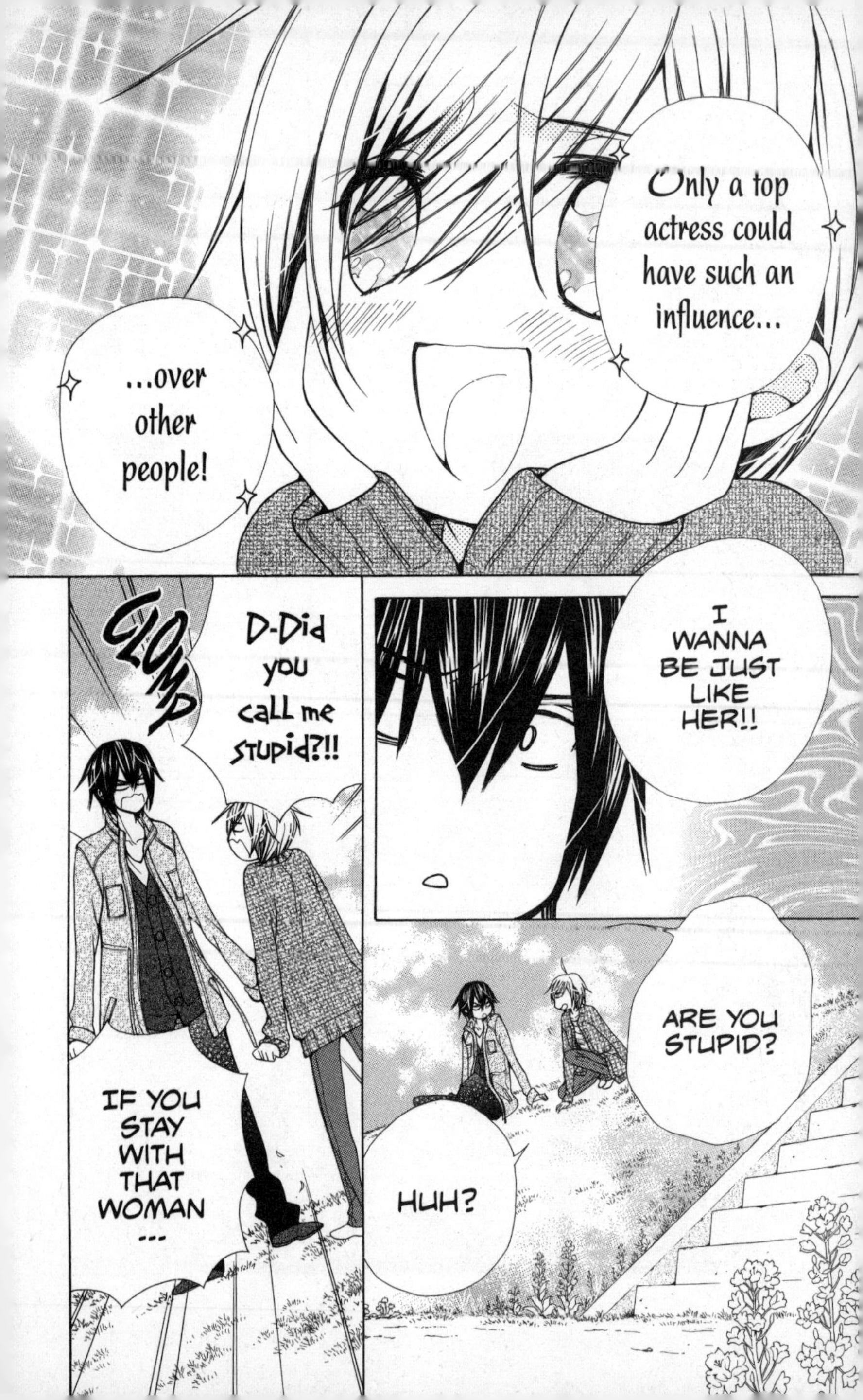
Only a top actress could have such an influence...
...over other people!
I WANNA BE JUST LIKE HER!!
ARE YOU STUPID?
HUH?
CLOMP
D-Did you call me stupid?!!
IF YOU STAY WITH THAT WOMAN ---

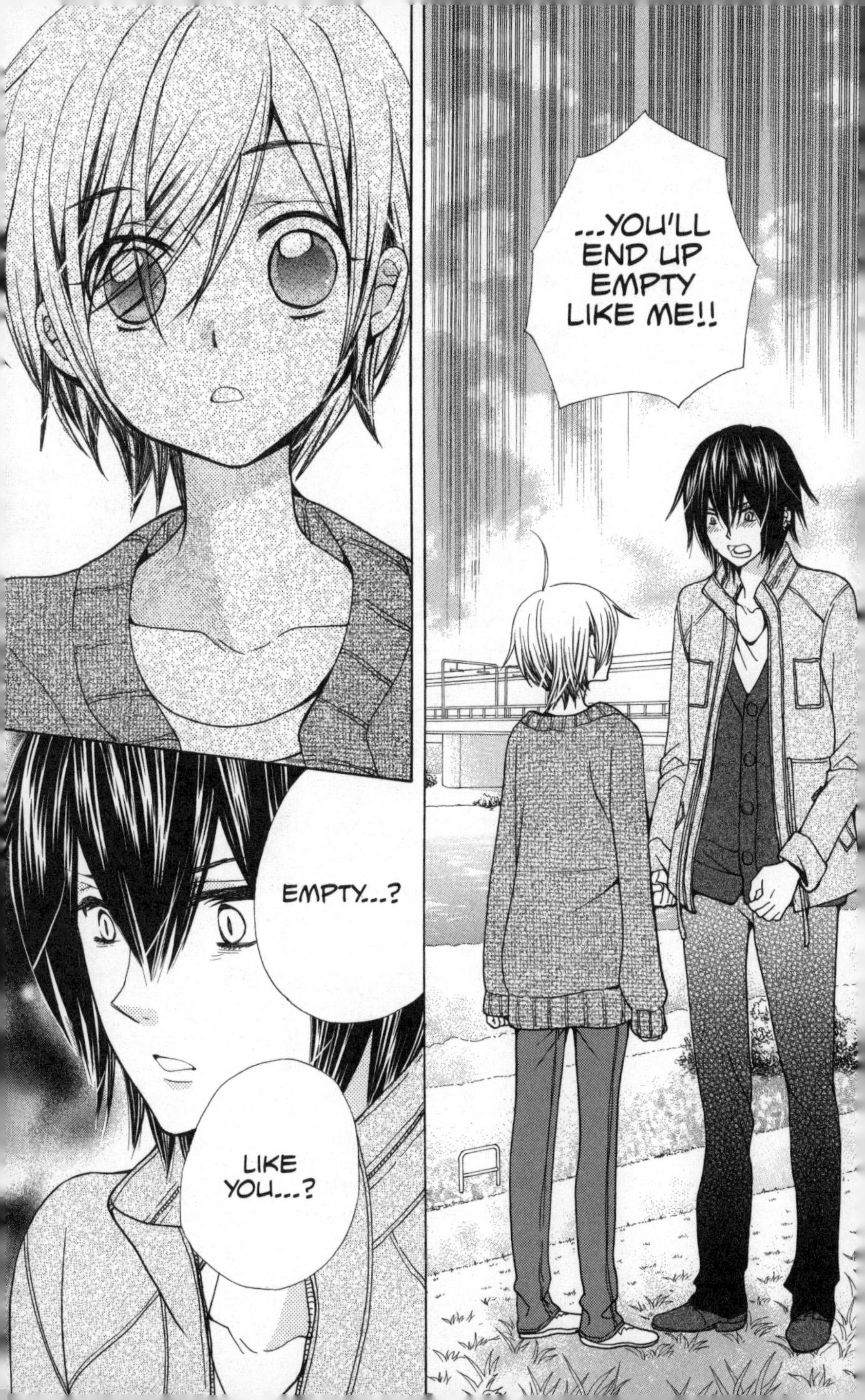
...YOU'LL END UP EMPTY LIKE ME!!
EMPTY...?
LIKE YOU...?

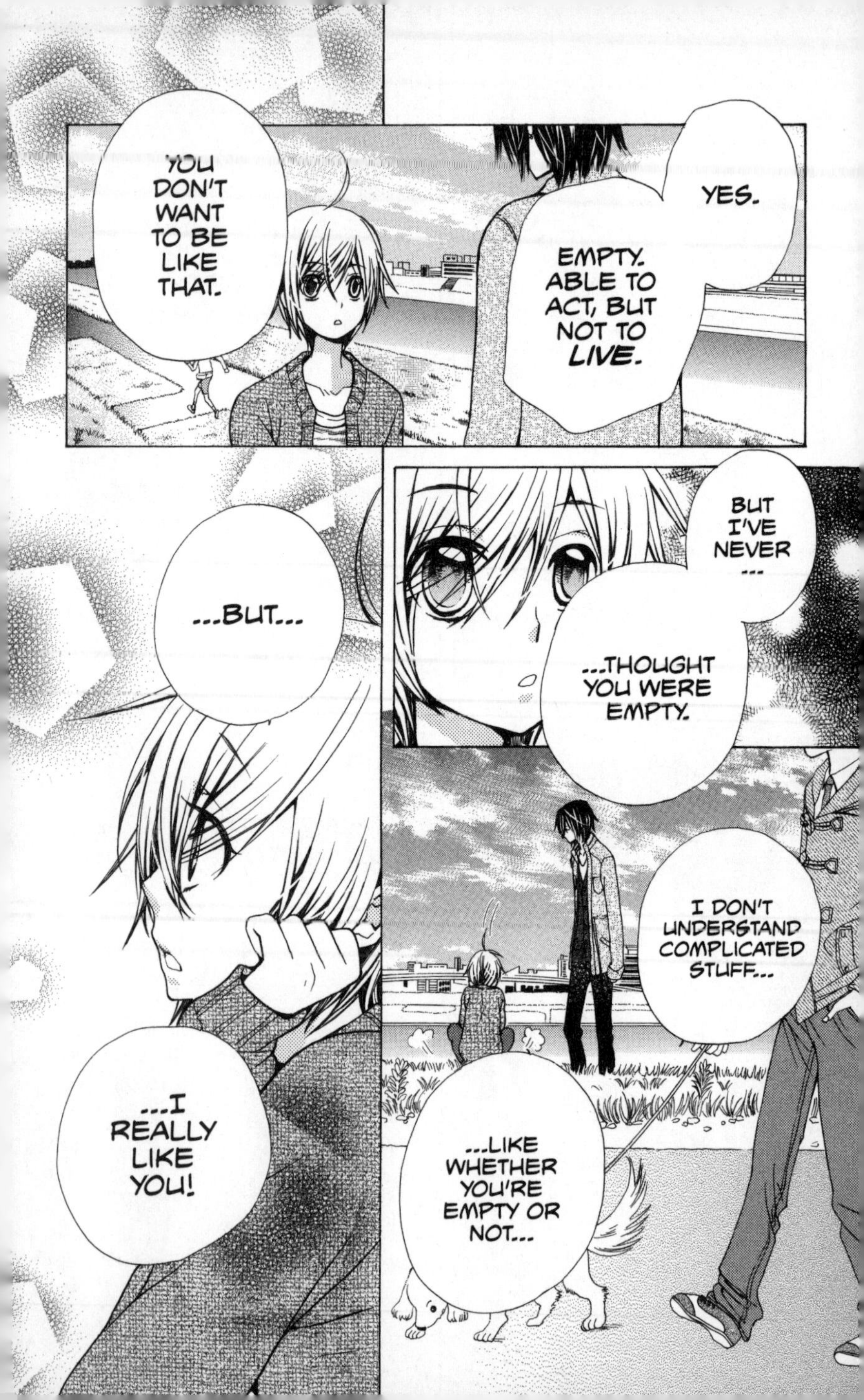
YES.
EMPTY. ABLE TO ACT, BUT NOT TO *LIVE*.
YOU DON'T WANT TO BE LIKE THAT.
BUT I'VE NEVER...
...THOUGHT YOU WERE EMPTY.
I DON'T UNDERSTAND COMPLICATED STUFF...
...LIKE WHETHER YOU'RE EMPTY OR NOT...
...BUT...
...I REALLY LIKE YOU!

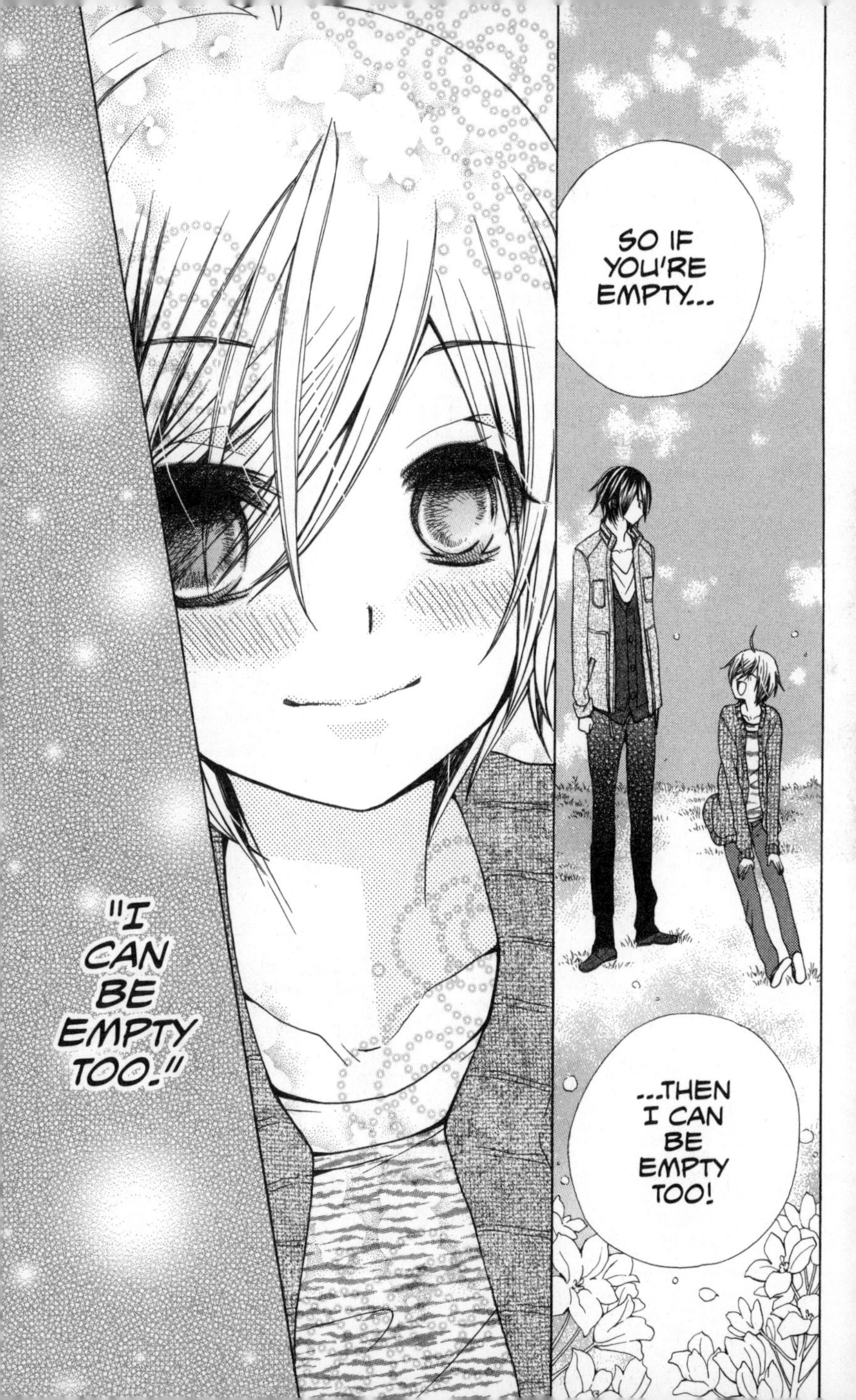
SO IF YOU'RE EMPTY...
...THEN I CAN BE EMPTY TOO!
"I CAN BE EMPTY TOO."

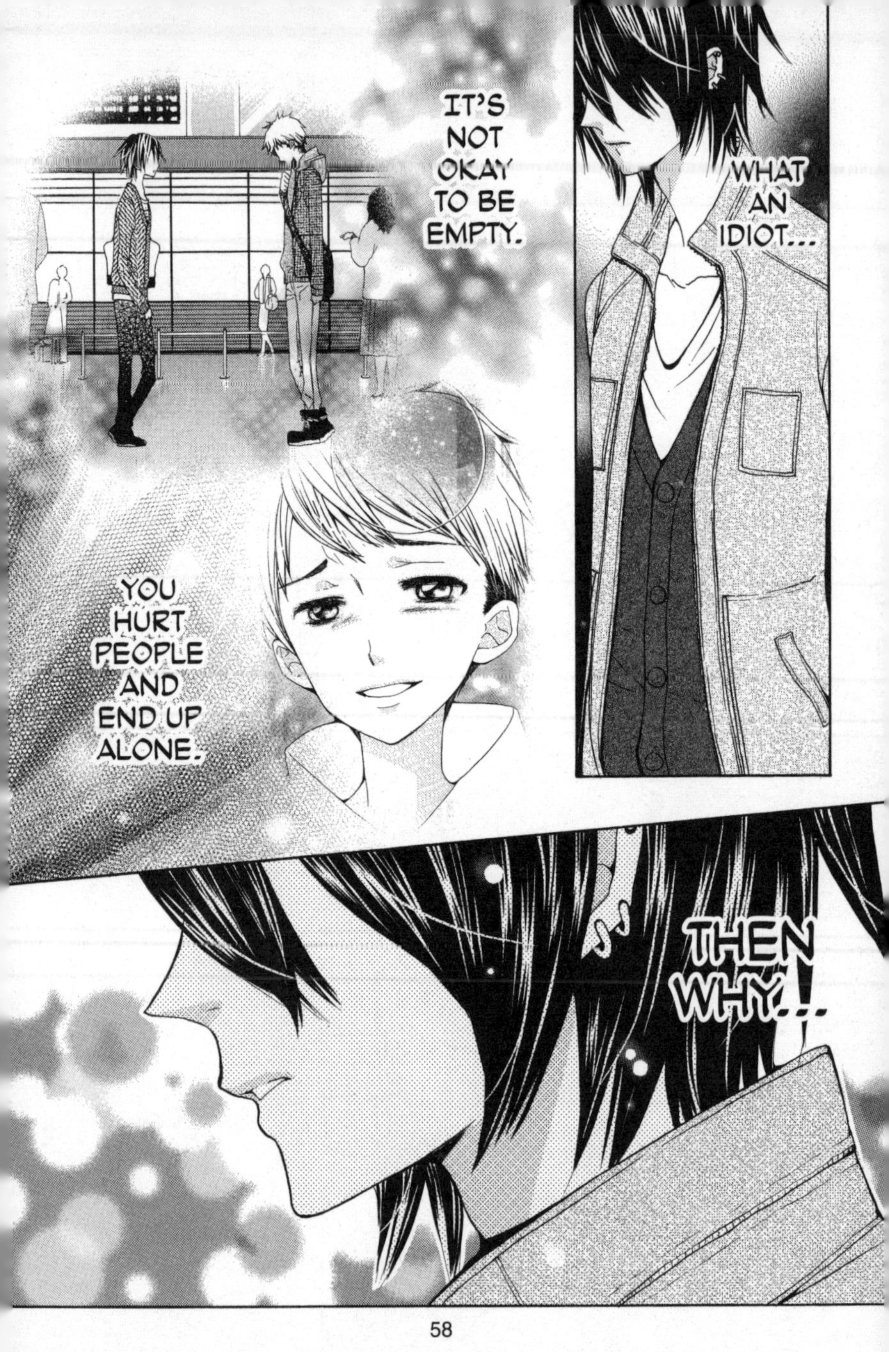
WHAT AN IDIOT...
IT'S NOT OKAY TO BE EMPTY.
YOU HURT PEOPLE AND END UP ALONE.
THEN WHY...

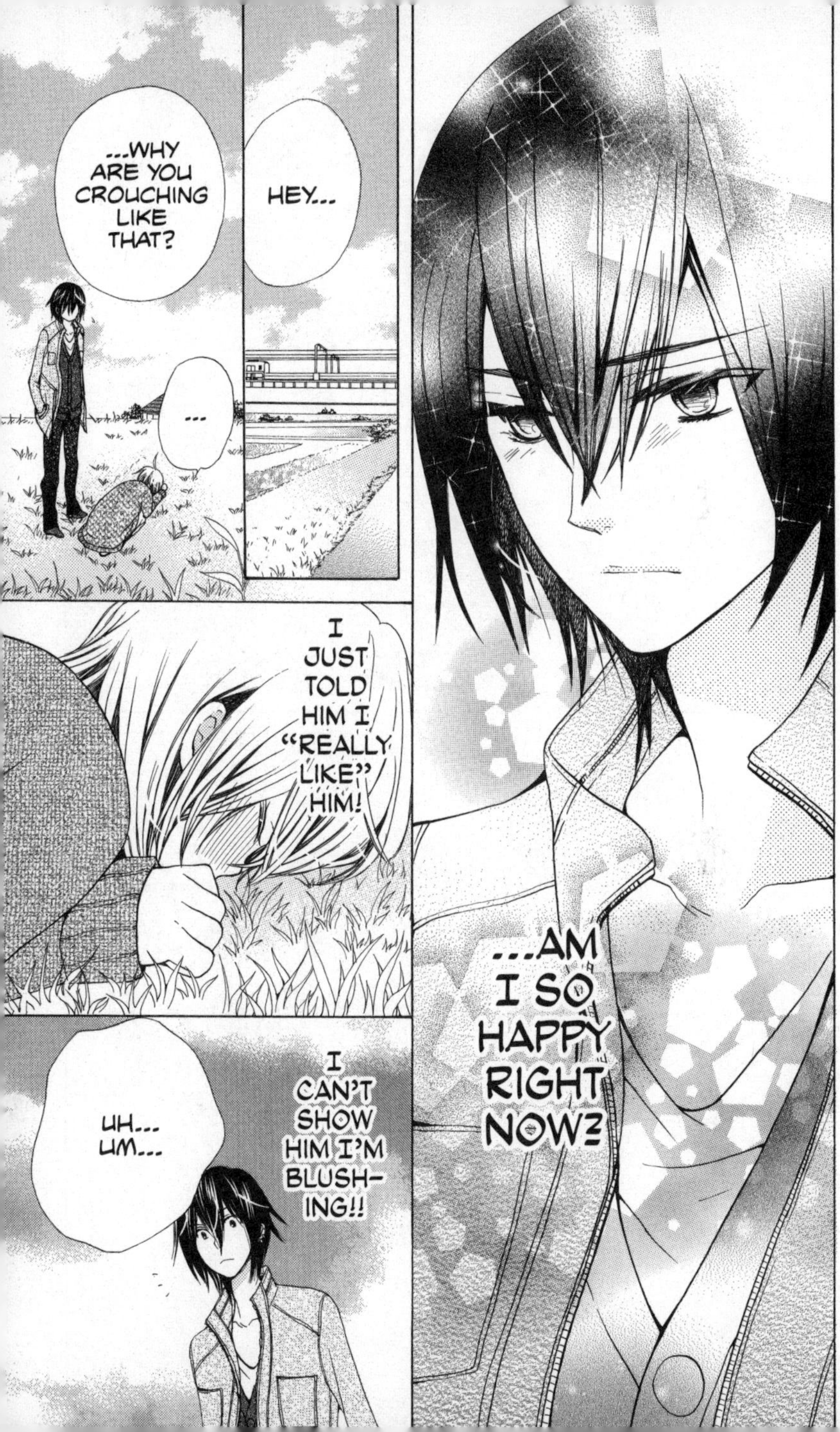
...AM I SO HAPPY RIGHT NOW?
HEY...
...WHY ARE YOU CROUCHING LIKE THAT?
...
I JUST TOLD HIM I "REALLY LIKE" HIM!
I CAN'T SHOW HIM I'M BLUSH-ING!!
UH... UM...

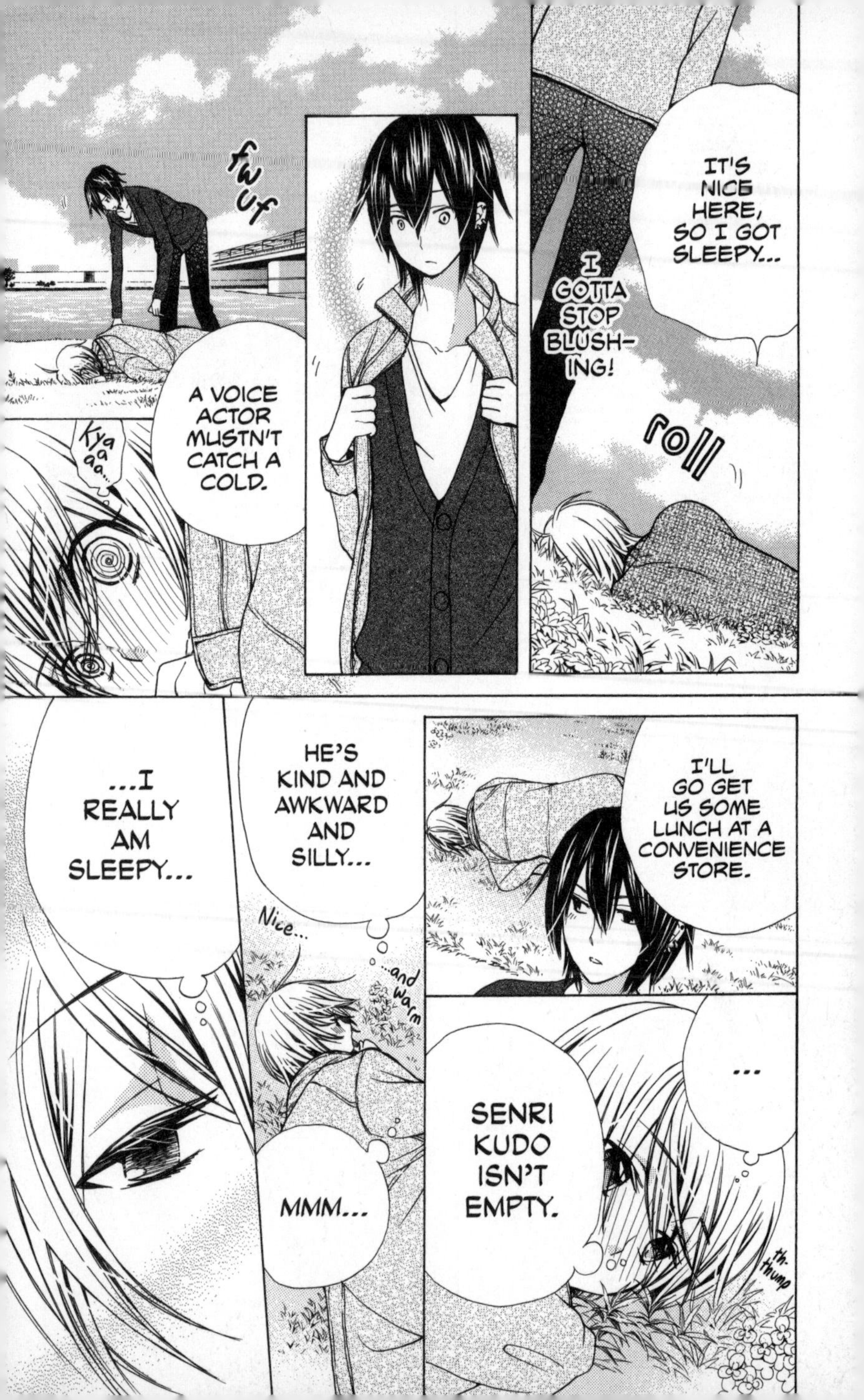
IT'S NICE HERE, SO I GOT SLEEPY...
I GOTTA STOP BLUSHING!
roll
fwuf
A VOICE ACTOR MUSTN'T CATCH A COLD.
Kyaaaa...
I'LL GO GET US SOME LUNCH AT A CONVENIENCE STORE.
...
SENRI KUDO ISN'T EMPTY.
th-thump
HE'S KIND AND AWKWARD AND SILLY...
Nice...
...and warm
MMM...
...I REALLY AM SLEEPY...

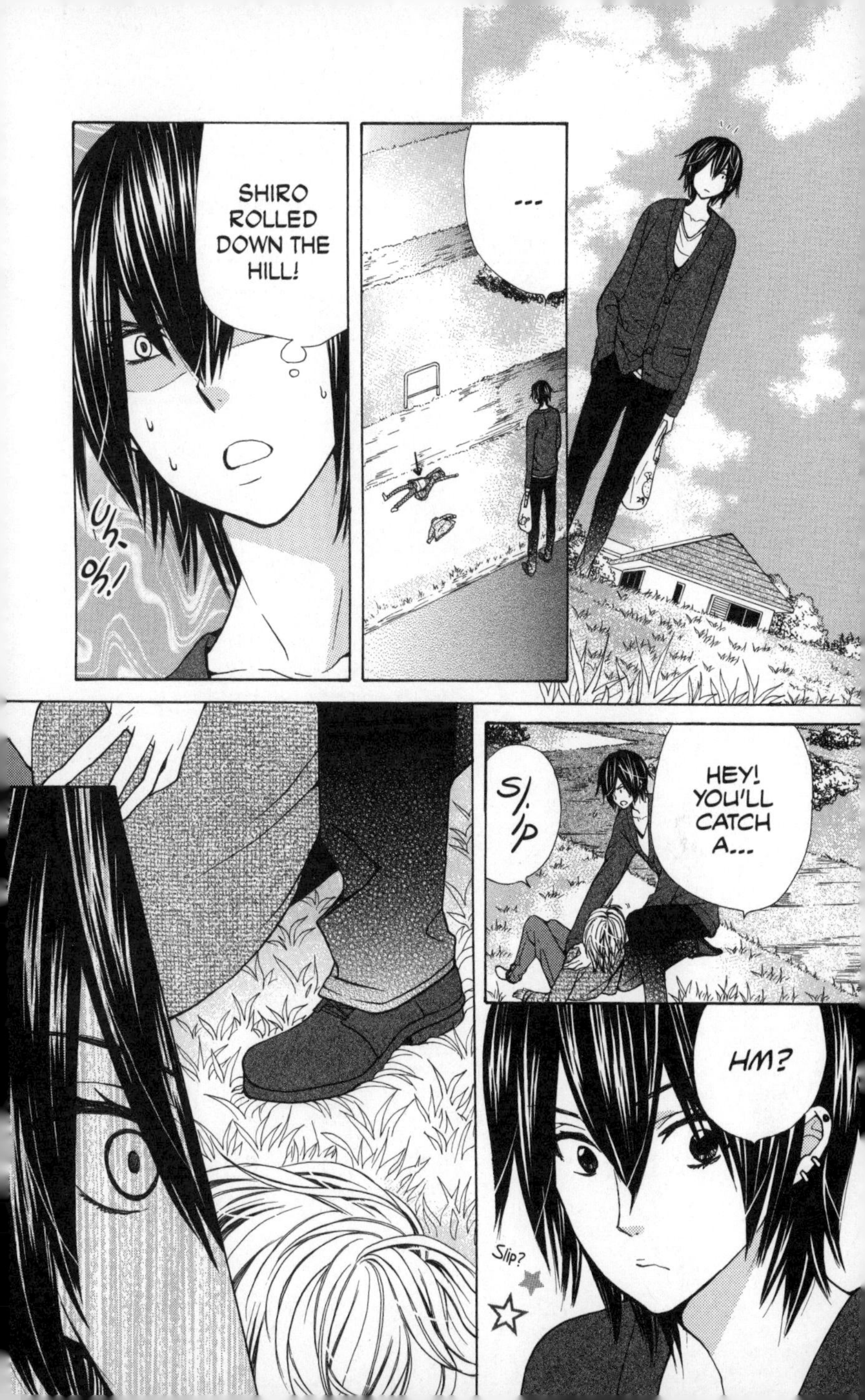
...
SHIRO ROLLED DOWN THE HILL!
Uh-oh!
HEY! YOU'LL CATCH A...
Slip
HM?
Slip?

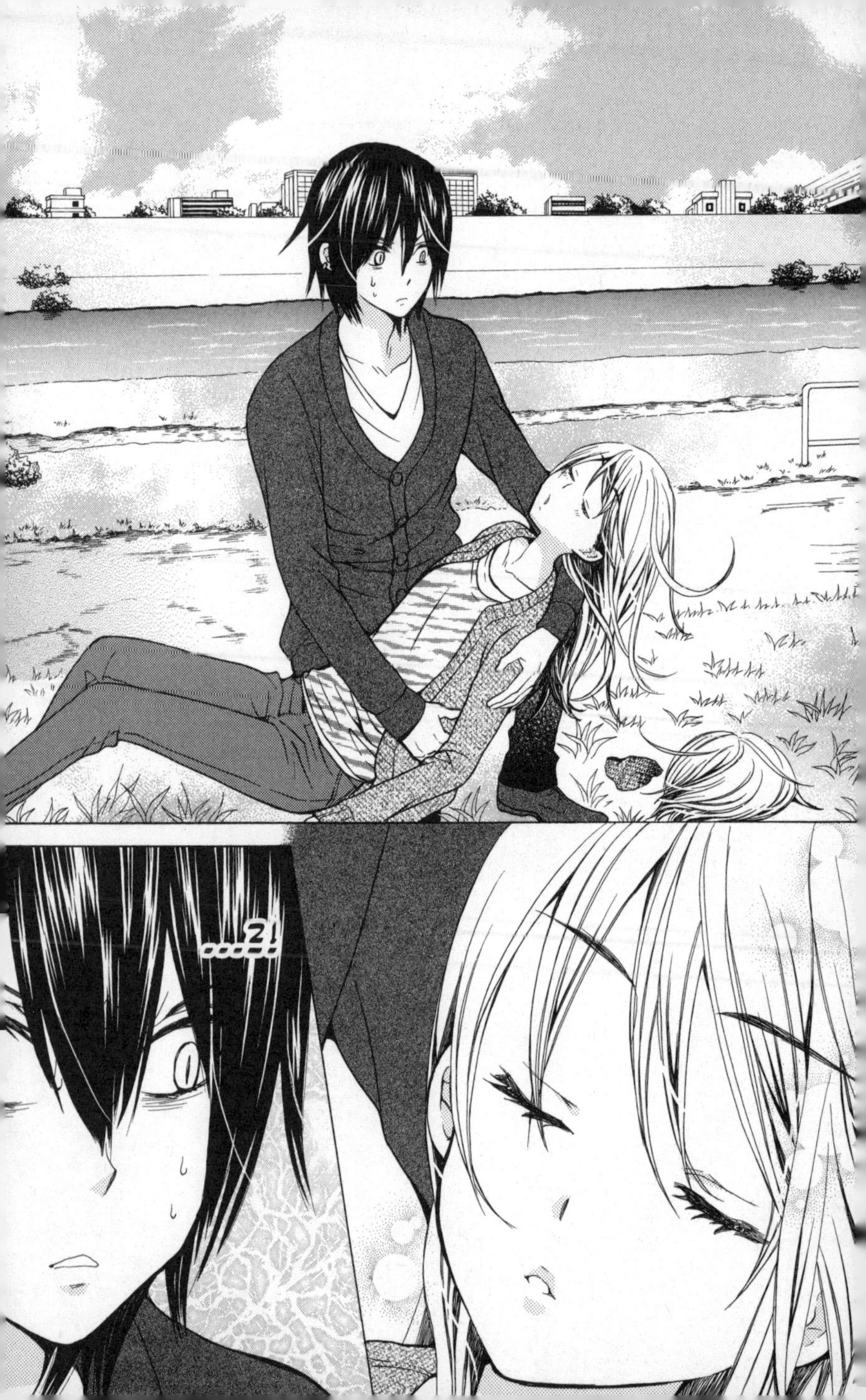
...?!

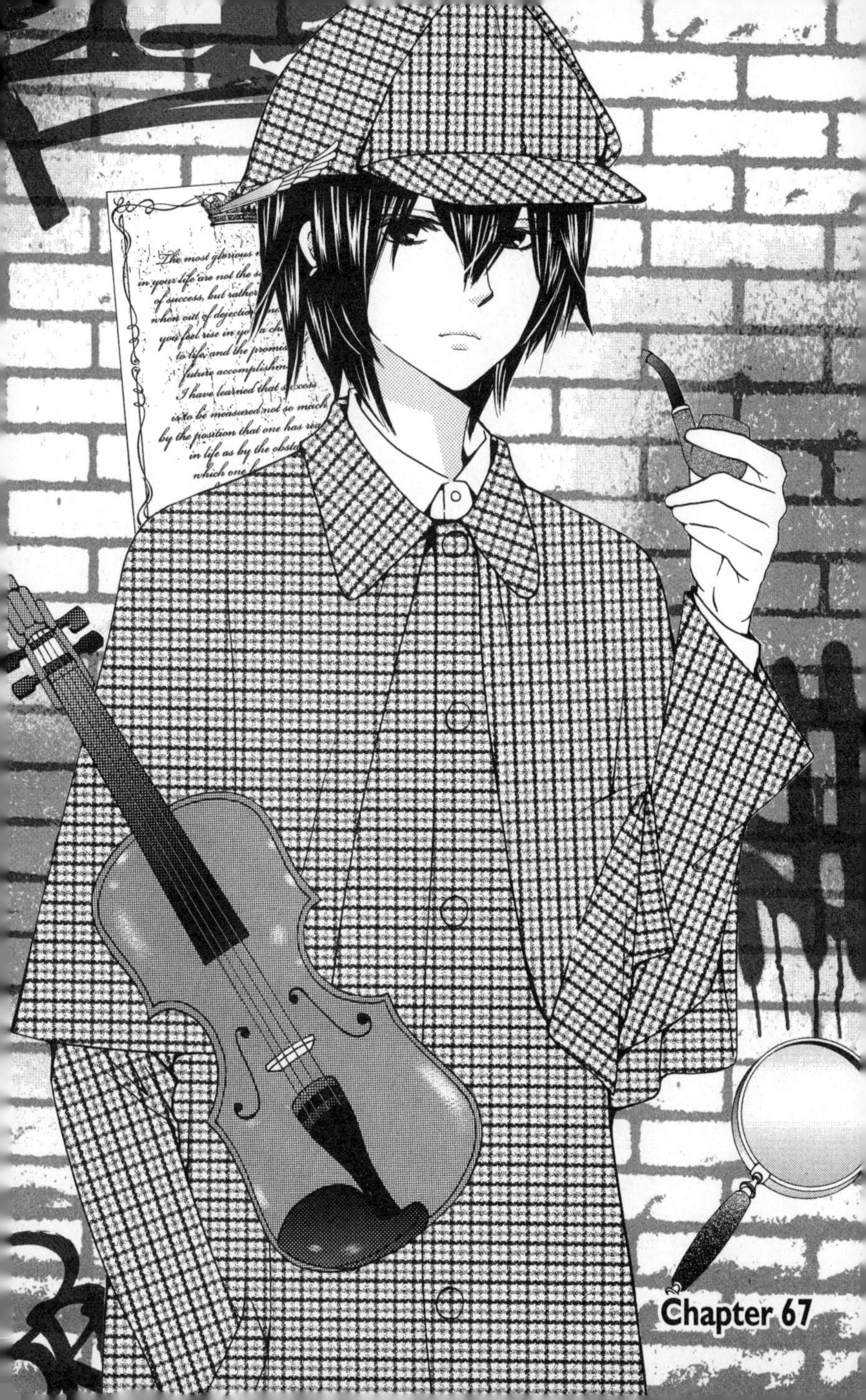
The most glorious
in your life are not the
of success, but rather
when out of dejection
you feel rise in yo a ch
to life and the promis
future accomplishm
I have learned that succes
is to be measured not so much
by the position that one has ri
in life as by the obst
which one

Chapter 67

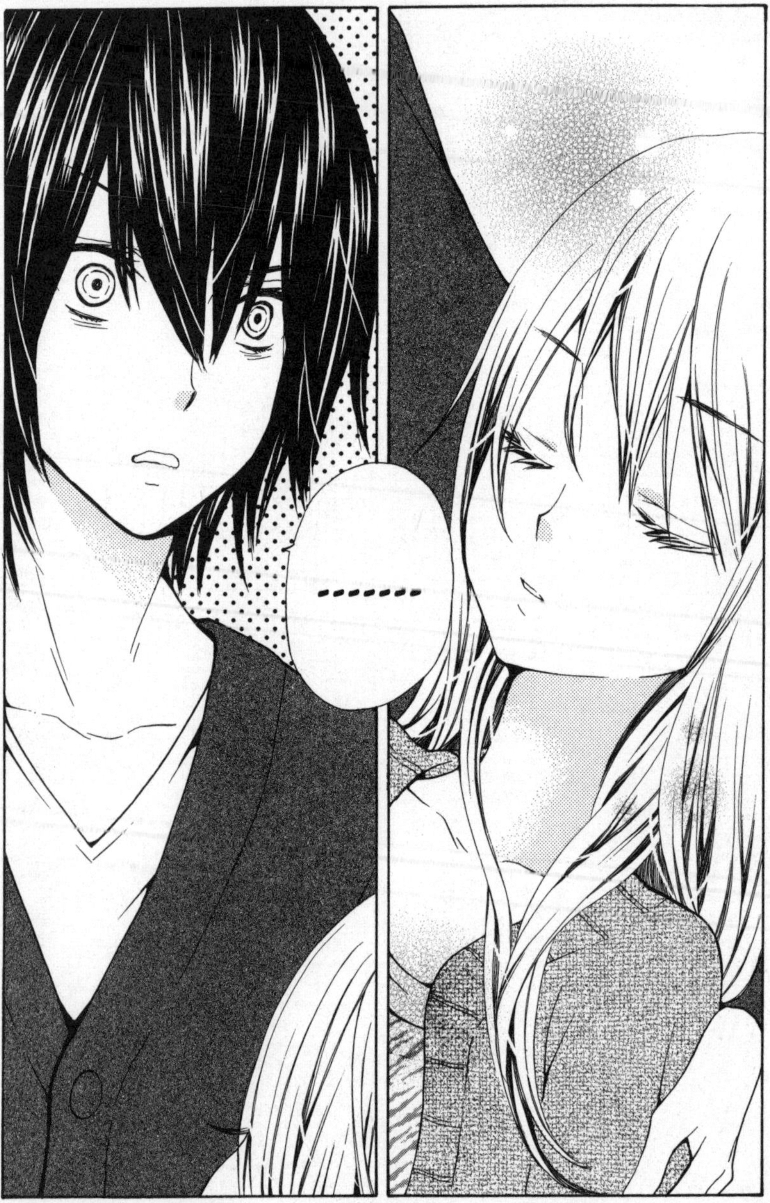
......

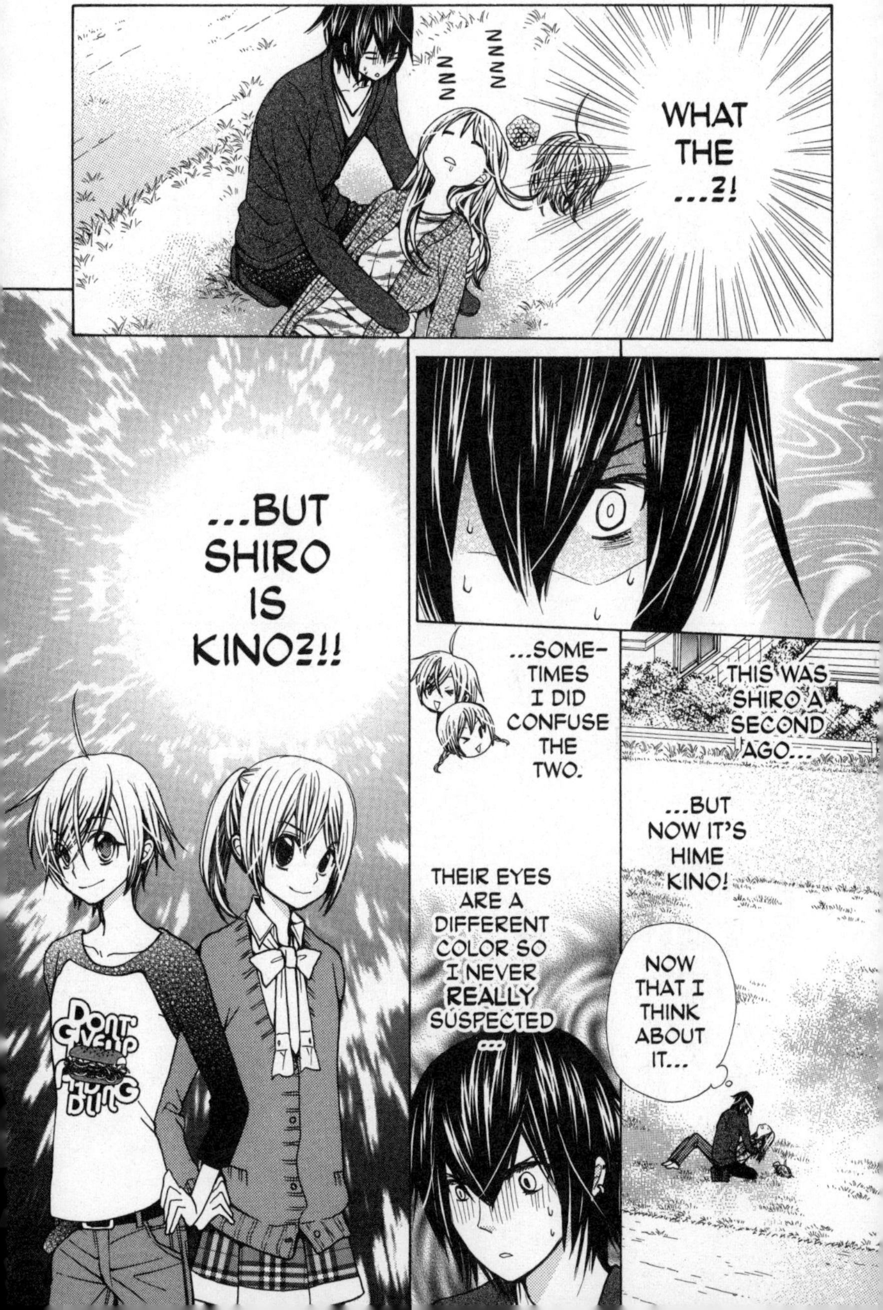
WHAT THE ...?!
THIS WAS SHIRO A SECOND AGO...
...BUT NOW IT'S HIME KINO!
NOW THAT I THINK ABOUT IT...
...SOMETIMES I DID CONFUSE THE TWO.
THEIR EYES ARE A DIFFERENT COLOR SO I NEVER REALLY SUSPECTED...
...BUT SHIRO IS KINO?!!

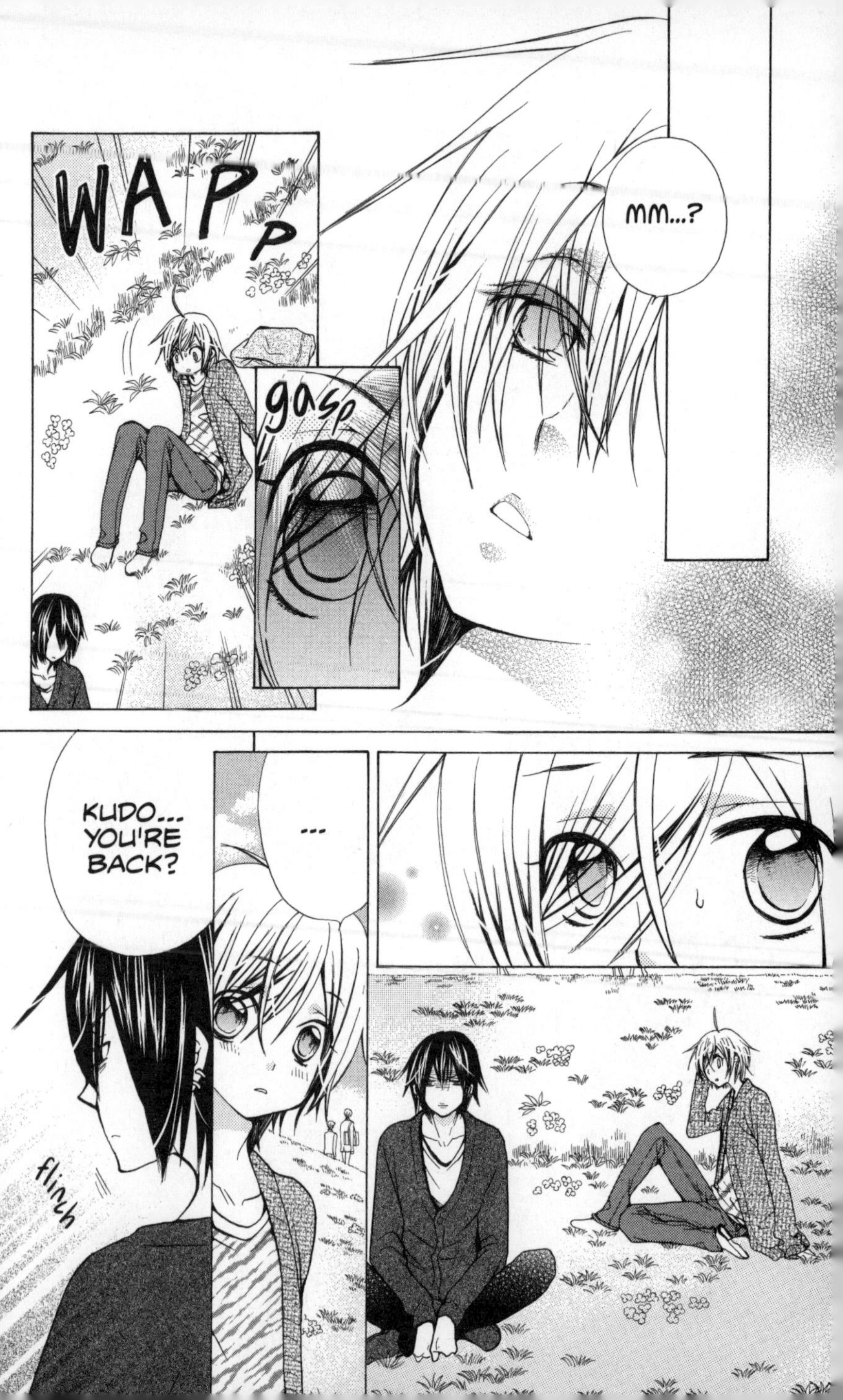
mm...?
gasp
WAPP
...
KUDO... YOU'RE BACK?
flinch

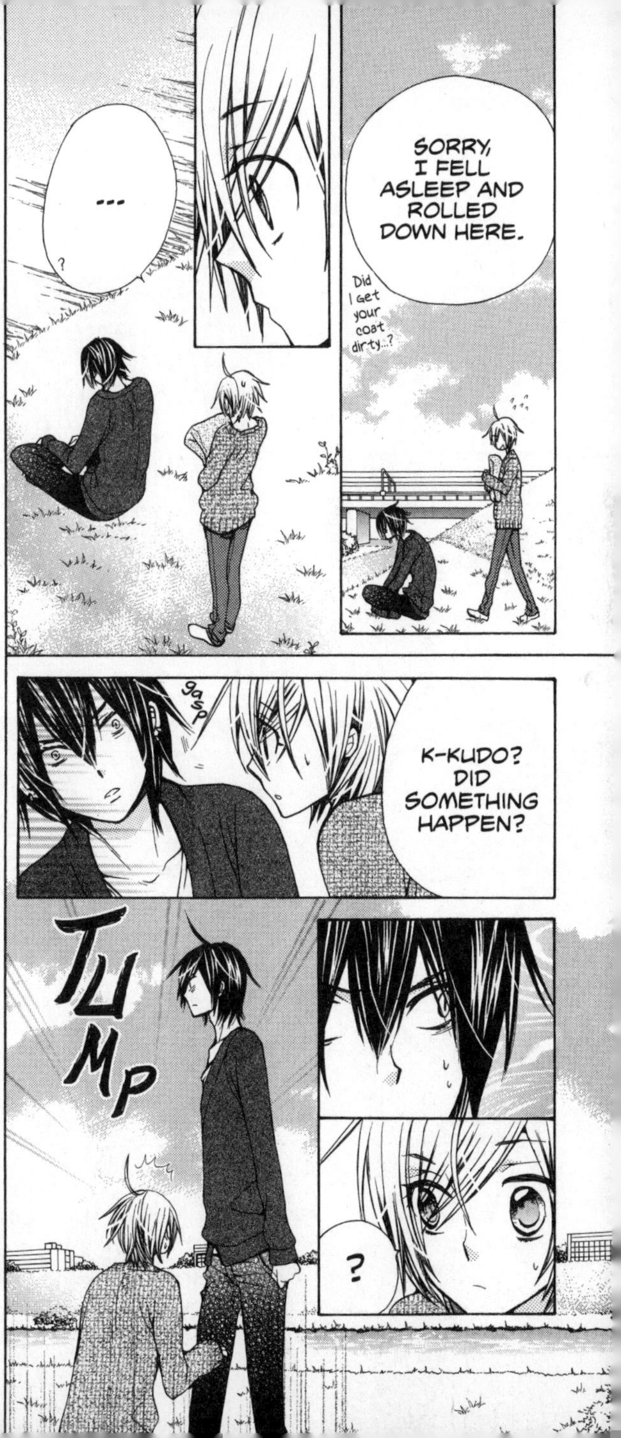
SORRY, I FELL ASLEEP AND ROLLED DOWN HERE.
Did I get your coat dirty...?
...
?
K-KUDO? DID SOMETHING HAPPEN?
gasp
?
TUMP

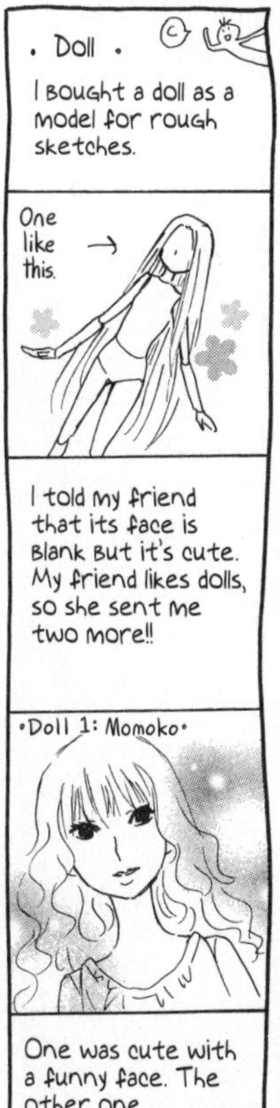
• Doll •
©
I bought a doll as a model for rough sketches.
One like this. →
I told my friend that its face is blank but it's cute. My friend likes dolls, so she sent me two more!!
•Doll 1: Momoko•
One was cute with a funny face. The other one...
RRMMMMMMMM
Amazon
This one's scary!
An assistant named her Bellona.

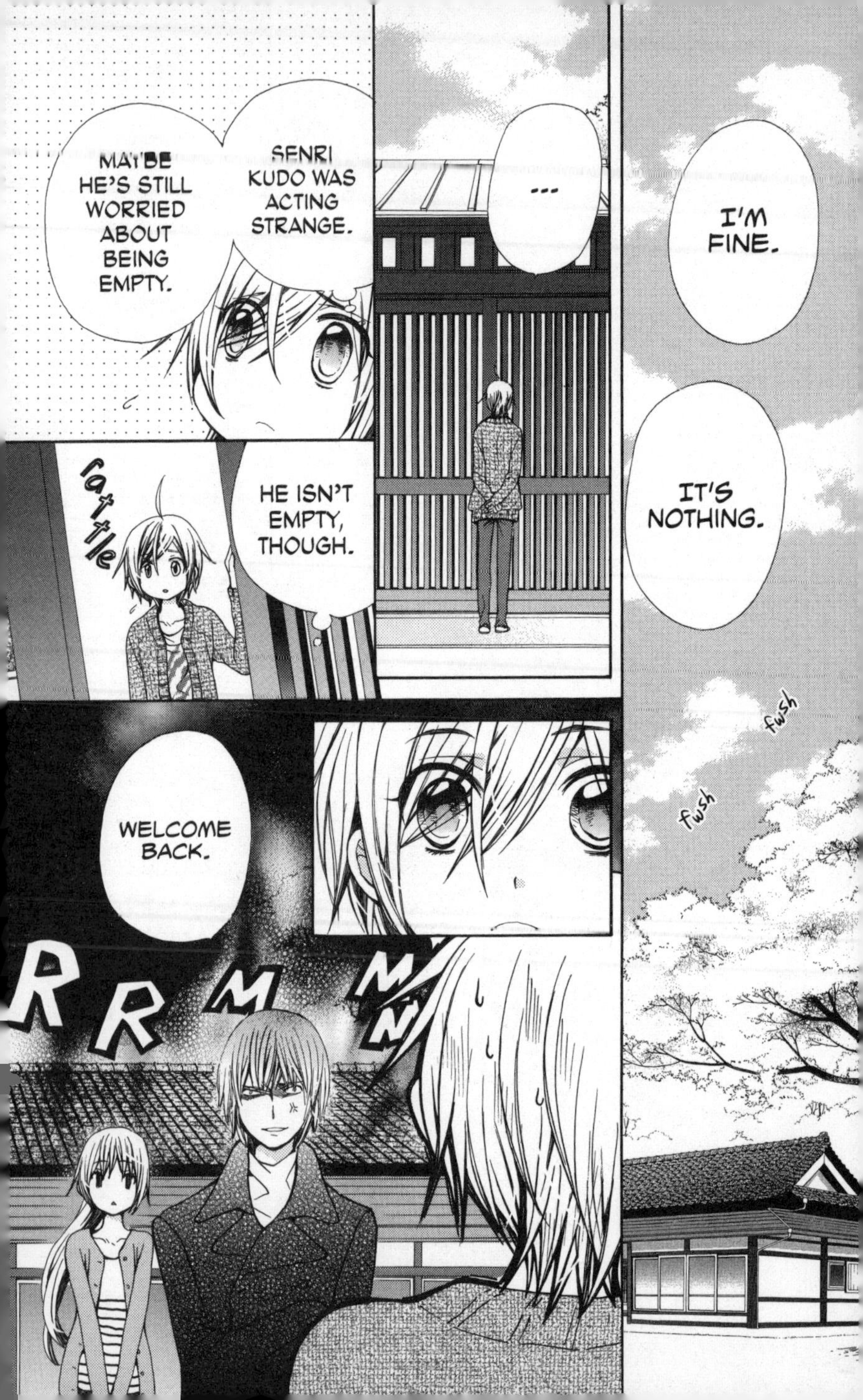
I'M FINE.
IT'S NOTHING.
fwsh
fwsh
...
SENRI KUDO WAS ACTING STRANGE.
MAYBE HE'S STILL WORRIED ABOUT BEING EMPTY.
HE ISN'T EMPTY, THOUGH.
rattle
WELCOME BACK.
RRMMMN

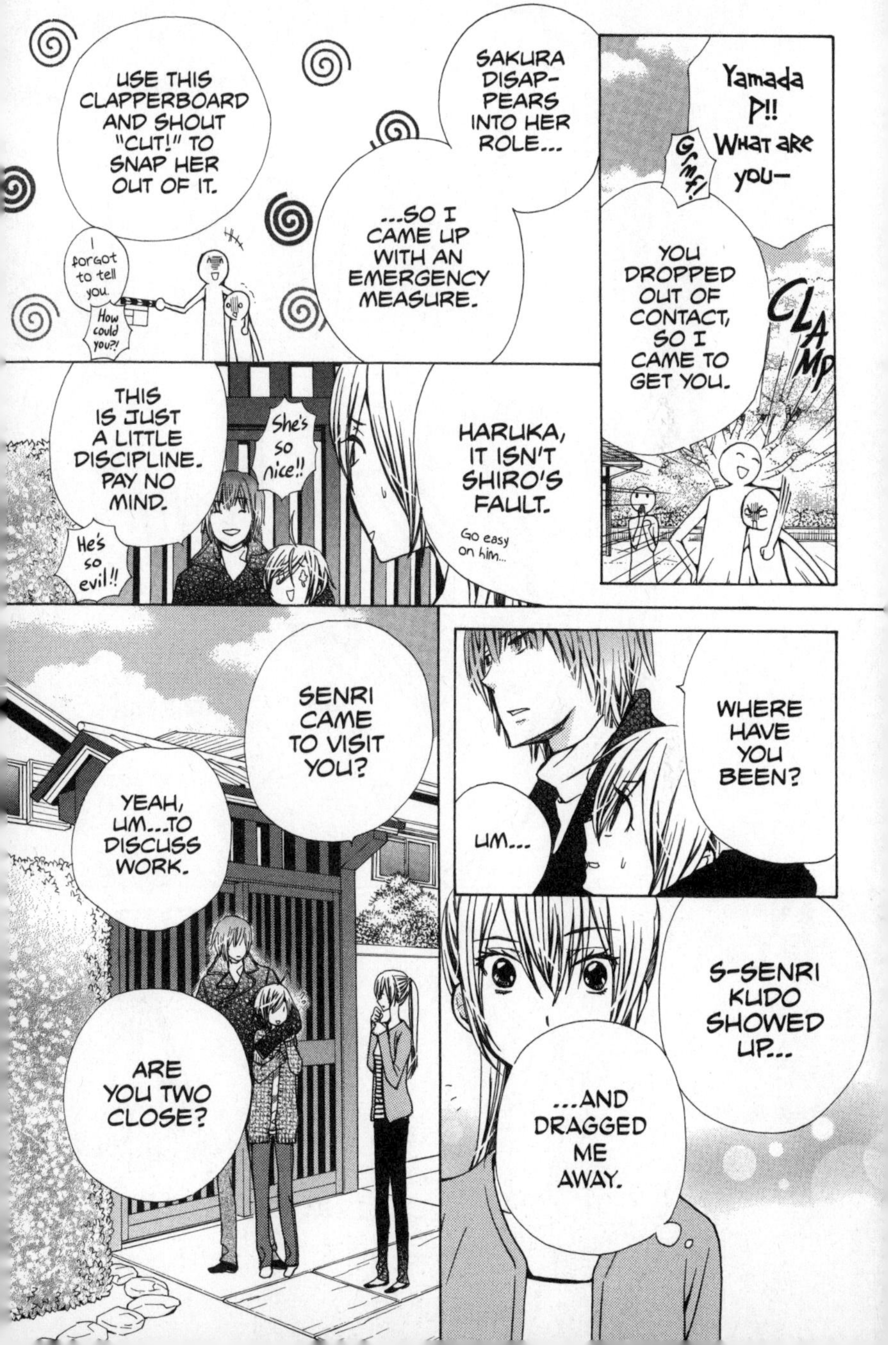
Yamada P!! What are you—
Grmf!
You dropped out of contact, so I came to get you.
CLAMP
Sakura disap-pears into her role...
...so I came up with an emergency measure.
Use this clapperboard and shout "Cut!" to snap her out of it.
I forgot to tell you.
How could you?!
Haruka, it isn't Shiro's fault.
Go easy on him...
This is just a little discipline. Pay no mind.
She's so nice!!
He's so evil!!
Where have you been?
Um...
S-Senri Kudo showed up...
...and dragged me away.
Senri came to visit you?
Yeah, um...to discuss work.
Are you two close?

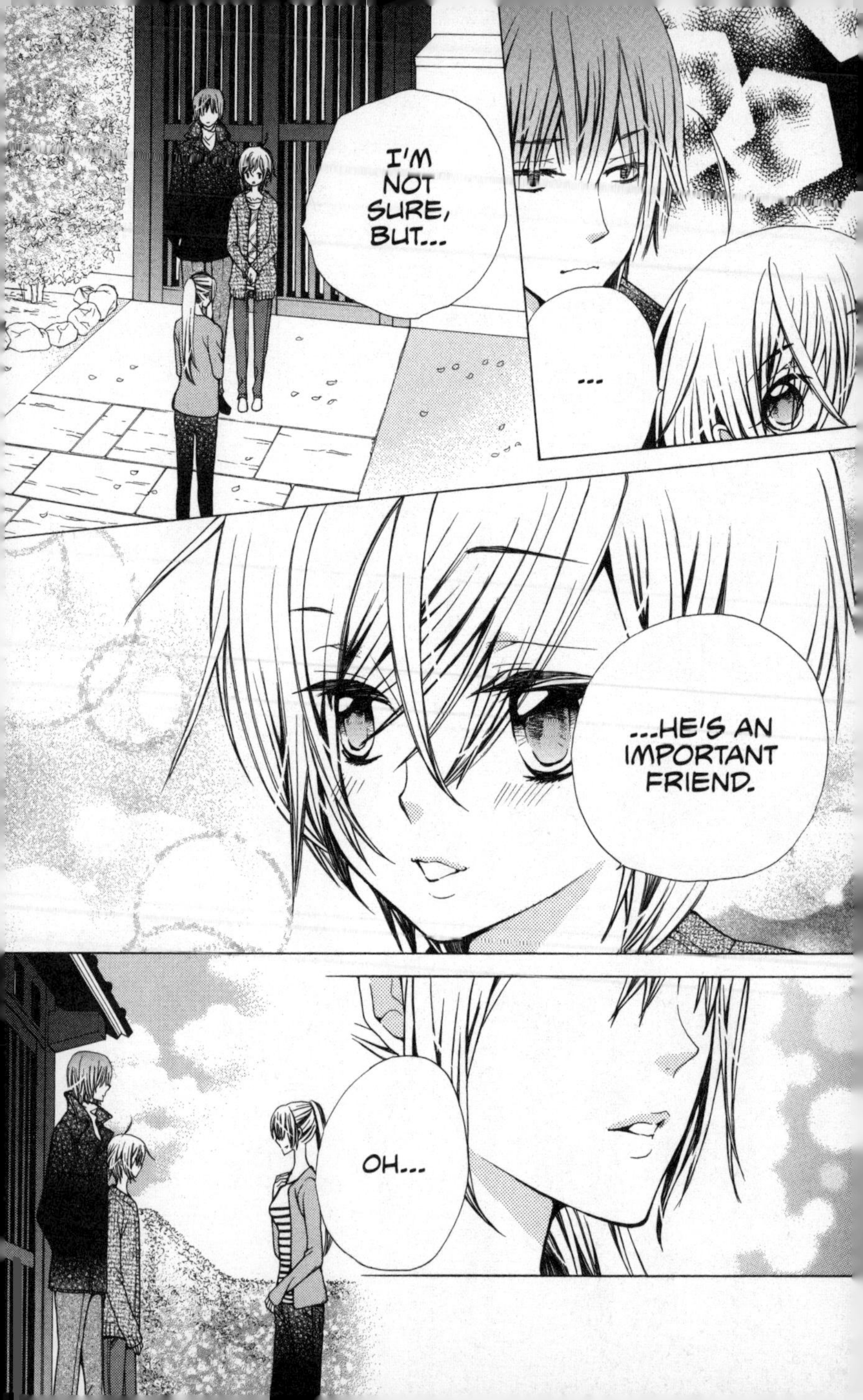
...
I'M NOT SURE, BUT...
...HE'S AN IMPORTANT FRIEND.
OH...

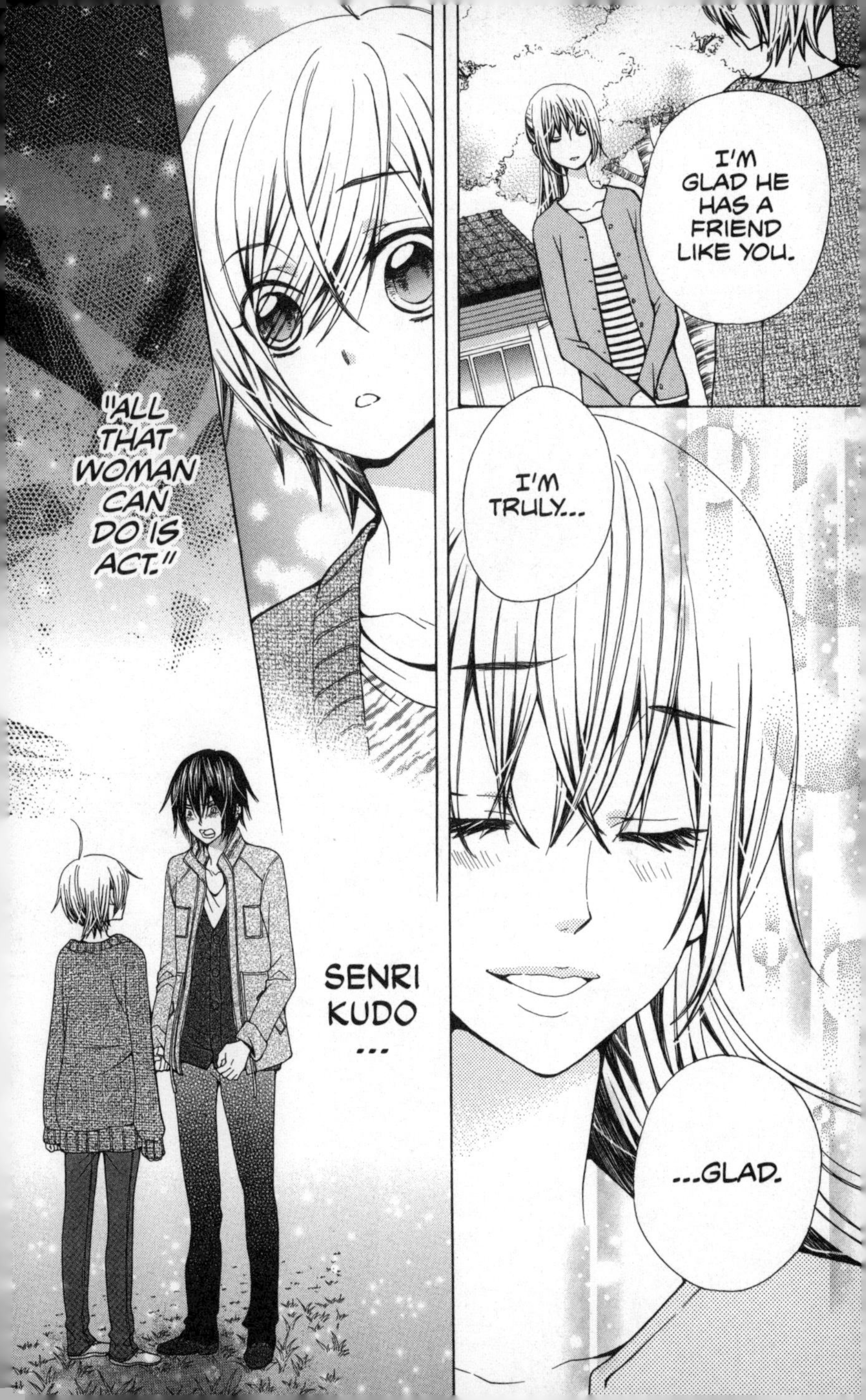
I'M GLAD HE HAS A FRIEND LIKE YOU.
I'M TRULY...
...GLAD.
"ALL THAT WOMAN CAN DO IS ACT."
SENRI KUDO ...

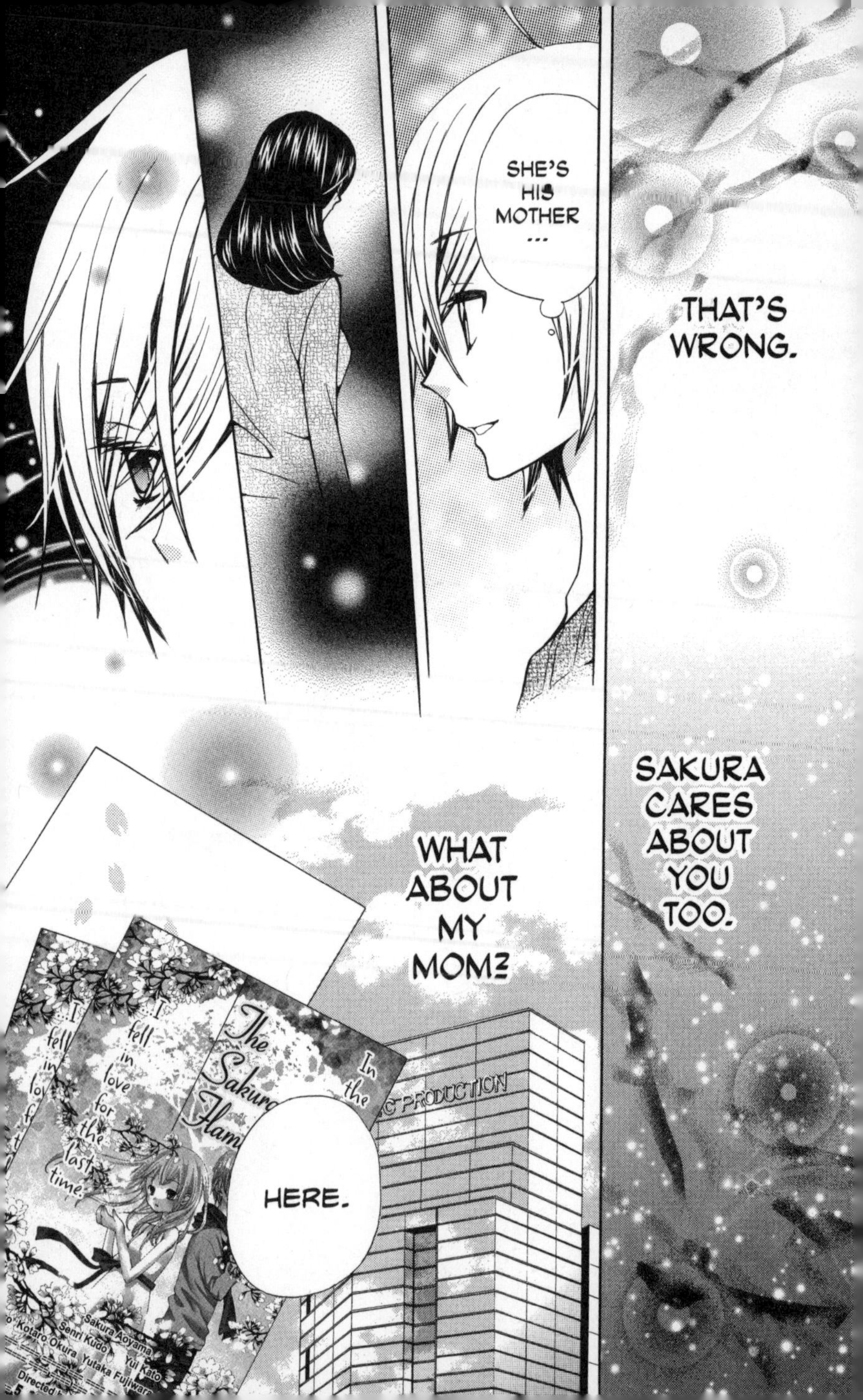
THAT'S WRONG.
SAKURA CARES ABOUT YOU TOO.
SHE'S HIS MOTHER...
WHAT ABOUT MY MOM?
...I fell in love for the last time.
Sakura Aoyama
Senri Kudo
Yui Kato
Kotaro Okura
Yutaka Fujiwara
HERE.

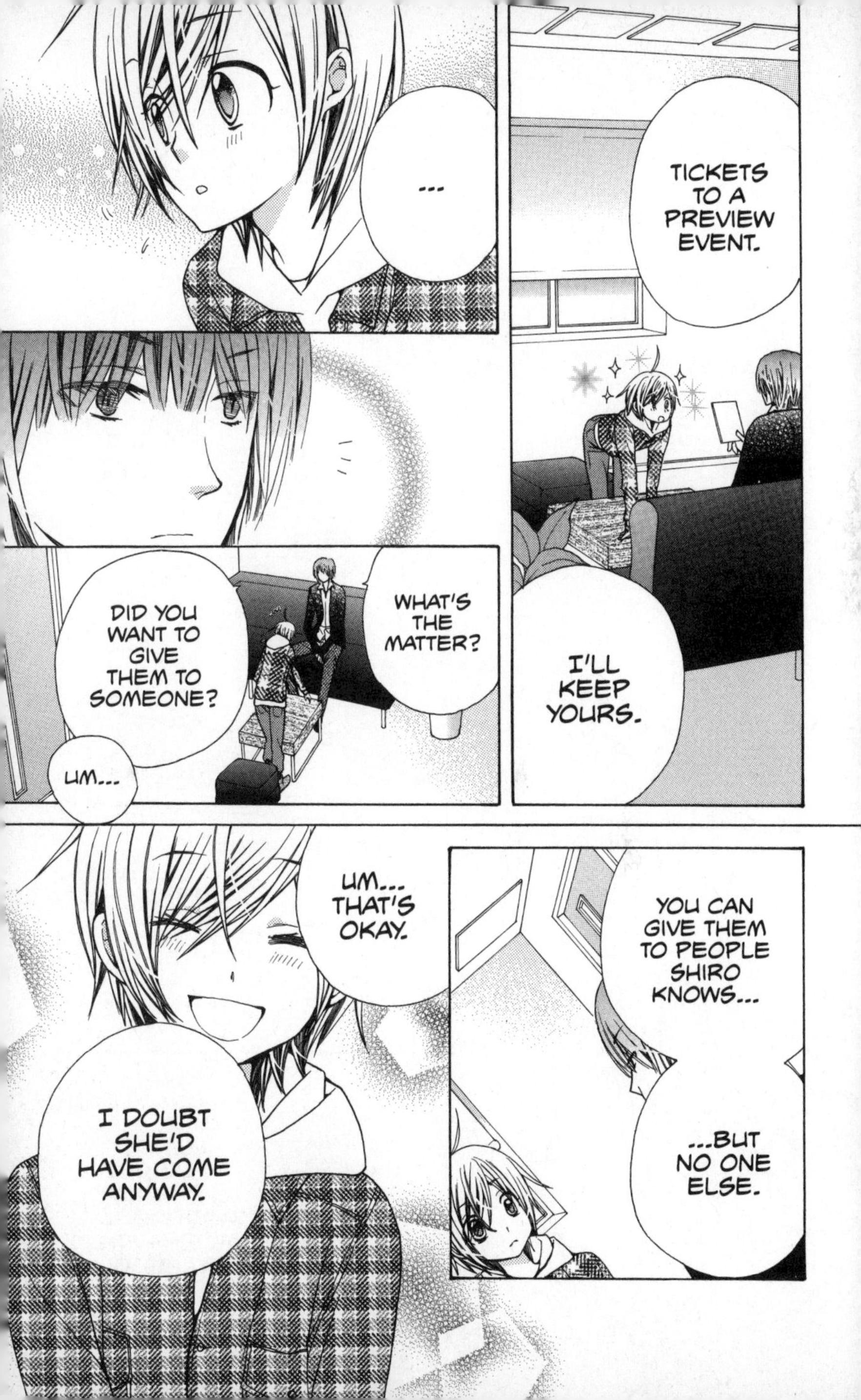
TICKETS TO A PREVIEW EVENT.
I'LL KEEP YOURS.
...
WHAT'S THE MATTER?
DID YOU WANT TO GIVE THEM TO SOMEONE?
UM...
YOU CAN GIVE THEM TO PEOPLE SHIRO KNOWS...
...BUT NO ONE ELSE.
UM... THAT'S OKAY.
I DOUBT SHE'D HAVE COME ANYWAY.

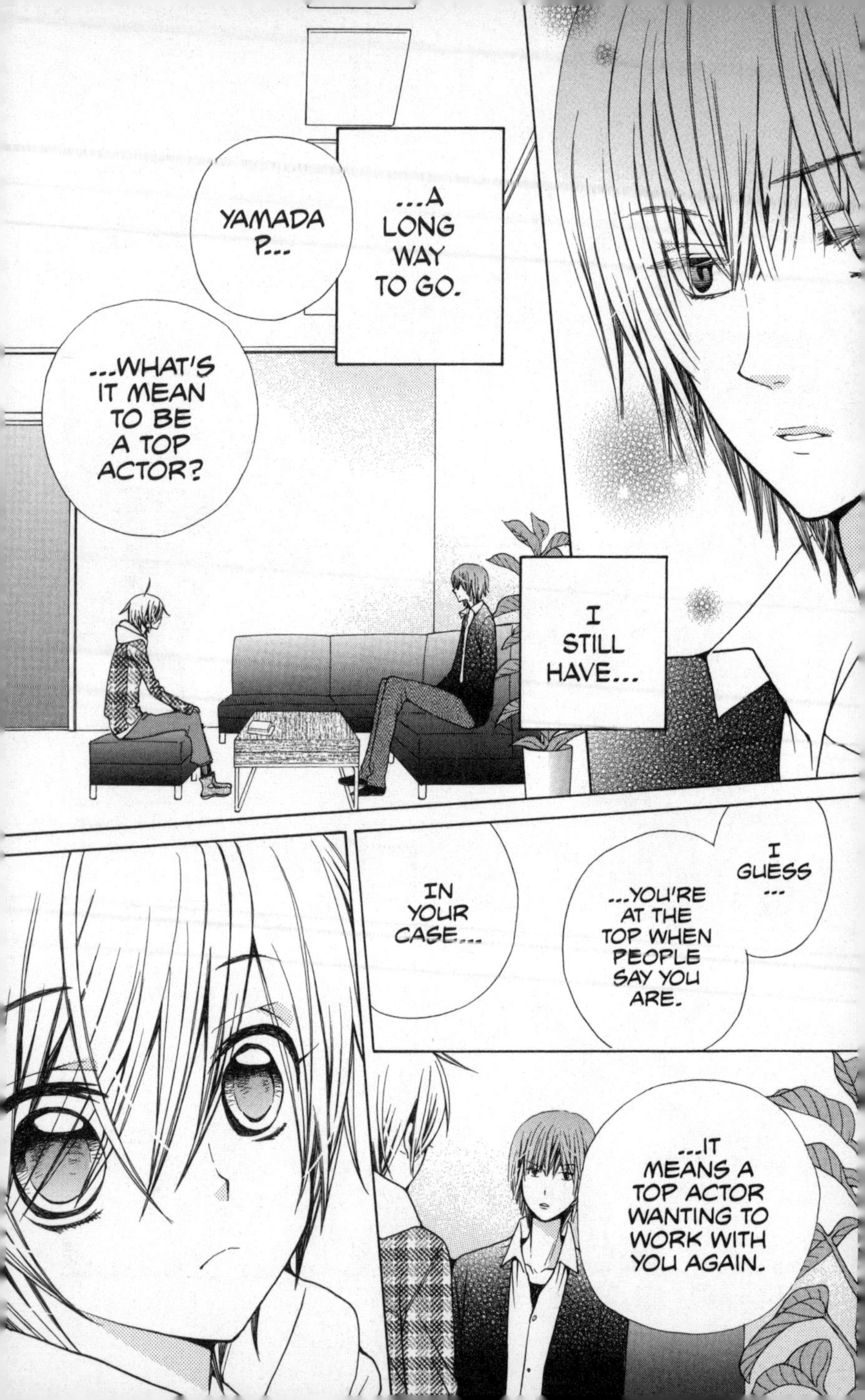
I STILL HAVE...
...A LONG WAY TO GO.
YAMADA P...
...WHAT'S IT MEAN TO BE A TOP ACTOR?
I GUESS...
...YOU'RE AT THE TOP WHEN PEOPLE SAY YOU ARE.
IN YOUR CASE...
...IT MEANS A TOP ACTOR WANTING TO WORK WITH YOU AGAIN.

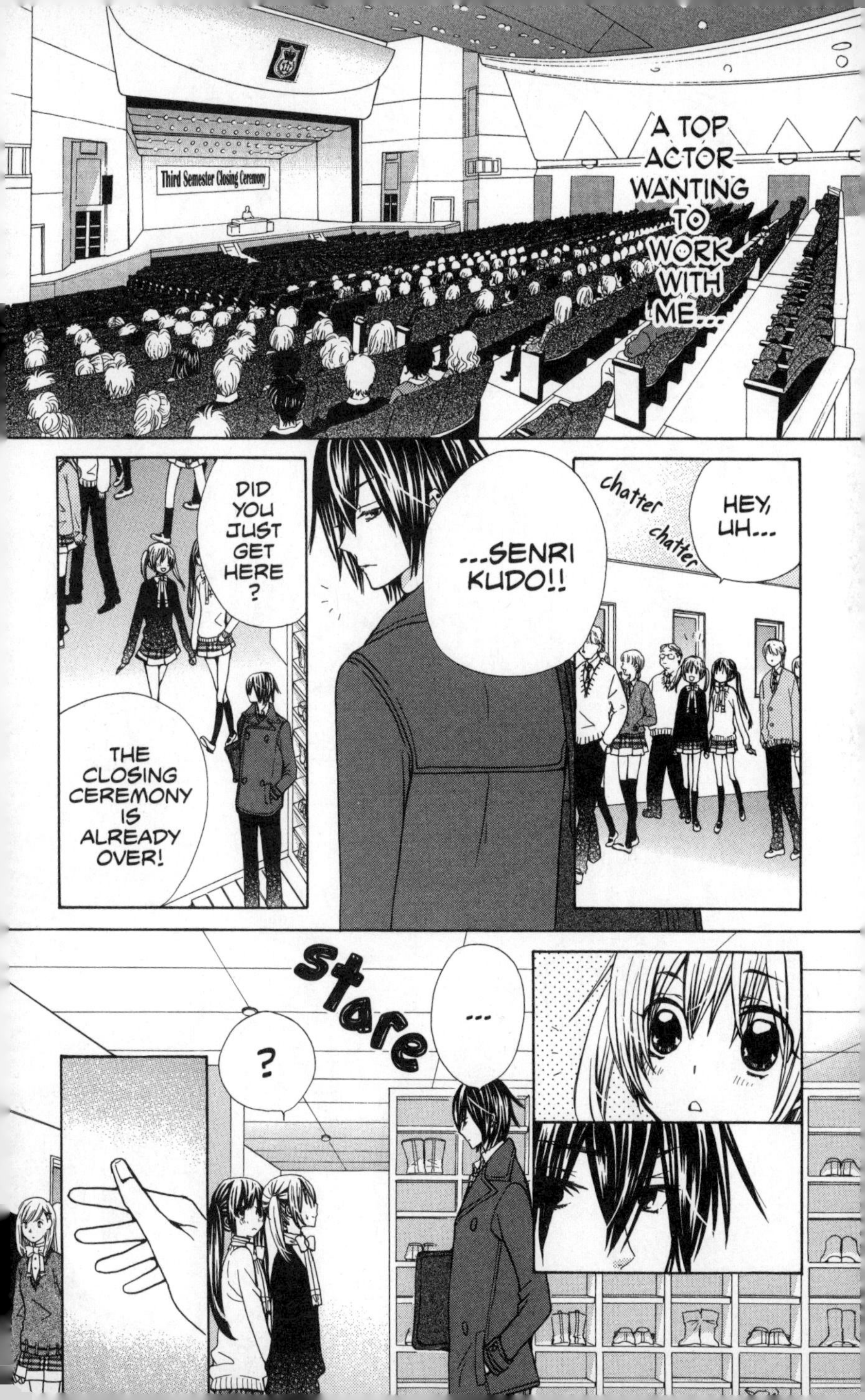
Third Semester Closing Ceremony
A TOP ACTOR WANTING TO WORK WITH ME...
chatter chatter
HEY, UH...
...SENRI KUDO!!
DID YOU JUST GET HERE?
THE CLOSING CEREMONY IS ALREADY OVER!
...
stare
?

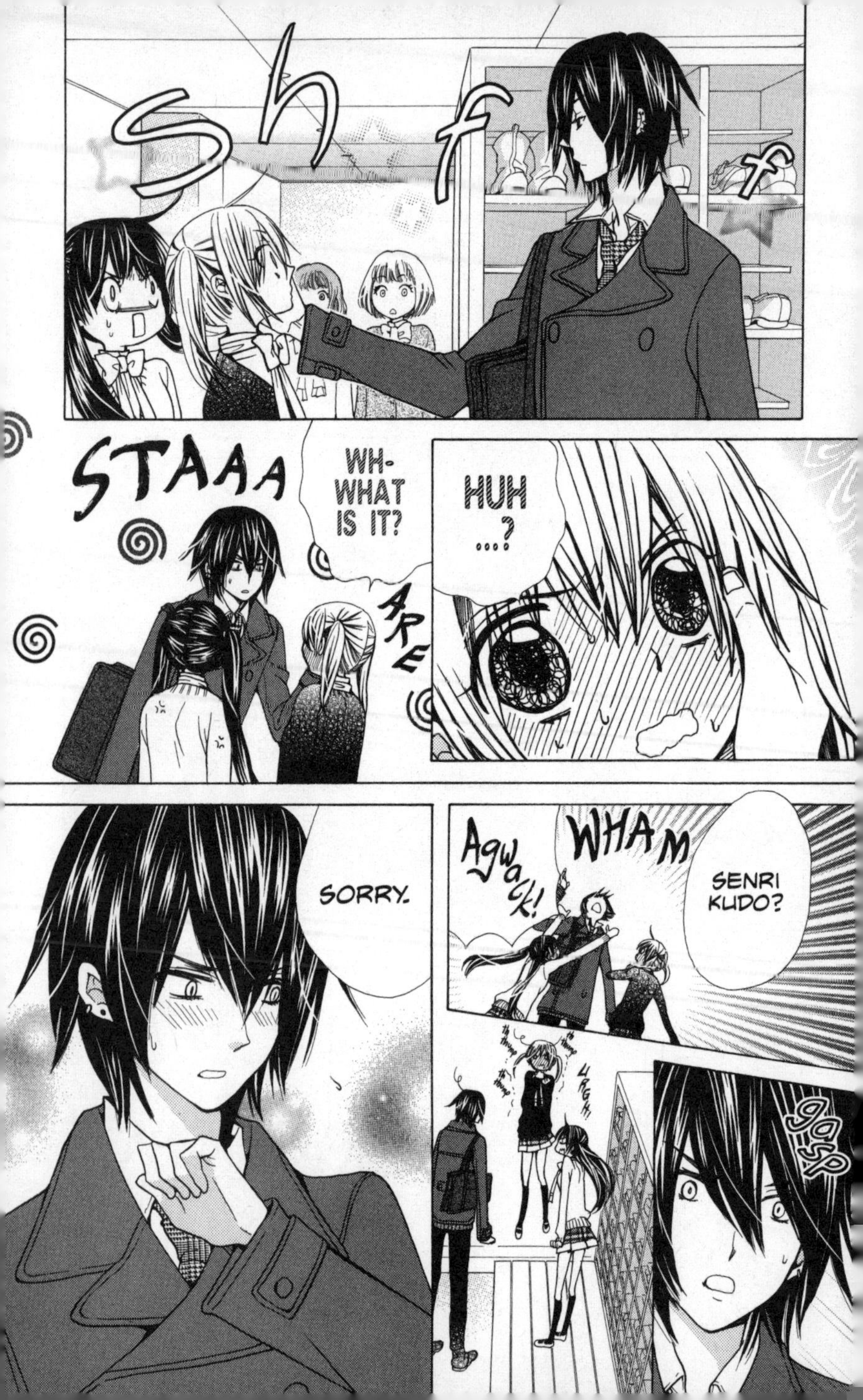
shff
HUH ...?
WH-WHAT IS IT?
STAAA
ARE
SENRI KUDO?
WHAM
Agwack!
th thump
th thump
th thump
URGH!
gasp
SORRY.

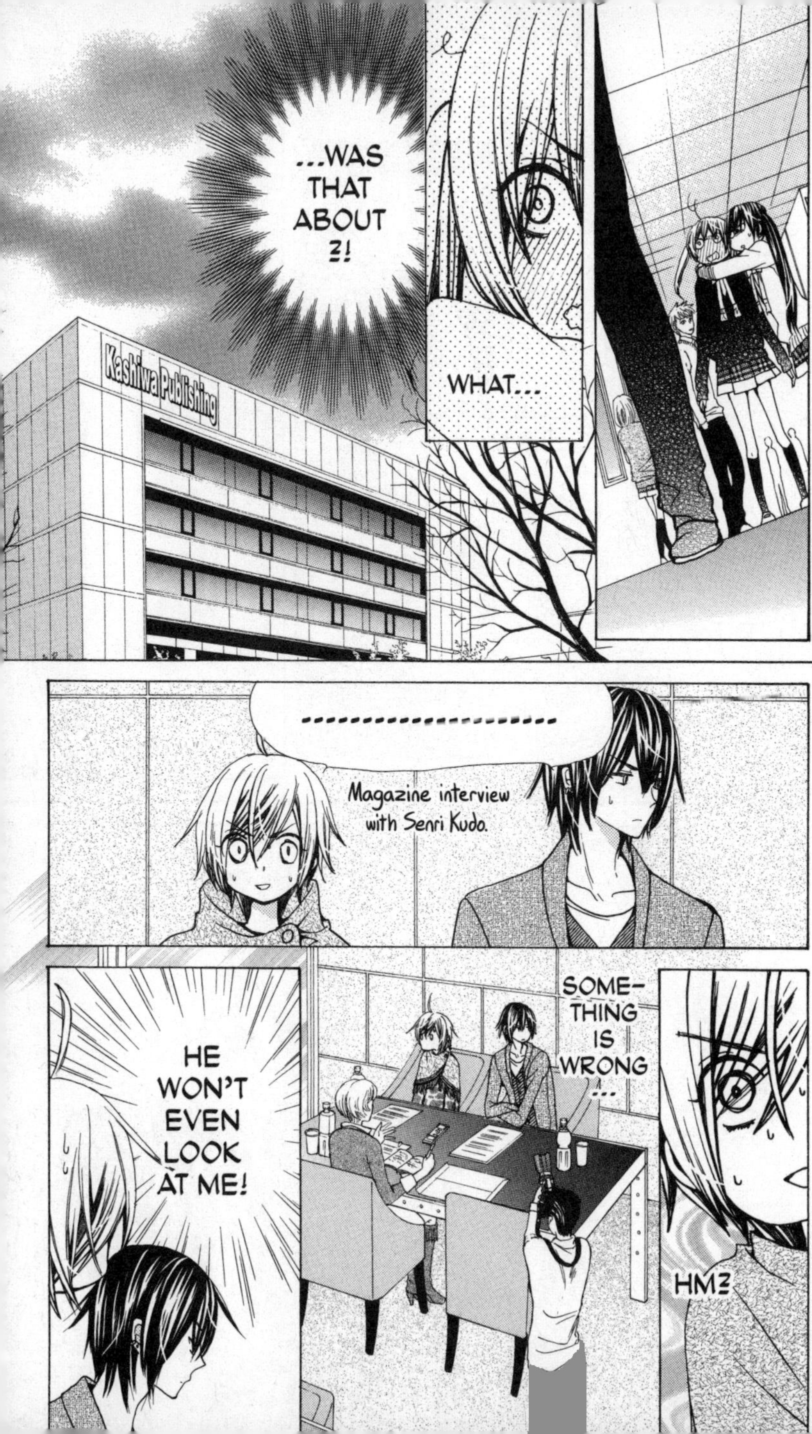
WHAT...
...WAS THAT ABOUT?!
Kashiwa Publishing

Magazine interview with Senri Kudo.
HM?
SOMETHING IS WRONG...
HE WON'T EVEN LOOK AT ME!

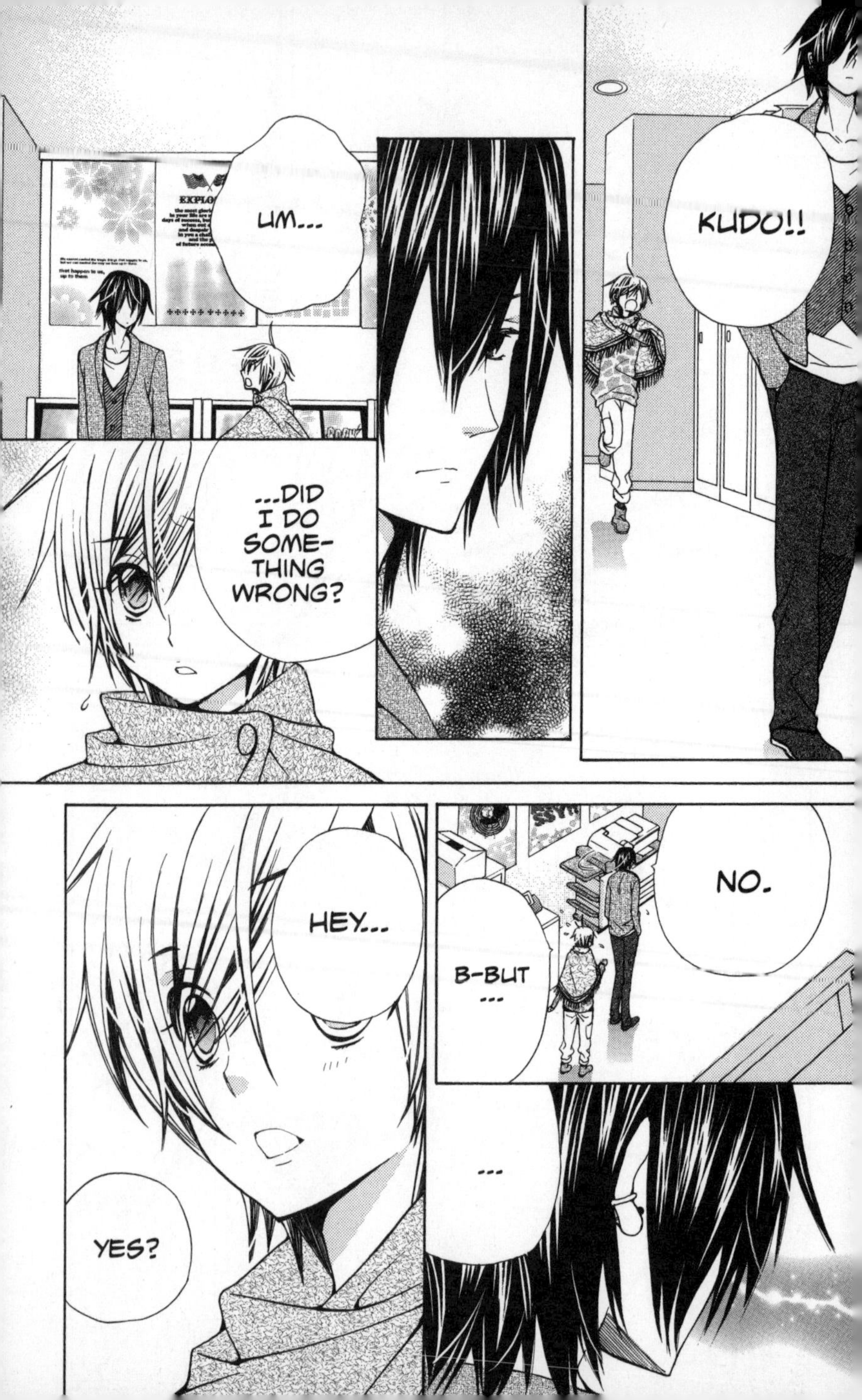
KUDO!!
UM...
...DID I DO SOMETHING WRONG?
NO.
B-BUT ...
...
HEY...
YES?

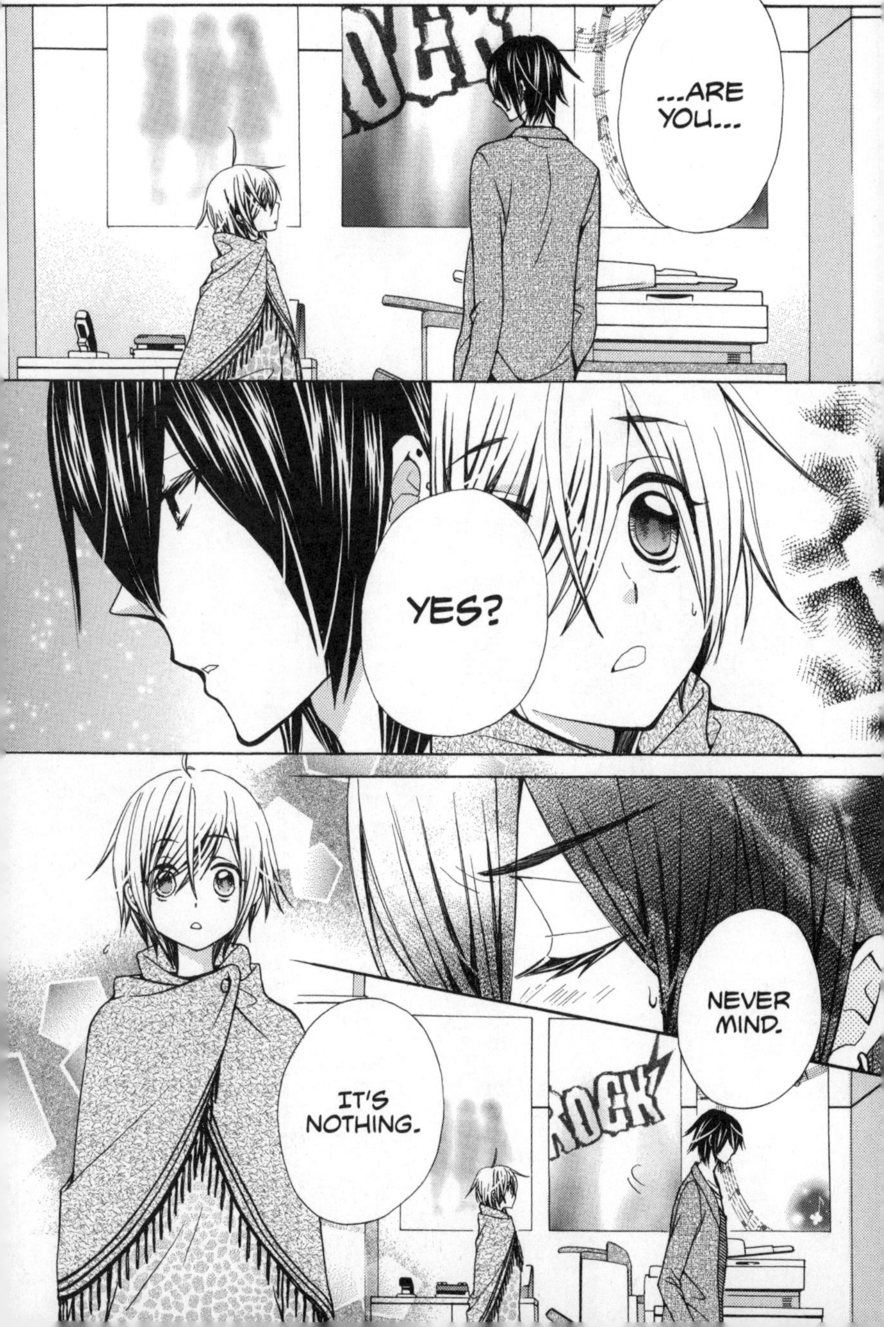
...ARE YOU...
YES?
NEVER MIND.
IT'S NOTHING.

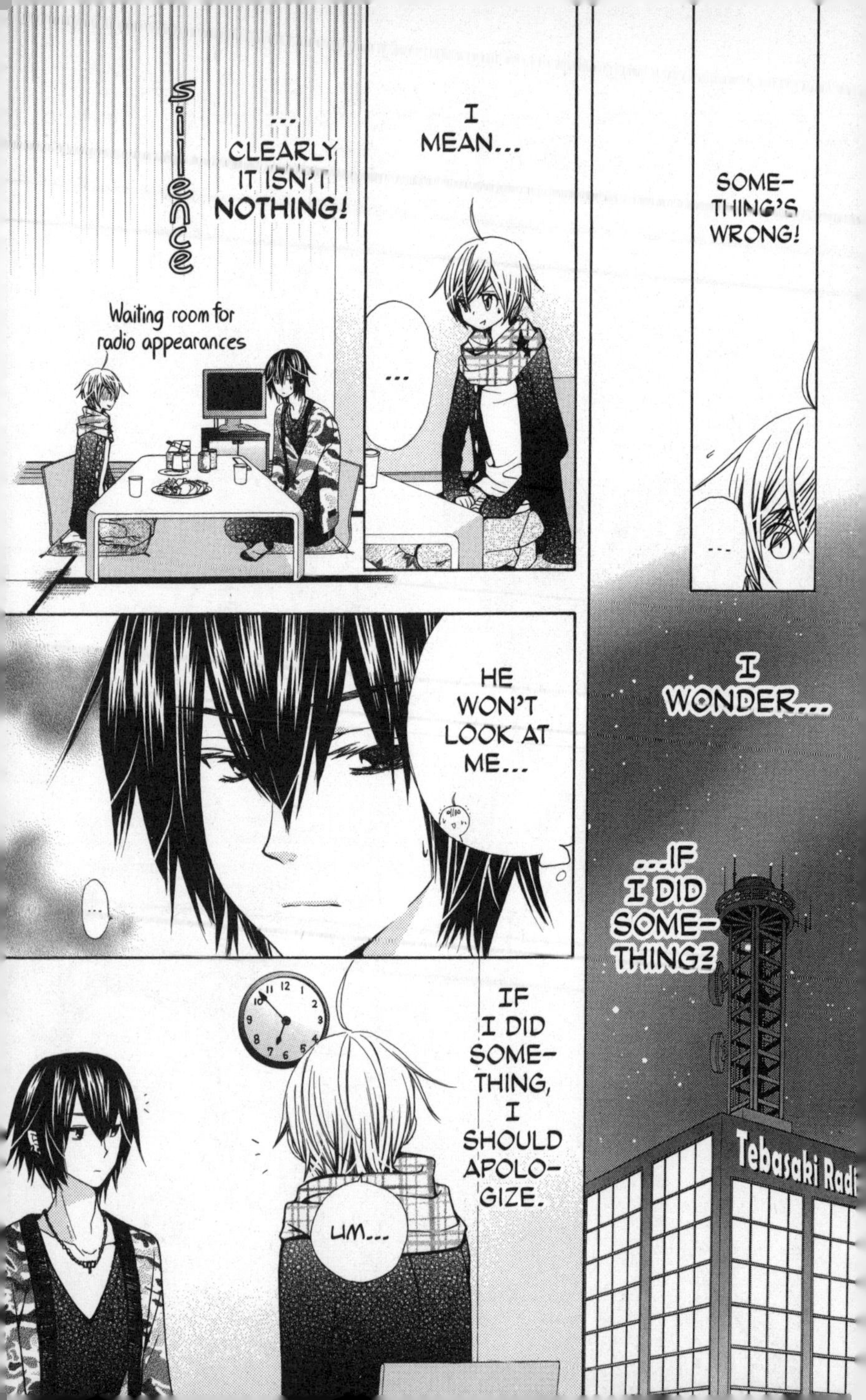
SOME-THING'S WRONG!
...
I WONDER...
...IF I DID SOME-THING?
Tebasaki Radi
I MEAN...
...
...CLEARLY IT ISN'T NOTHING!
Silence
Waiting room for radio appearances
HE WON'T LOOK AT ME...
...
IF I DID SOME-THING, I SHOULD APOLO-GIZE.
UM...

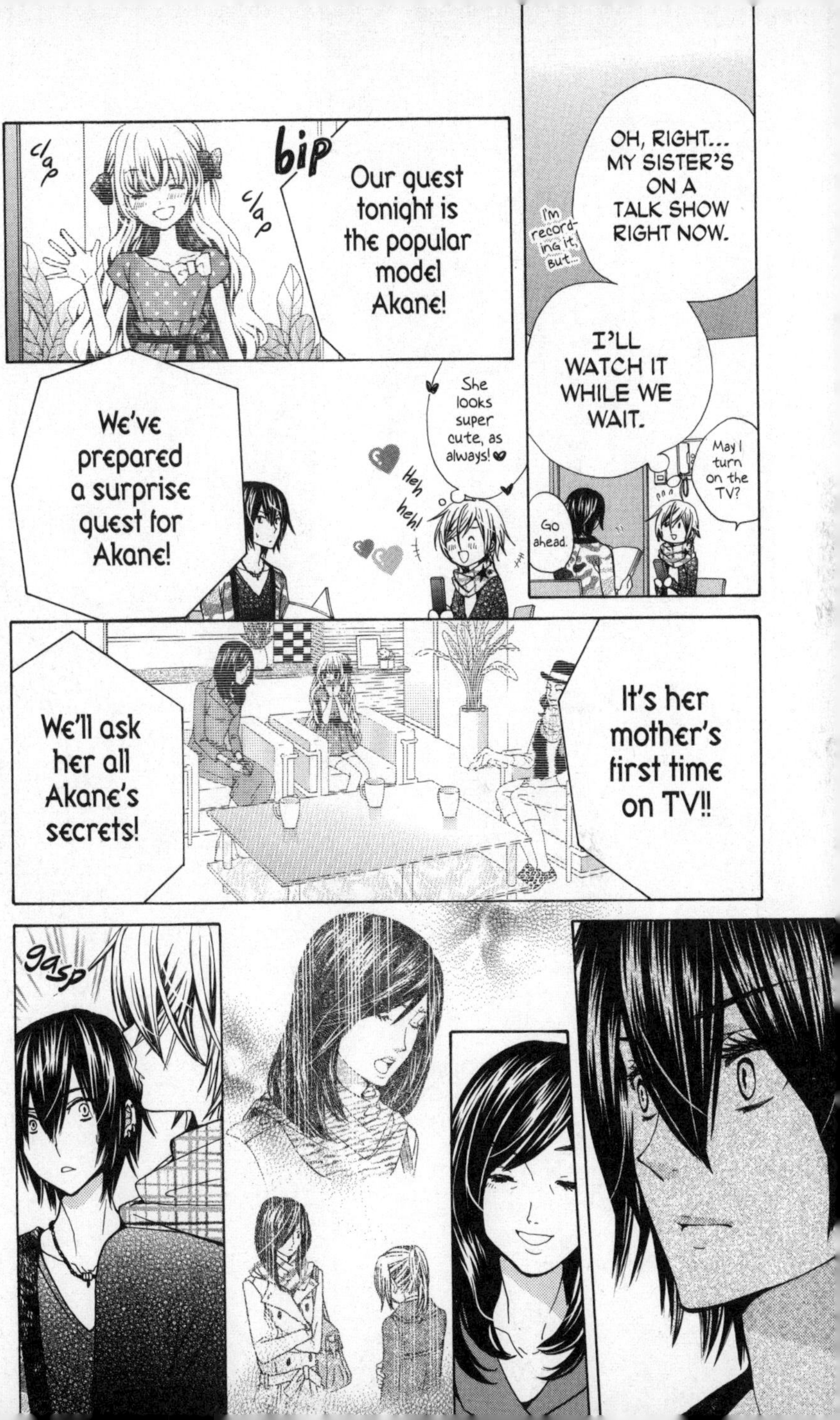
OH, RIGHT... MY SISTER'S ON A TALK SHOW RIGHT NOW.
I'm recording it, but...
I'LL WATCH IT WHILE WE WAIT.
May I turn on the TV?
Go ahead.
bip
Our guest tonight is the popular model Akane!
clap
clap
She looks super cute, as always!
Heh heh!
We've prepared a surprise guest for Akane!
It's her mother's first time on TV!!
We'll ask her all Akane's secrets!
gasp

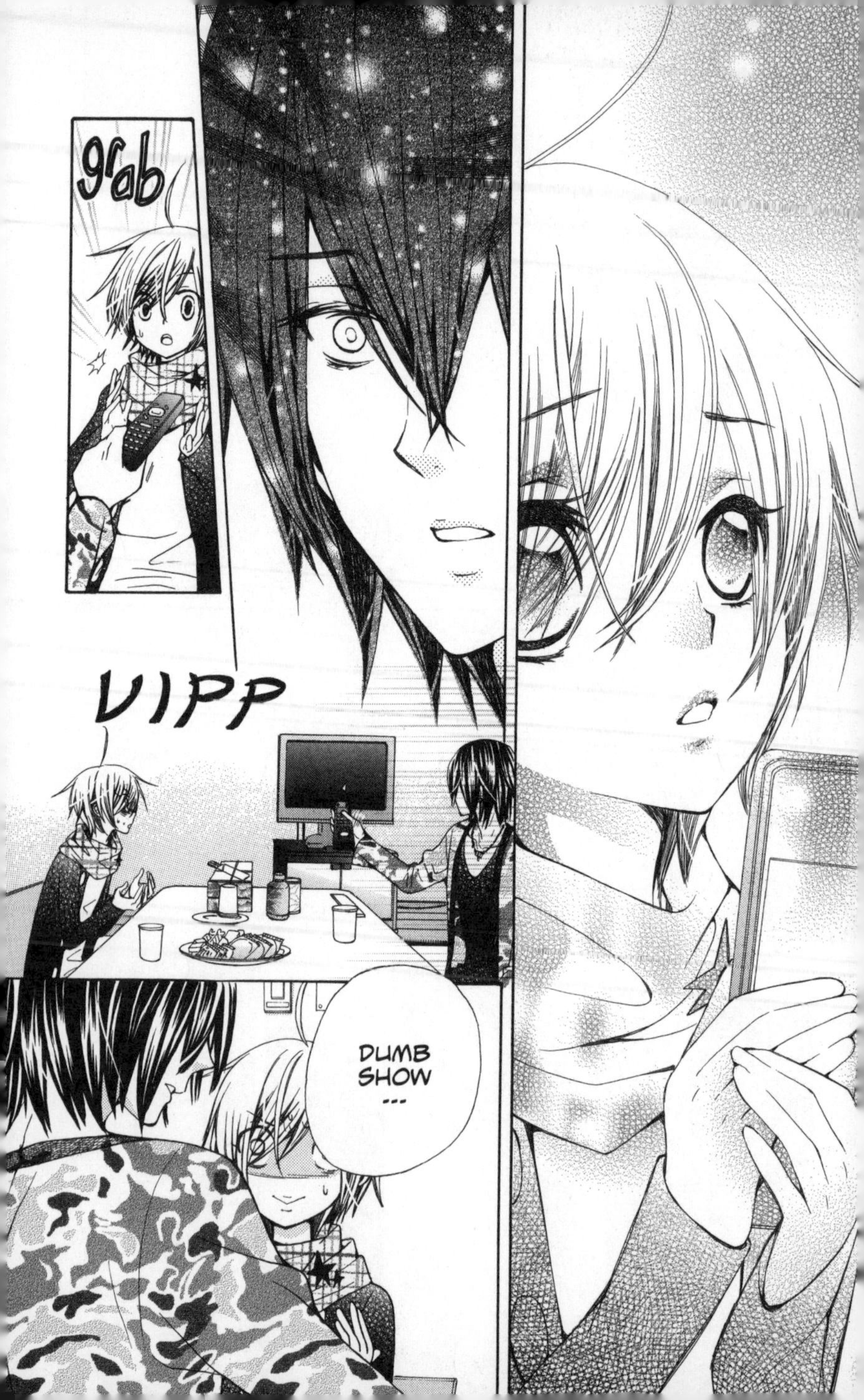
grab
VIPP
DUMB SHOW ...

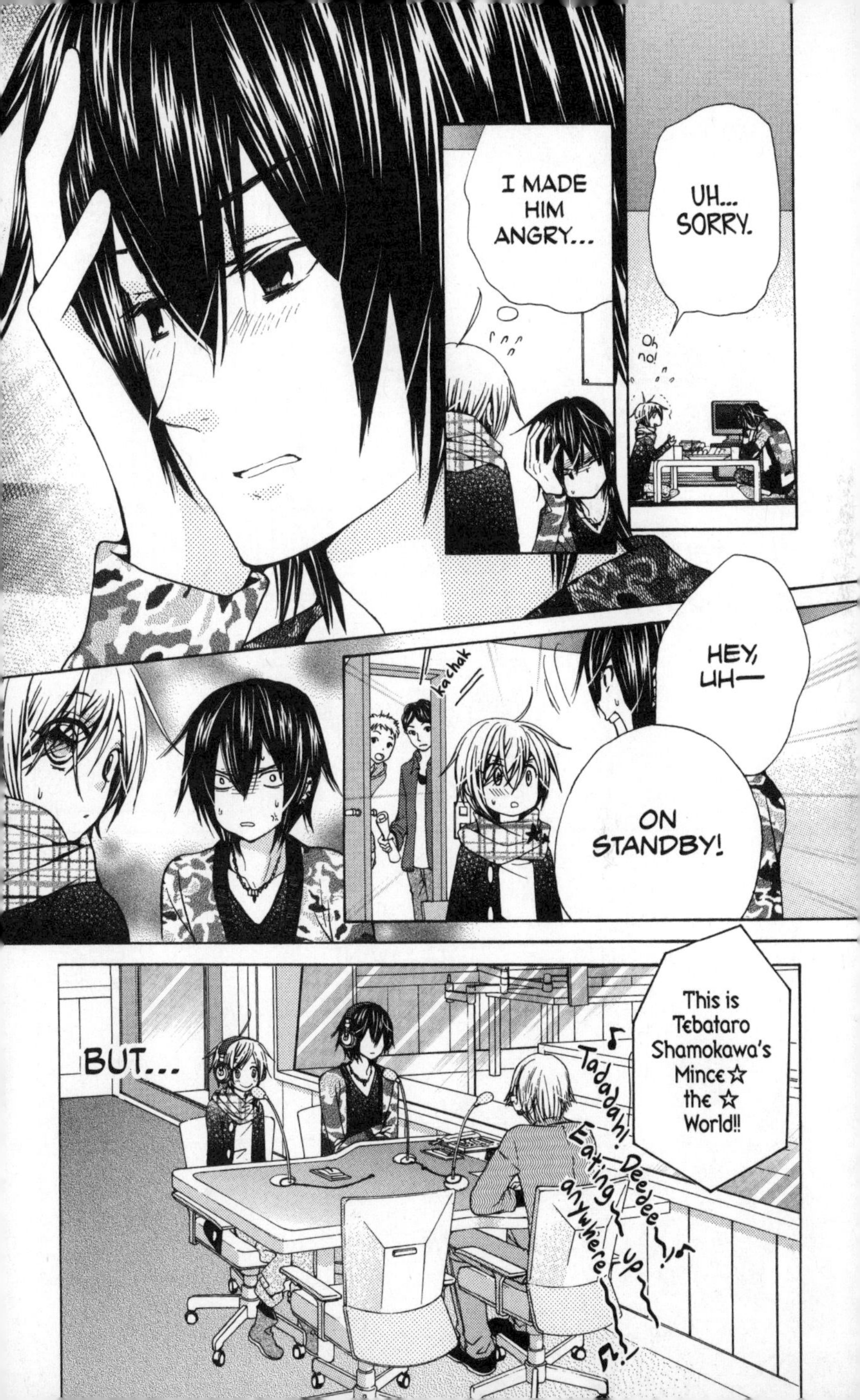
UH... SORRY.
Oh no!
I MADE HIM ANGRY...
HEY, UH—
kachak
ON STANDBY!
This is Tebataro Shamokawa's Mince☆ the ☆ World!!
Tadadah! Deedee~!
Eating~ up~ anywhere~
BUT...

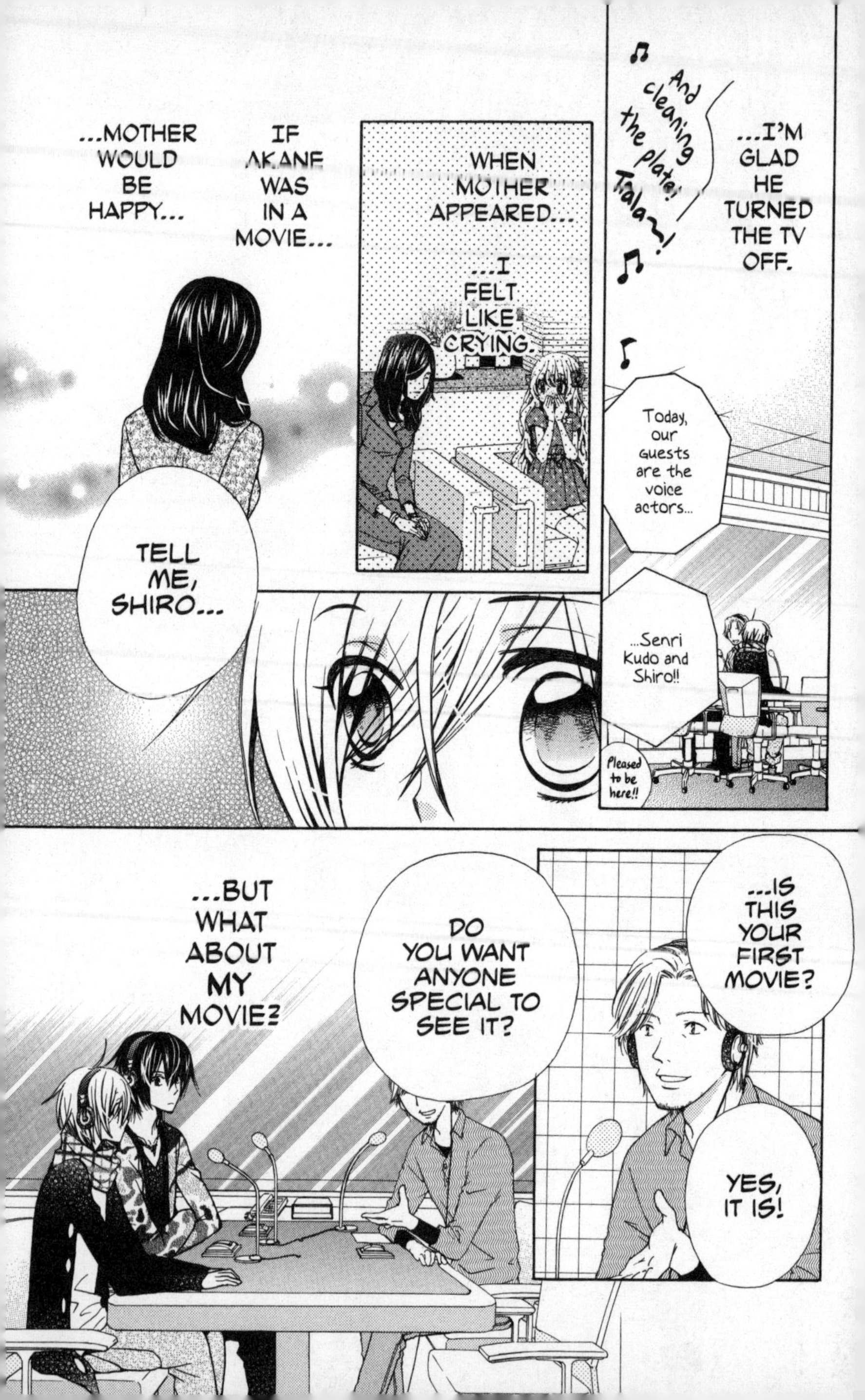

...I'M GLAD HE TURNED THE TV OFF.
And cleaning the plate! Tala~!
Today, our guests are the voice actors...
...Senri Kudo and Shiro!!
Pleased to be here!!
WHEN MOTHER APPEARED...
...I FELT LIKE CRYING.
IF AKANE WAS IN A MOVIE...
...MOTHER WOULD BE HAPPY...
TELL ME, SHIRO...
...IS THIS YOUR FIRST MOVIE?
YES, IT IS!
DO YOU WANT ANYONE SPECIAL TO SEE IT?
...BUT WHAT ABOUT MY MOVIE?

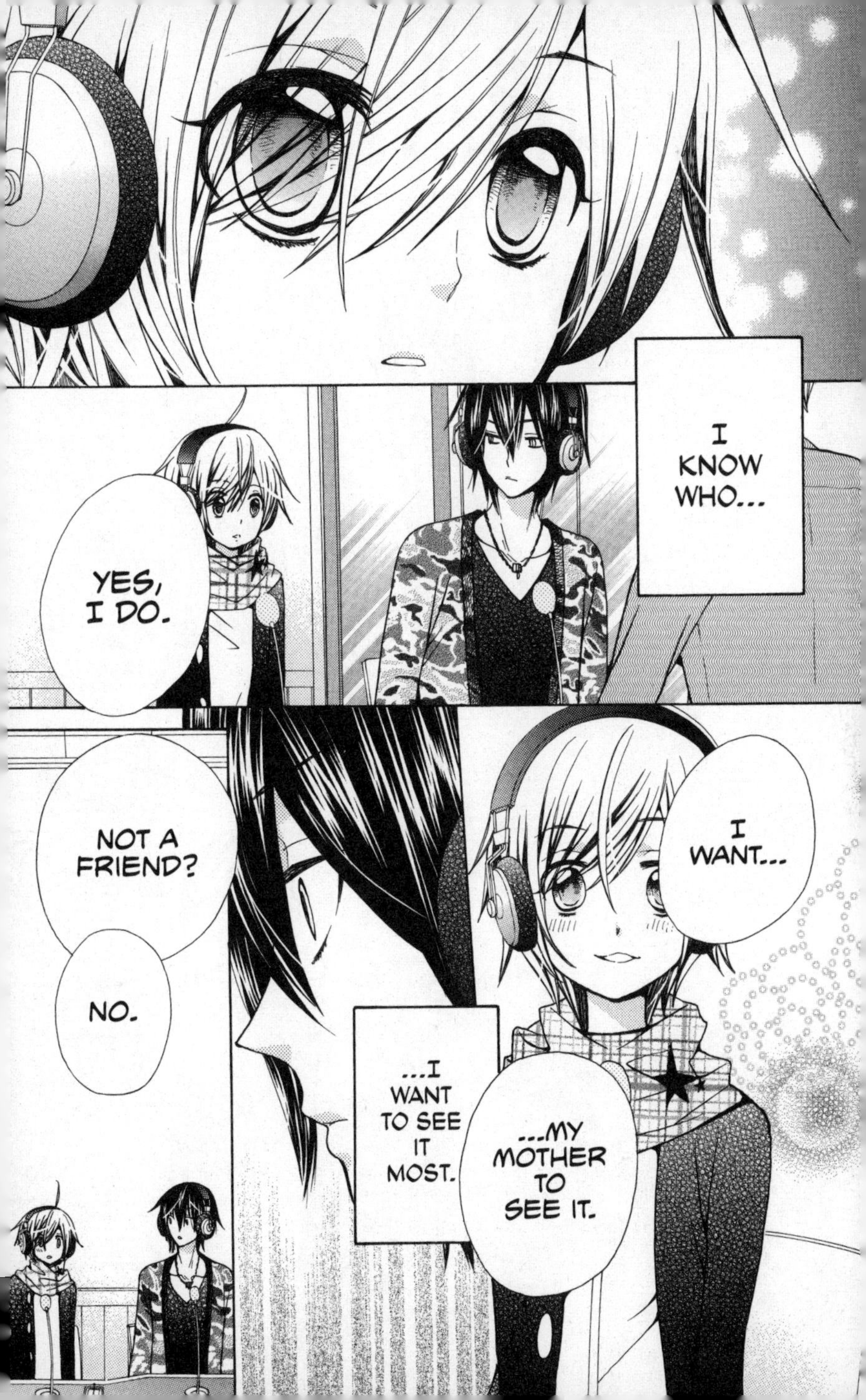
I KNOW WHO...
YES, I DO.
I WANT...
...MY MOTHER TO SEE IT.
...I WANT TO SEE IT MOST.
NOT A FRIEND?
NO.

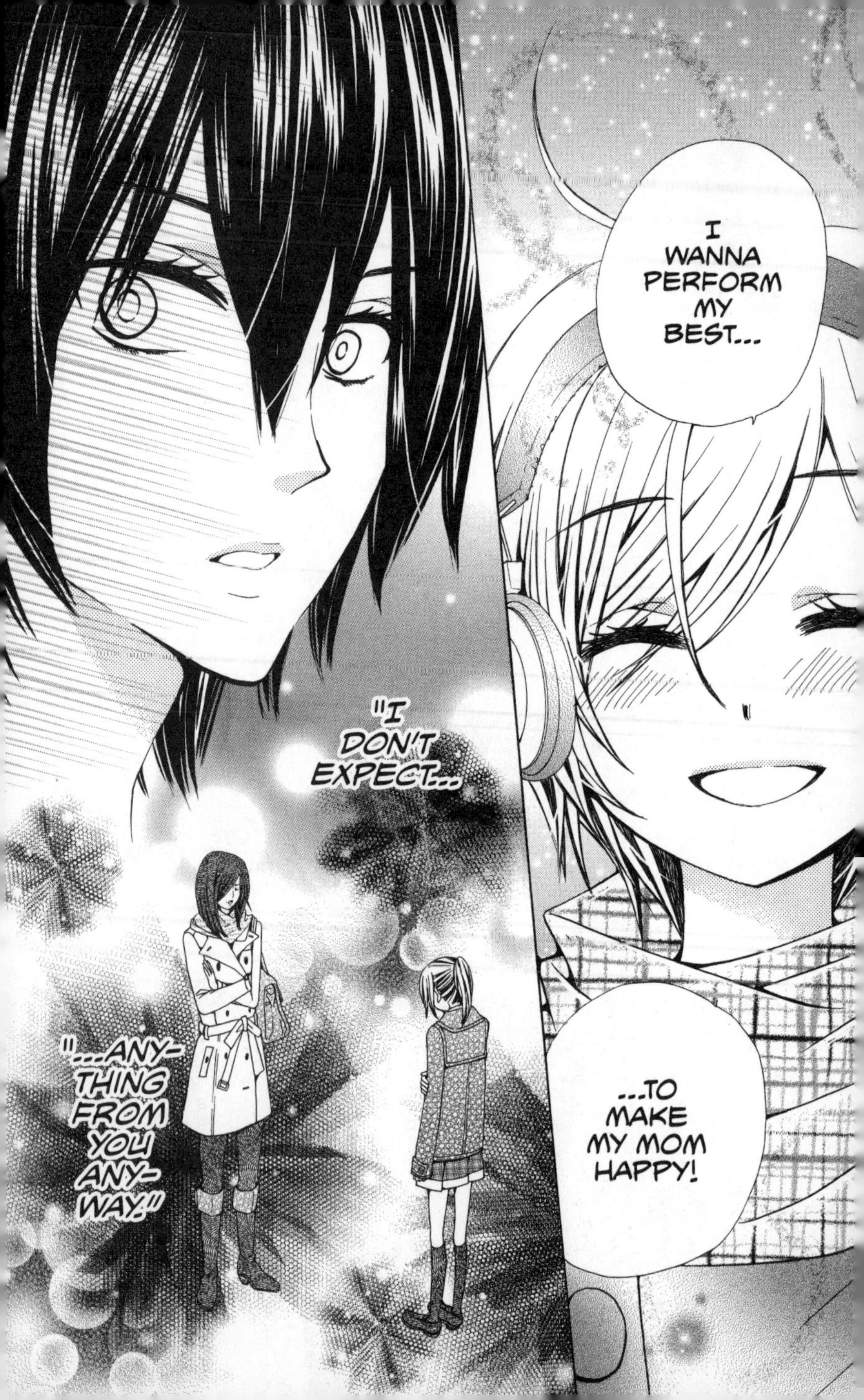
I WANNA PERFORM MY BEST...
...TO MAKE MY MOM HAPPY!
"I DON'T EXPECT...
"...ANYTHING FROM YOU ANYWAY."

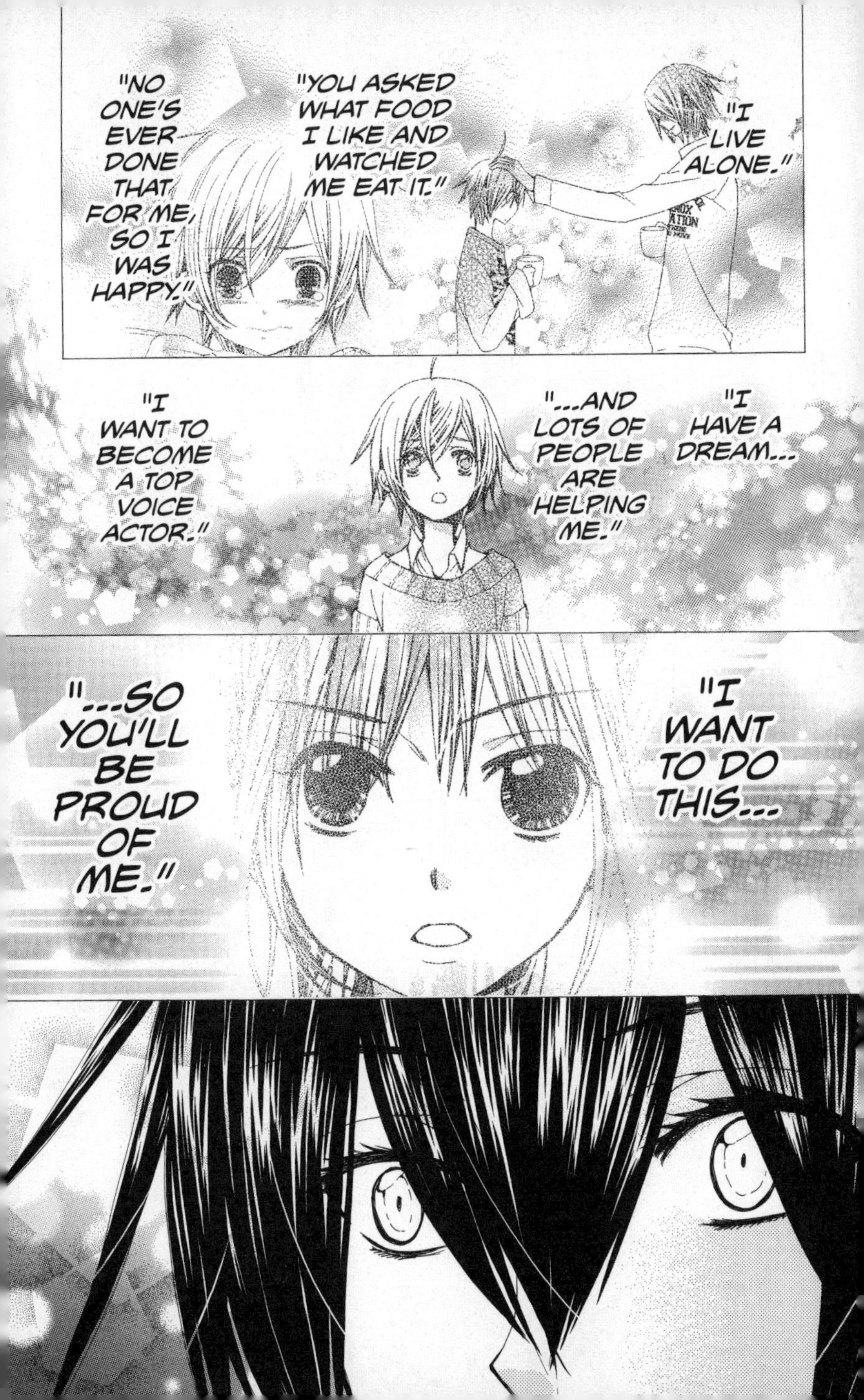
"I LIVE ALONE."
"YOU ASKED WHAT FOOD I LIKE AND WATCHED ME EAT IT."
"NO ONE'S EVER DONE THAT FOR ME, SO I WAS HAPPY."
"I HAVE A DREAM...
"...AND LOTS OF PEOPLE ARE HELPING ME."
"I WANT TO BECOME A TOP VOICE ACTOR."
"I WANT TO DO THIS...
"...SO YOU'LL BE PROUD OF ME."

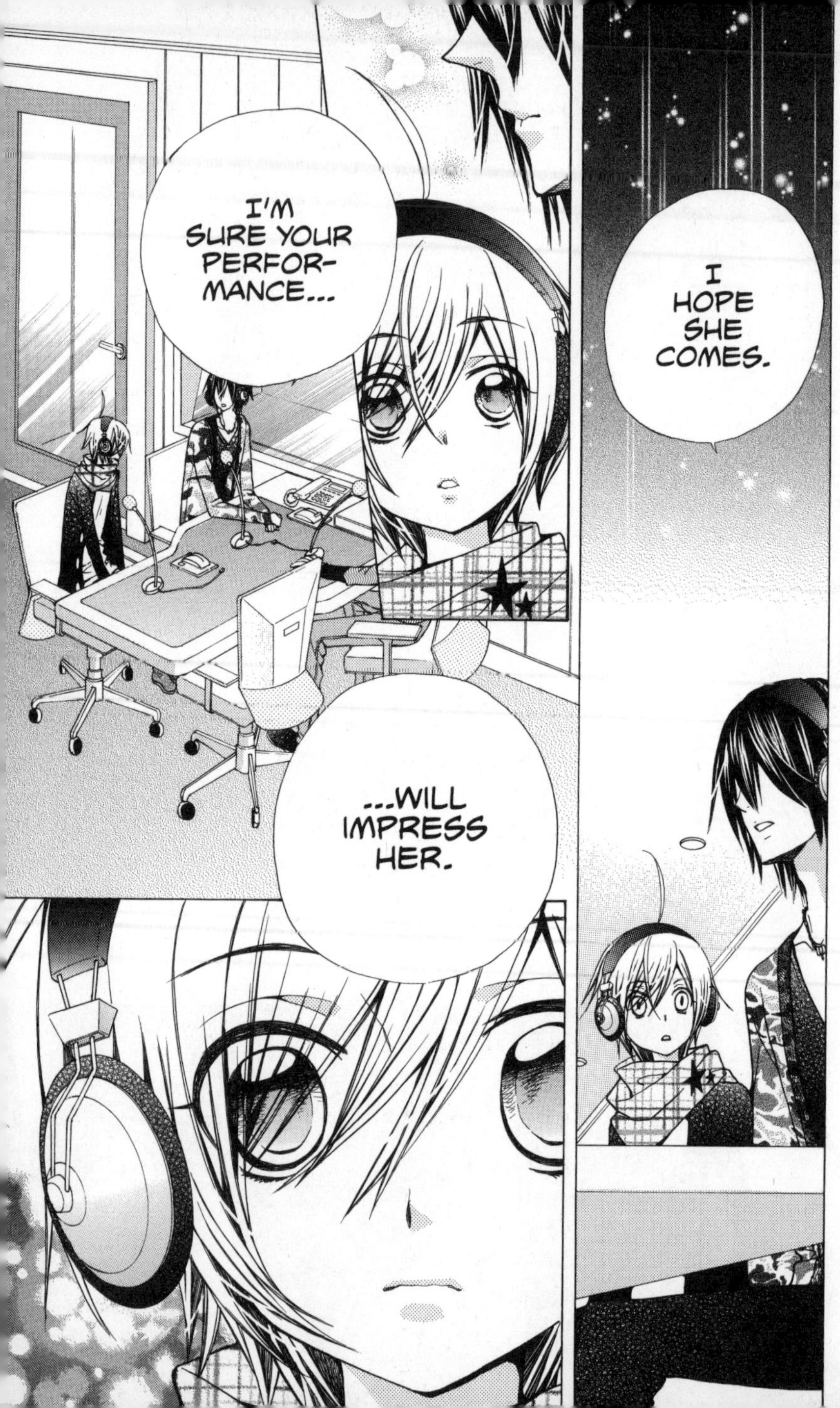
I HOPE SHE COMES.
I'M SURE YOUR PERFOR-MANCE...
...WILL IMPRESS HER.

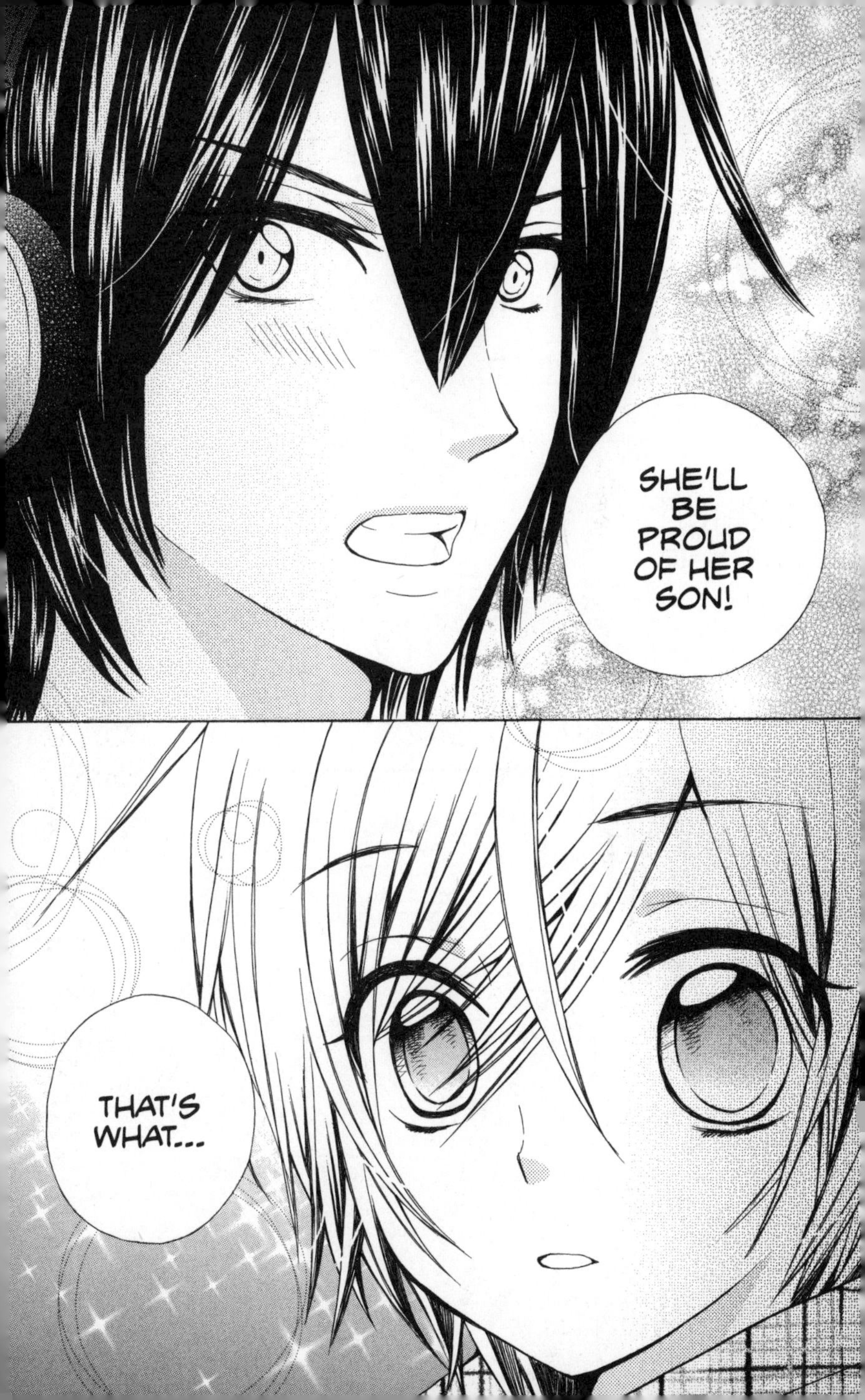
SHE'LL BE PROUD OF HER SON!
THAT'S WHAT...

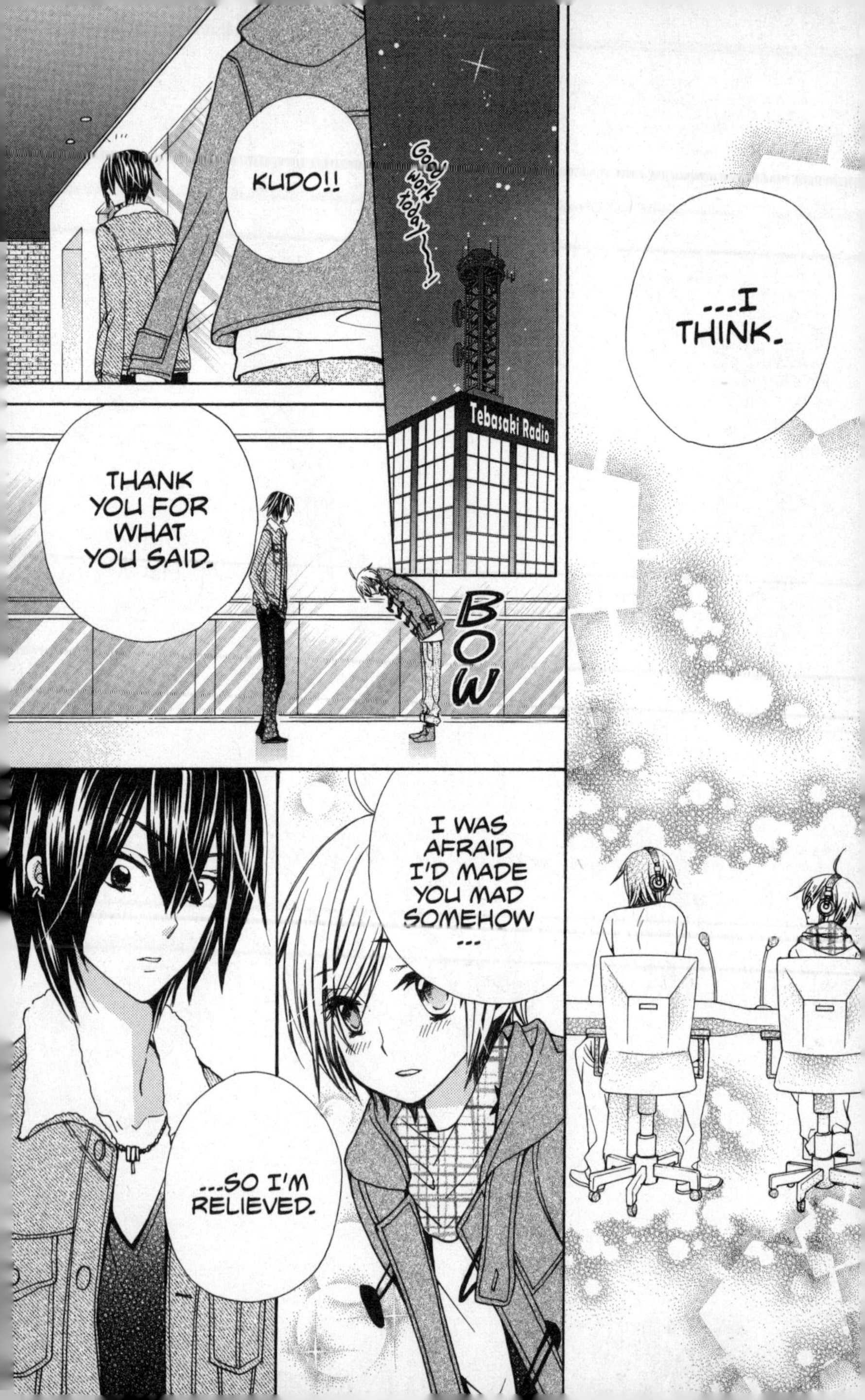
...I THINK.
Good work today~!
Tebasaki Radio
KUDO!!
THANK YOU FOR WHAT YOU SAID.
BOW
I WAS AFRAID I'D MADE YOU MAD SOMEHOW...
...SO I'M RELIEVED.

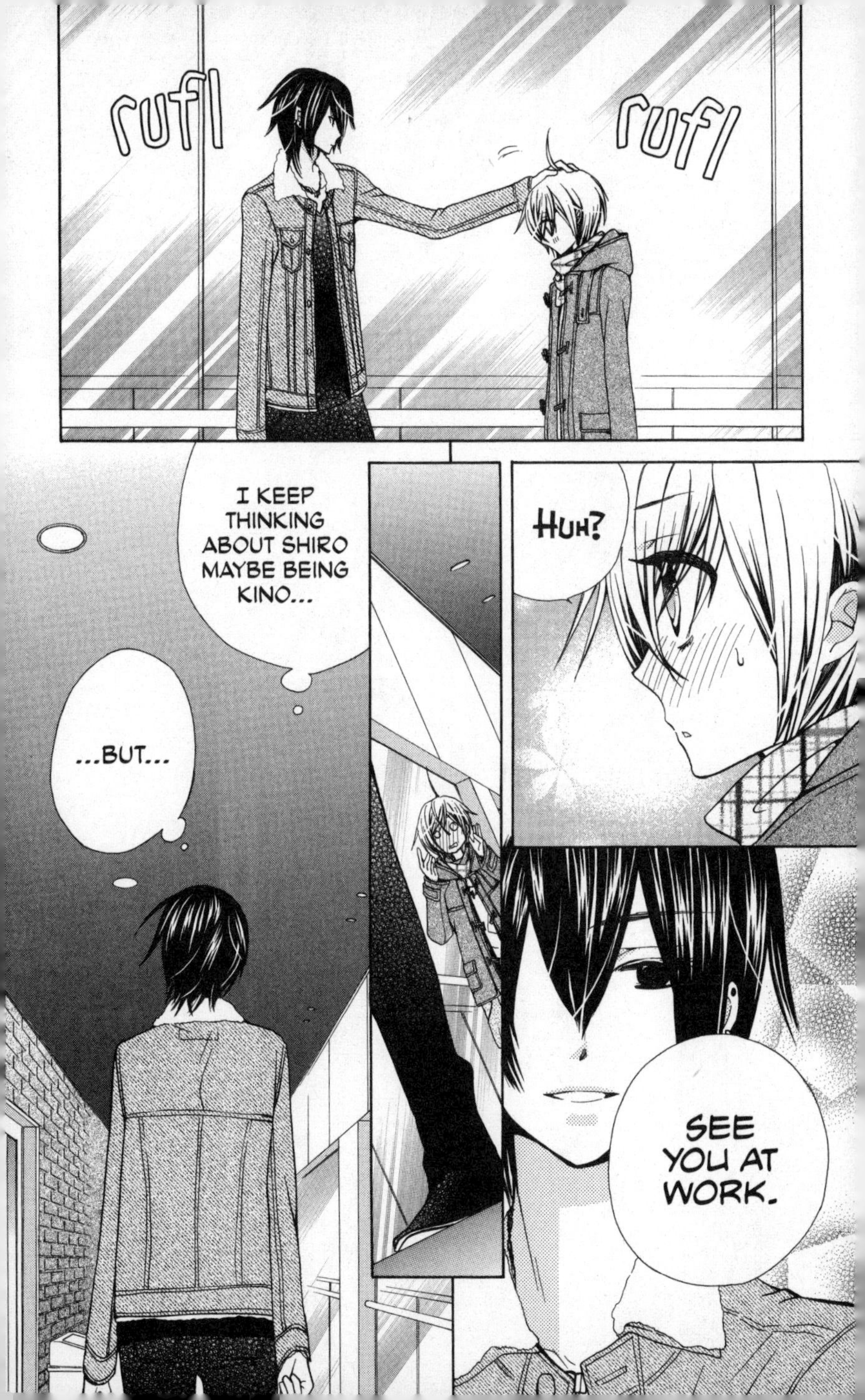
rufl
rufl
HUH?
SEE YOU AT WORK.
I KEEP THINKING ABOUT SHIRO MAYBE BEING KINO...
...BUT...

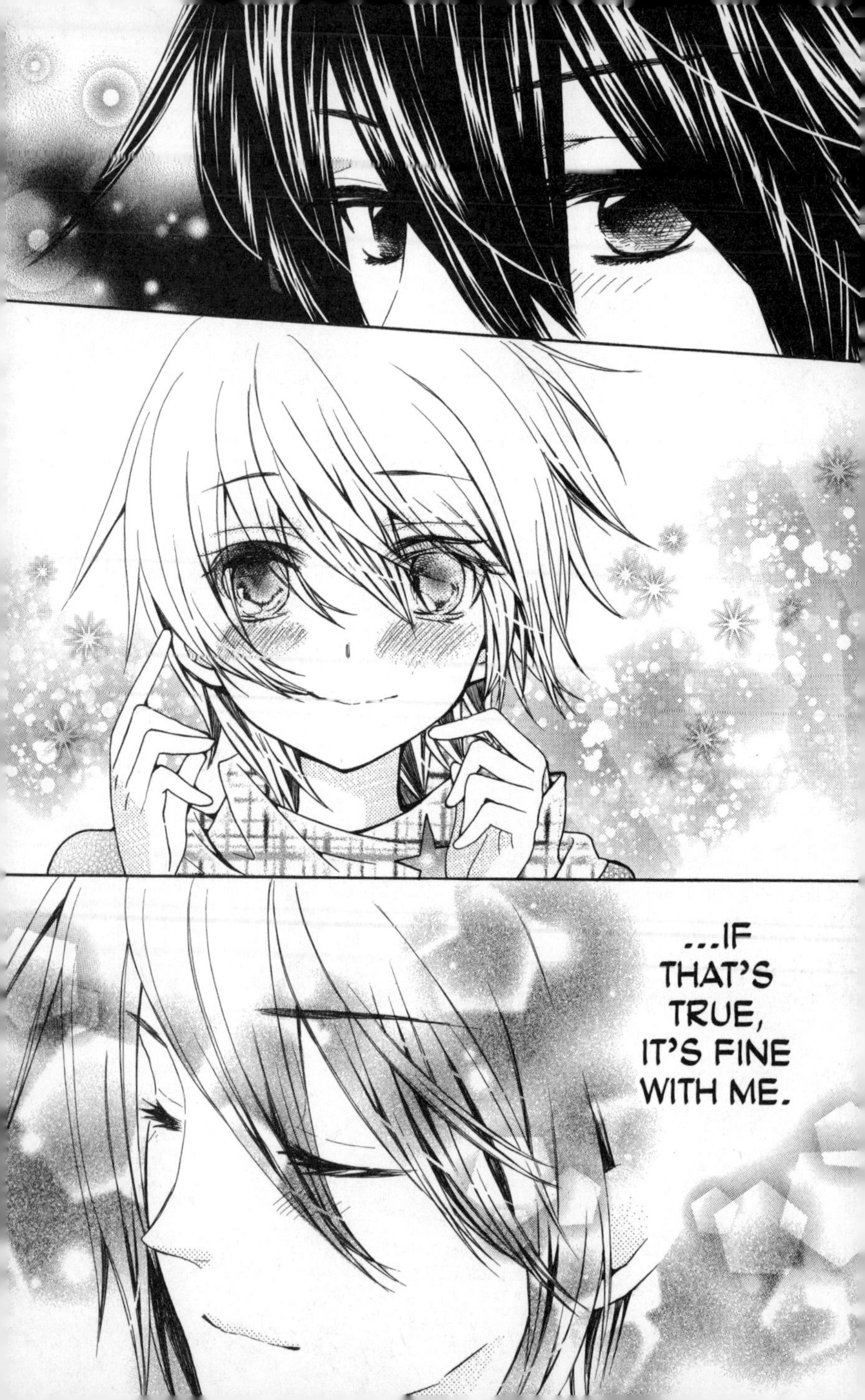
...IF THAT'S TRUE, IT'S FINE WITH ME.

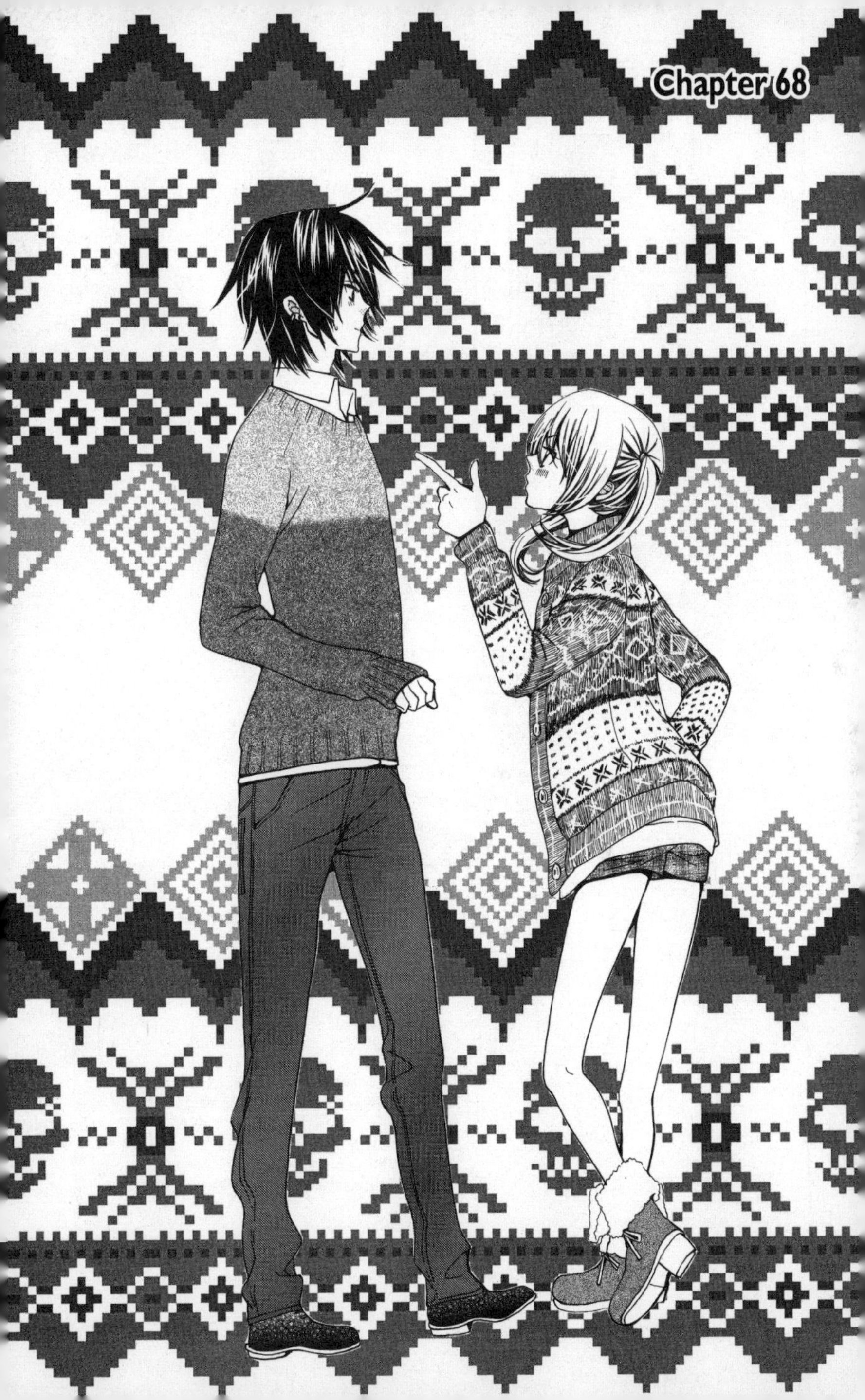
Chapter 68

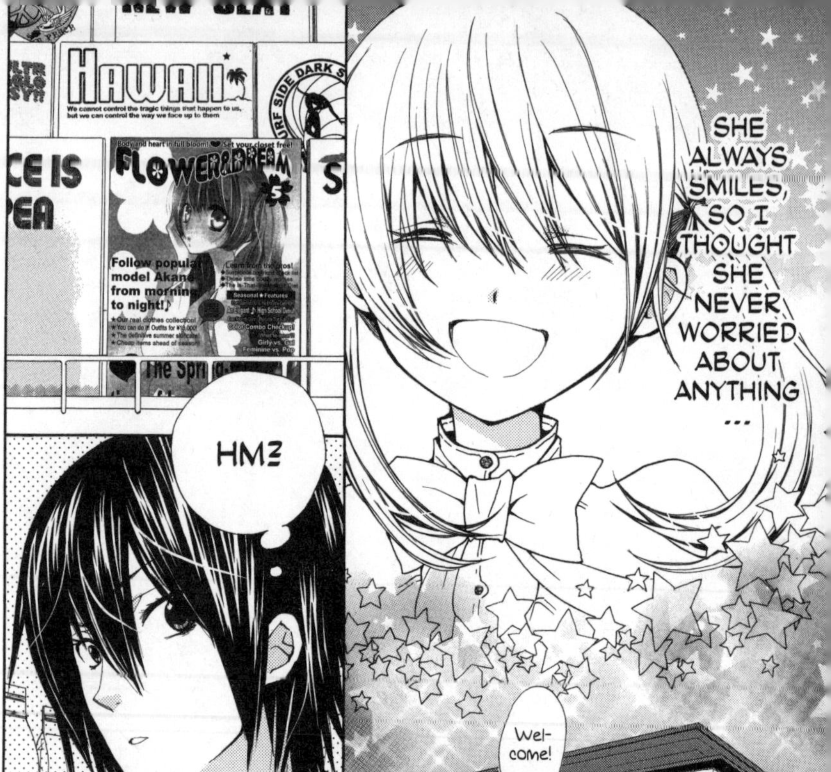
SHE ALWAYS SMILES, SO I THOUGHT SHE NEVER WORRIED ABOUT ANYTHING...
Wel-come!
yonKus
Rice Balls!
HAWAII
We cannot control the tragic things that happen to us, but we can control the way we face up to them
Body and heart in full bloom! Set your closet free!
FLOWER&DREAM
5
Follow popula model Akane from morning to night!♪
HM?

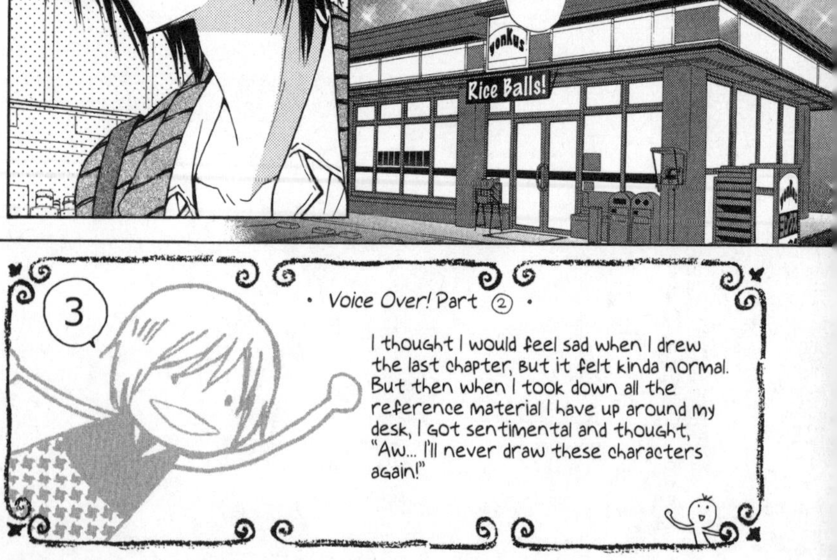
3

• *Voice Over! Part* ② •

I thought I would feel sad when I drew the last chapter, but it felt kinda normal. But then when I took down all the reference material I have up around my desk, I got sentimental and thought, "Aw... I'll never draw these characters again!"

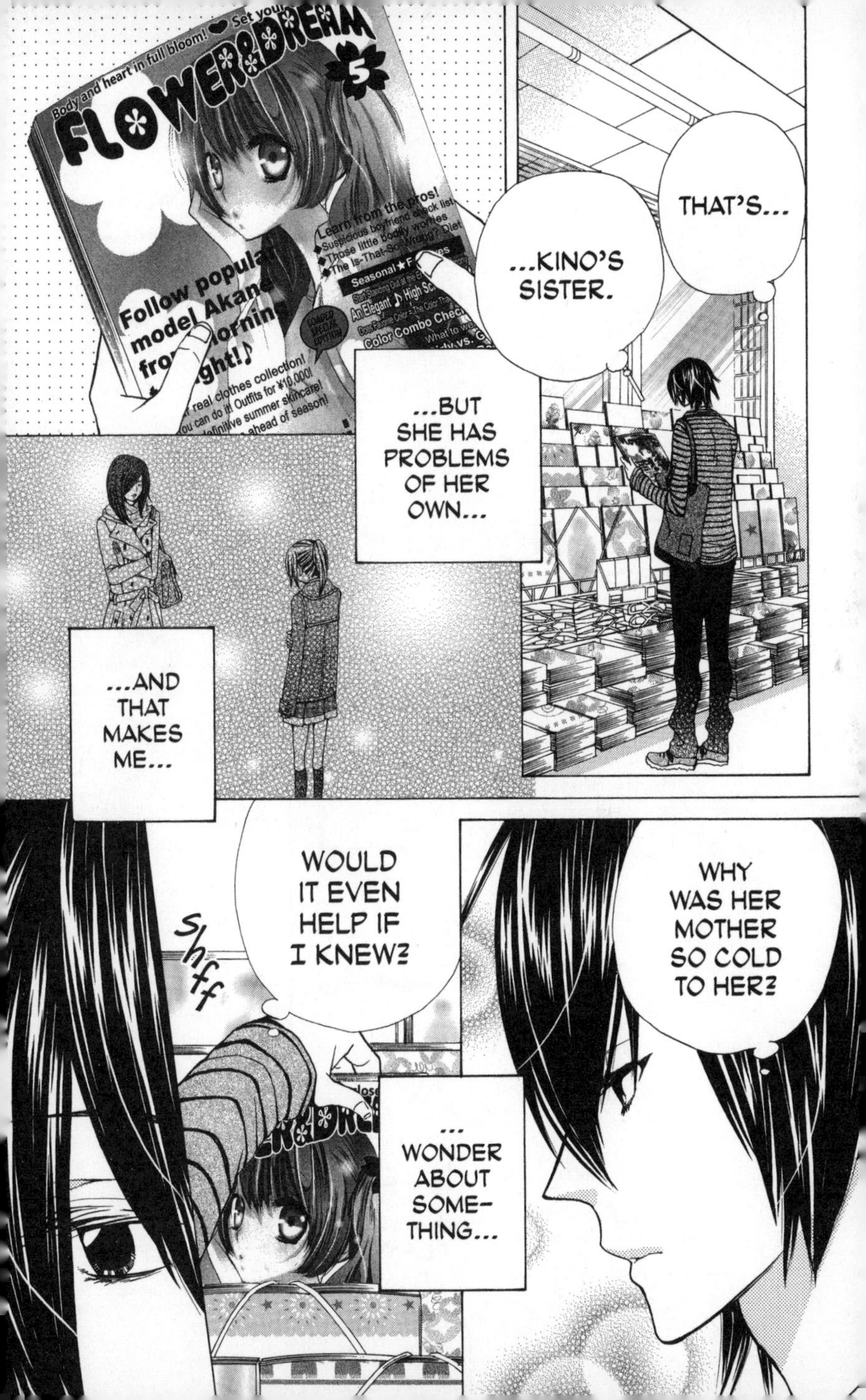

THAT'S...
...KINO'S SISTER.
...BUT SHE HAS PROBLEMS OF HER OWN...
FLOWER&DREAM
5
Learn from the pros!
...AND THAT MAKES ME...
...WONDER ABOUT SOMETHING...
WHY WAS HER MOTHER SO COLD TO HER?
WOULD IT EVEN HELP IF I KNEW?
Shff

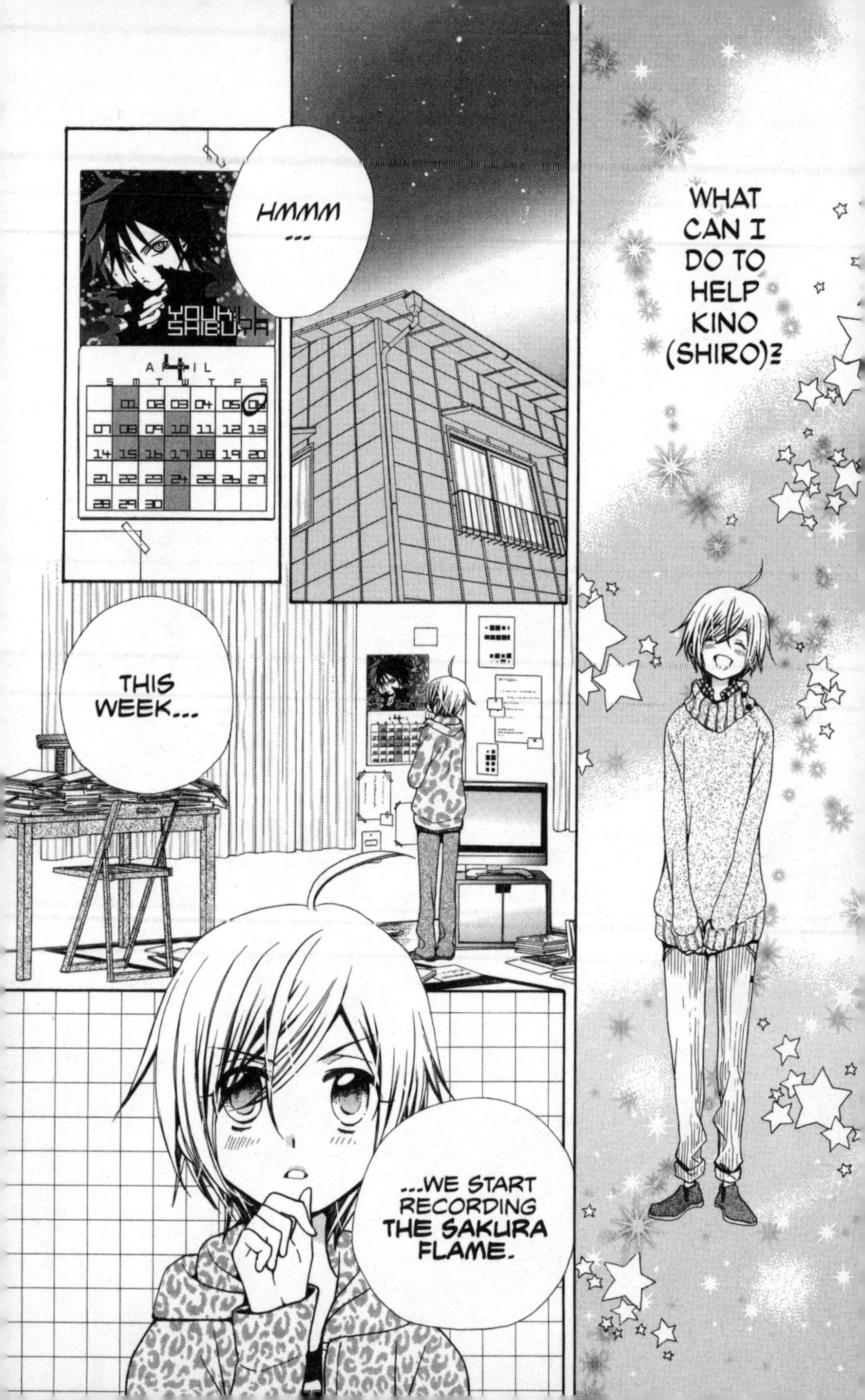
WHAT CAN I DO TO HELP KINO (SHIRO)?
HMMM...
YOUKI SHIBUYA
APRIL
THIS WEEK...
...WE START RECORDING THE SAKURA FLAME.

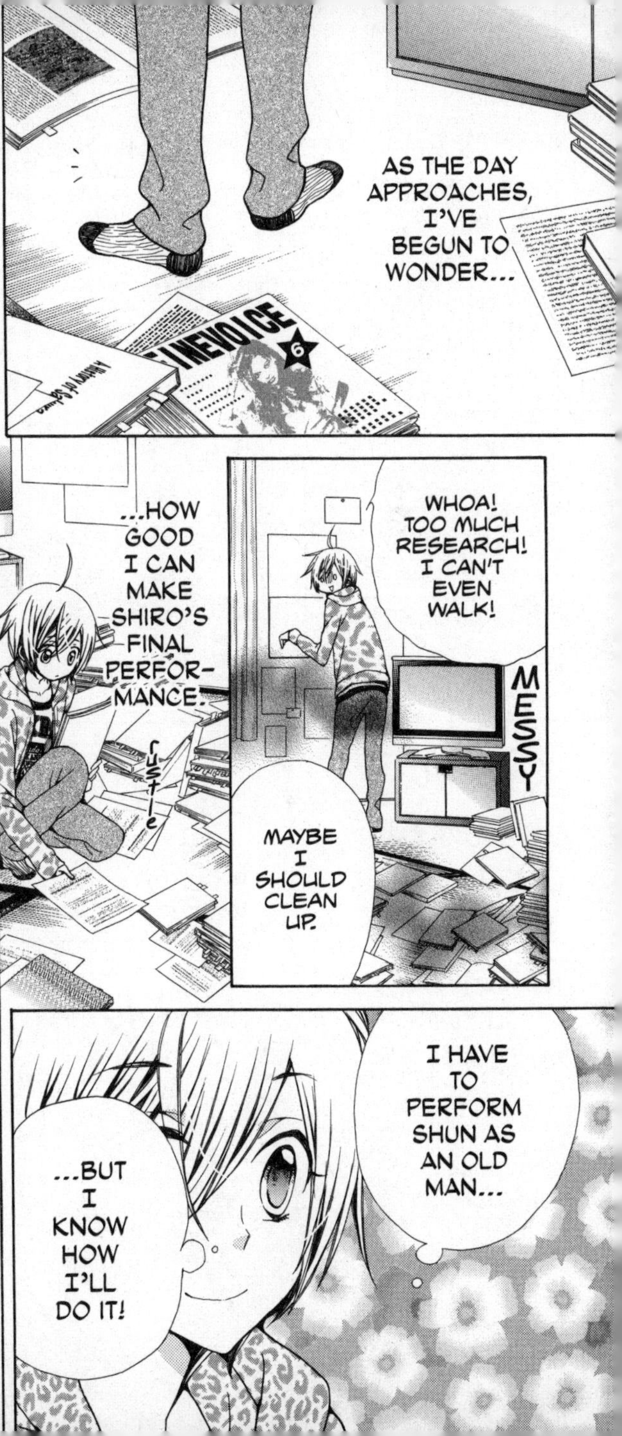
AS THE DAY APPROACHES, I'VE BEGUN TO WONDER...
6
WHOA! TOO MUCH RESEARCH! I CAN'T EVEN WALK!
MESSY
MAYBE I SHOULD CLEAN UP.
...HOW GOOD I CAN MAKE SHIRO'S FINAL PERFORMANCE.
rustle
I HAVE TO PERFORM SHUN AS AN OLD MAN...
...BUT I KNOW HOW I'LL DO IT!

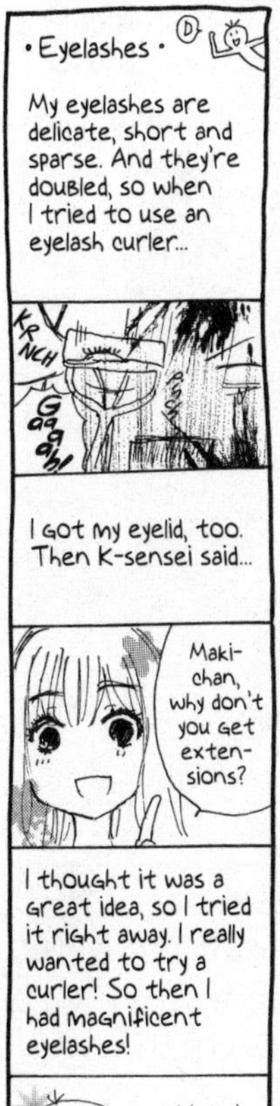
• Eyelashes •
My eyelashes are delicate, short and sparse. And they're doubled, so when I tried to use an eyelash curler...
KRNCH
Gaaaah!
I got my eyelid, too. Then K-sensei said...
Maki-chan, why don't you get extensions?
I thought it was a great idea, so I tried it right away. I really wanted to try a curler! So then I had magnificent eyelashes!
Now I won't pinch my eyelid in the curler!!
Mirror
But the manual said never to use an eyelash curler on them...
For the extensions.
OMG!! Oh well!!
Your right eyelashes must be in a resting phase.
The girl who did my extensions said...
No, they're naturally like that...

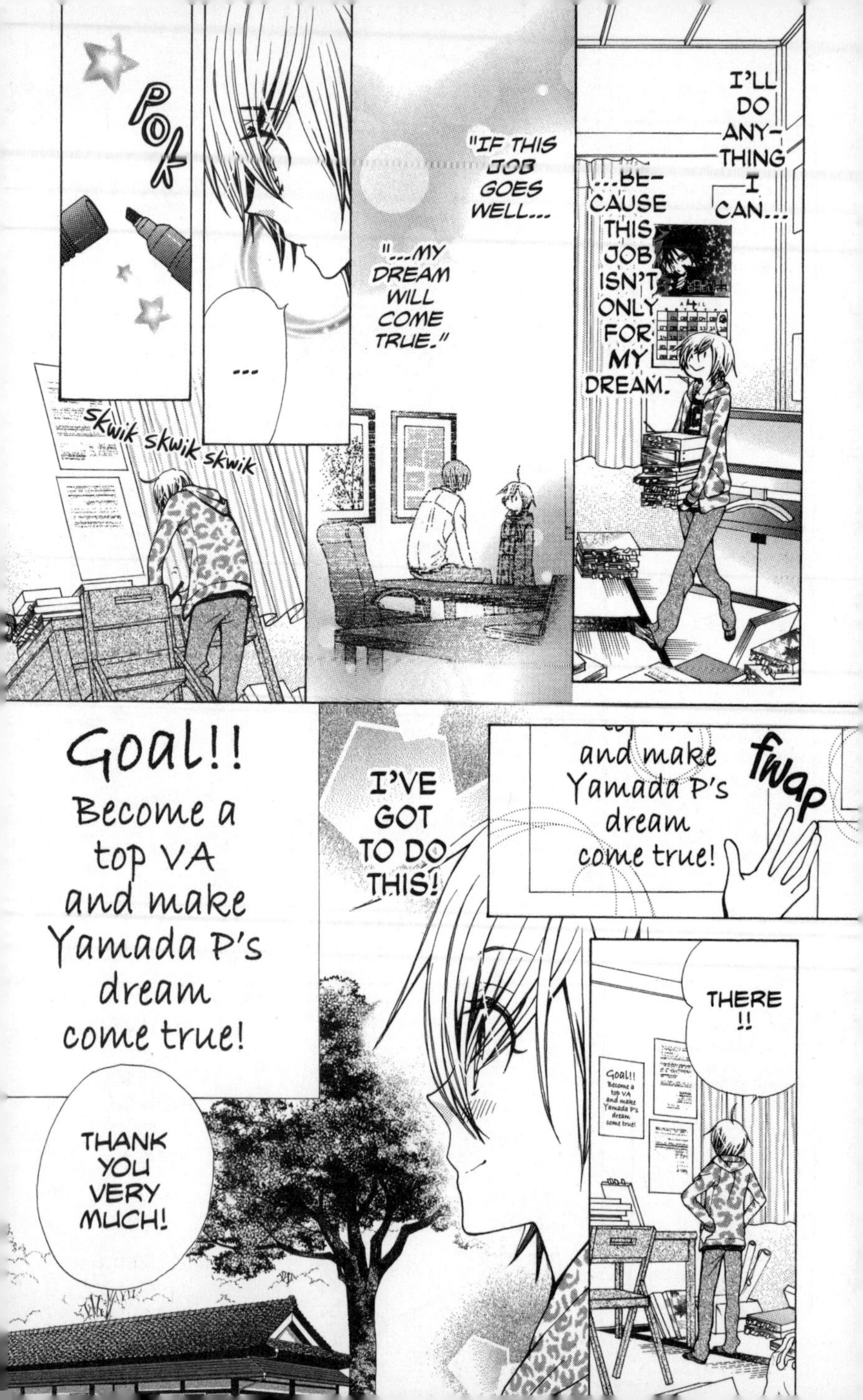
I'LL DO ANYTHING I CAN...
...BECAUSE THIS JOB ISN'T ONLY FOR MY DREAM.
"IF THIS JOB GOES WELL...
"...MY DREAM WILL COME TRUE."
...
POK
SKWIK SKWIK SKWIK
FWAP
and make Yamada P's dream come true!
I'VE GOT TO DO THIS!
THERE!!
Goal!! Become a top VA and make Yamada P's dream come true!
THANK YOU VERY MUCH!

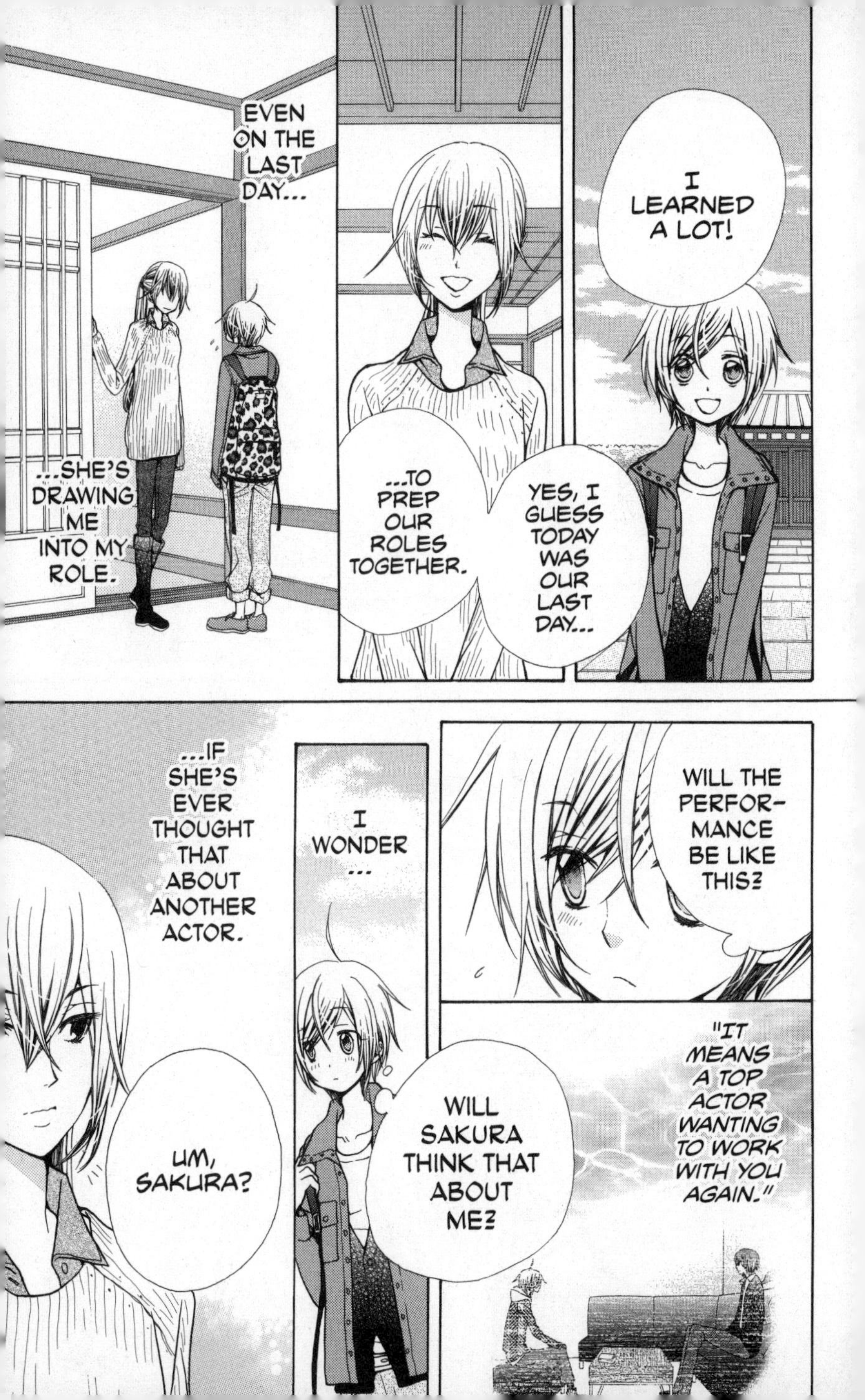
I LEARNED A LOT!
YES, I GUESS TODAY WAS OUR LAST DAY...
...TO PREP OUR ROLES TOGETHER.
EVEN ON THE LAST DAY...
...SHE'S DRAWING ME INTO MY ROLE.
WILL THE PERFOR-MANCE BE LIKE THIS?
"IT MEANS A TOP ACTOR WANTING TO WORK WITH YOU AGAIN."
I WONDER...
WILL SAKURA THINK THAT ABOUT ME?
...IF SHE'S EVER THOUGHT THAT ABOUT ANOTHER ACTOR.
UM, SAKURA?

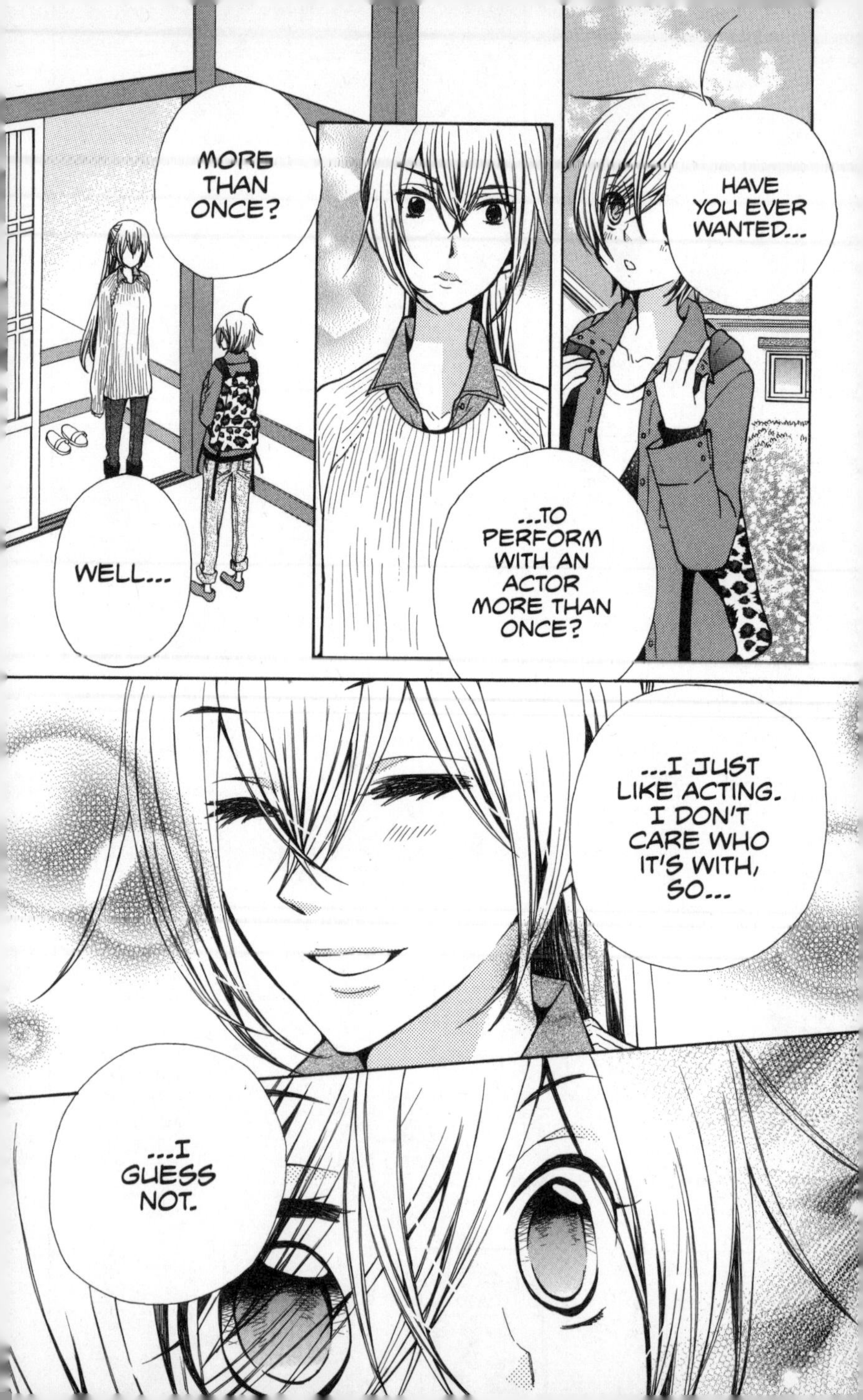
HAVE YOU EVER WANTED...
...TO PERFORM WITH AN ACTOR MORE THAN ONCE?
MORE THAN ONCE?
WELL...
...I JUST LIKE ACTING. I DON'T CARE WHO IT'S WITH, SO...
...I GUESS NOT.

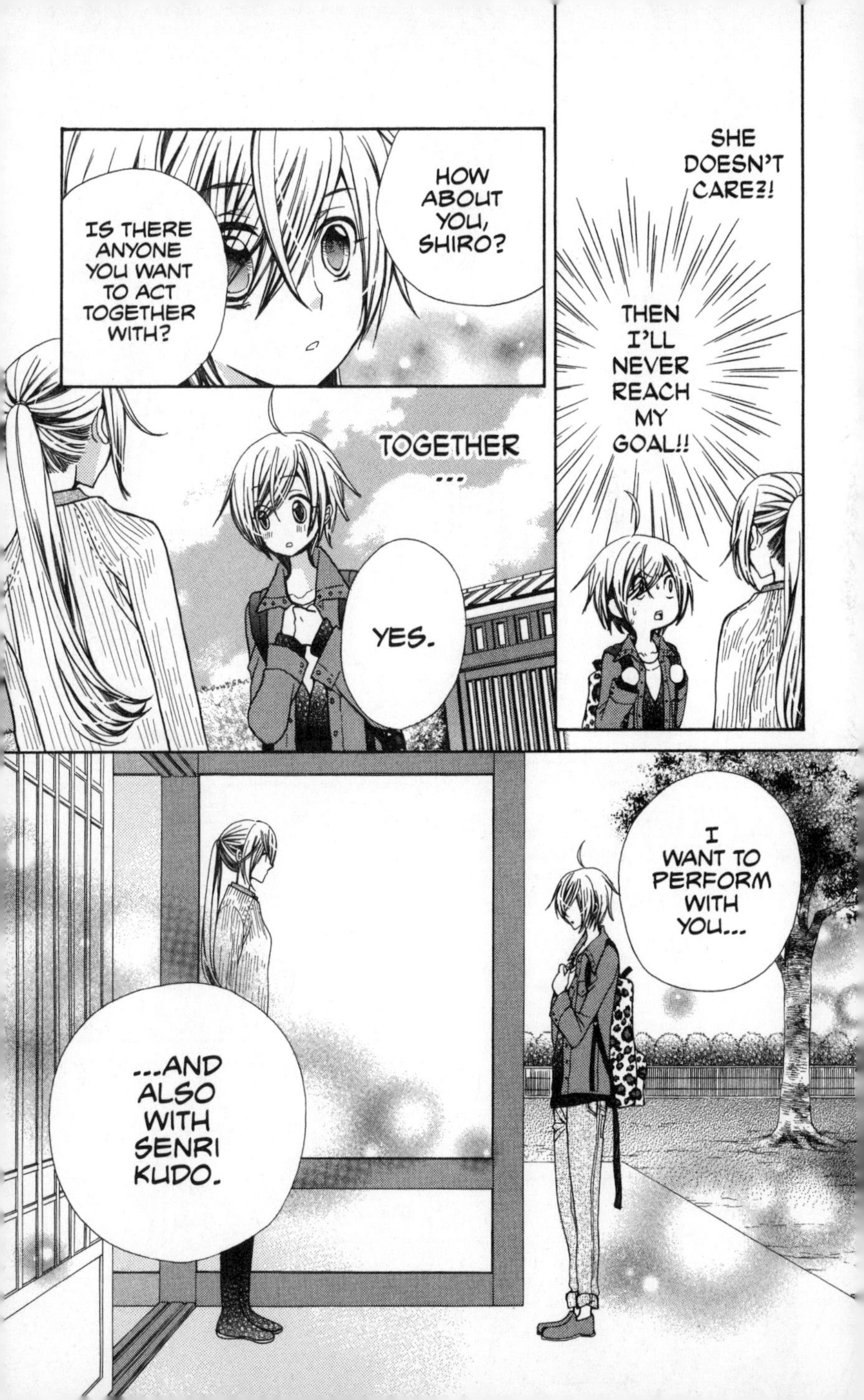
SHE DOESN'T CARE?!
THEN I'LL NEVER REACH MY GOAL!!
HOW ABOUT YOU, SHIRO?
IS THERE ANYONE YOU WANT TO ACT TOGETHER WITH?
TOGETHER ...
YES.
I WANT TO PERFORM WITH YOU...
...AND ALSO WITH SENRI KUDO.

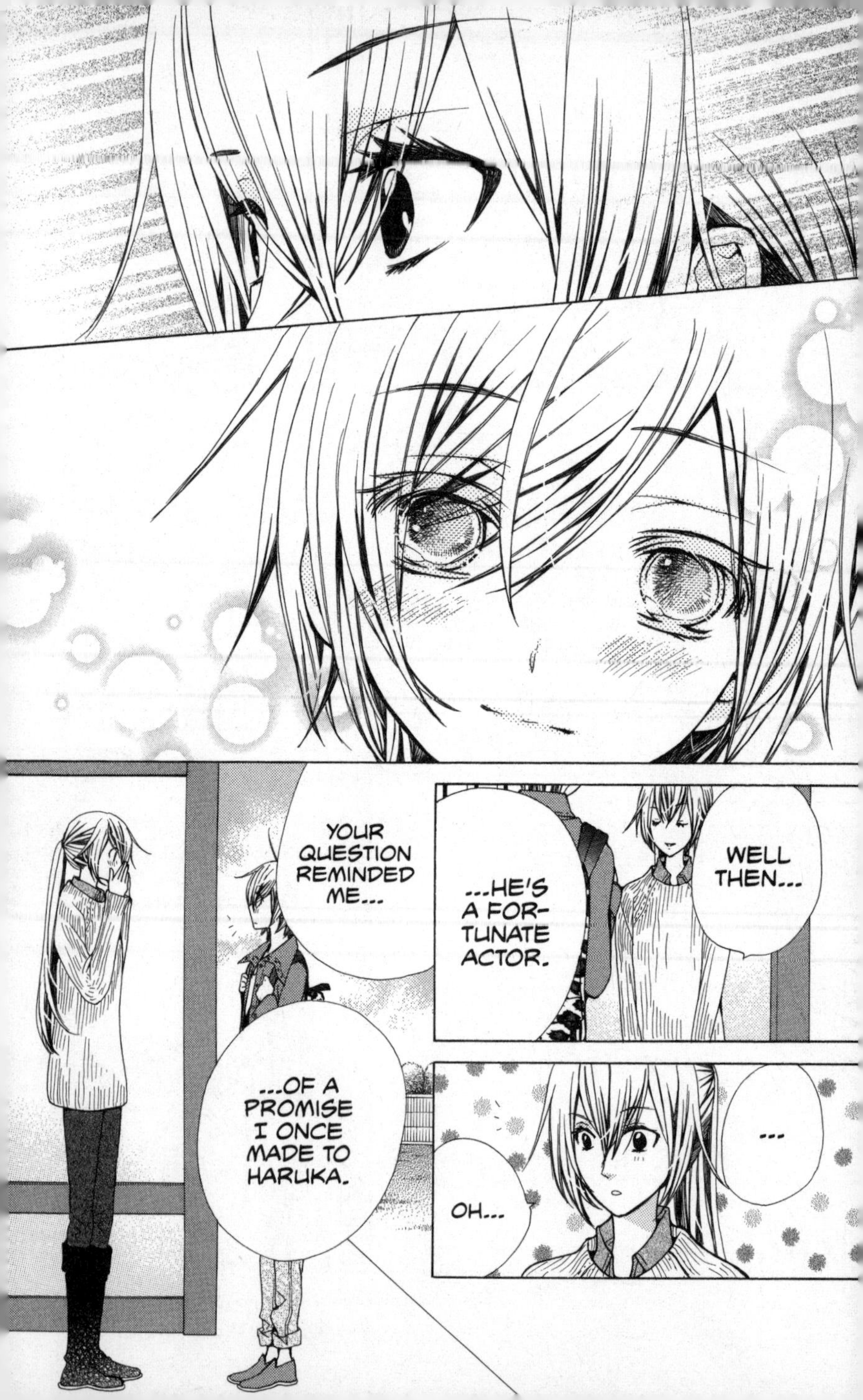
WELL THEN...
...HE'S A FORTUNATE ACTOR.
...
OH...
YOUR QUESTION REMINDED ME...
...OF A PROMISE I ONCE MADE TO HARUKA.

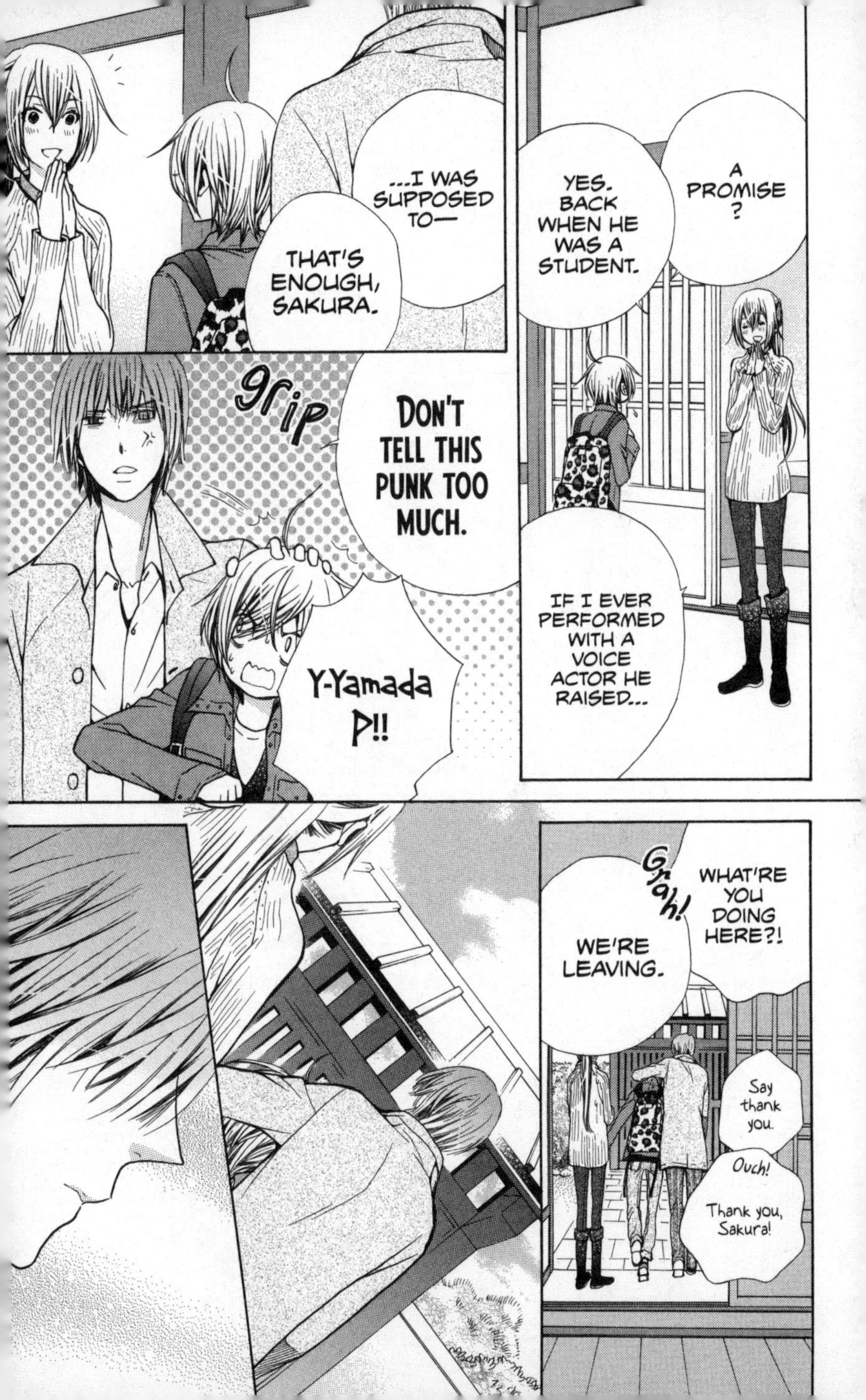
A PROMISE?
YES. BACK WHEN HE WAS A STUDENT.
IF I EVER PERFORMED WITH A VOICE ACTOR HE RAISED...
...I WAS SUPPOSED TO—
THAT'S ENOUGH, SAKURA.
grip
DON'T TELL THIS PUNK TOO MUCH.
Y-Yamada P!!
WHAT'RE YOU DOING HERE?!
Grah!
WE'RE LEAVING.
Say thank you.
Ouch!
Thank you, Sakura!

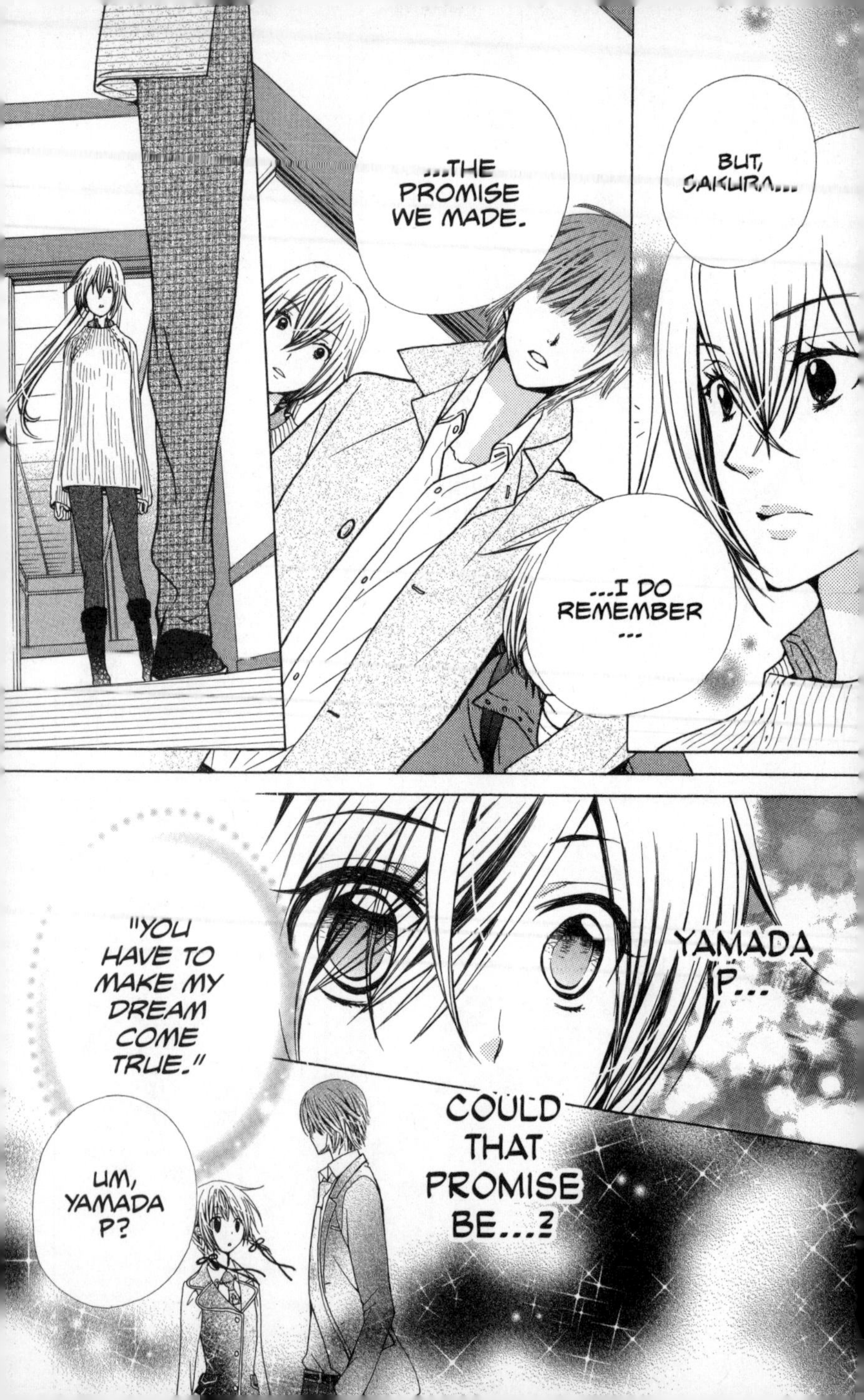
BUT, SAKURA...
...I DO REMEMBER ...
...THE PROMISE WE MADE.
YAMADA P...
"YOU HAVE TO MAKE MY DREAM COME TRUE."
COULD THAT PROMISE BE...?
UM, YAMADA P?

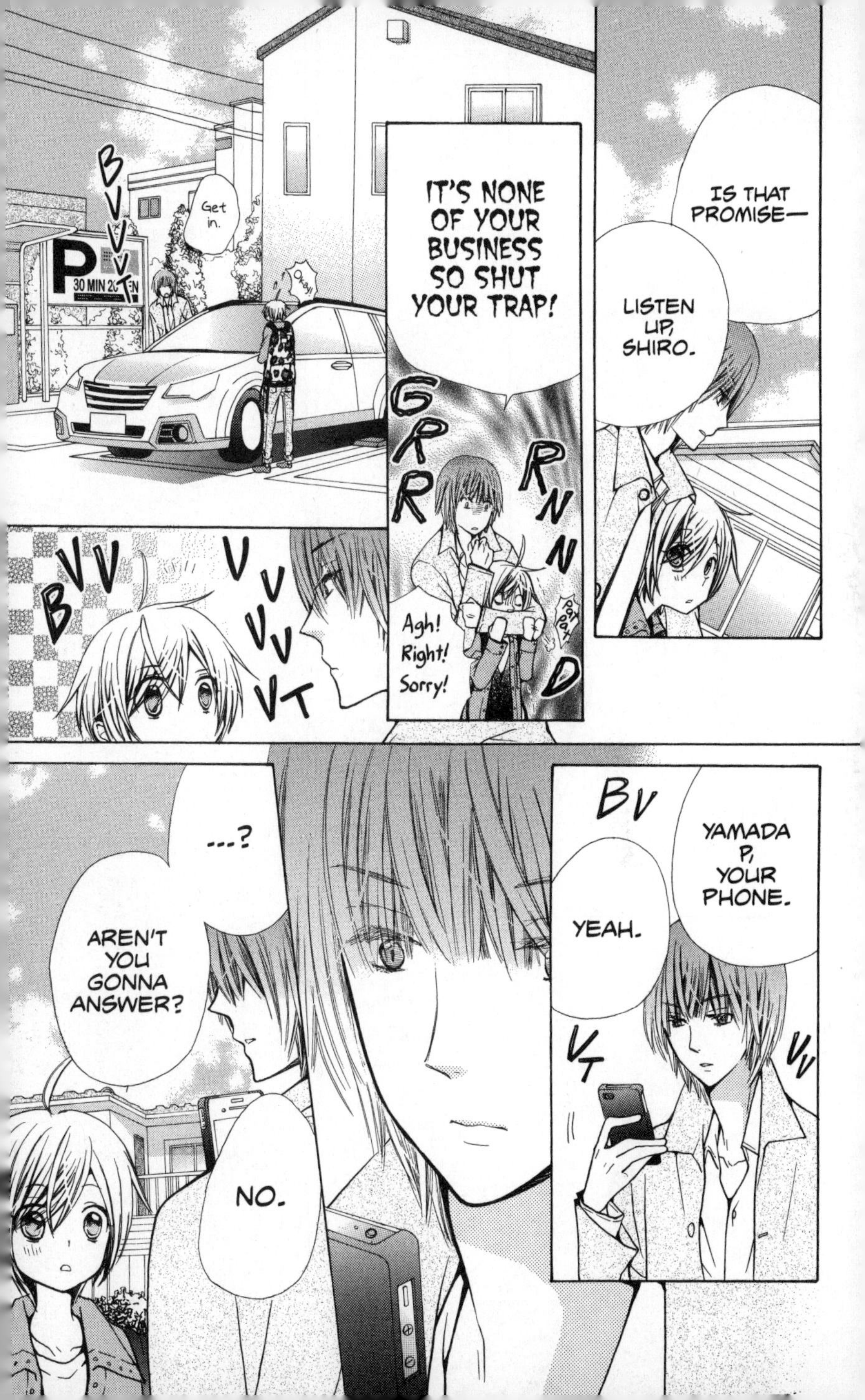
IS THAT PROMISE—
LISTEN UP, SHIRO.
IT'S NONE OF YOUR BUSINESS SO SHUT YOUR TRAP!
GRRRRNND
Pat pat
Agh! Right! Sorry!
Get in.
BVVVVT
Okay!
P
30 MIN
BVVVVVVT
BV
YAMADA P, YOUR PHONE.
YEAH.
VT
VV
...?
AREN'T YOU GONNA ANSWER?
NO.

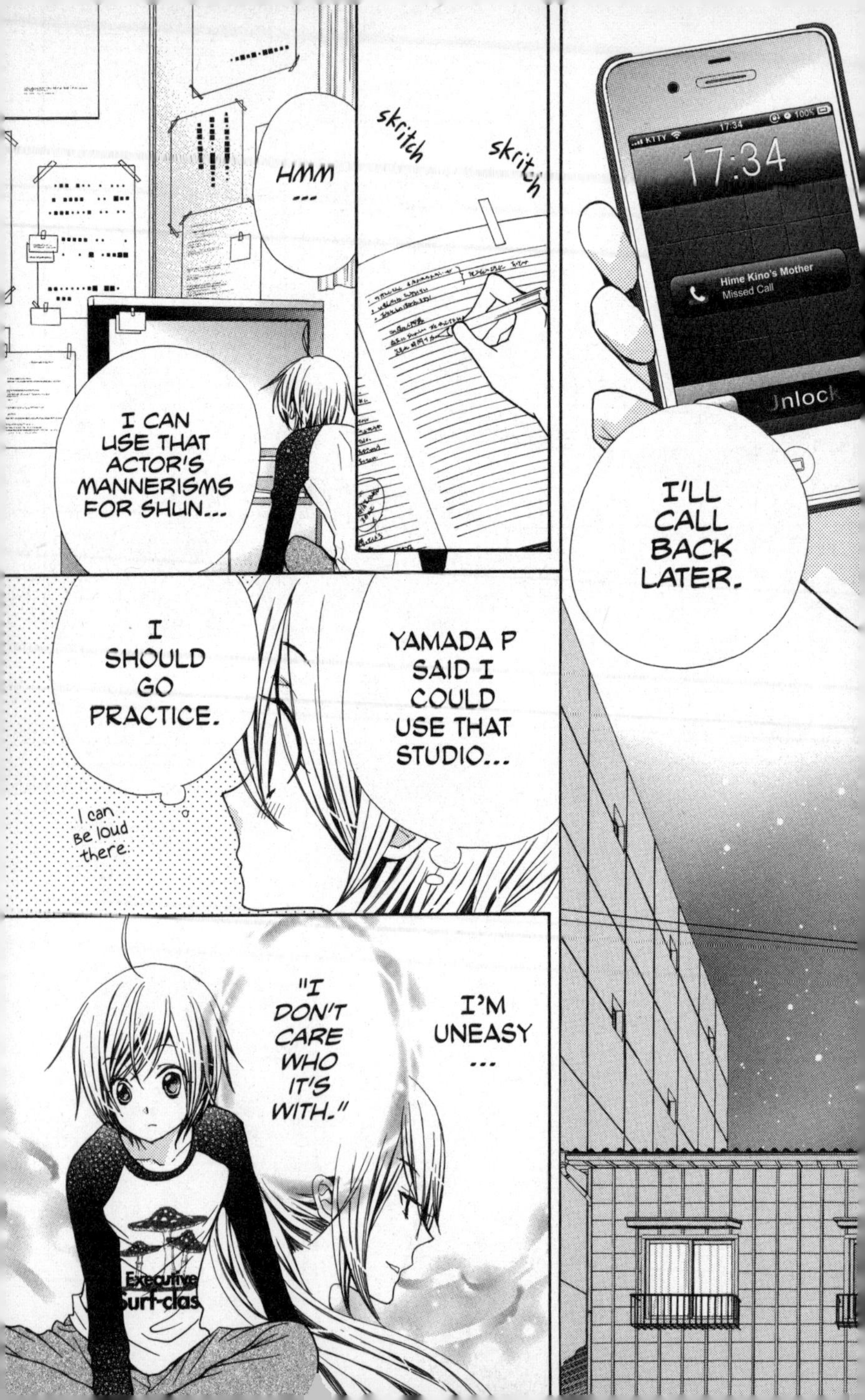
17:34
Hime Kino's Mother
Missed Call
Unlock
I'LL CALL BACK LATER.
skritch
skritch
HMM...
I CAN USE THAT ACTOR'S MANNERISMS FOR SHUN...
YAMADA P SAID I COULD USE THAT STUDIO...
I SHOULD GO PRACTICE.
I can be loud there.
I'M UNEASY...
"I DON'T CARE WHO IT'S WITH."
Executive
Surf-clas

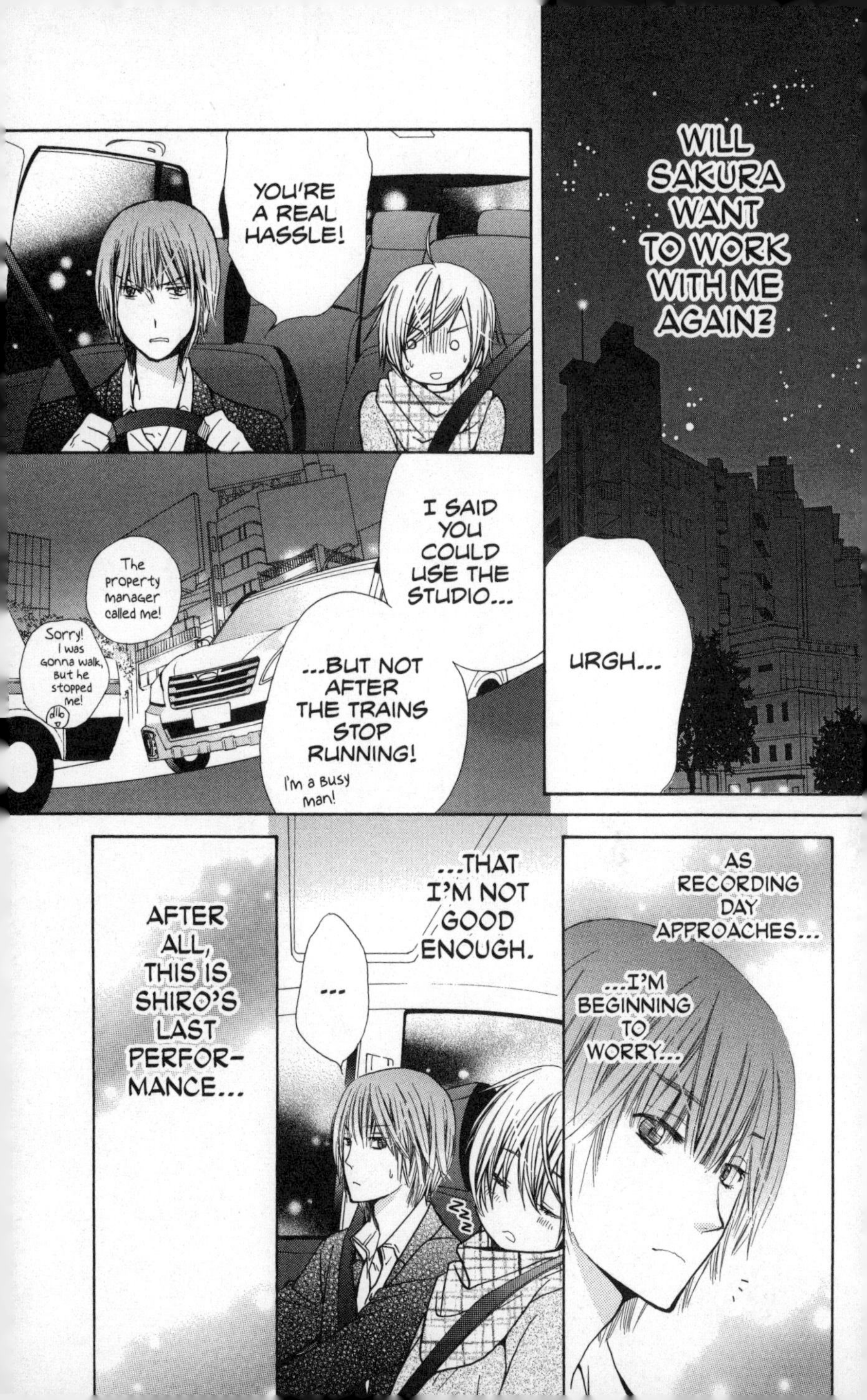
WILL SAKURA WANT TO WORK WITH ME AGAIN?
YOU'RE A REAL HASSLE!
I SAID YOU COULD USE THE STUDIO...
...BUT NOT AFTER THE TRAINS STOP RUNNING!
I'm a busy man!
URGH...
The property manager called me!
Sorry! I was gonna walk, but he stopped me!
AS RECORDING DAY APPROACHES...
...I'M BEGINNING TO WORRY...
...THAT I'M NOT GOOD ENOUGH.
...
AFTER ALL, THIS IS SHIRO'S LAST PERFORMANCE...

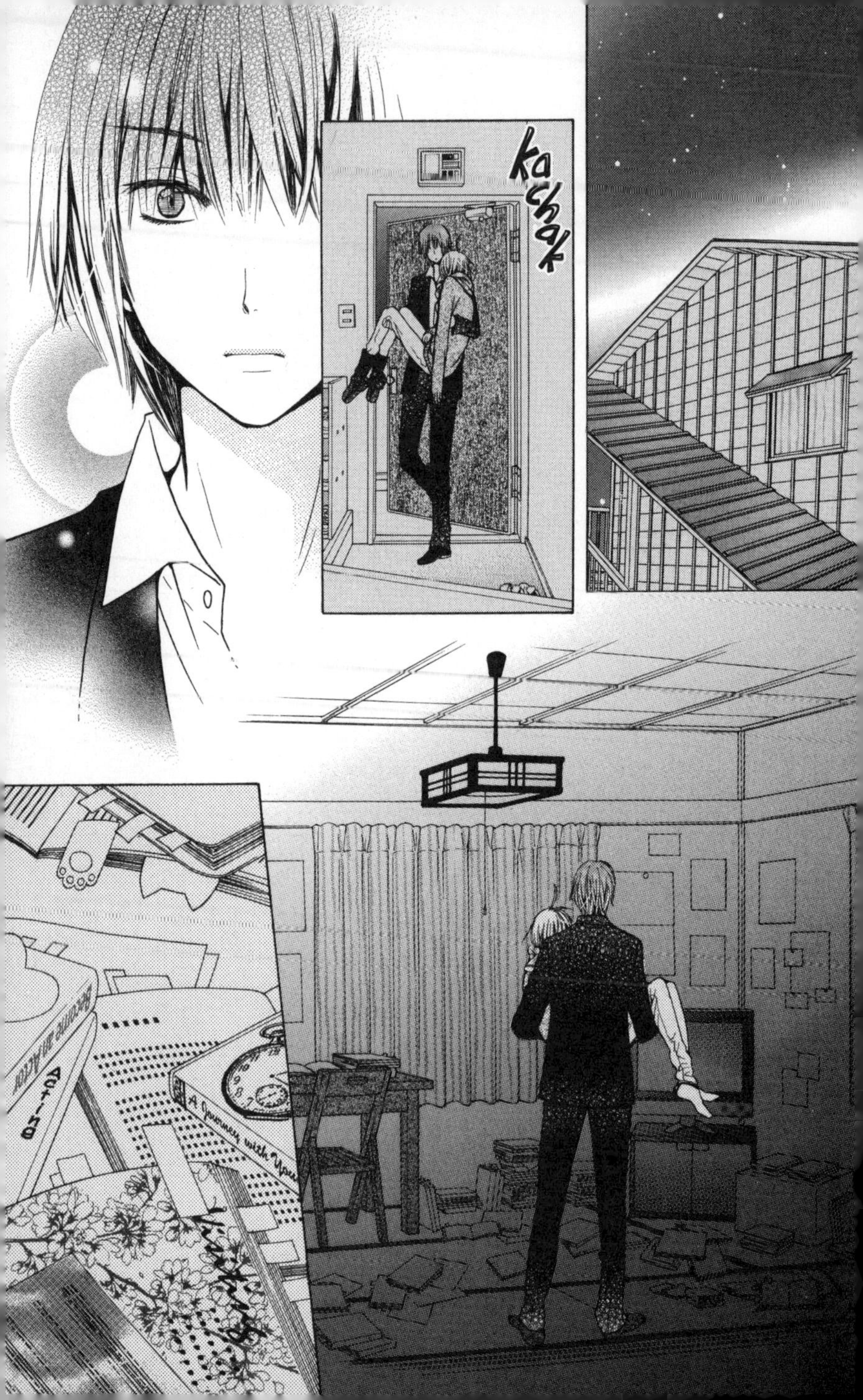

ka chak
Acting
A Journey with You

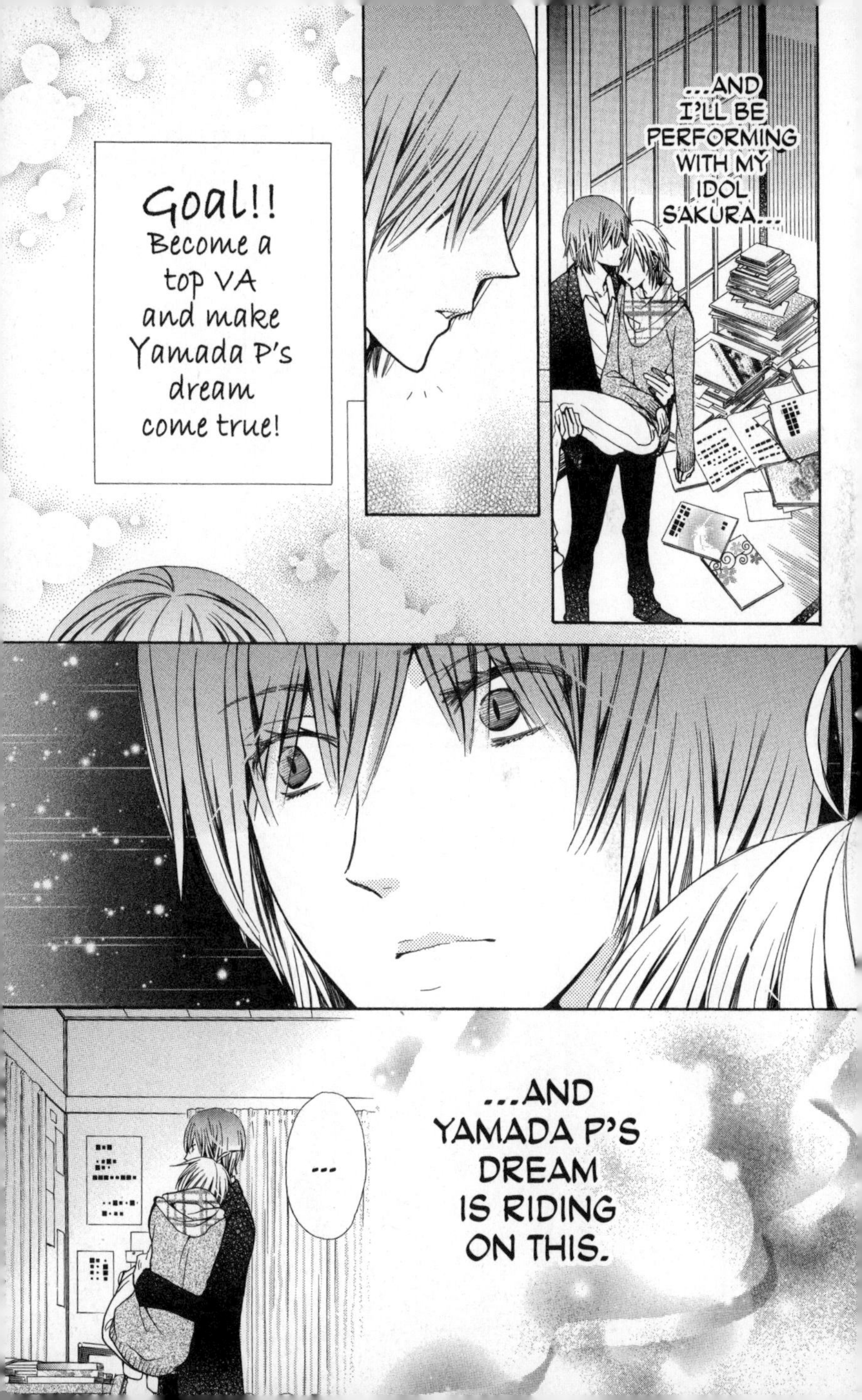
...AND I'LL BE PERFORMING WITH MY IDOL SAKURA...
Goal!! Become a top VA and make Yamada P's dream come true!
...AND YAMADA P'S DREAM IS RIDING ON THIS.
...

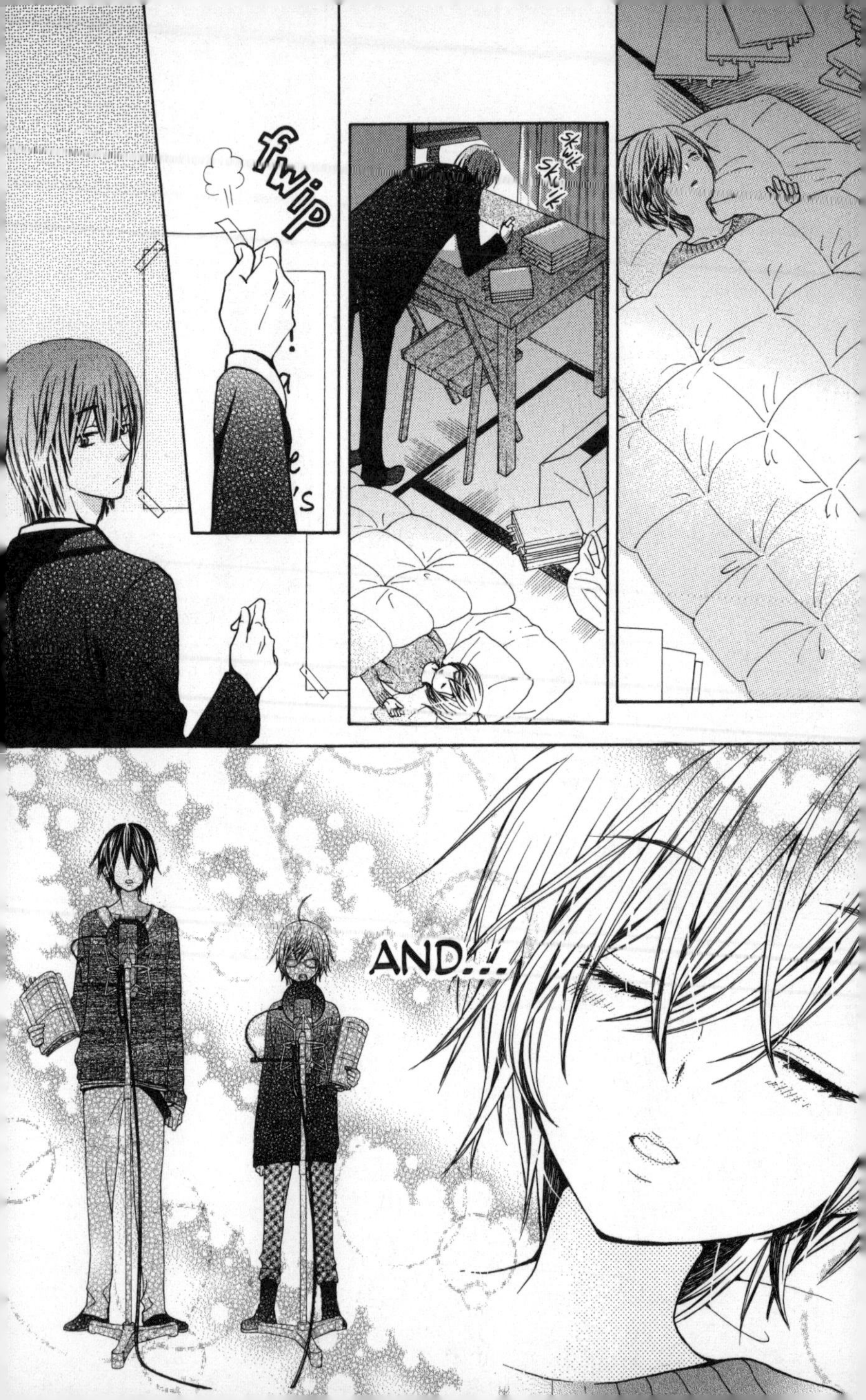
skwik
skwik
fwip
AND...

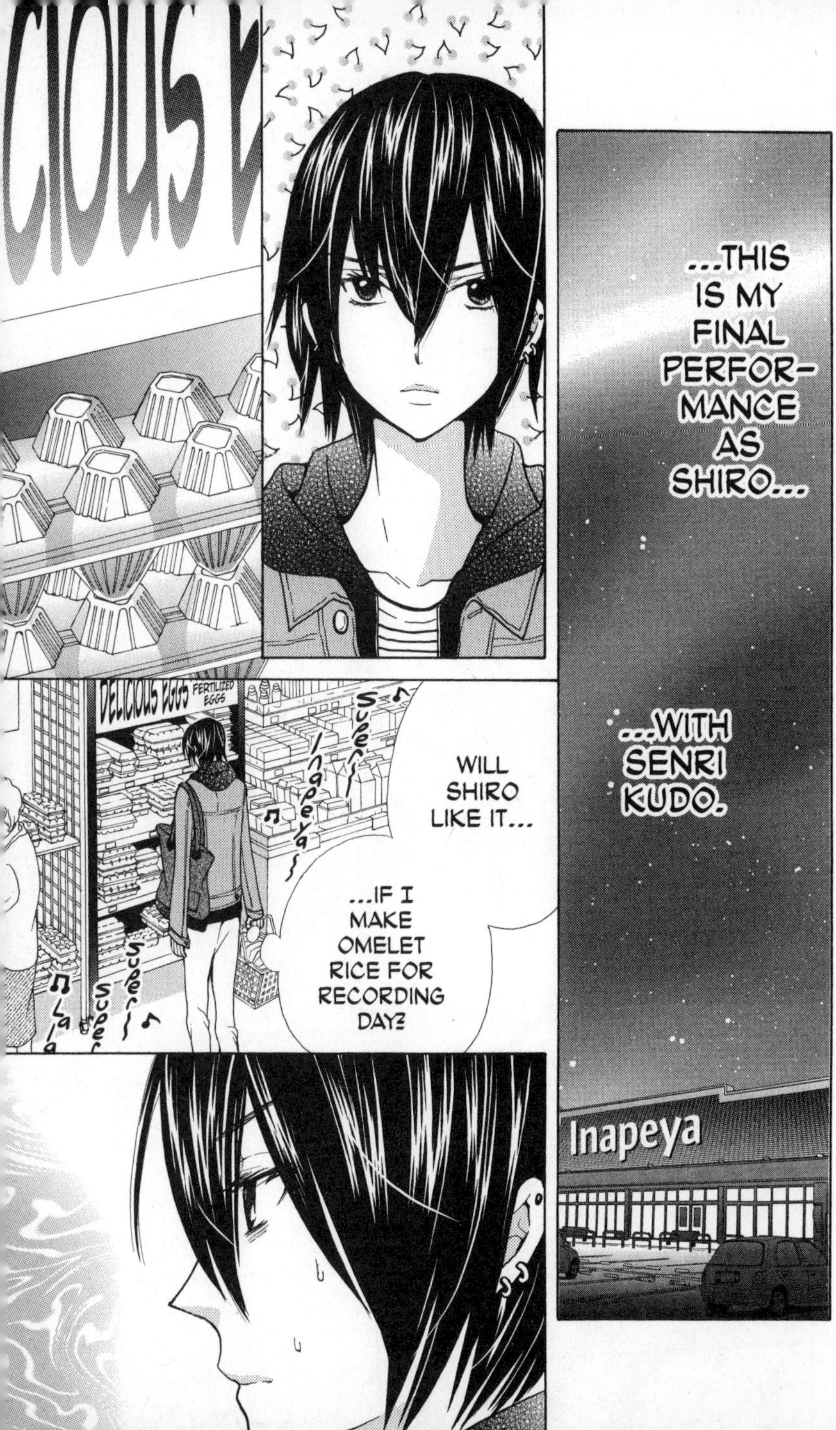
...THIS IS MY FINAL PERFORMANCE AS SHIRO...
...WITH SENRI KUDO.
Inapeya
DELICIOUS EGGS
FERTILIZED EGGS
Super~ Inapeya~
Super~ Super Lala
WILL SHIRO LIKE IT...
...IF I MAKE OMELET RICE FOR RECORDING DAY?

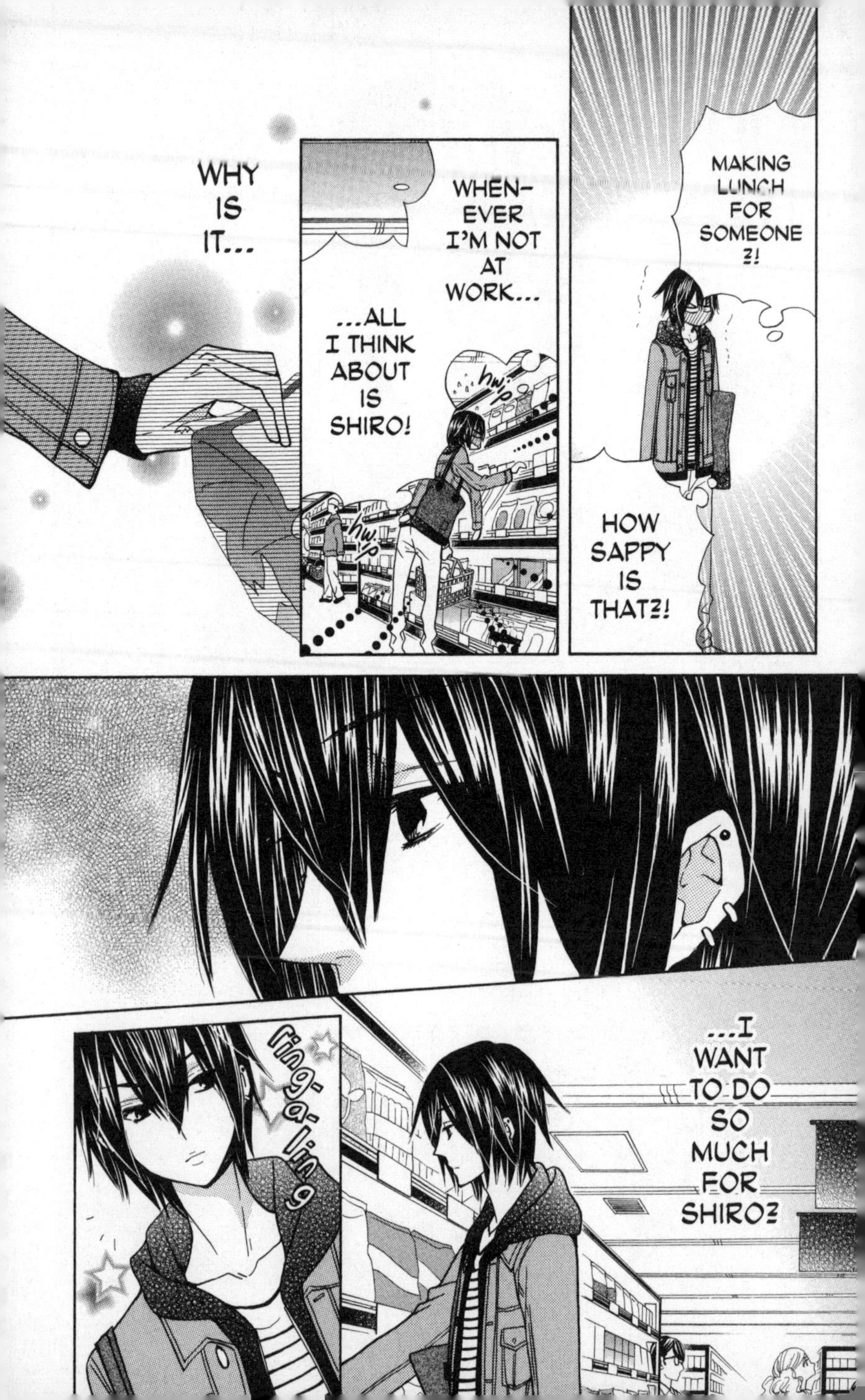
MAKING LUNCH FOR SOMEONE?!
HOW SAPPY IS THAT?!
WHEN-EVER I'M NOT AT WORK...
hwip
...ALL I THINK ABOUT IS SHIRO!
hwip
WHY IS IT...
...I WANT TO DO SO MUCH FOR SHIRO?
ring-a-ling

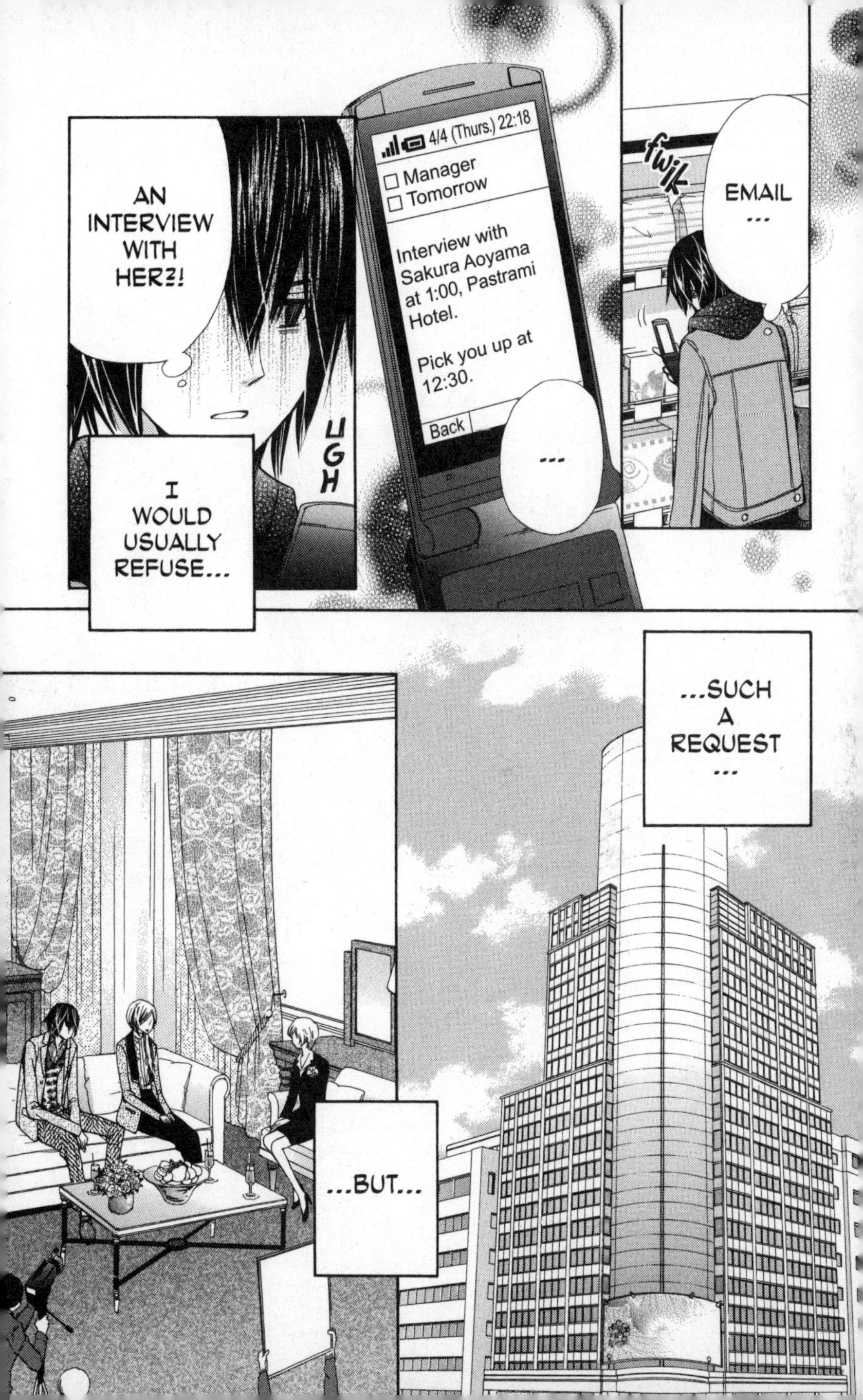
fwik
EMAIL...
4/4 (Thurs.) 22:18
Manager
Tomorrow
Interview with Sakura Aoyama at 1:00, Pastrami Hotel.
Pick you up at 12:30.
Back
...
AN INTERVIEW WITH HER?!
UGH
I WOULD USUALLY REFUSE...
...SUCH A REQUEST...
...BUT...

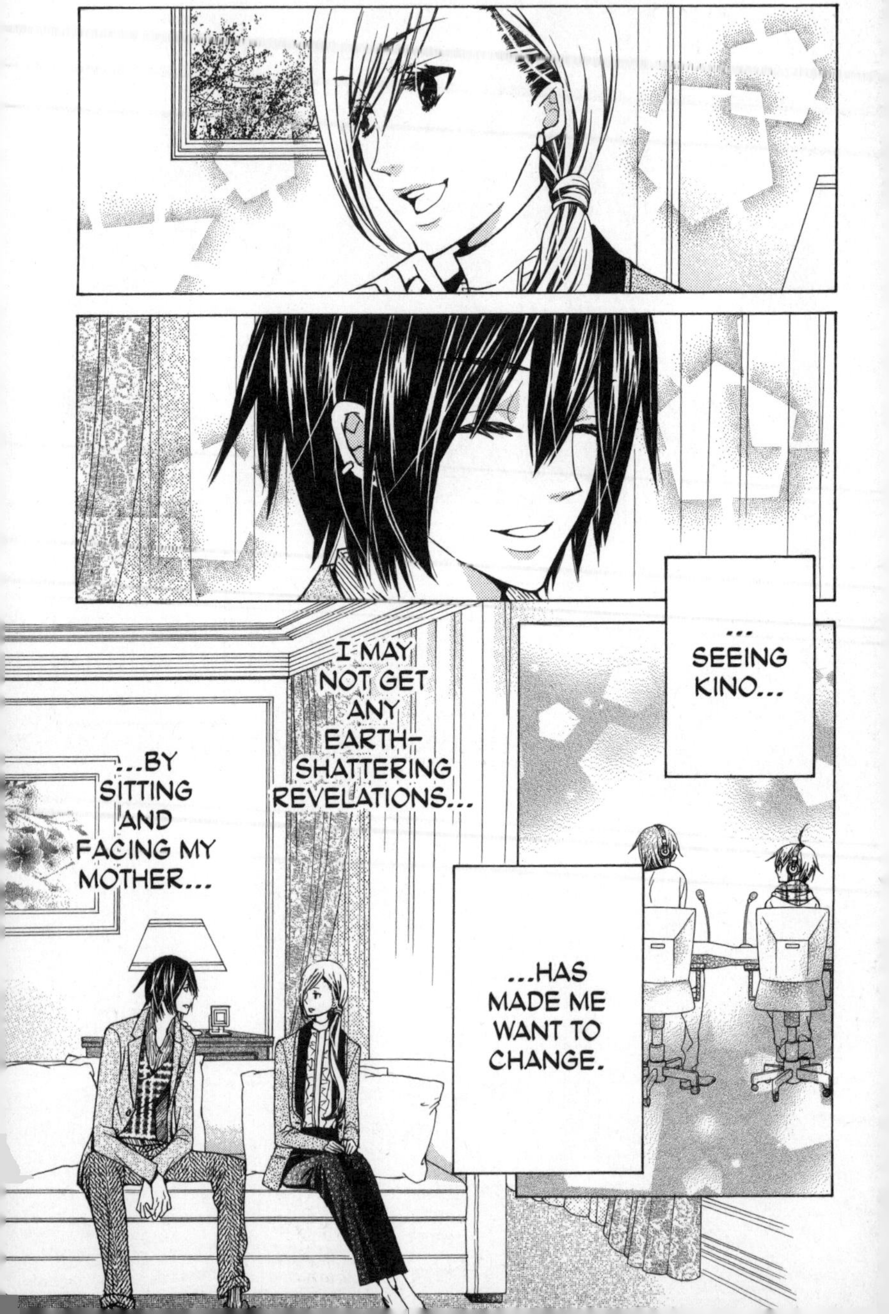
...
SEEING KINO...
...HAS MADE ME WANT TO CHANGE.
I MAY NOT GET ANY EARTH-SHATTERING REVELATIONS...
...BY SITTING AND FACING MY MOTHER...

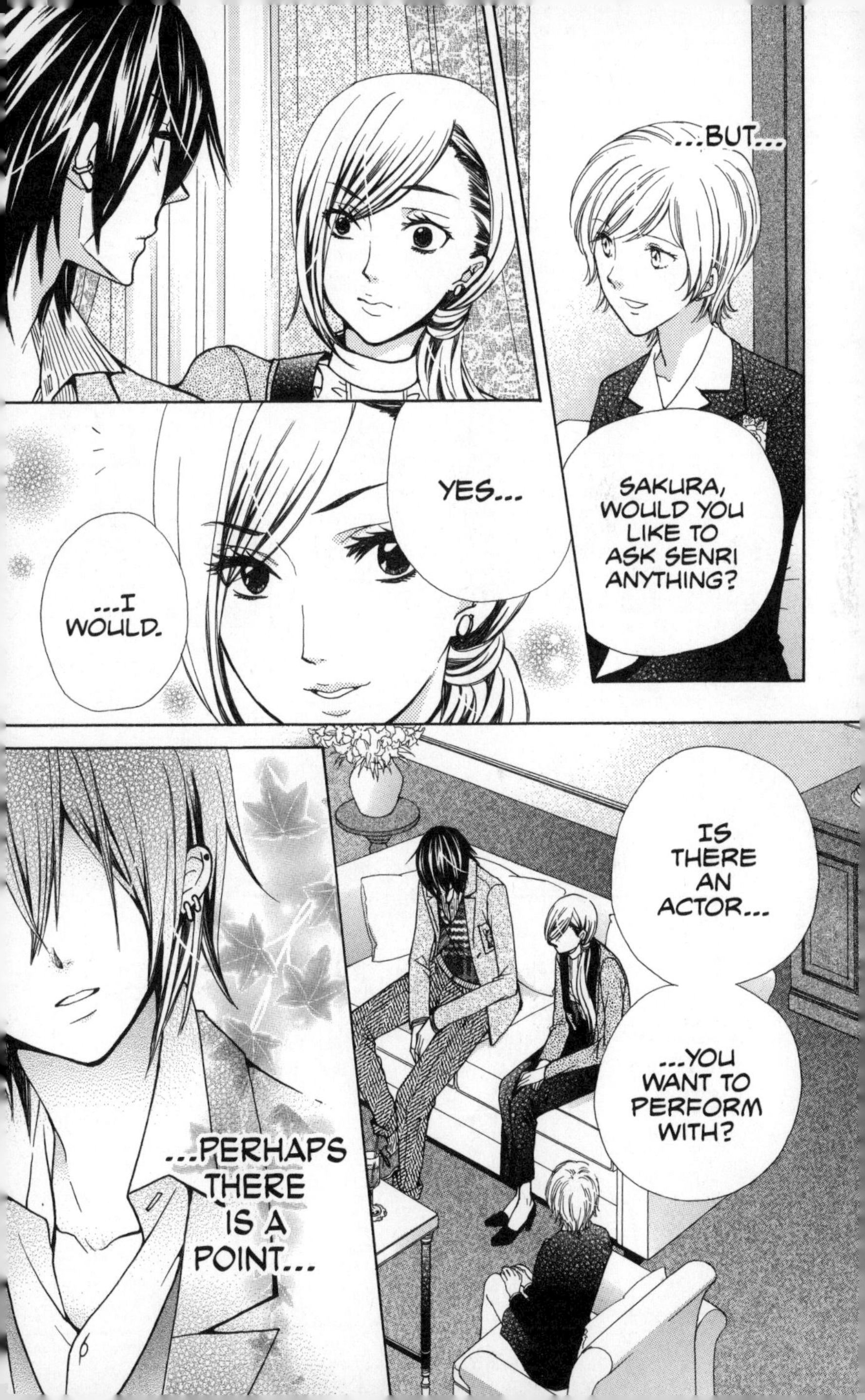
...BUT...
SAKURA, WOULD YOU LIKE TO ASK SENRI ANYTHING?
YES...
...I WOULD.
IS THERE AN ACTOR...
...YOU WANT TO PERFORM WITH?
...PERHAPS THERE IS A POINT...

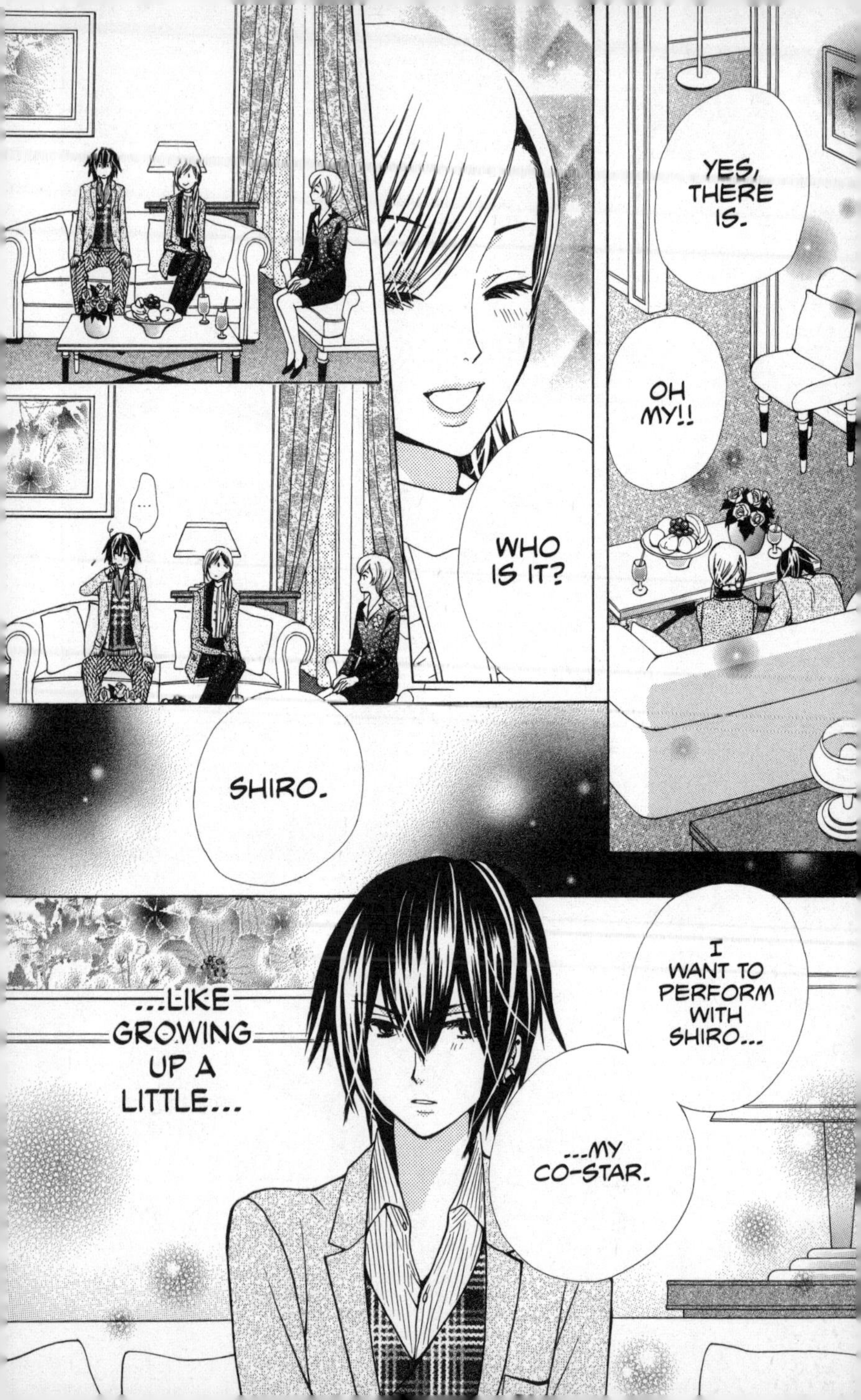
YES, THERE IS.
OH MY!!
WHO IS IT?
...
SHIRO.
I WANT TO PERFORM WITH SHIRO...
...MY CO-STAR.
...LIKE GROWING UP A LITTLE...

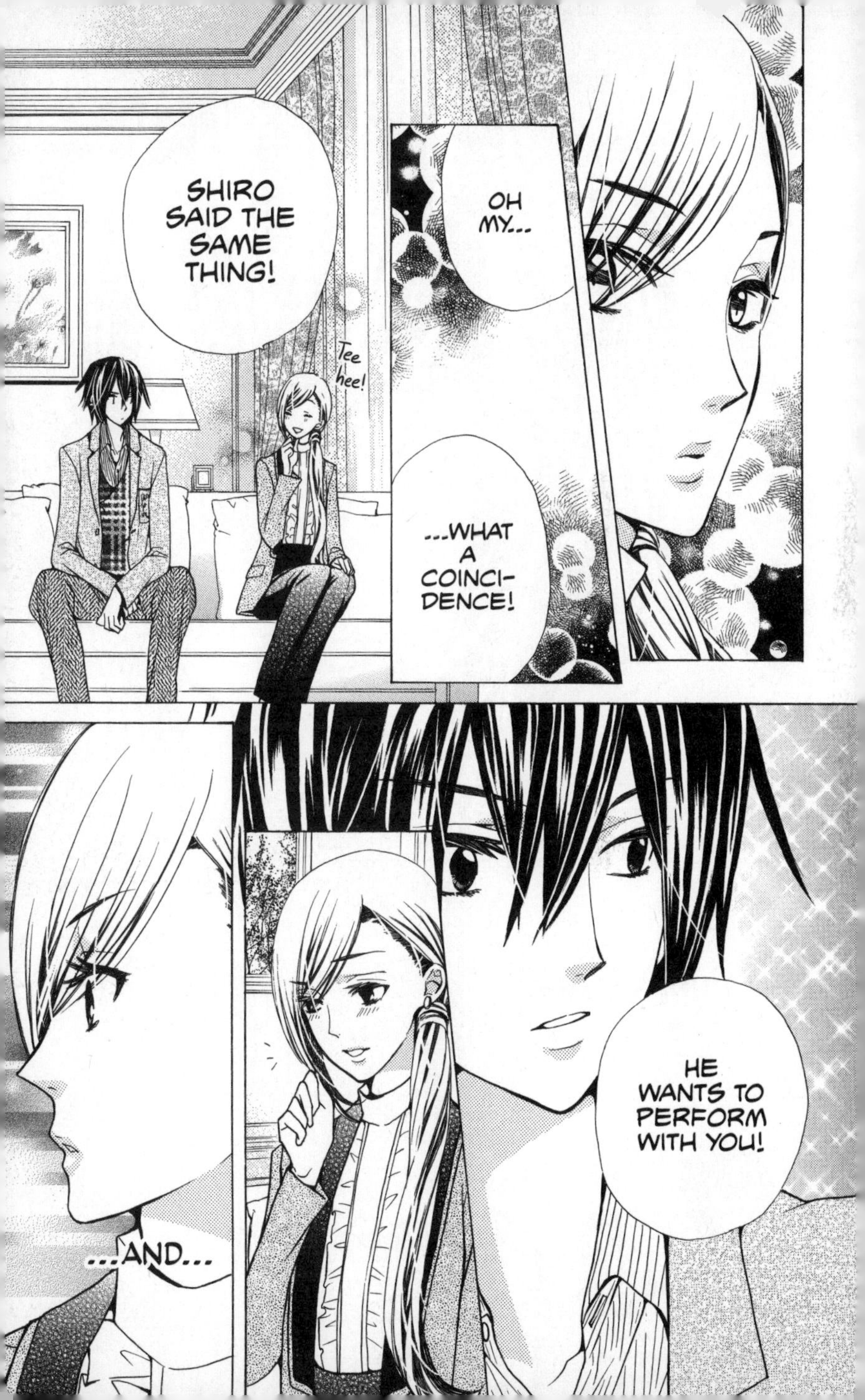
OH MY...
...WHAT A COINCIDENCE!
SHIRO SAID THE SAME THING!
Tee hee!
HE WANTS TO PERFORM WITH YOU!
...AND...

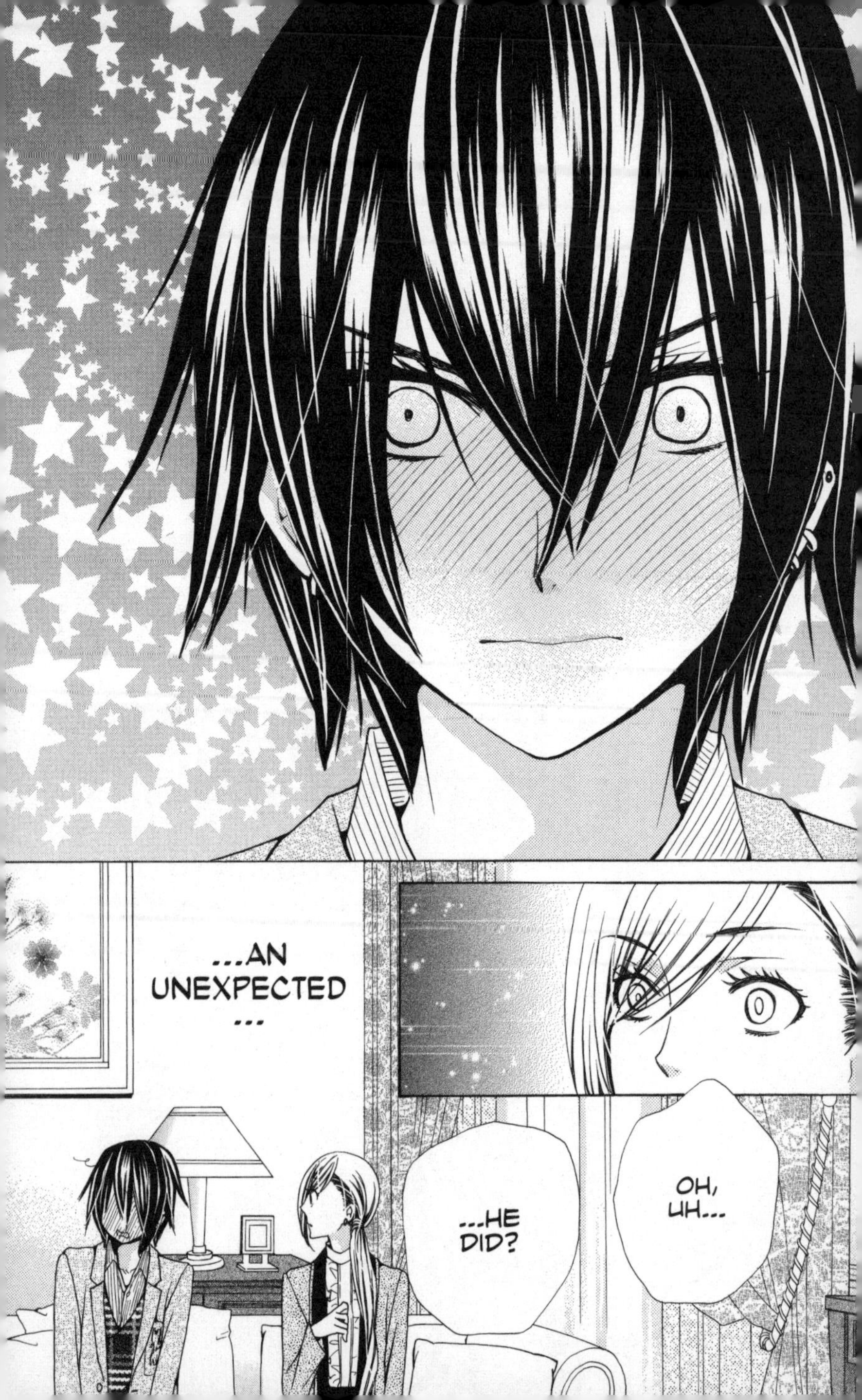
...AN UNEXPECTED ...
OH, UH...
...HE DID?

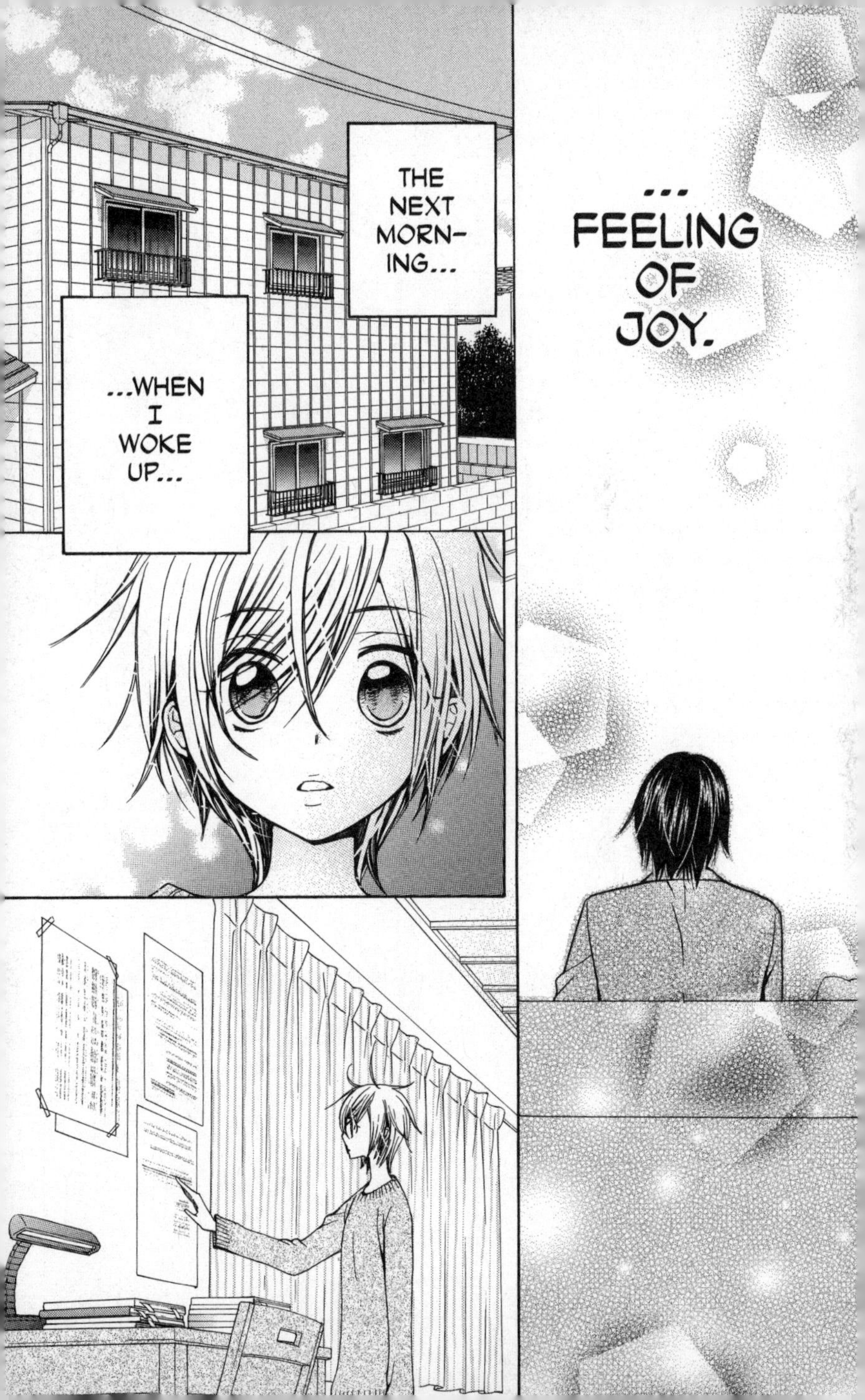
...FEELING OF JOY.
THE NEXT MORNING...
...WHEN I WOKE UP...

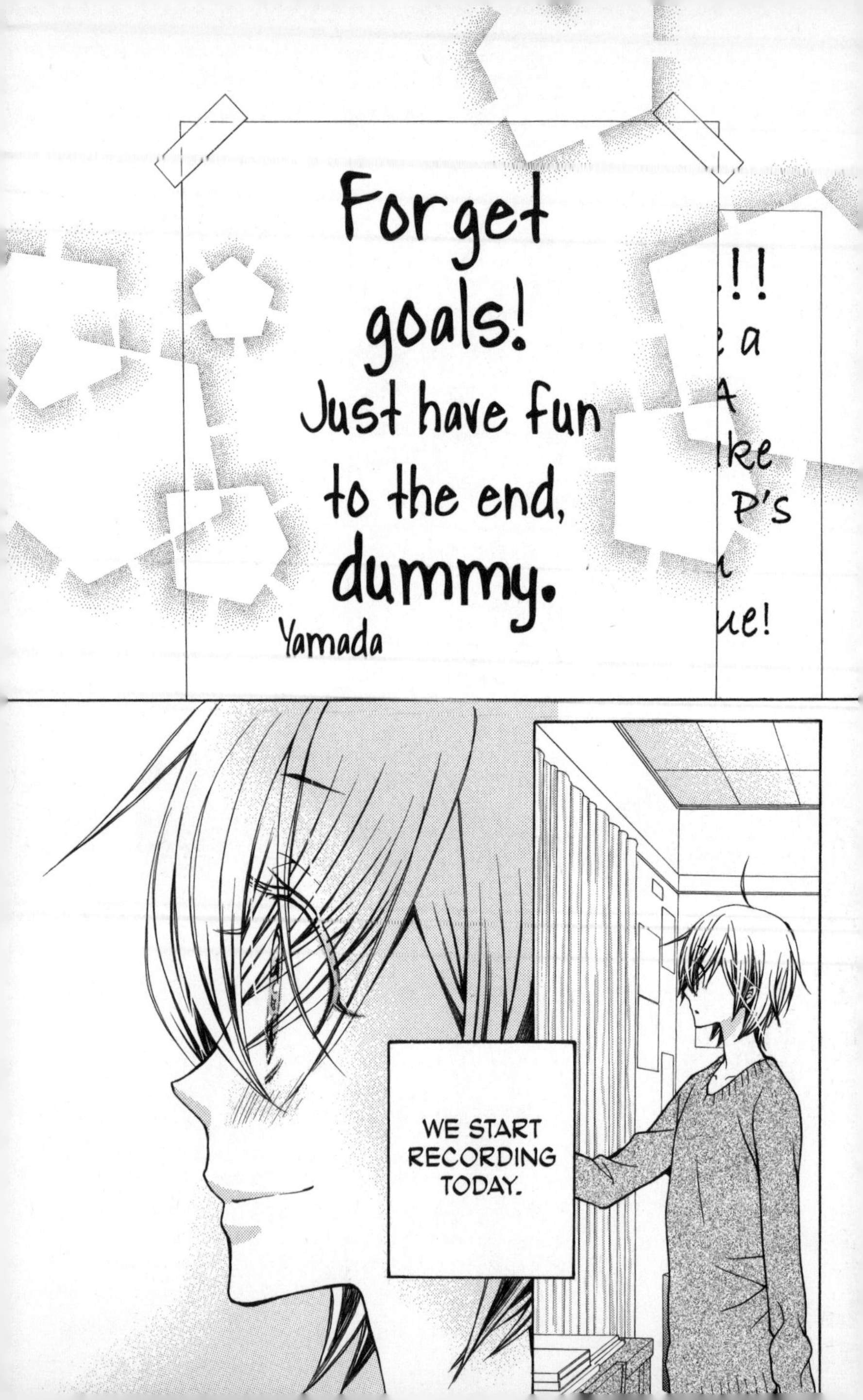
Forget goals! Just have fun to the end, dummy.
Yamada
WE START RECORDING TODAY.

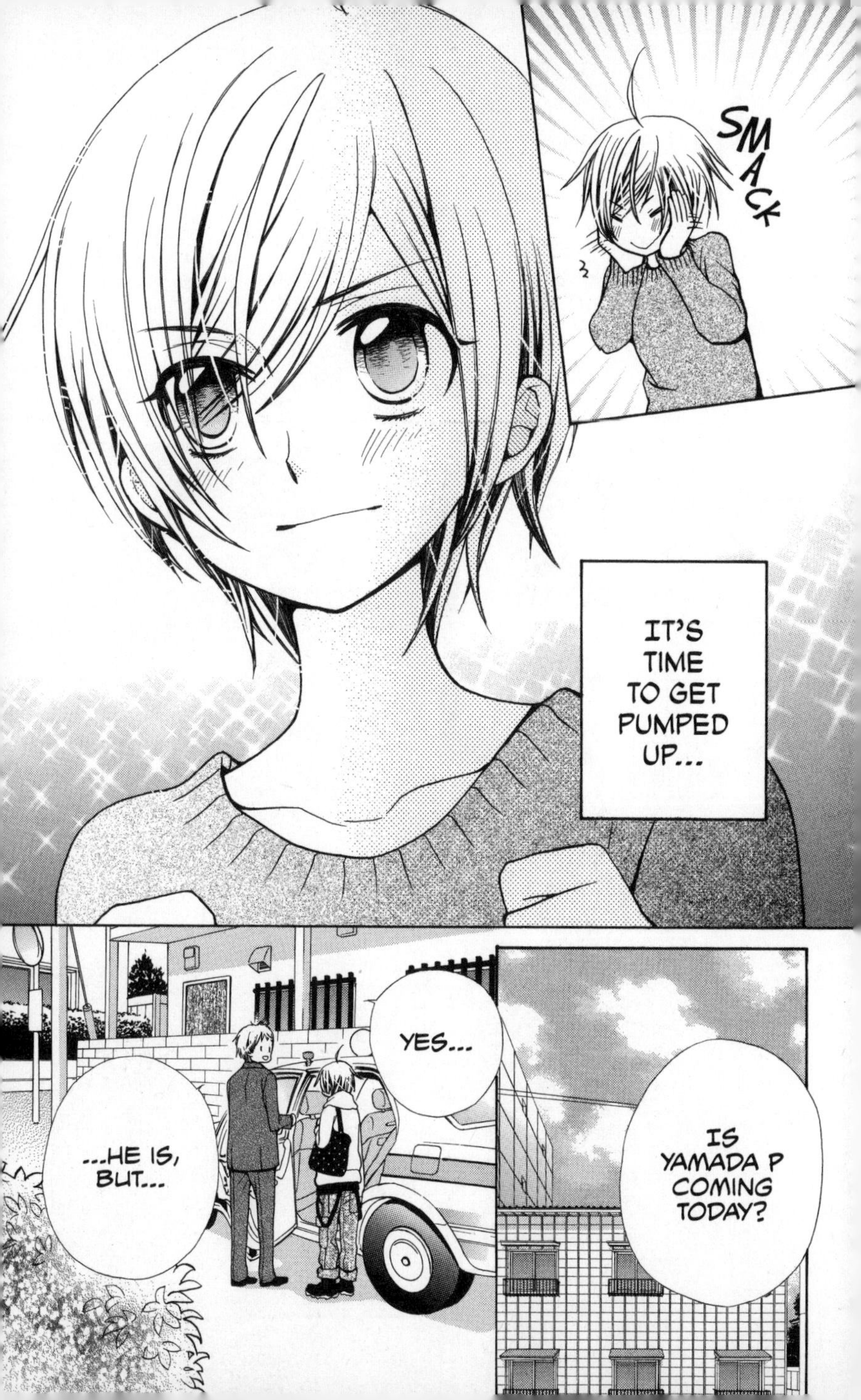
SMACK
IT'S TIME TO GET PUMPED UP...
IS YAMADA P COMING TODAY?
YES...
...HE IS, BUT...

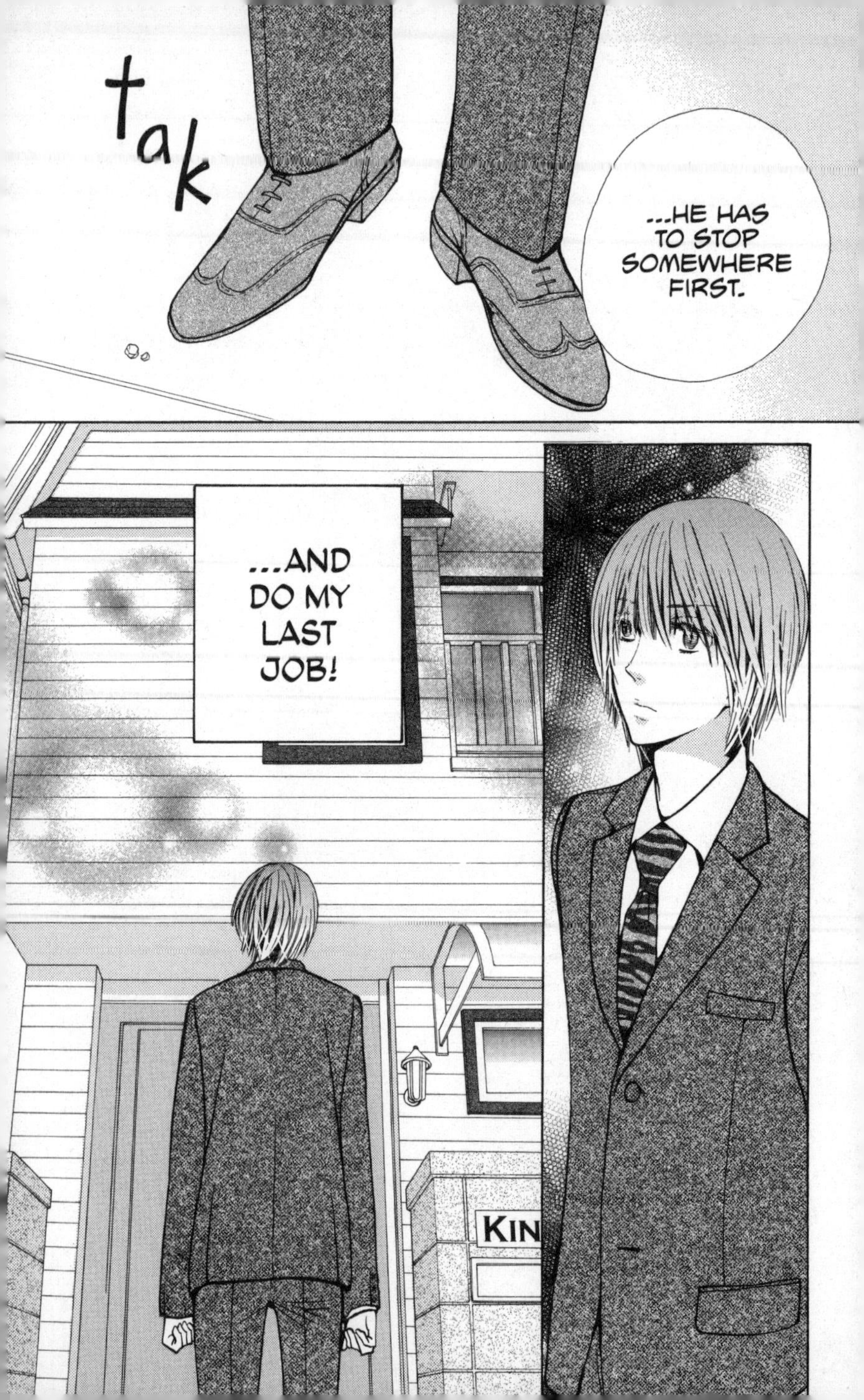
...HE HAS TO STOP SOMEWHERE FIRST.
tak
...AND DO MY LAST JOB!
KIN

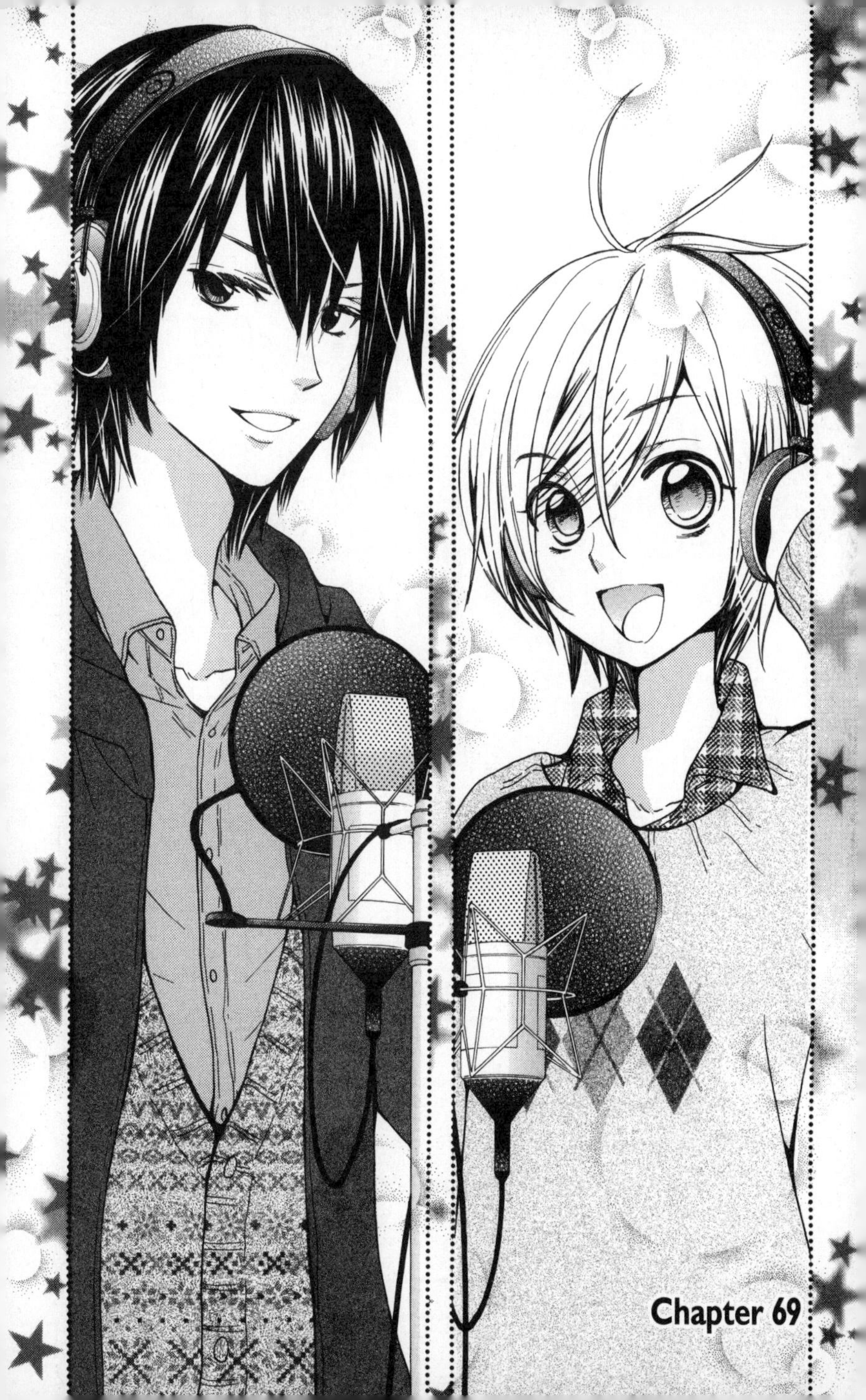
Chapter 69

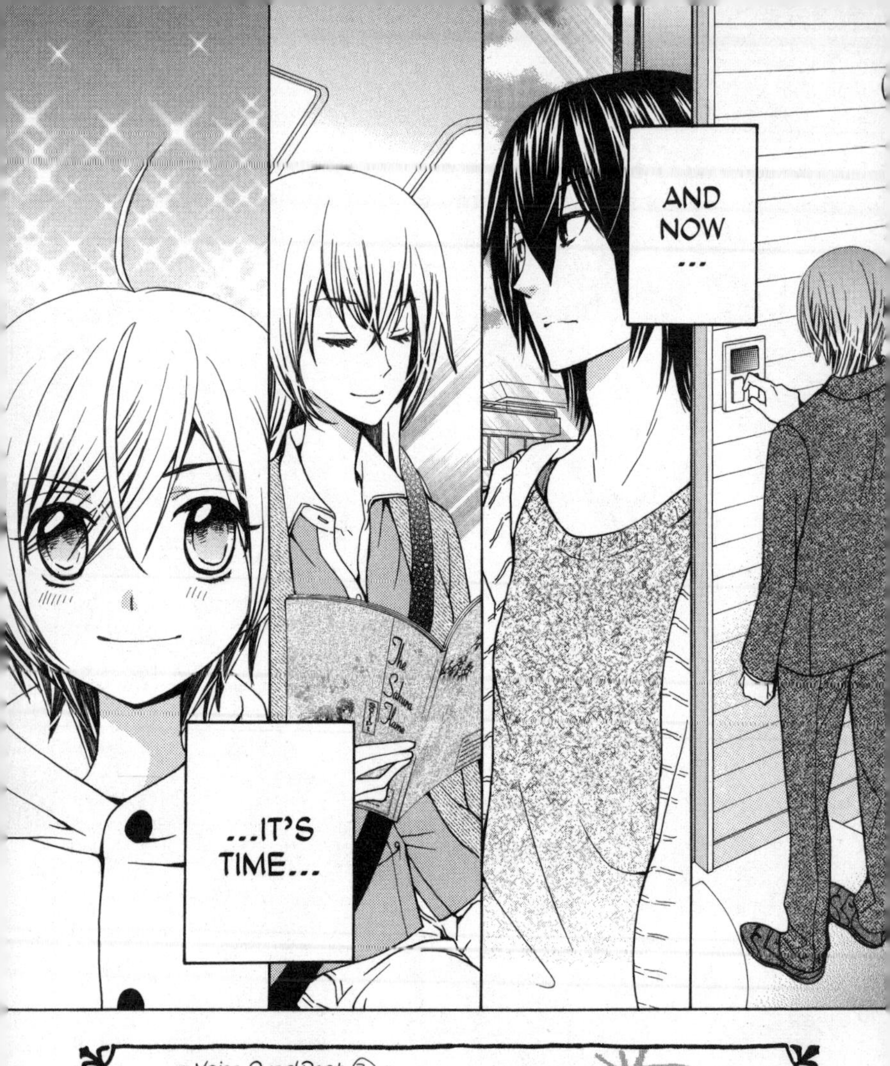
AND NOW ...
...IT'S TIME...

• *Voice Over!* Part ③ •

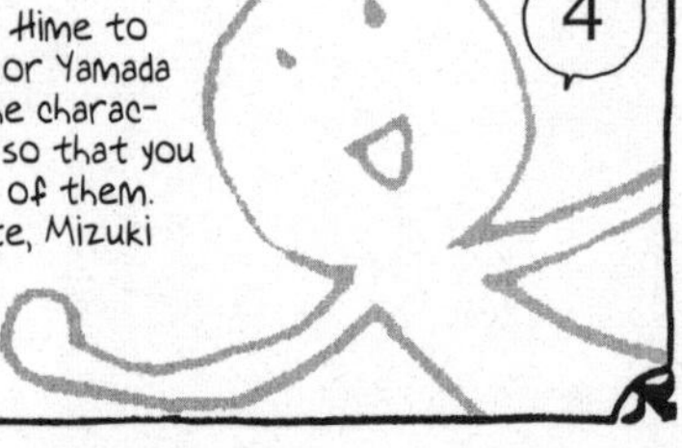
4

In letters, fans often say they want Hime to get together with Senri, or Mizuki or Yamada P and so on. I'm glad they get into the characters so much. For a while, I wrote it so that you might want Hime to end up with any of them. Actually, I did consider the Senri route, Mizuki route, and Yamada P route... Vaguely, anyway!!!

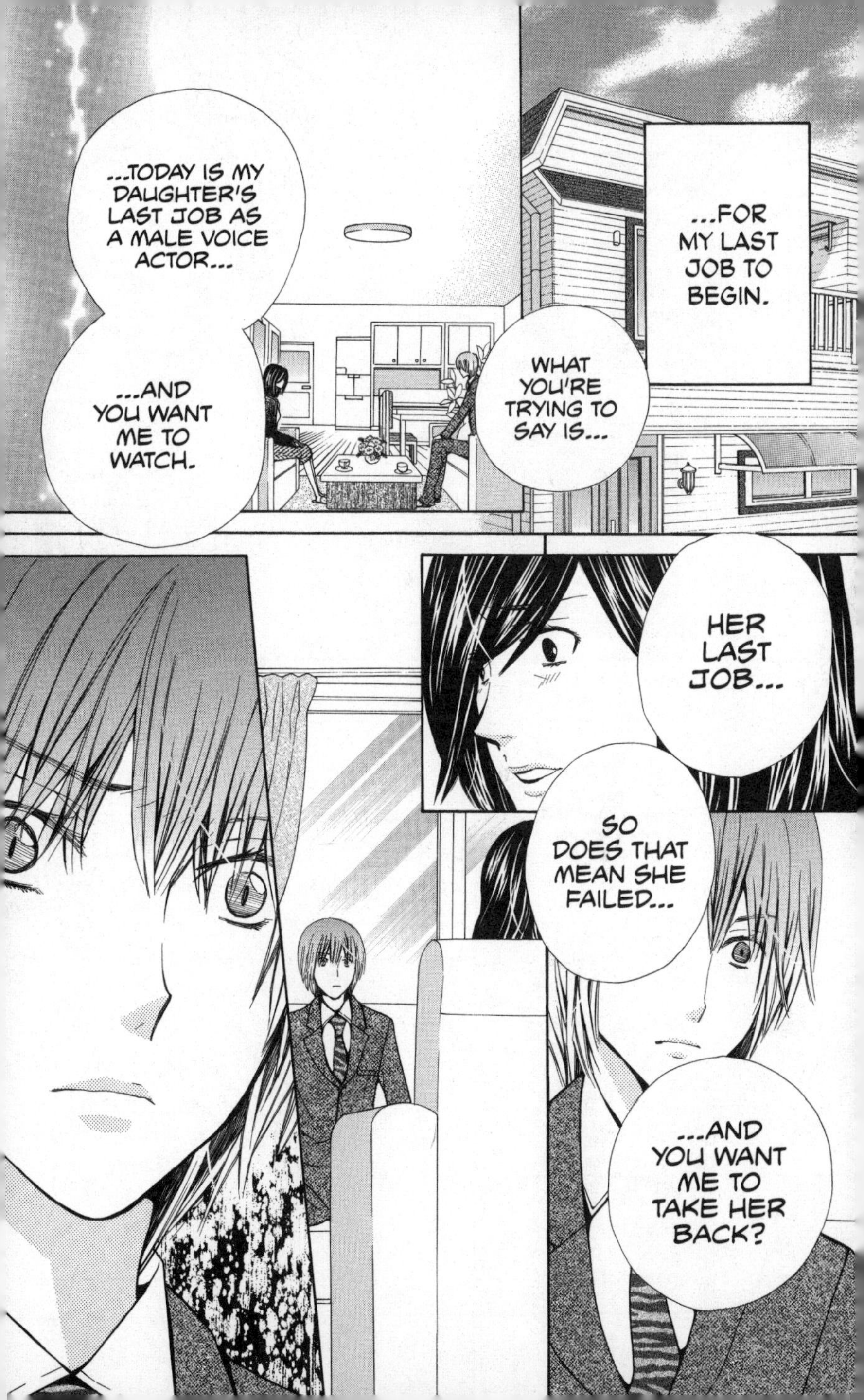
...FOR MY LAST JOB TO BEGIN.
WHAT YOU'RE TRYING TO SAY IS...
...TODAY IS MY DAUGHTER'S LAST JOB AS A MALE VOICE ACTOR...
...AND YOU WANT ME TO WATCH.
HER LAST JOB...
SO DOES THAT MEAN SHE FAILED...
...AND YOU WANT ME TO TAKE HER BACK?

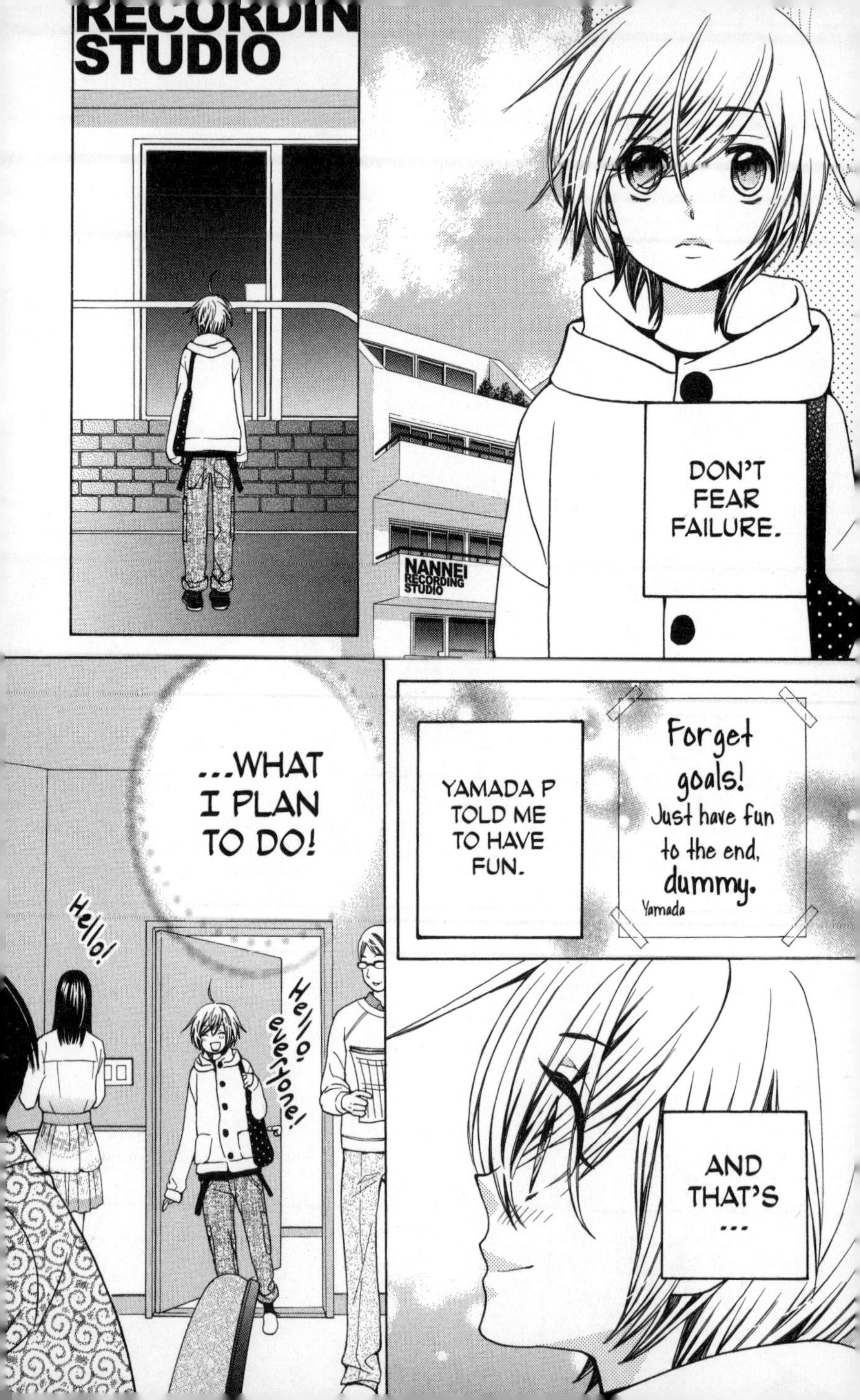
DON'T FEAR FAILURE.
RECORDIN STUDIO
NANNEI RECORDING STUDIO
YAMADA P TOLD ME TO HAVE FUN.
Forget goals! Just have fun to the end, dummy.
Yamada
AND THAT'S...
...WHAT I PLAN TO DO!
Hello, everyone!
Hello!

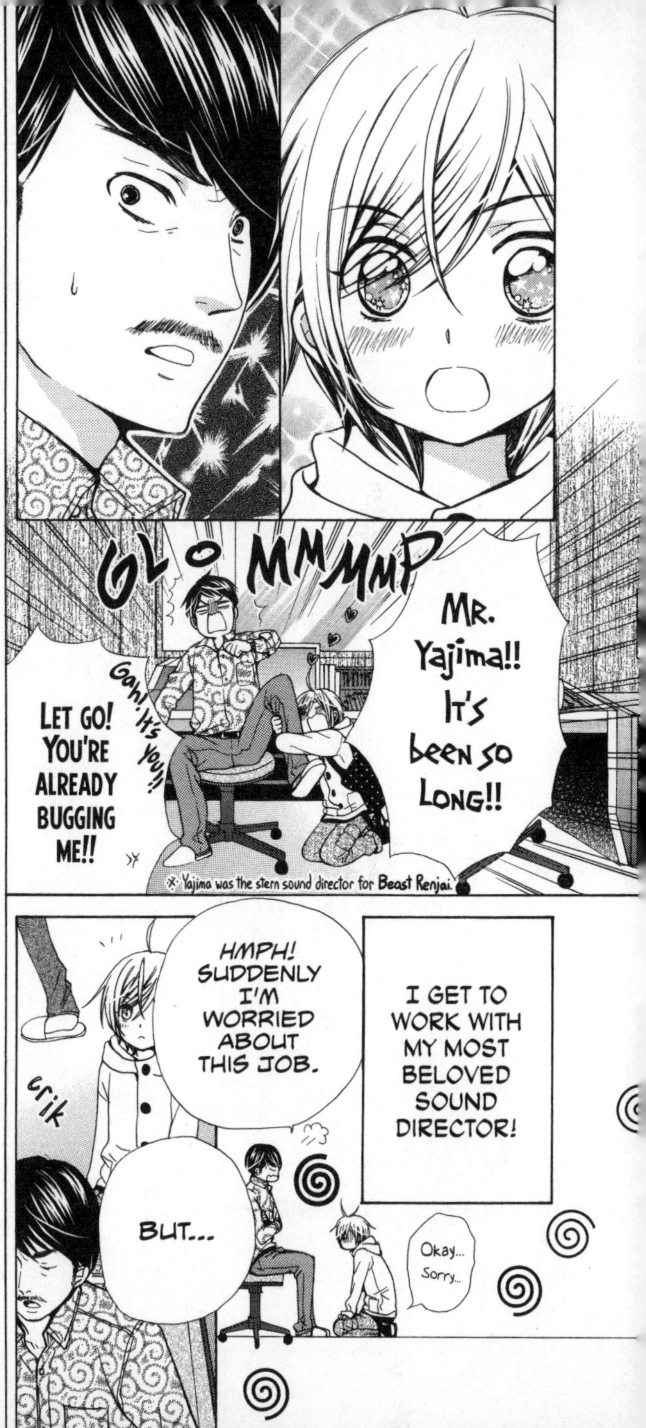
GLOMMMMP
MR. Yajima!! It's been so Long!!
Gah! It's you!!
LET GO! YOU'RE ALREADY BUGGING ME!!
※ Yajima was the stern sound director for Beast Renjai.
I GET TO WORK WITH MY MOST BELOVED SOUND DIRECTOR!
HMPH! SUDDENLY I'M WORRIED ABOUT THIS JOB.
Okay... Sorry...
crik
BUT...

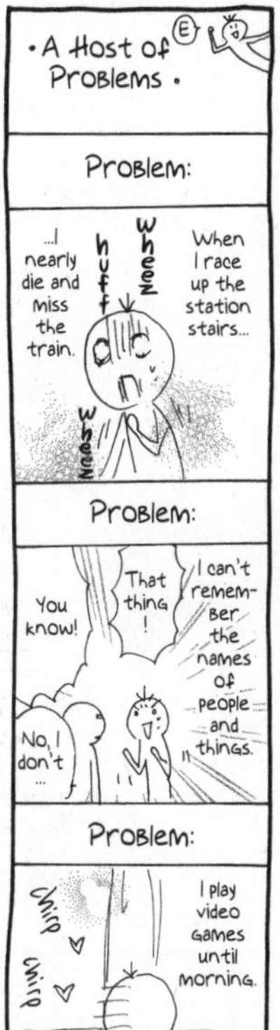
• A Host of Problems •
Problem:
When I race up the station stairs...
wheez
huff
...I nearly die and miss the train.
wheez
Problem:
I can't remember the names of people and things.
That thing!
You know!
No, I don't...
Problem:
I play video games until morning.
chirp
chirp
Problem:
I'm out of sidebar topics...
It's blank...
But it's the last volume!!
I'll improve my ways...

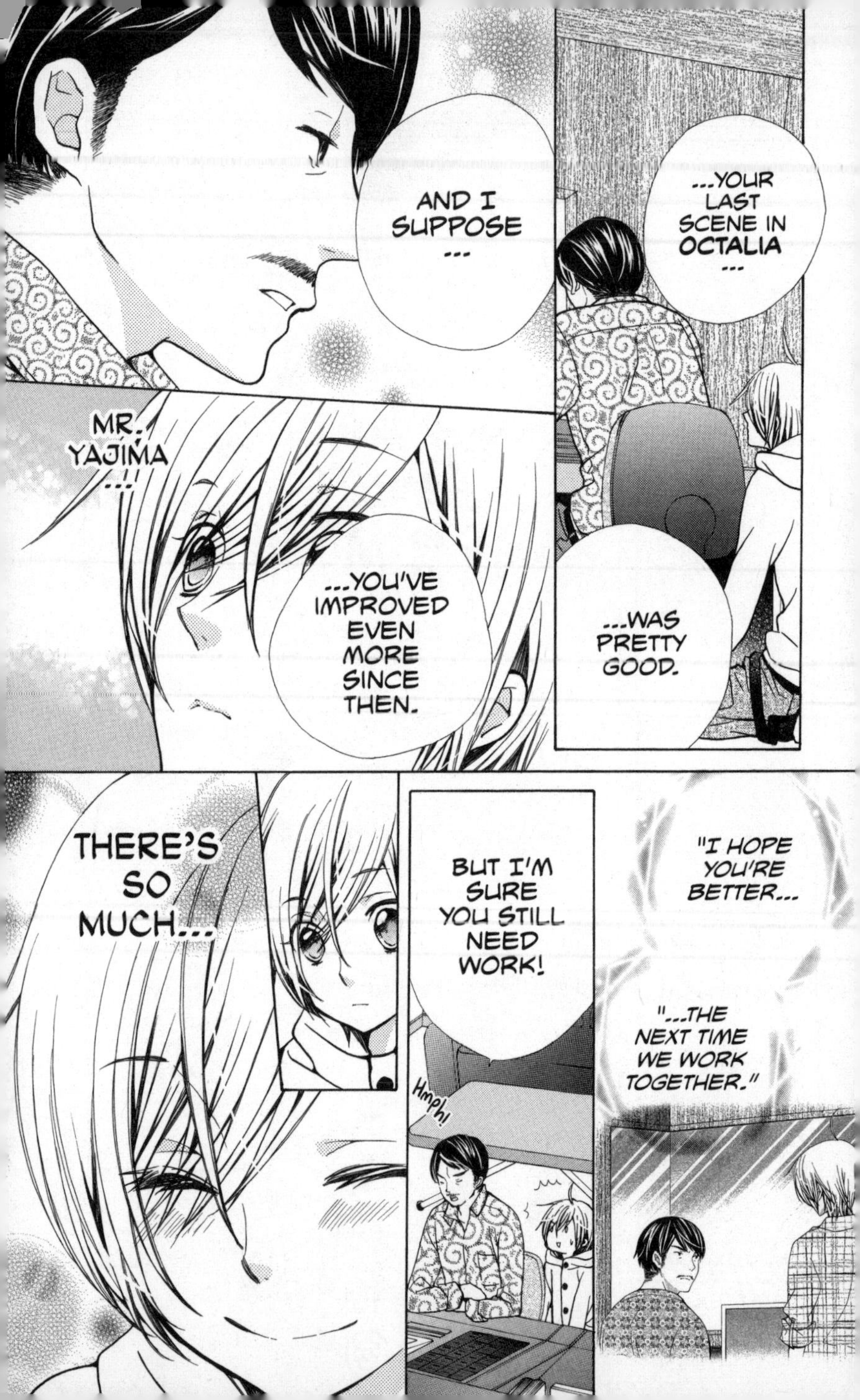
...YOUR LAST SCENE IN OCTALIA ...
...WAS PRETTY GOOD.
AND I SUPPOSE ...
...YOU'VE IMPROVED EVEN MORE SINCE THEN.
MR. YAJIMA ...!!
"I HOPE YOU'RE BETTER...
"...THE NEXT TIME WE WORK TOGETHER."
BUT I'M SURE YOU STILL NEED WORK!
Hmph!
THERE'S SO MUCH...

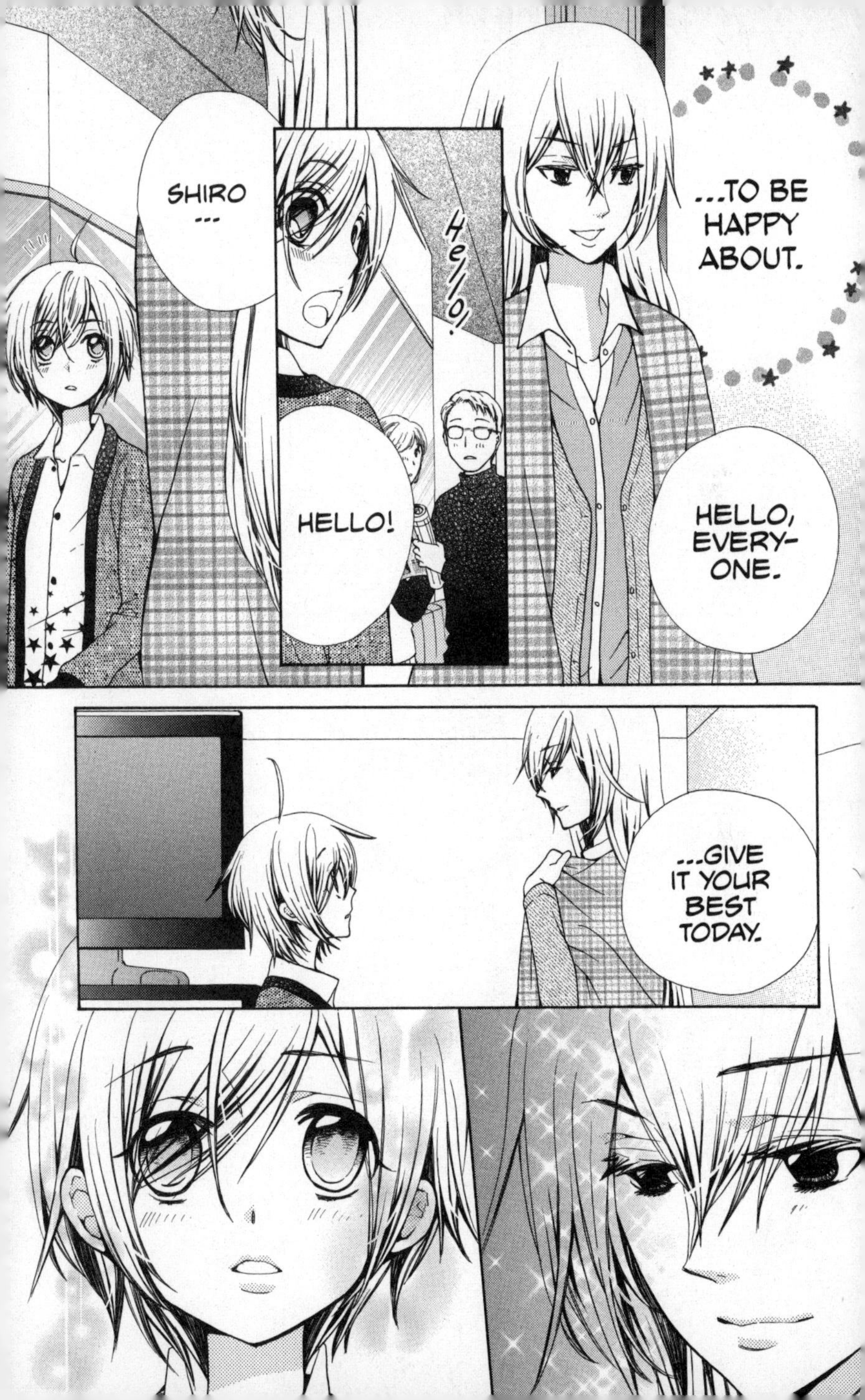
...TO BE HAPPY ABOUT.
HELLO, EVERYONE.
Hello!
HELLO!
SHIRO...
...GIVE IT YOUR BEST TODAY.

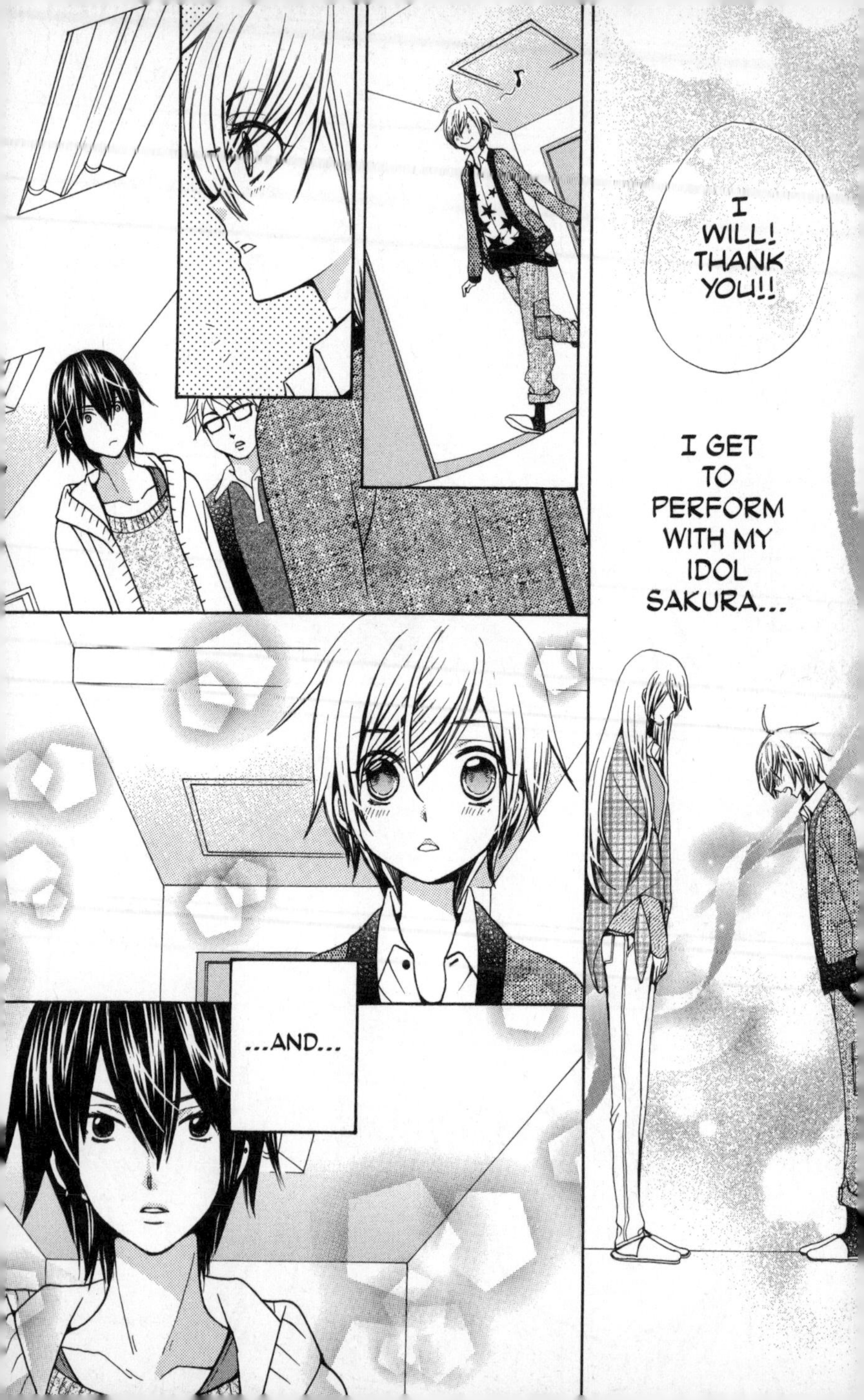
I WILL! THANK YOU!!
I GET TO PERFORM WITH MY IDOL SAKURA...
...AND...

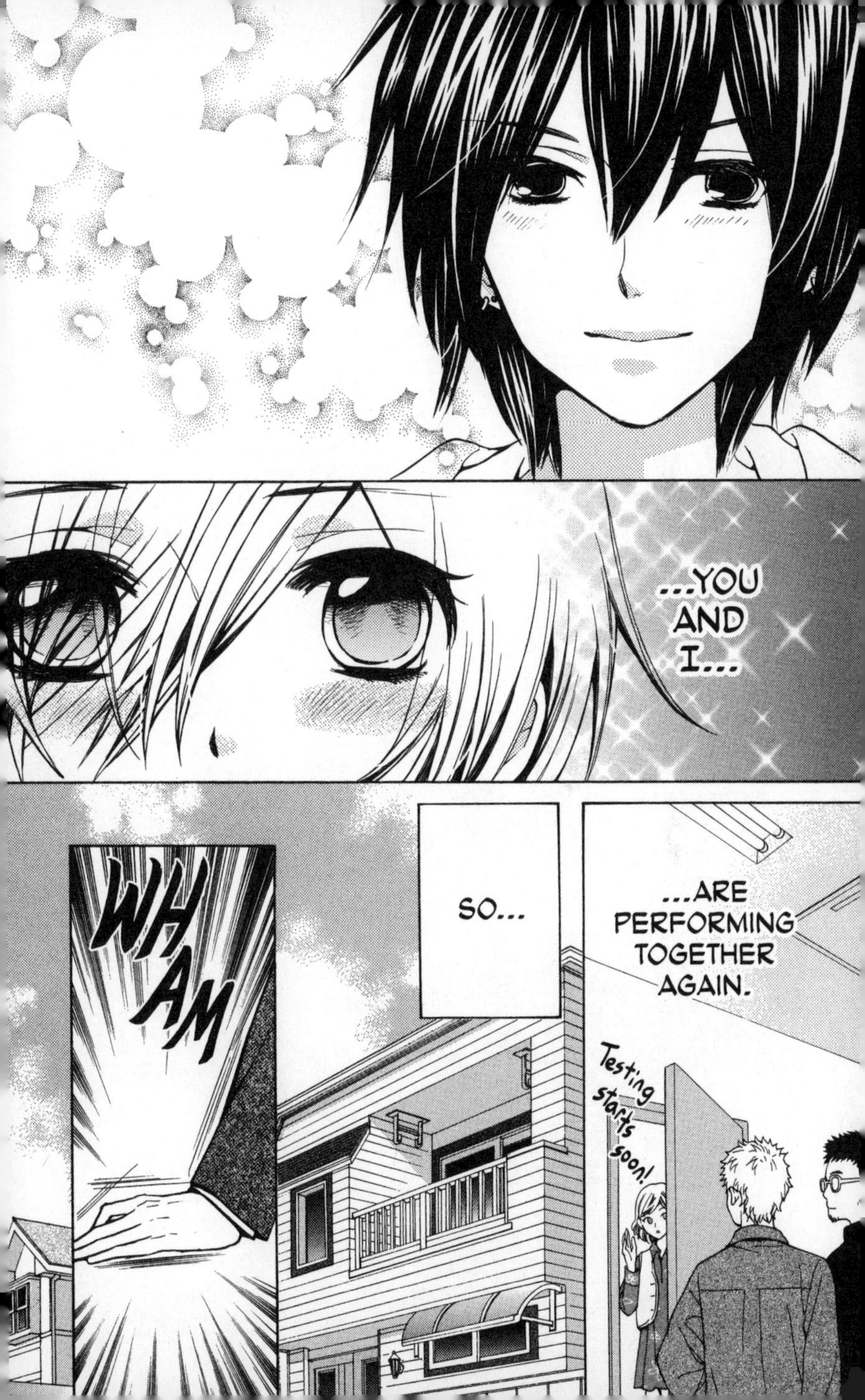
...YOU AND I...
...ARE PERFORMING TOGETHER AGAIN.
SO...
Testing starts soon!
WHAM

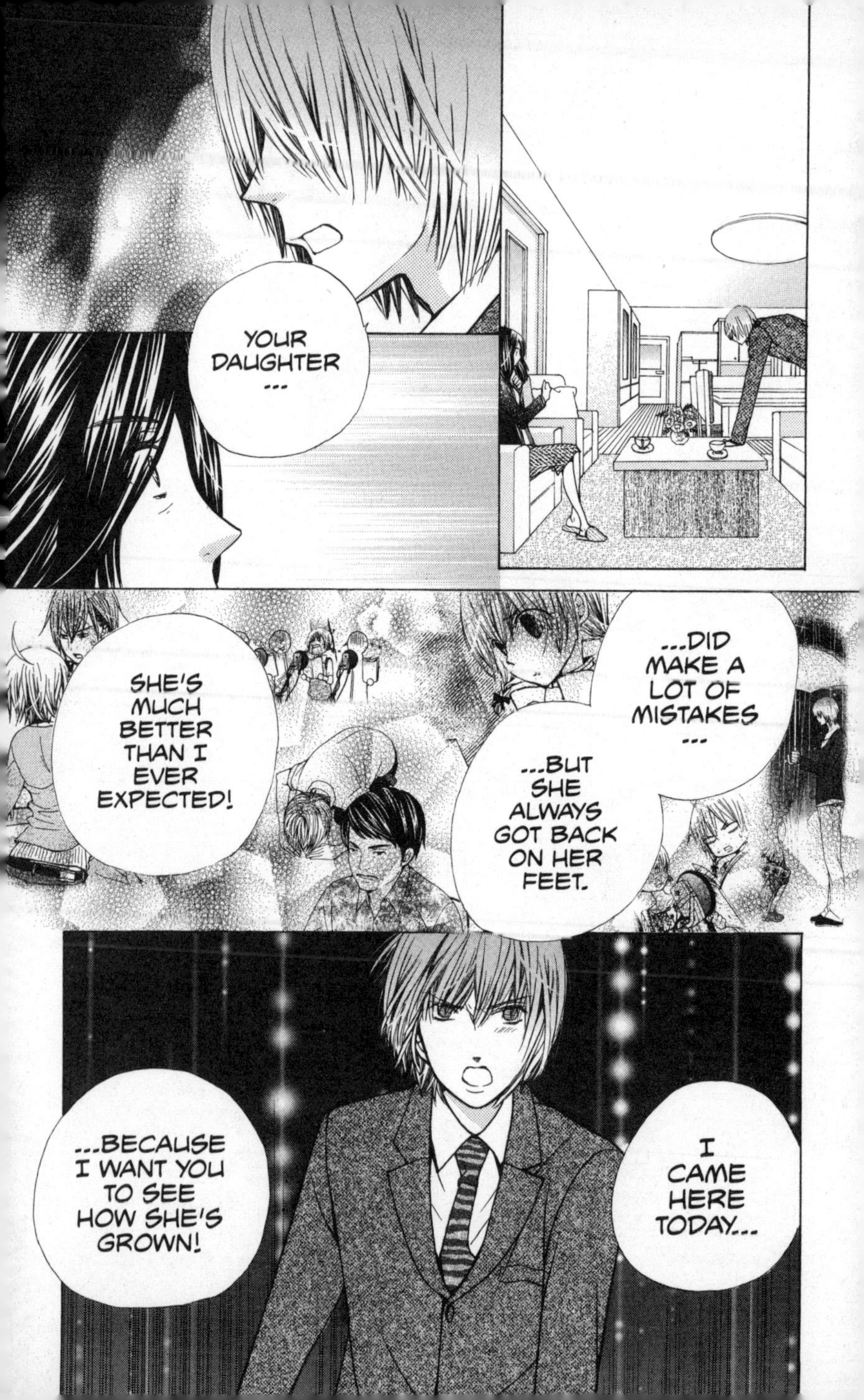
YOUR DAUGHTER ...
...DID MAKE A LOT OF MISTAKES ...
...BUT SHE ALWAYS GOT BACK ON HER FEET.
SHE'S MUCH BETTER THAN I EVER EXPECTED!
I CAME HERE TODAY...
...BECAUSE I WANT YOU TO SEE HOW SHE'S GROWN!

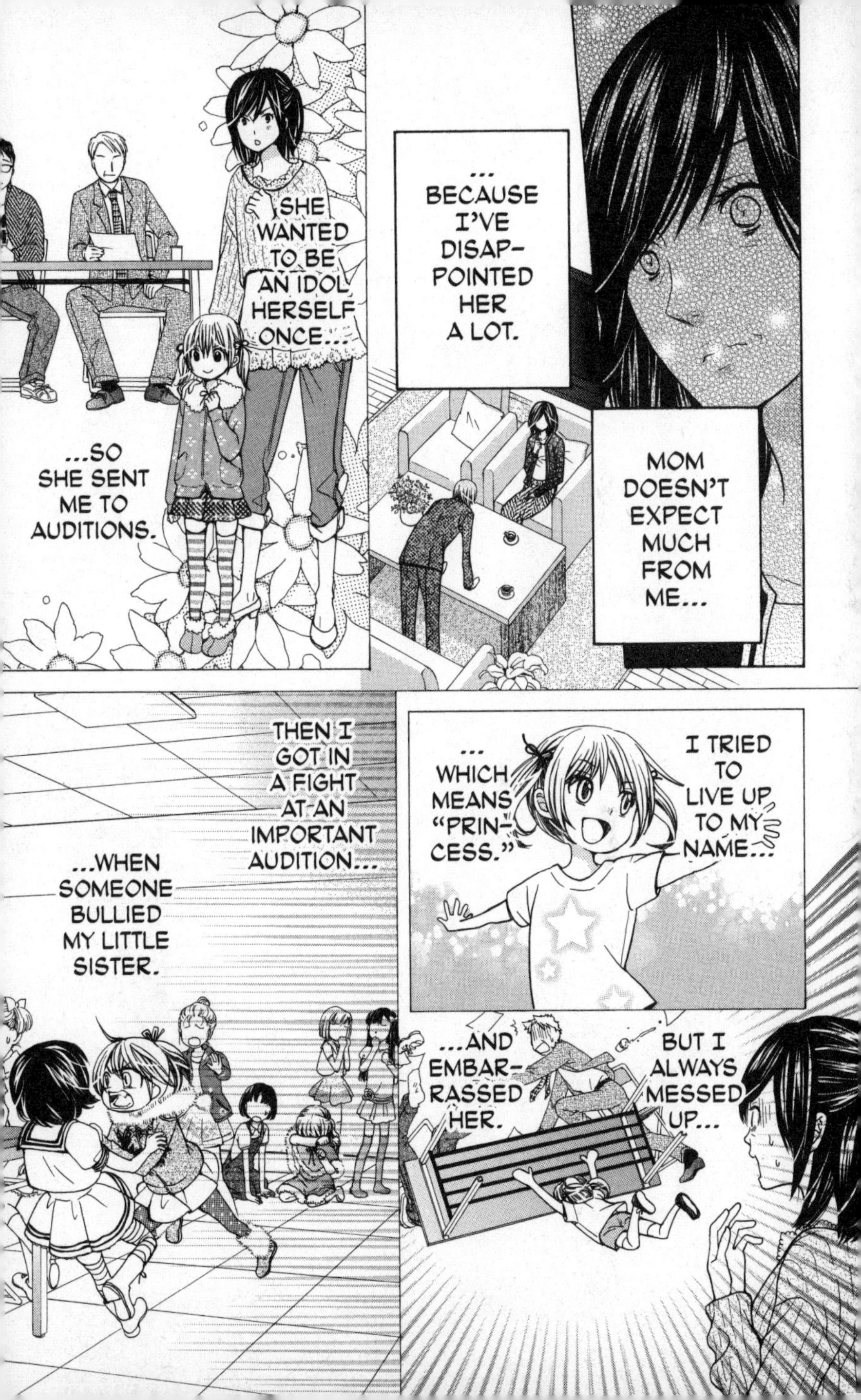
MOM DOESN'T EXPECT MUCH FROM ME...
...BECAUSE I'VE DISAPPOINTED HER A LOT.
SHE WANTED TO BE AN IDOL HERSELF ONCE...
...SO SHE SENT ME TO AUDITIONS.
I TRIED TO LIVE UP TO MY NAME...
...WHICH MEANS "PRINCESS."
BUT I ALWAYS MESSED UP...
...AND EMBARRASSED HER.
THEN I GOT IN A FIGHT AT AN IMPORTANT AUDITION...
...WHEN SOMEONE BULLIED MY LITTLE SISTER.

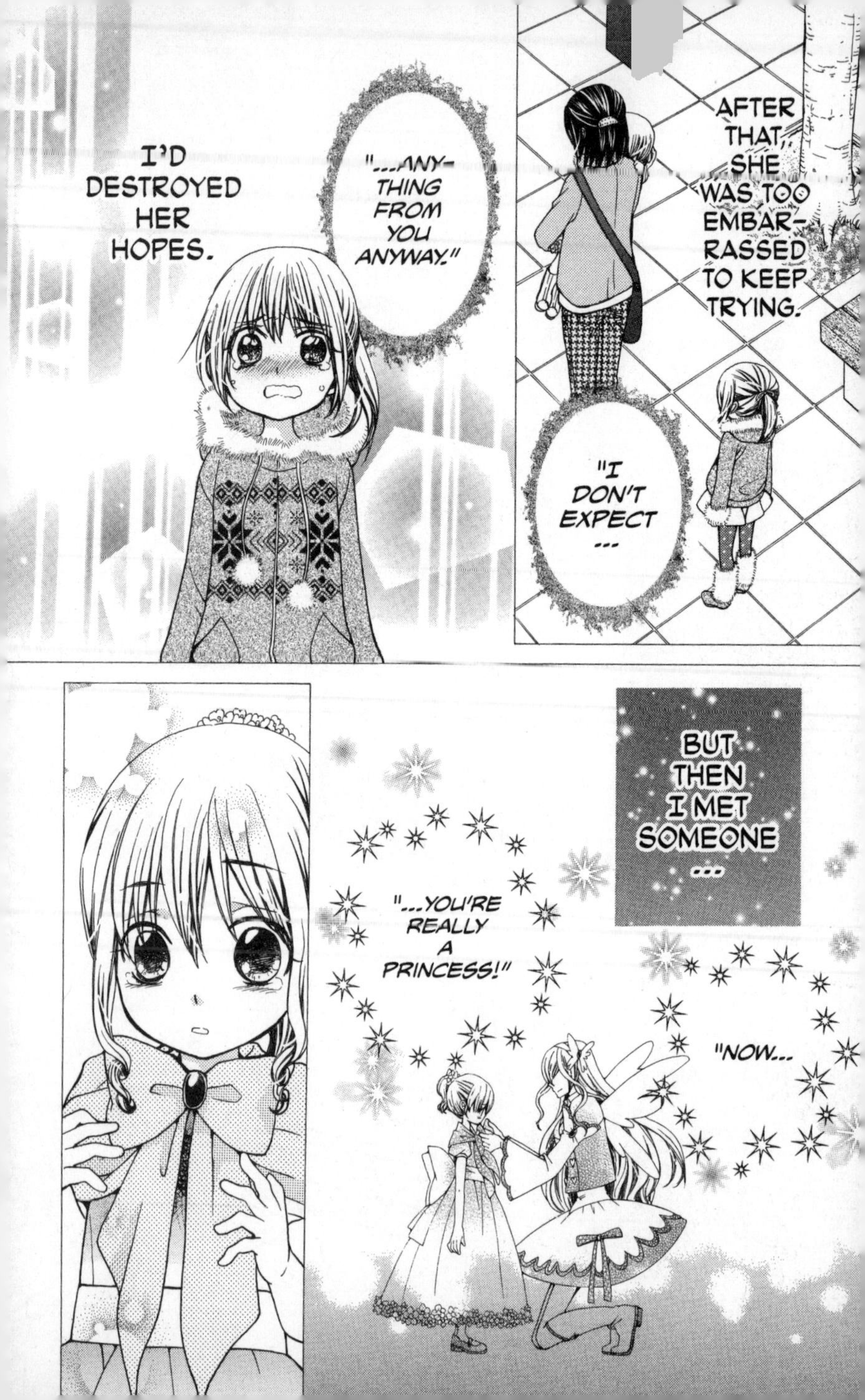
AFTER THAT, SHE WAS TOO EMBARRASSED TO KEEP TRYING.
"I DON'T EXPECT...
"...ANYTHING FROM YOU ANYWAY."
I'D DESTROYED HER HOPES.
BUT THEN I MET SOMEONE...
"NOW...
"...YOU'RE REALLY A PRINCESS!"

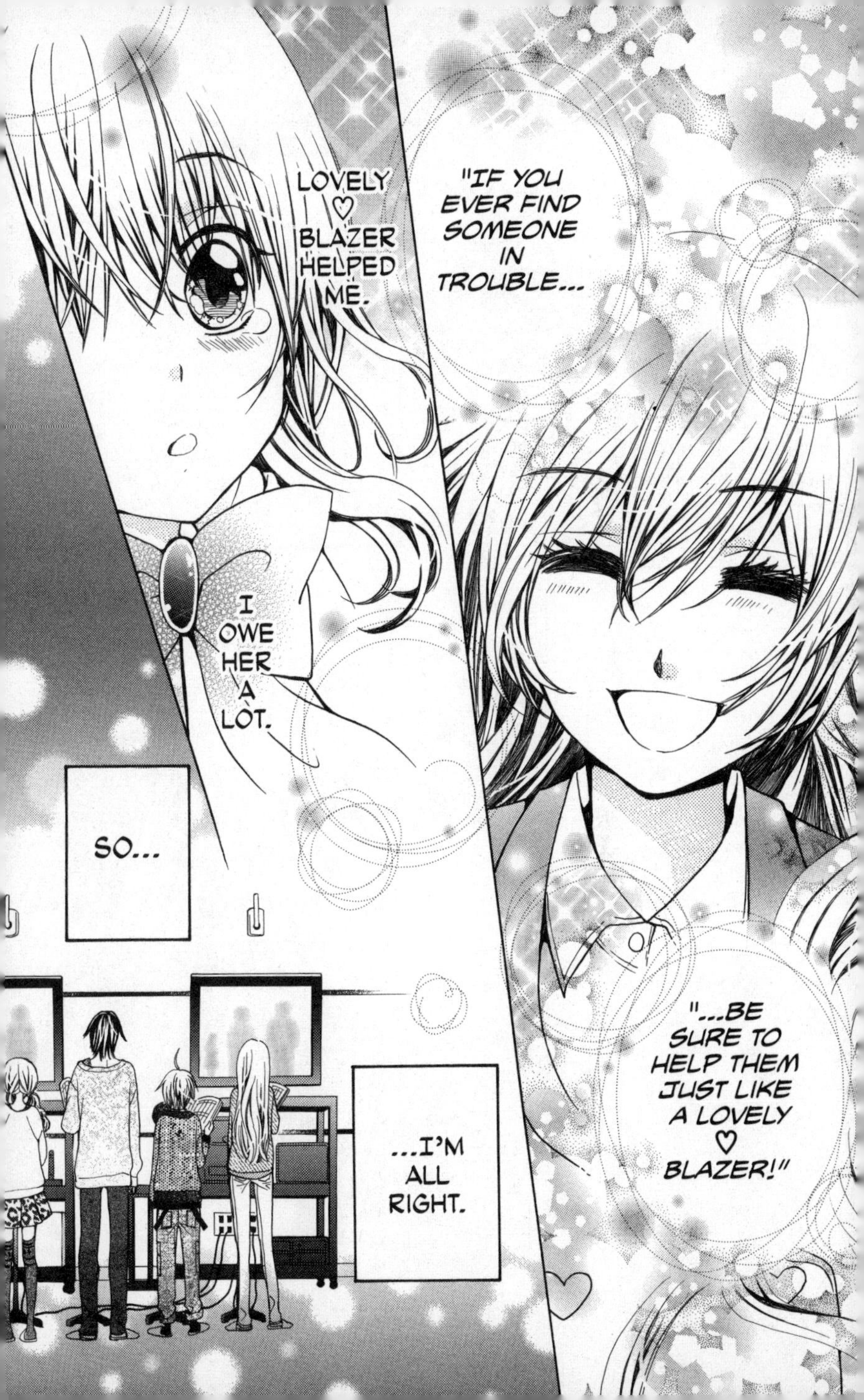
"IF YOU EVER FIND SOMEONE IN TROUBLE...
"...BE SURE TO HELP THEM JUST LIKE A LOVELY ♡ BLAZER!"
LOVELY ♡ BLAZER HELPED ME.
I OWE HER A LOT.
SO...
...I'M ALL RIGHT.

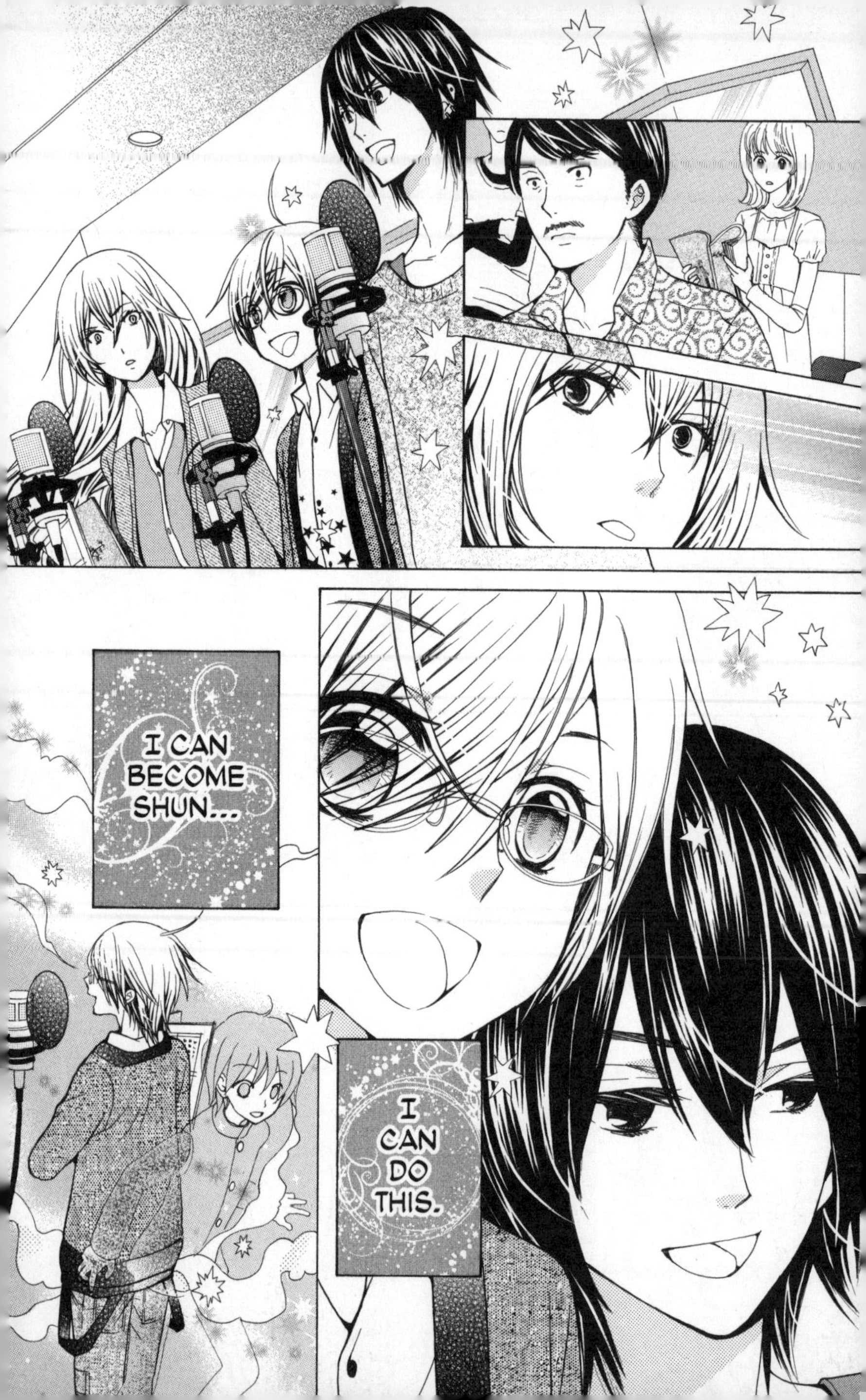
I CAN DO THIS.
I CAN BECOME SHUN...

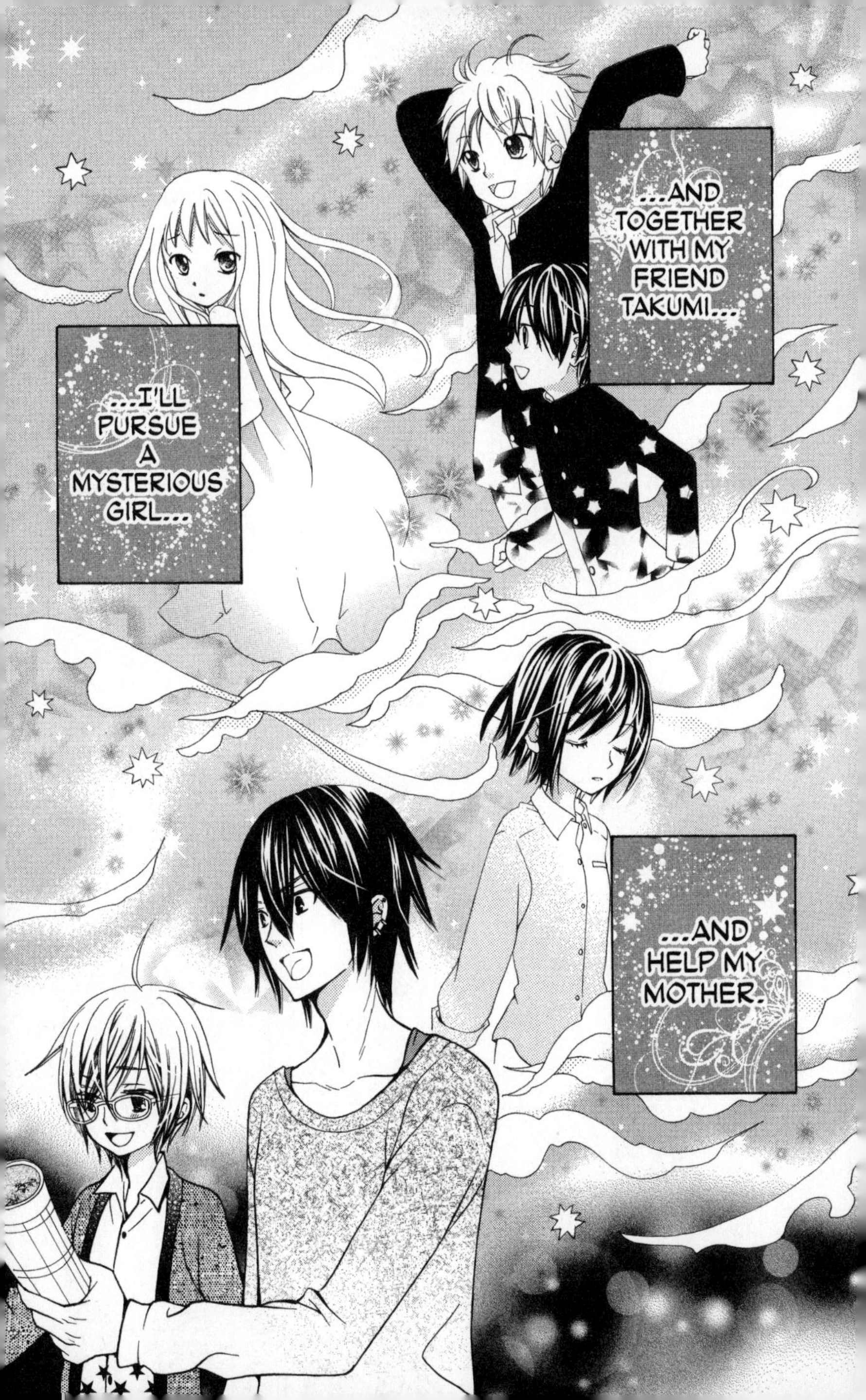
...AND TOGETHER WITH MY FRIEND TAKUMI...
...I'LL PURSUE A MYSTERIOUS GIRL...
...AND HELP MY MOTHER.

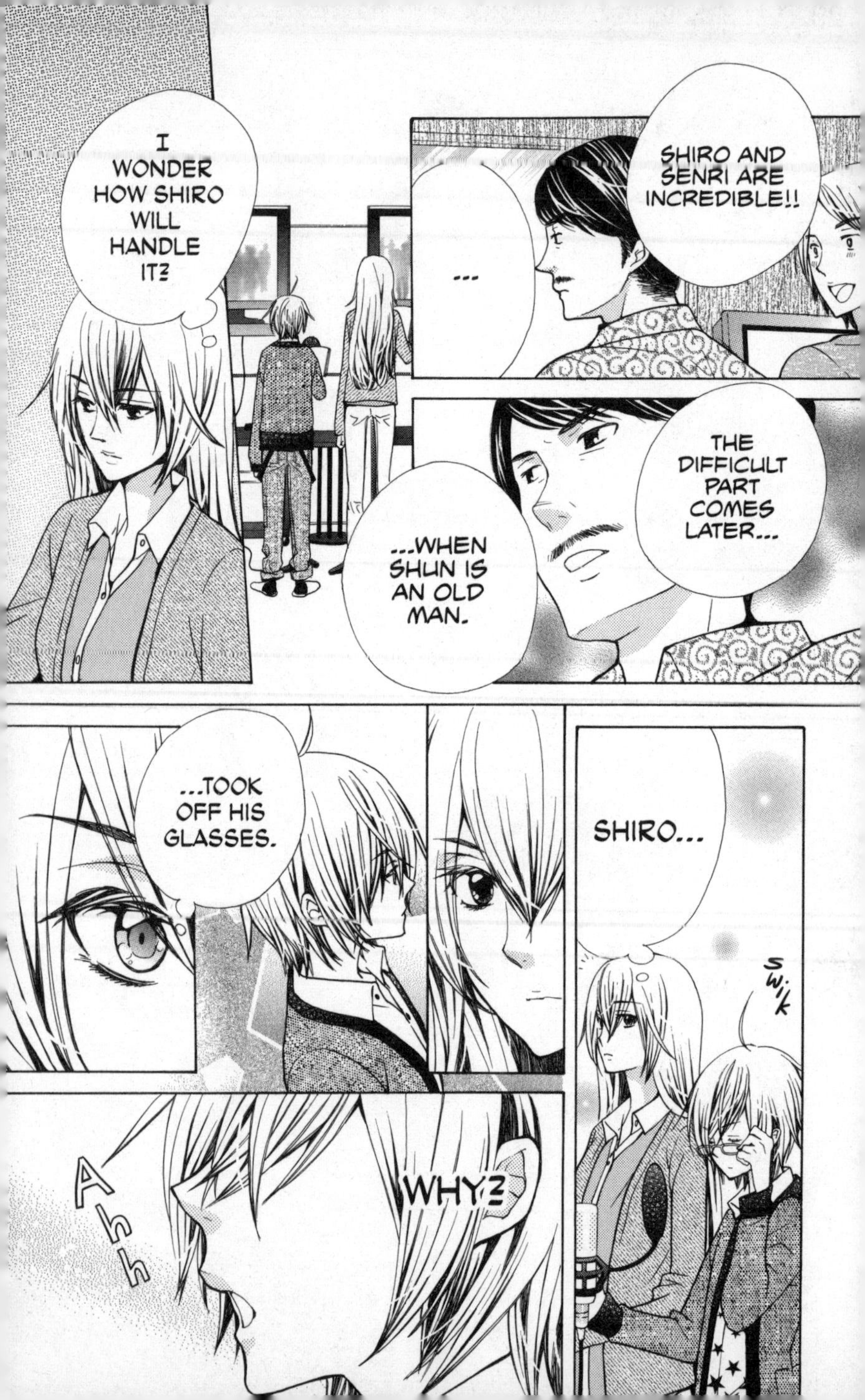
SHIRO AND SENRI ARE INCREDIBLE!!
...
THE DIFFICULT PART COMES LATER...
...WHEN SHUN IS AN OLD MAN.
I WONDER HOW SHIRO WILL HANDLE IT?
SHIRO...
SWIK
...TOOK OFF HIS GLASSES.
WHY?
Ahh

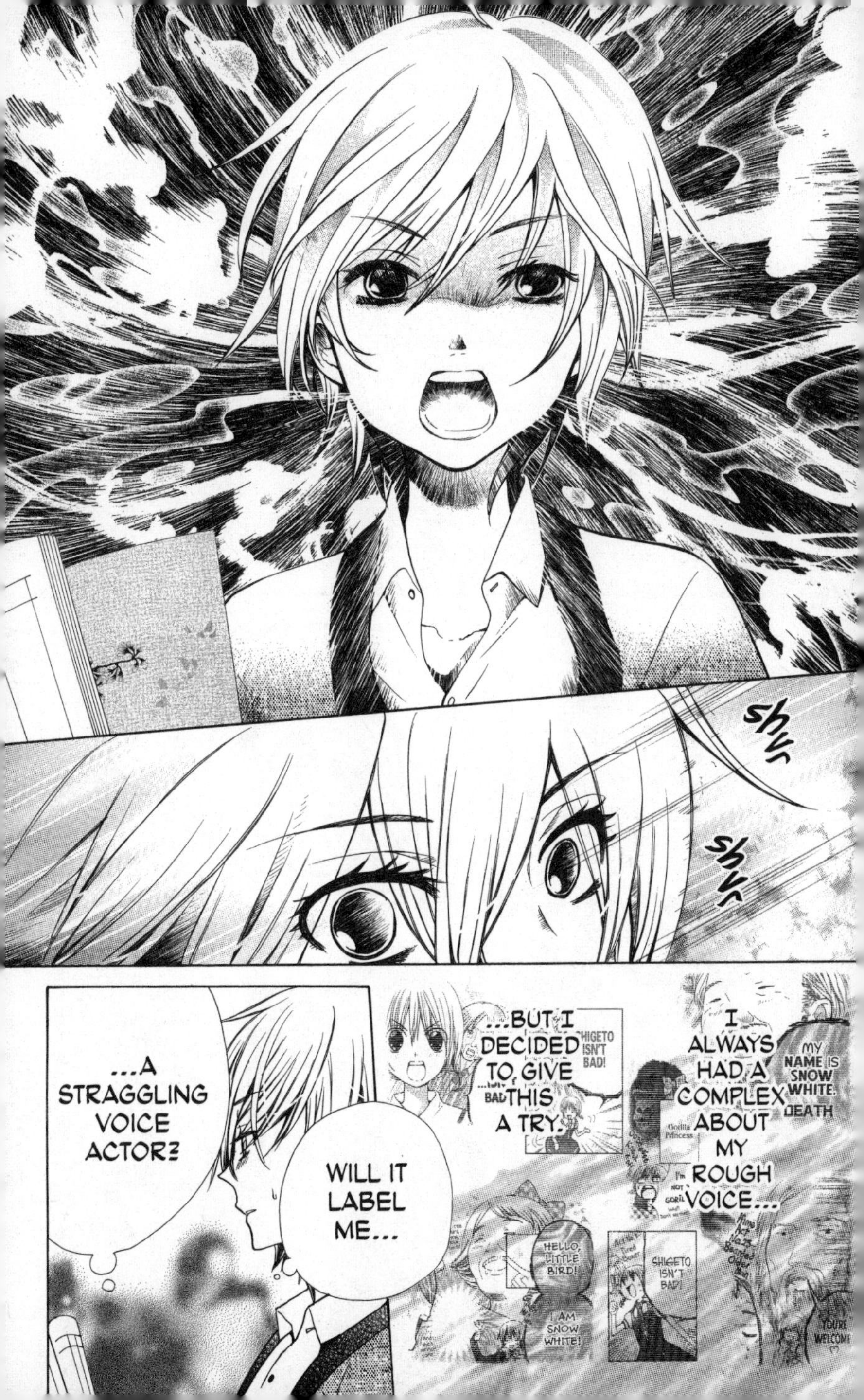
shur
shur
I ALWAYS HAD A COMPLEX ABOUT MY ROUGH VOICE...
MY NAME IS SNOW WHITE. DEATH
Gorilla Princess
YOU'RE WELCOME!
SHIGETO ISN'T BAD!
...BUT I DECIDED TO GIVE THIS A TRY.
SHIGETO ISN'T BAD!
HELLO, LITTLE BIRD!
I AM SNOW WHITE!
WILL IT LABEL ME...
...A STRAGGLING VOICE ACTOR?

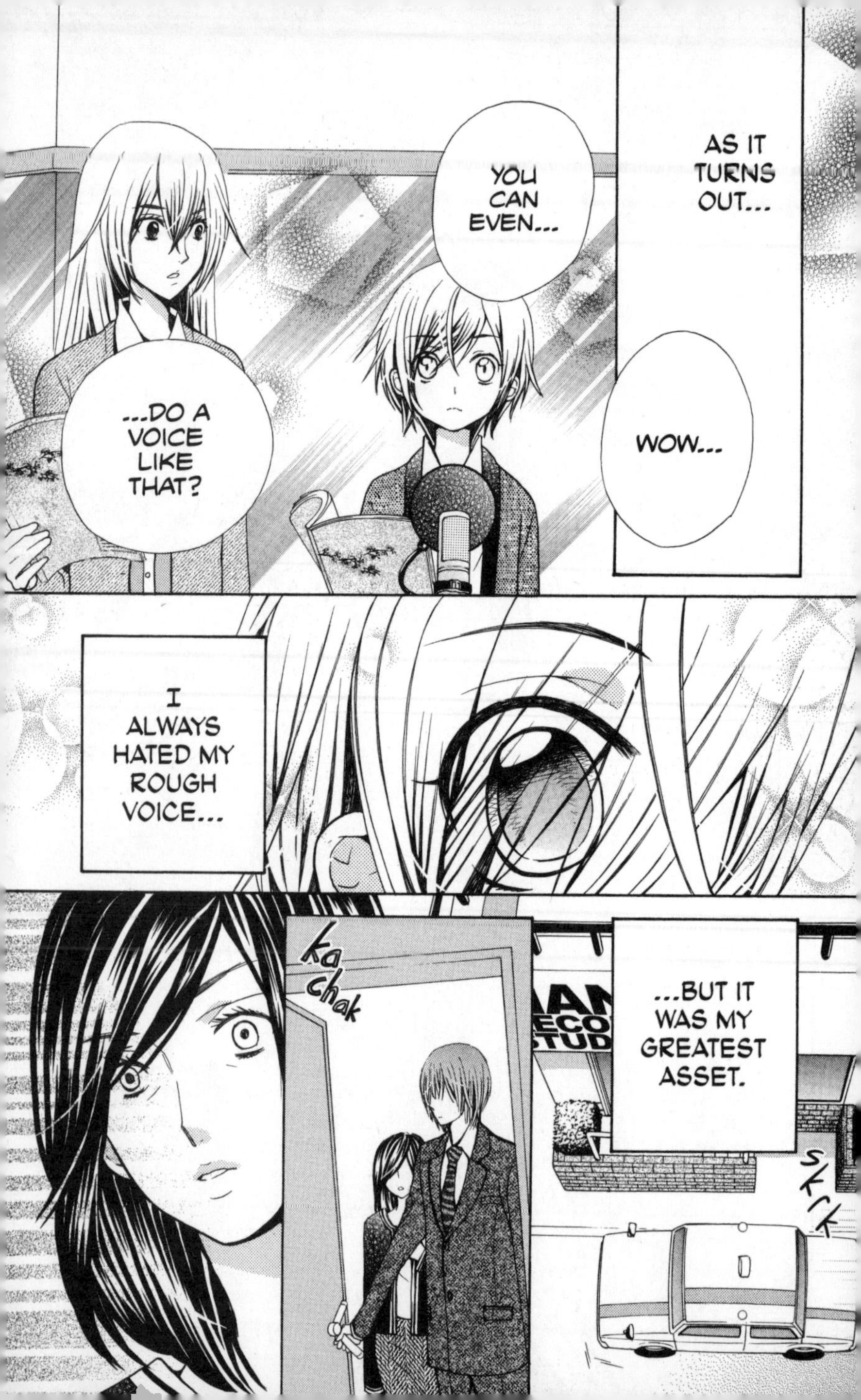
AS IT TURNS OUT...
WOW...
YOU CAN EVEN...
...DO A VOICE LIKE THAT?
I ALWAYS HATED MY ROUGH VOICE...
...BUT IT WAS MY GREATEST ASSET.
SKCK
ka chak

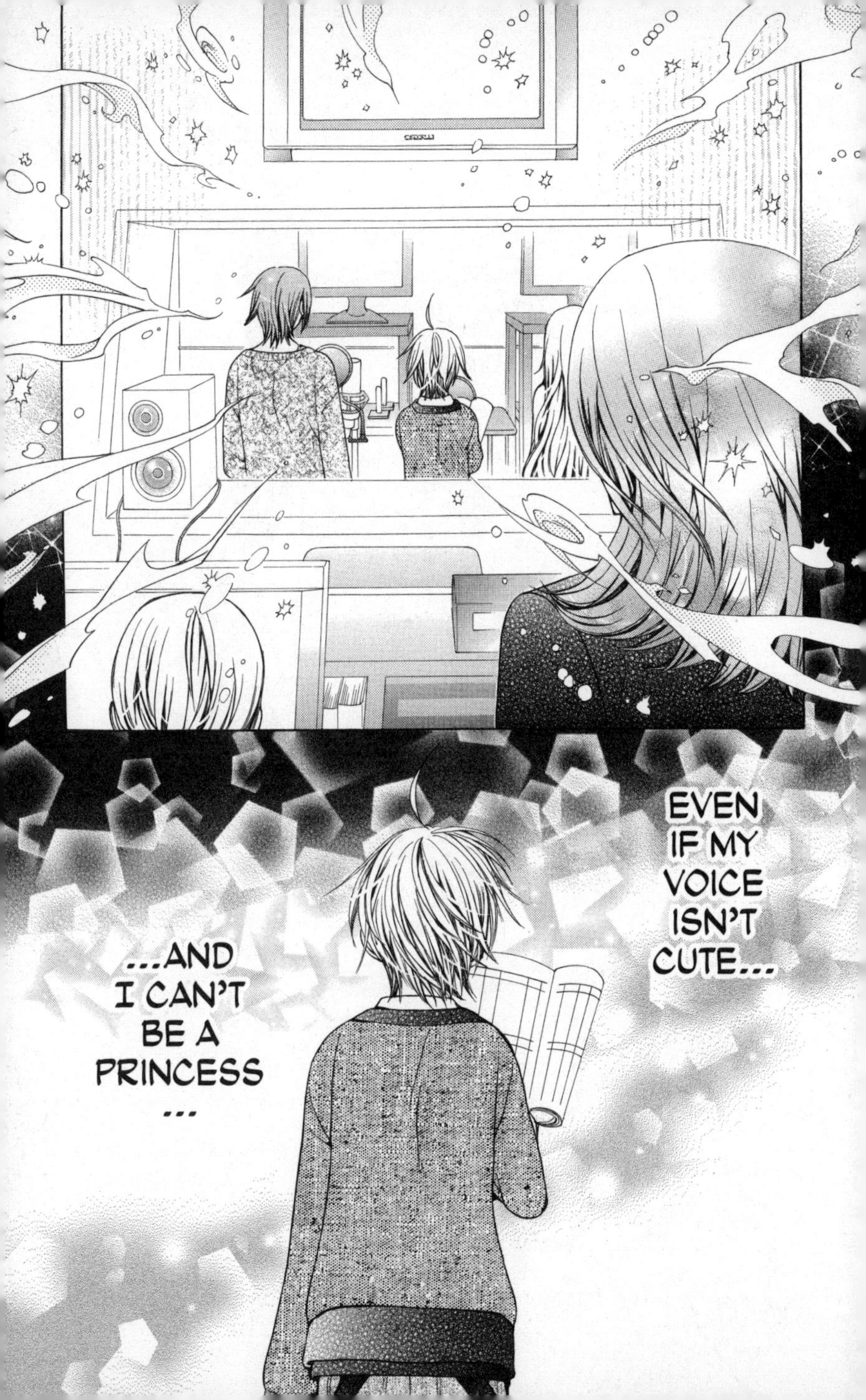
EVEN IF MY VOICE ISN'T CUTE...
...AND I CAN'T BE A PRINCESS ...

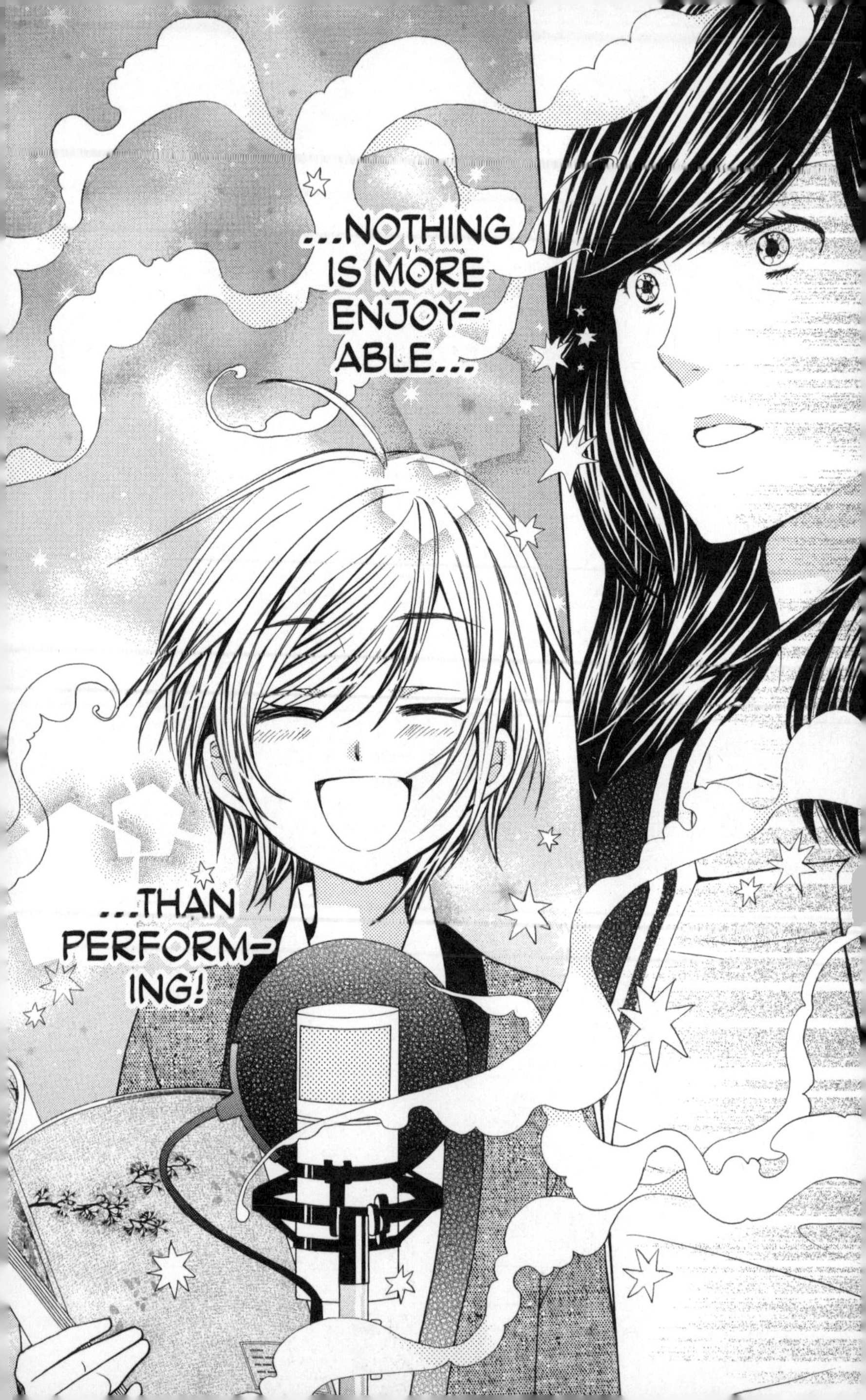
...NOTHING IS MORE ENJOY-ABLE...
...THAN PERFORM-ING!

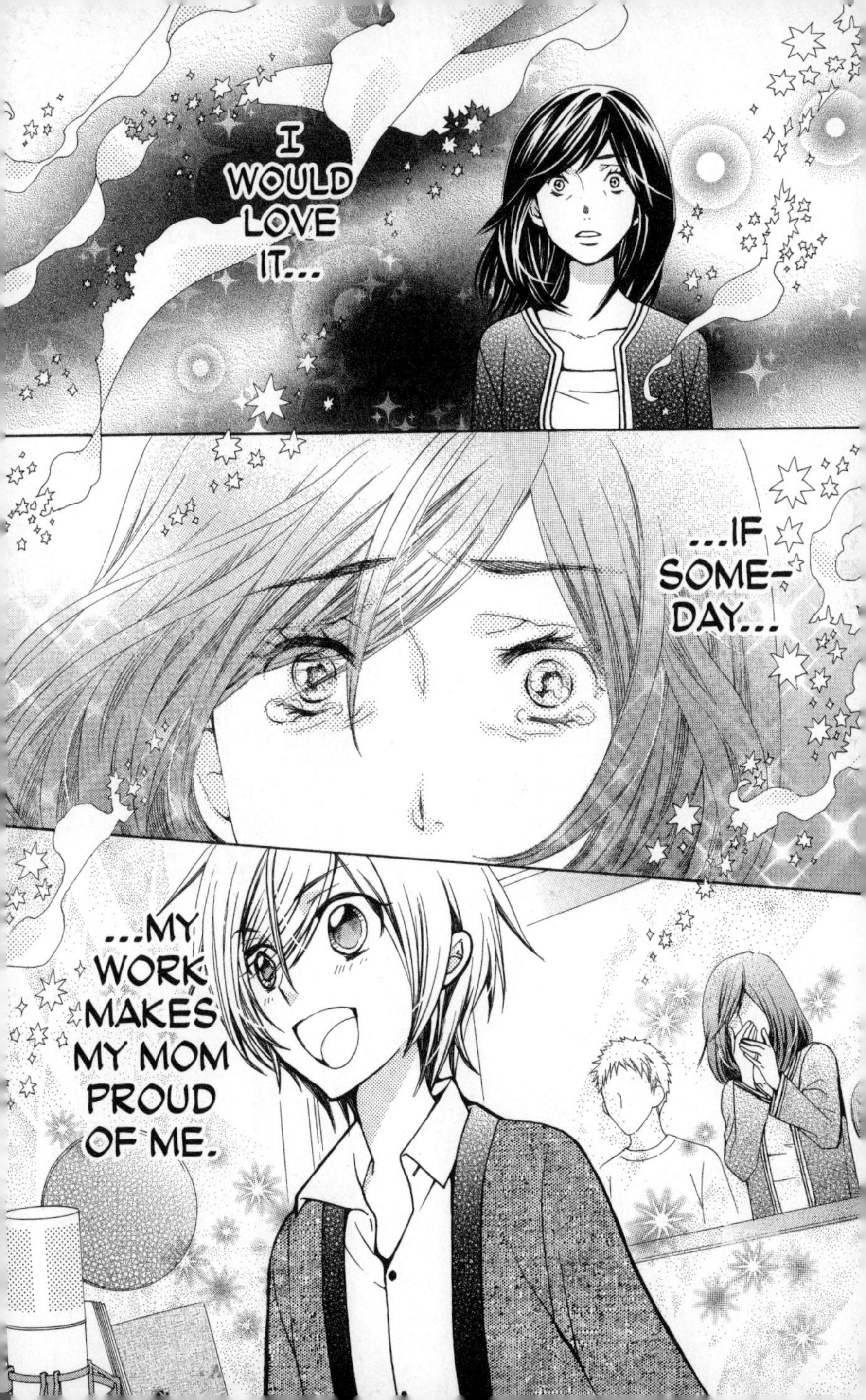
I WOULD LOVE IT...
...IF SOME-DAY...
...MY WORK MAKES MY MOM PROUD OF ME.

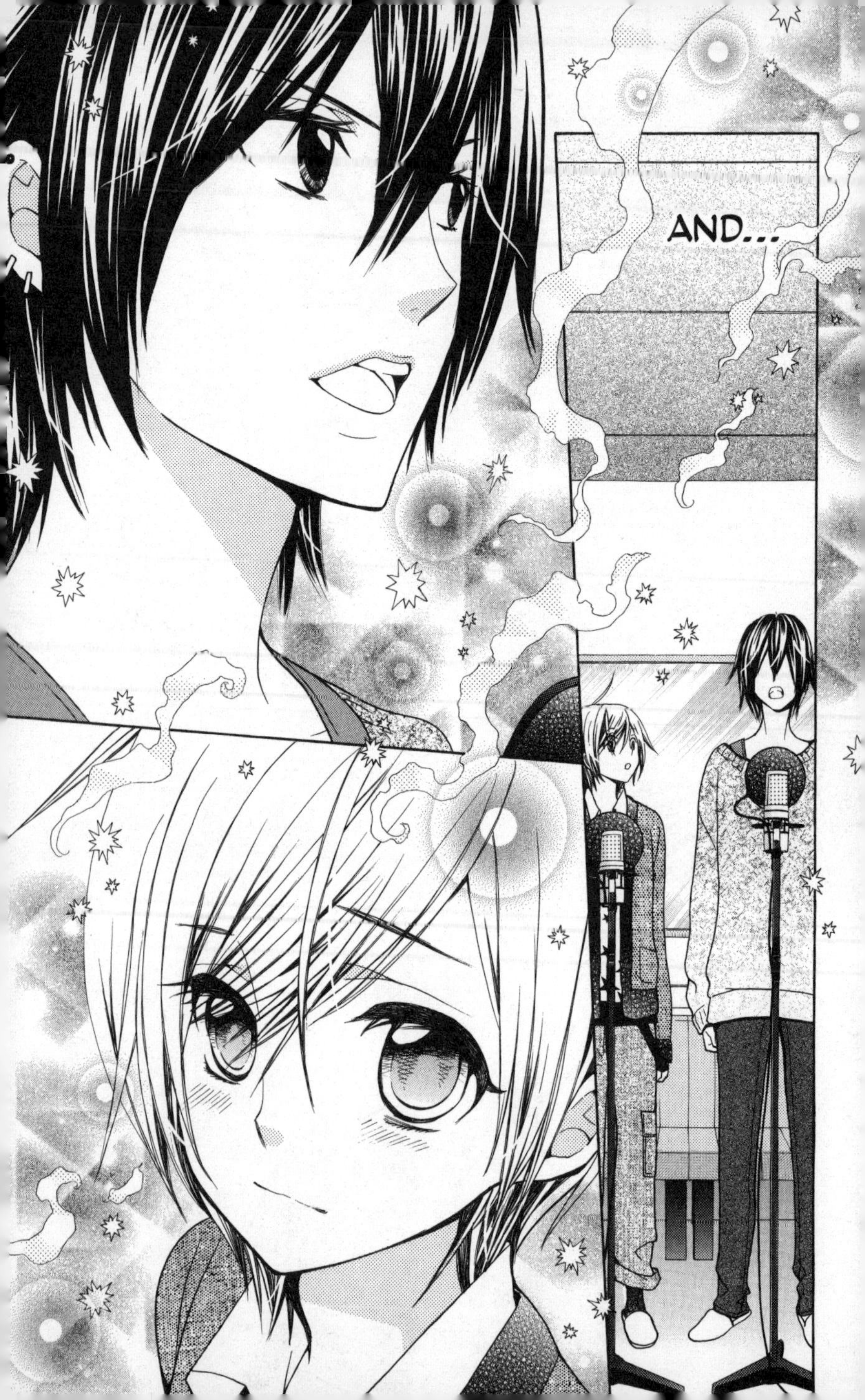
AND...

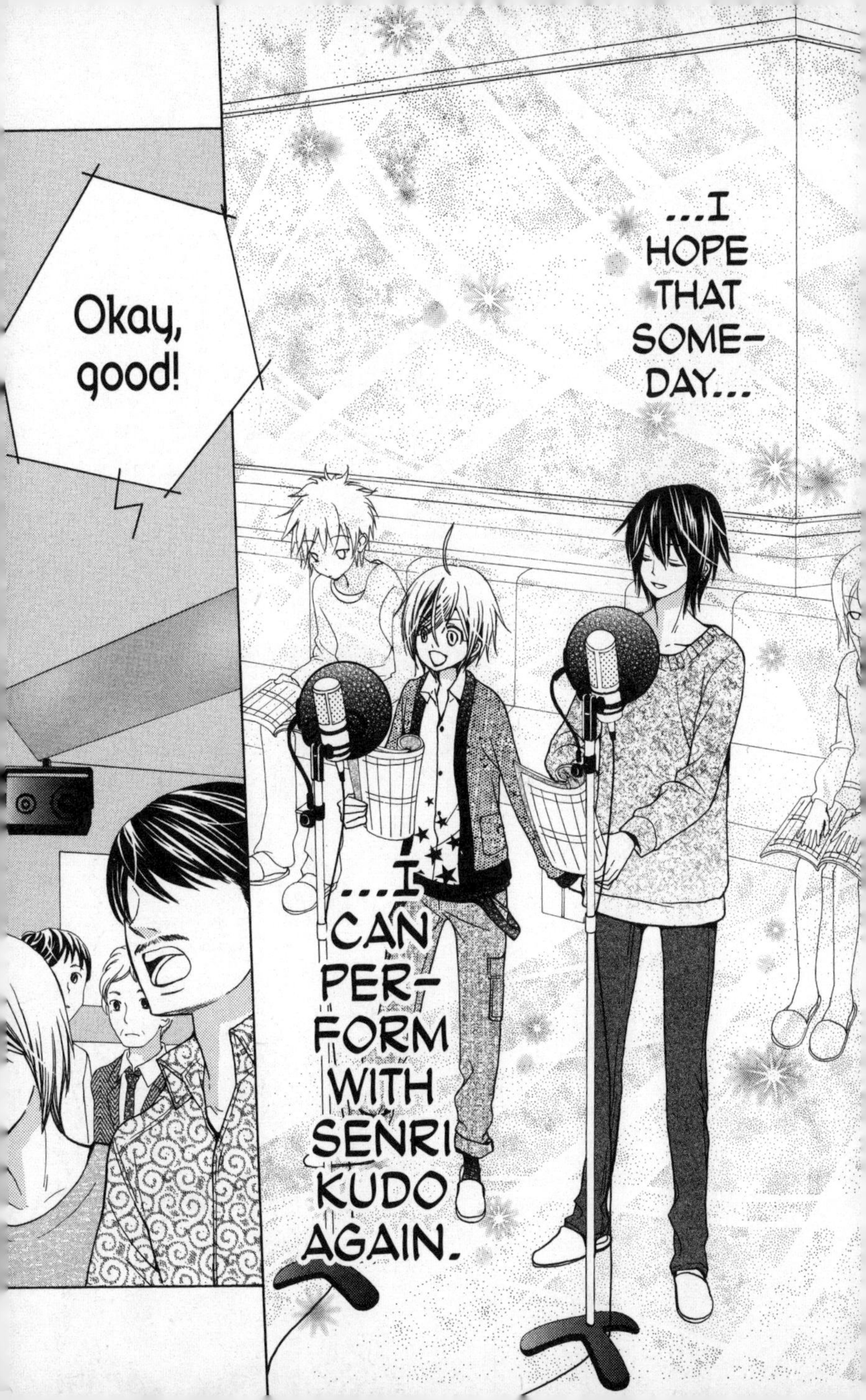
...I HOPE THAT SOME-DAY...
...I CAN PER-FORM WITH SENRI KUDO AGAIN.
Okay, good!

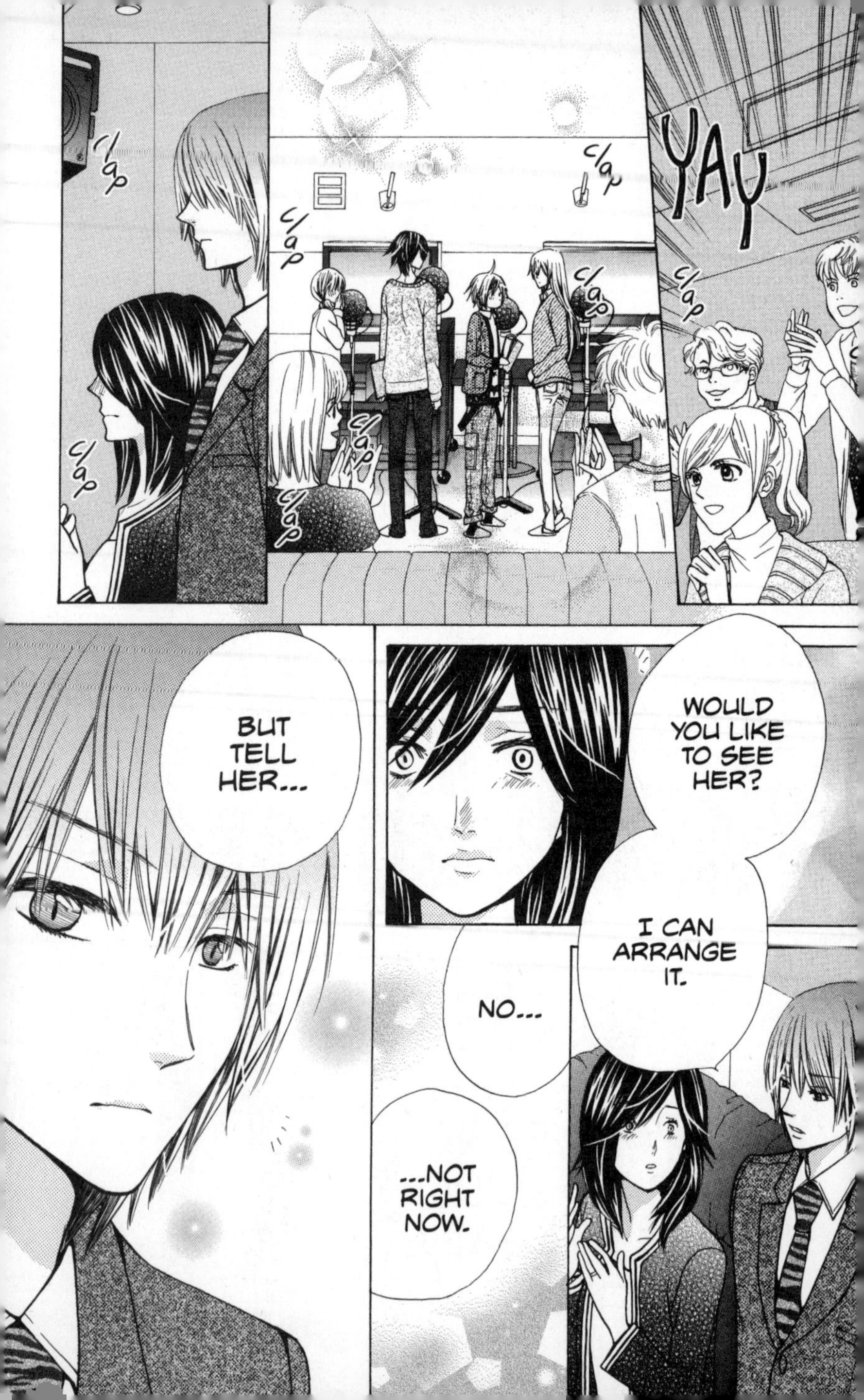
YAY
clap
clap
clap
clap
clap
clap
clap
clap
WOULD YOU LIKE TO SEE HER?
I CAN ARRANGE IT.
NO...
...NOT RIGHT NOW.
BUT TELL HER...

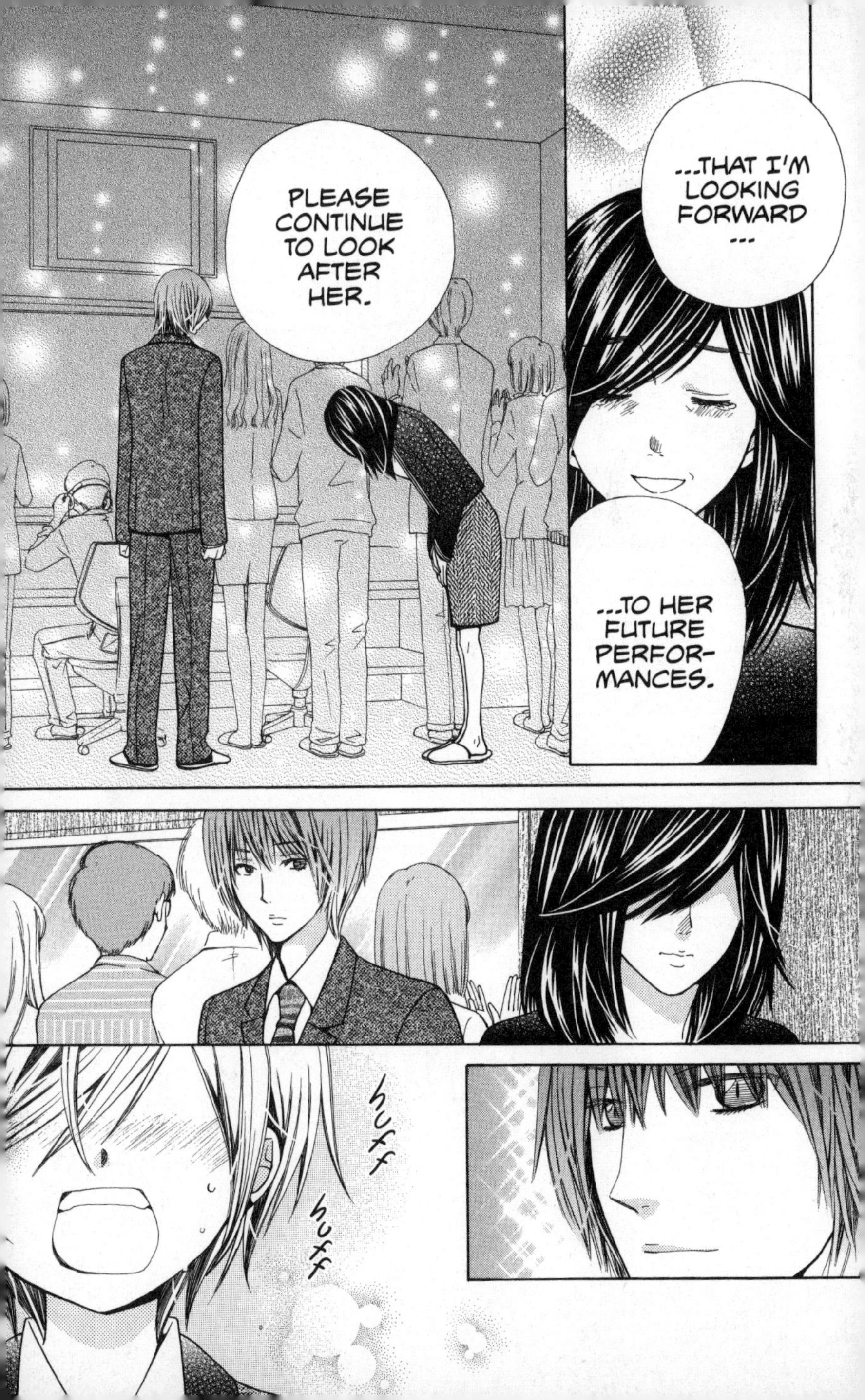
...THAT I'M LOOKING FORWARD ...
...TO HER FUTURE PERFORMANCES.
PLEASE CONTINUE TO LOOK AFTER HER.
huff huff

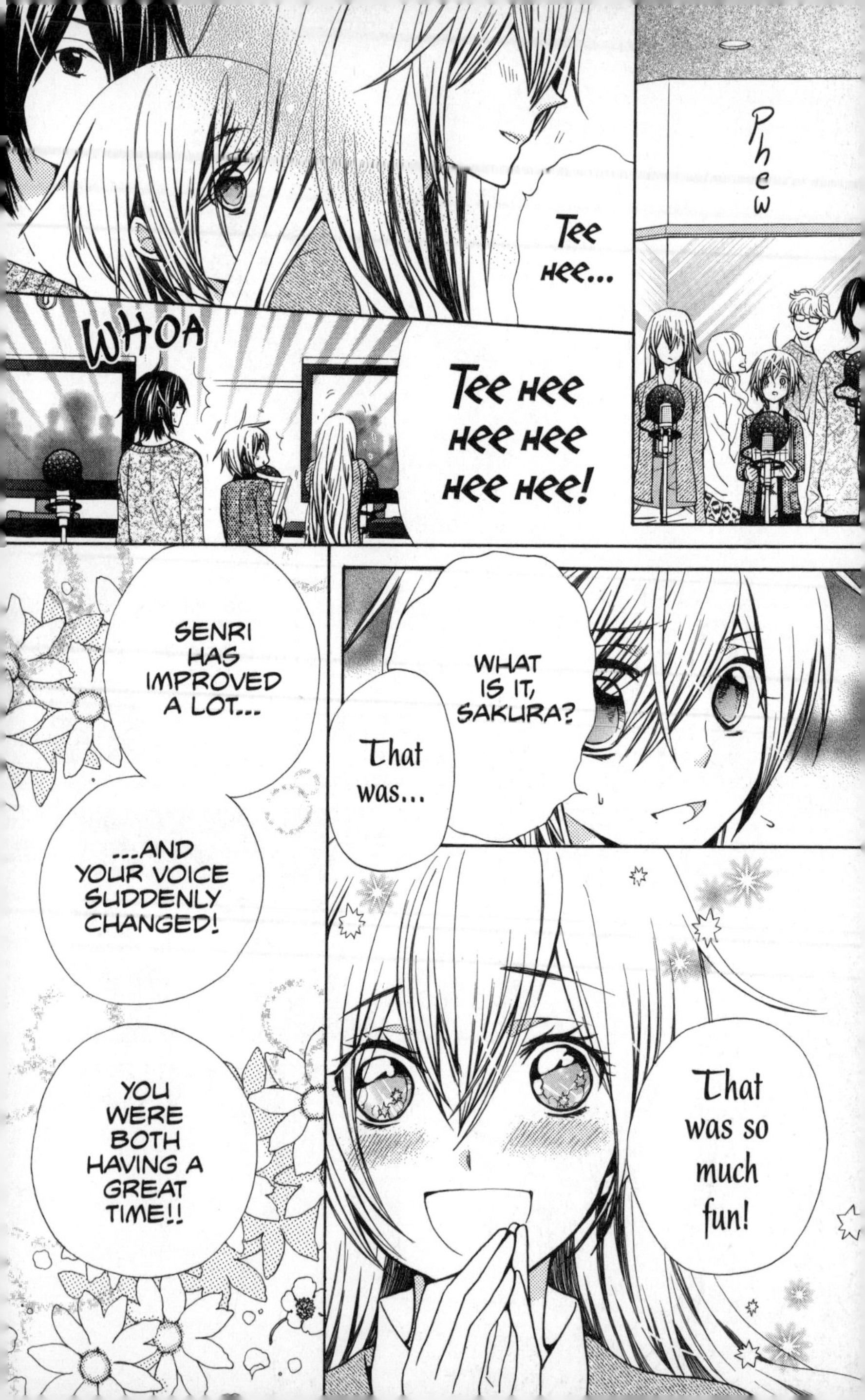
Phew
Tee hee...
Tee hee hee hee hee hee!
WHOA
WHAT IS IT, SAKURA?
That was...
That was so much fun!
SENRI HAS IMPROVED A LOT...
...AND YOUR VOICE SUDDENLY CHANGED!
YOU WERE BOTH HAVING A GREAT TIME!!

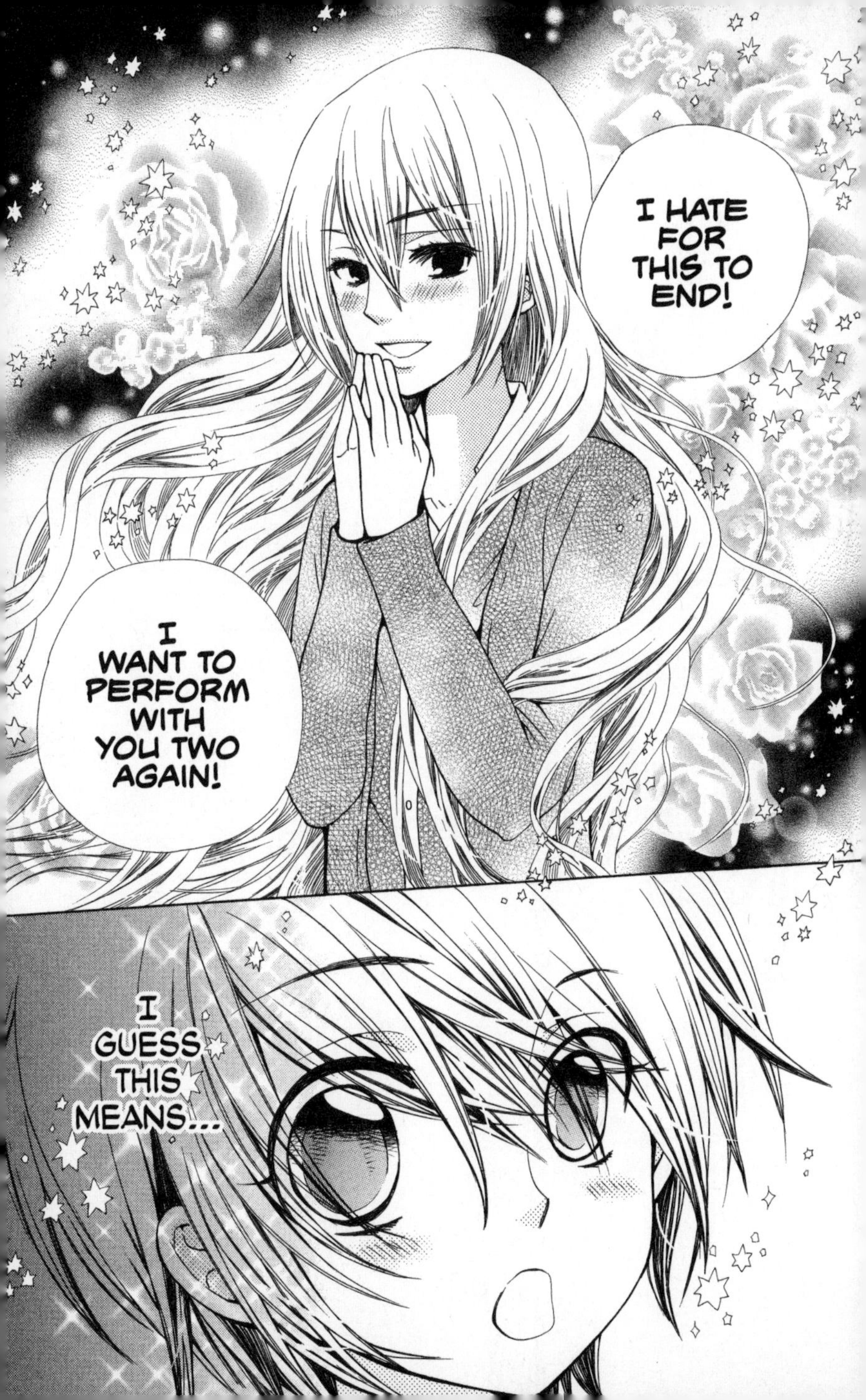
I HATE FOR THIS TO END!
I WANT TO PERFORM WITH YOU TWO AGAIN!
I GUESS THIS MEANS...

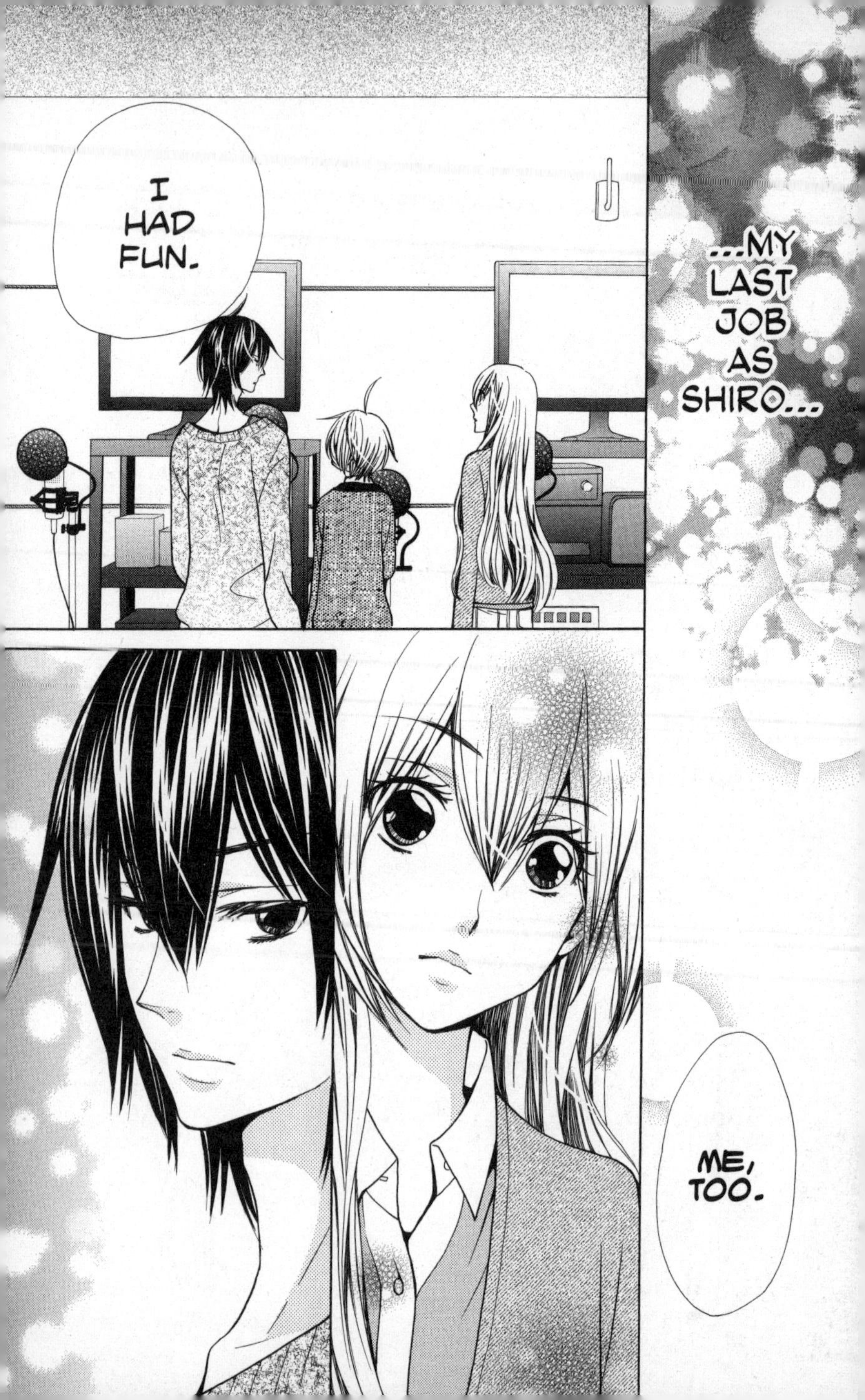
...MY LAST JOB AS SHIRO...
I HAD FUN.
ME, TOO.

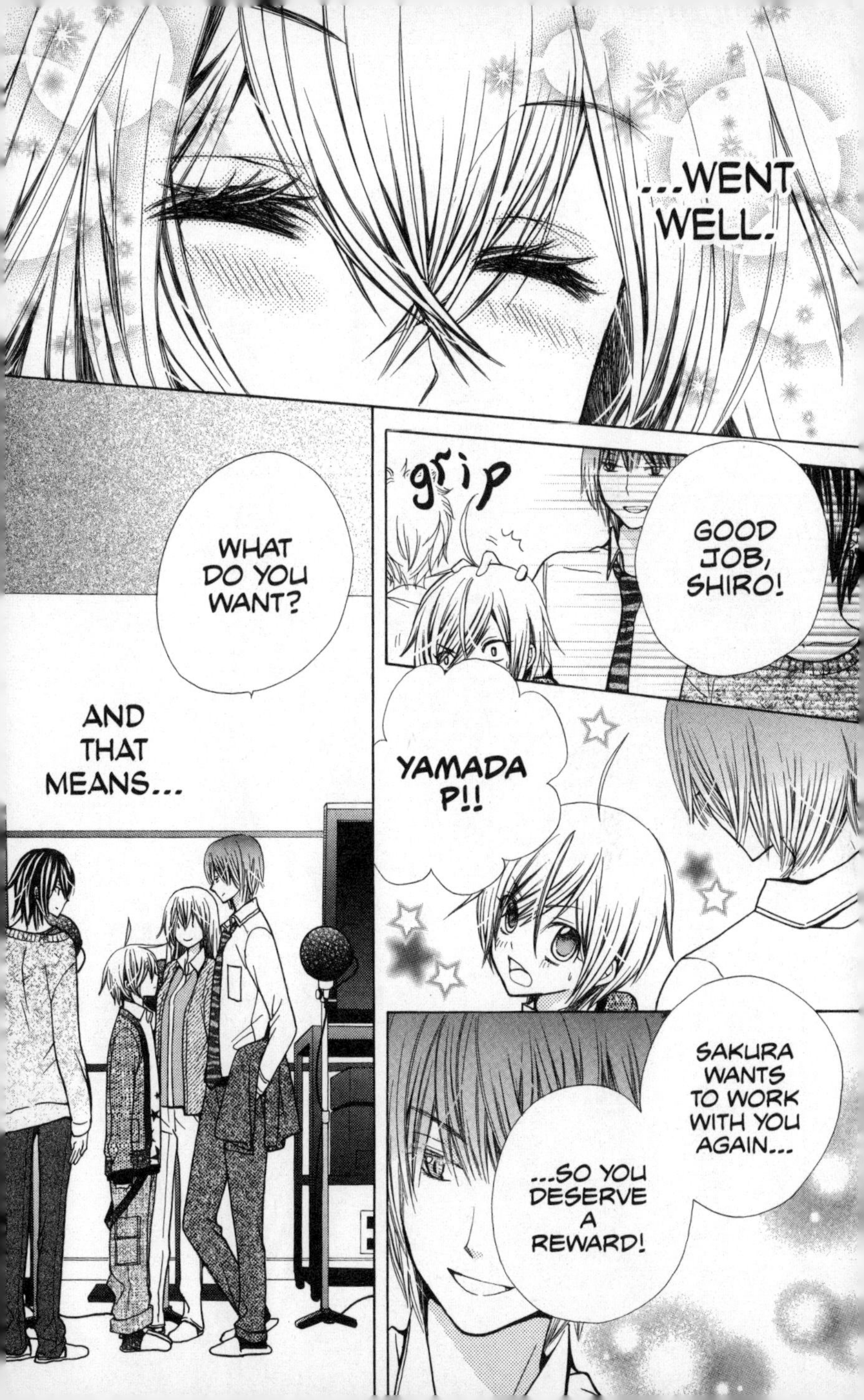
...WENT WELL.
grip
GOOD JOB, SHIRO!
YAMADA P!!
SAKURA WANTS TO WORK WITH YOU AGAIN...
...SO YOU DESERVE A REWARD!
WHAT DO YOU WANT?
AND THAT MEANS...

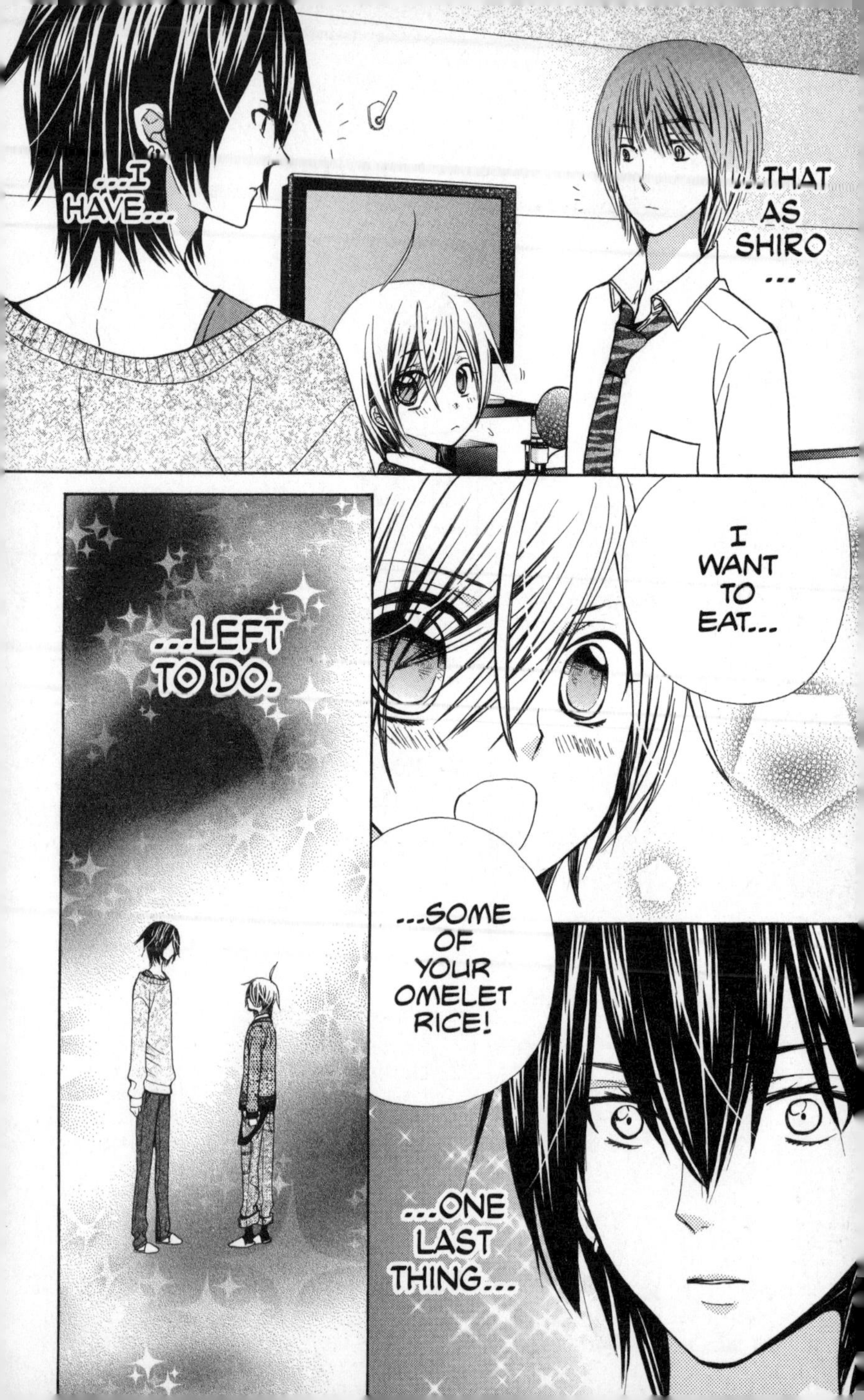
...THAT AS SHIRO...
...I HAVE...
I WANT TO EAT...
...SOME OF YOUR OMELET RICE!
...ONE LAST THING...
...LEFT TO DO.

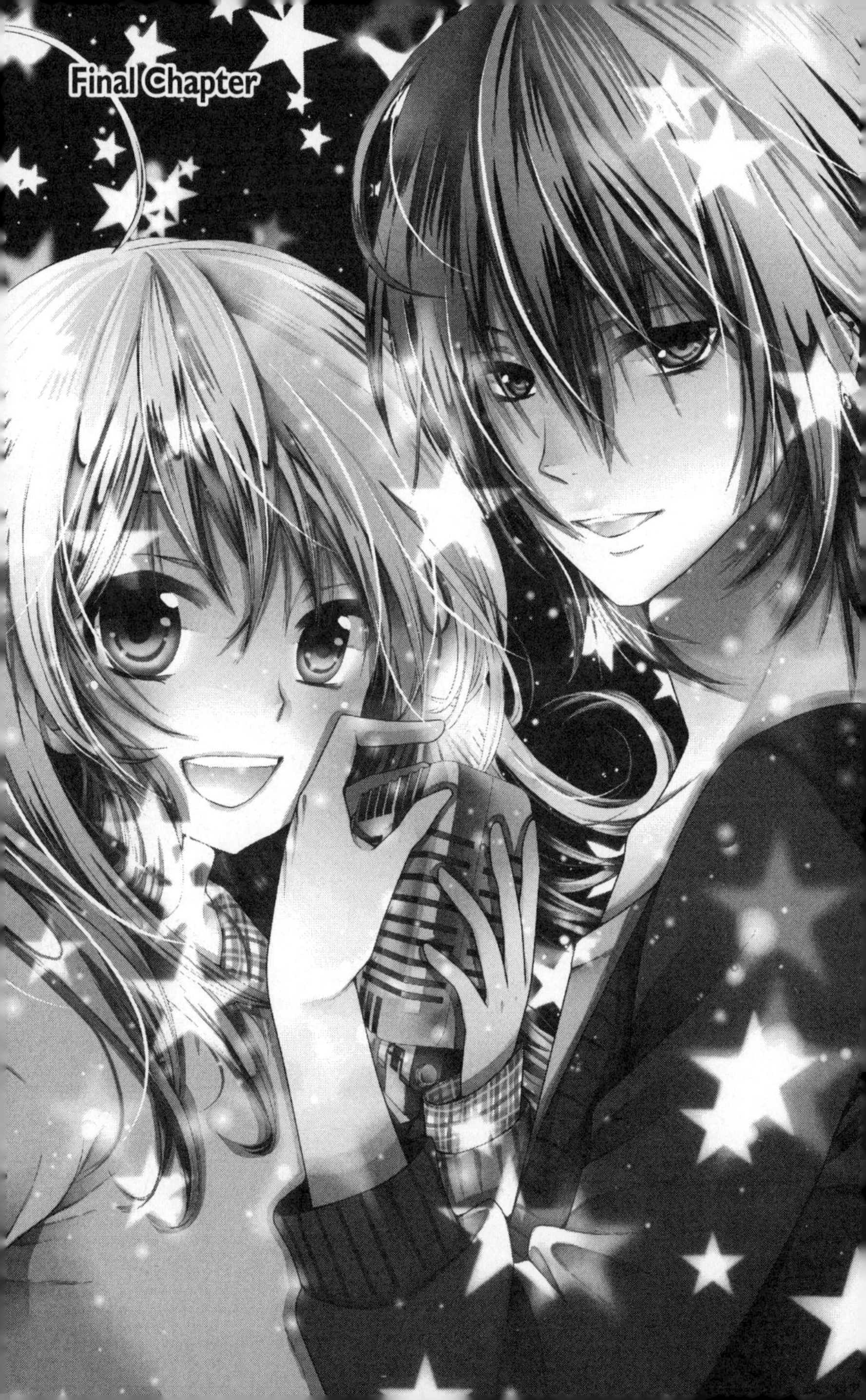
Final Chapter

Sudden Bonus Content Corner!!

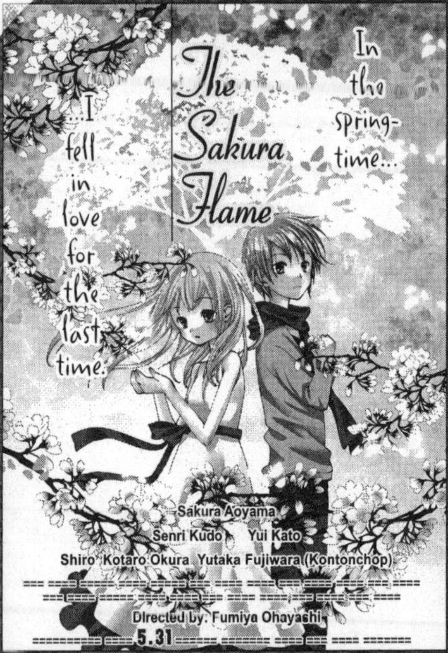
The Sakura Flame
In the spring-time...
...I fell in love for the last time.
Sakura Aoyama
Senri Kudo Yui Kato
Shiro Kotaro Okura Yutaka Fujiwara (Kontonchop)
Directed by: Fumiya Ohayashi
5.31

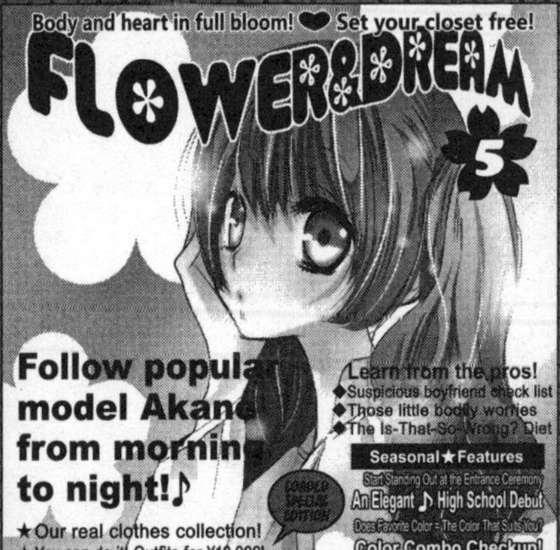
Body and heart in full bloom! ❤ Set your closet free!
FLOWER&DREAM
5
Follow popular model Akane from morning to night!♪
Learn from the pros!
◆Suspicious boyfriend check list
◆Those little bodily worries
◆The Is-That-So-Wrong? Diet
Seasonal★Features
Start Standing Out at the Entrance Ceremony
An Elegant ♪ High School Debut
Does Favorite Color = The Color That Suits You?
Color Combo Checkup!
What to wear?!
Girly vs. Gal
Feminine vs. Pop
★Our real clothes collection!
★You can do it! Outfits for ¥10,000!
★The definitive summer skincare!
★Cheap items ahead of season!
❤ The Spring-time of Love Begins! ❤

↑

This poster is for the movie that Shiro & Senri & Sakura were in. MB-chan drew the illustration in color and M-yama-san did the lettering and applied other touches!! It turned out pretty slick!

This is the cover of the magazine Hime's little sister Akane was in. This was drawn in color, too. I-guchi-san did the layout and lettering!! →

Let the springtime of love begin!!

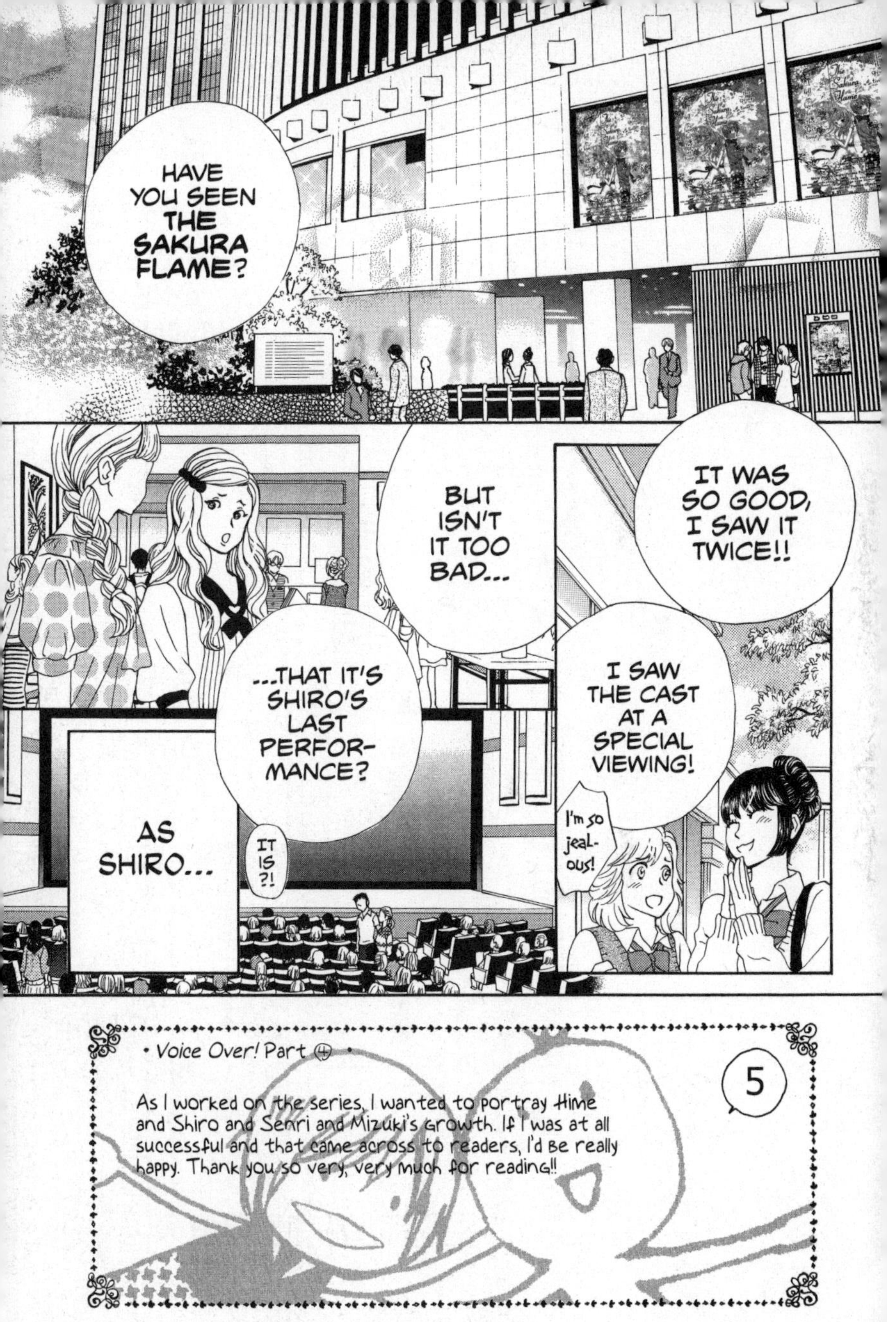
HAVE YOU SEEN THE SAKURA FLAME?
IT WAS SO GOOD, I SAW IT TWICE!!
I SAW THE CAST AT A SPECIAL VIEWING!
I'm so jeal-ous!
BUT ISN'T IT TOO BAD...
...THAT IT'S SHIRO'S LAST PERFOR-MANCE?
IT IS?!
AS SHIRO...

• *Voice Over!* Part ④ •

5

As I worked on the series, I wanted to portray Hime and Shiro and Senri and Mizuki's growth. If I was at all successful and that came across to readers, I'd be really happy. Thank you so very, very much for reading!!

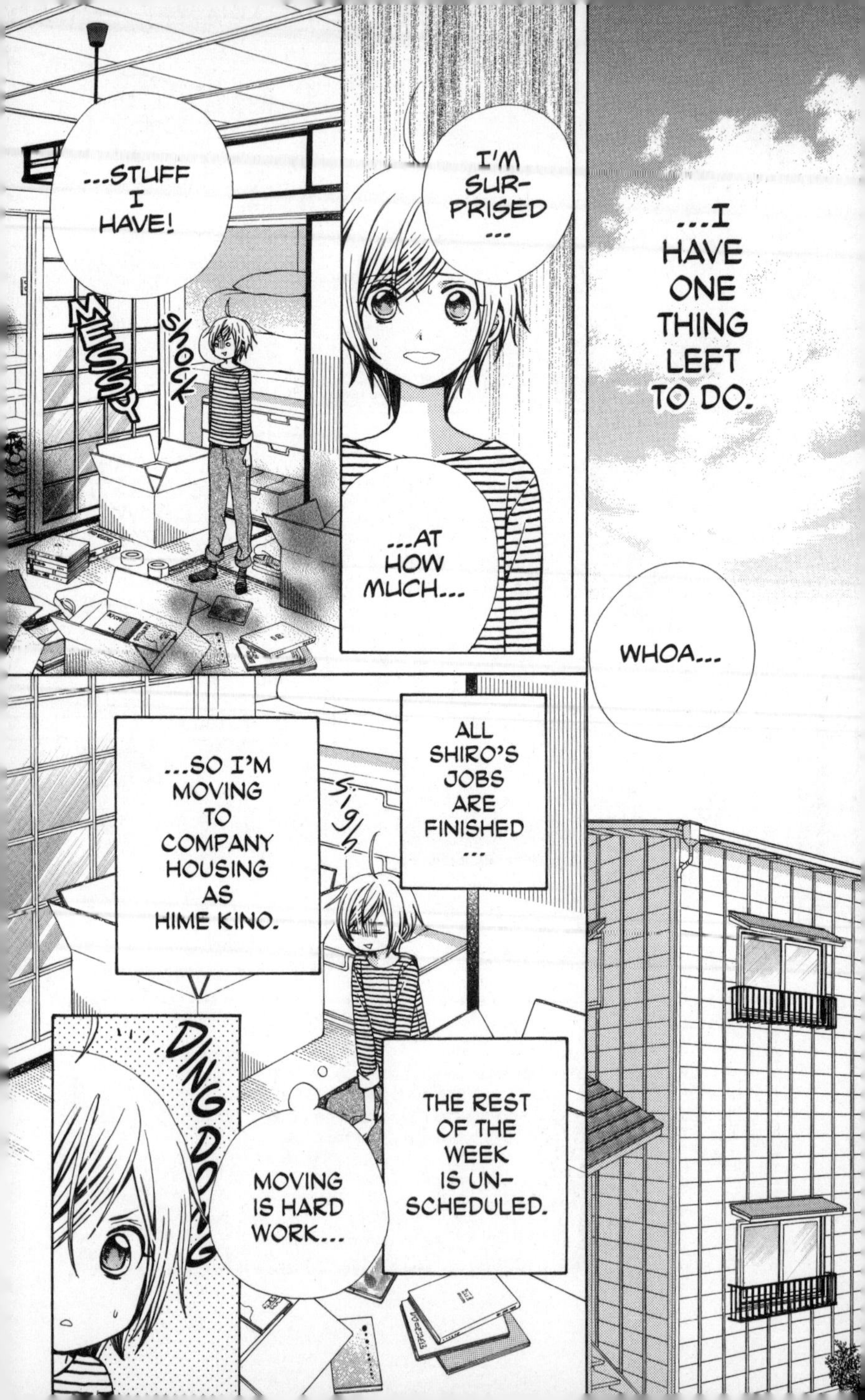
...I HAVE ONE THING LEFT TO DO.
WHOA...
I'M SUR-PRISED...
...AT HOW MUCH...
...STUFF I HAVE!
SHOCK
MESSY
ALL SHIRO'S JOBS ARE FINISHED...
...SO I'M MOVING TO COMPANY HOUSING AS HIME KINO.
SIGH
THE REST OF THE WEEK IS UN-SCHEDULED.
MOVING IS HARD WORK...
DING DONG

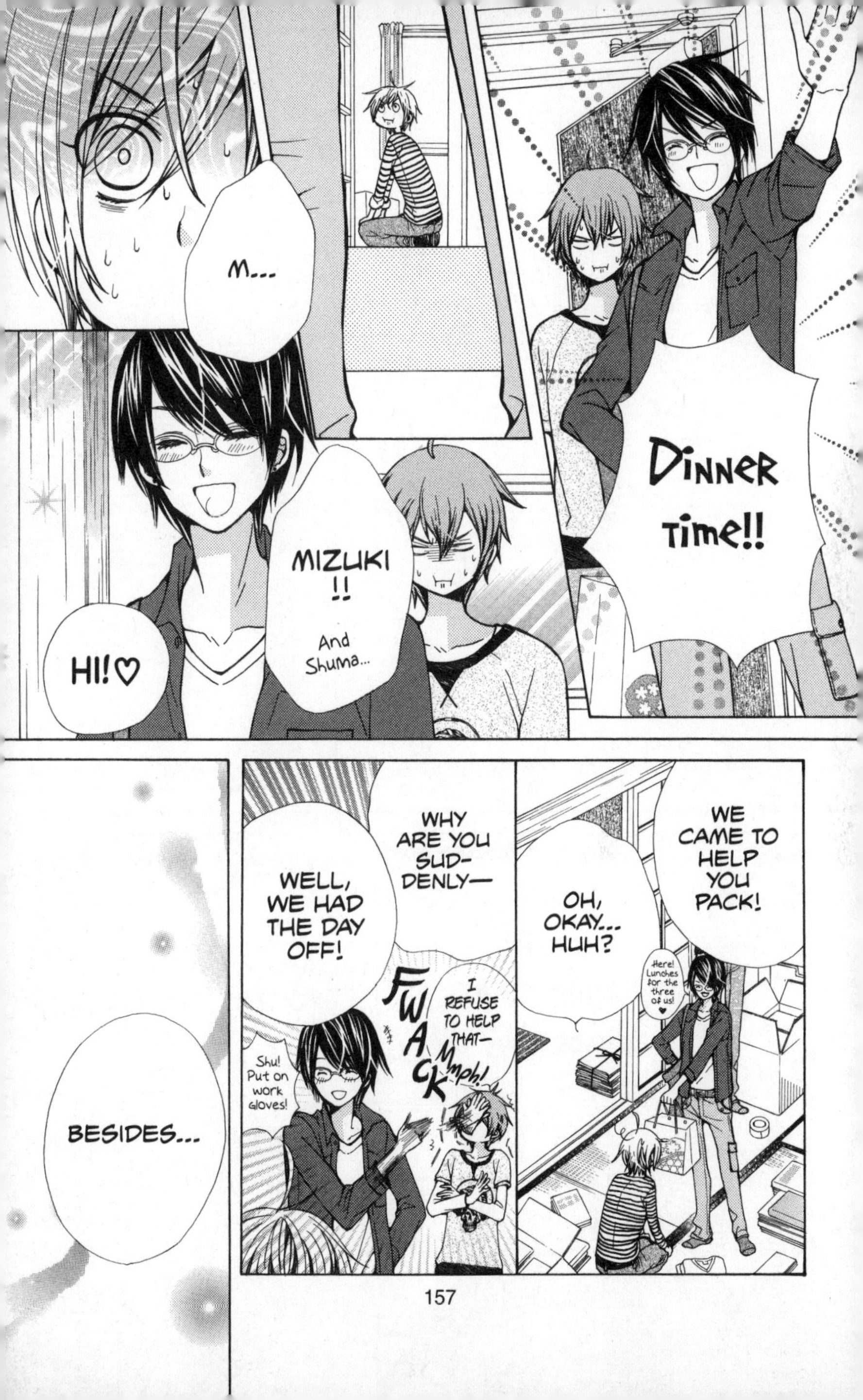
Dinner time!!
M...
MIZUKI !!
And Shuma...
HI!♡
WE CAME TO HELP YOU PACK!
OH, OKAY... HUH?
Here! Lunches for the three of us! ♥
WHY ARE YOU SUD-DENLY—
WELL, WE HAD THE DAY OFF!
I REFUSE TO HELP THAT—
Mmph!
FWACK
Shu! Put on work gloves!
BESIDES...

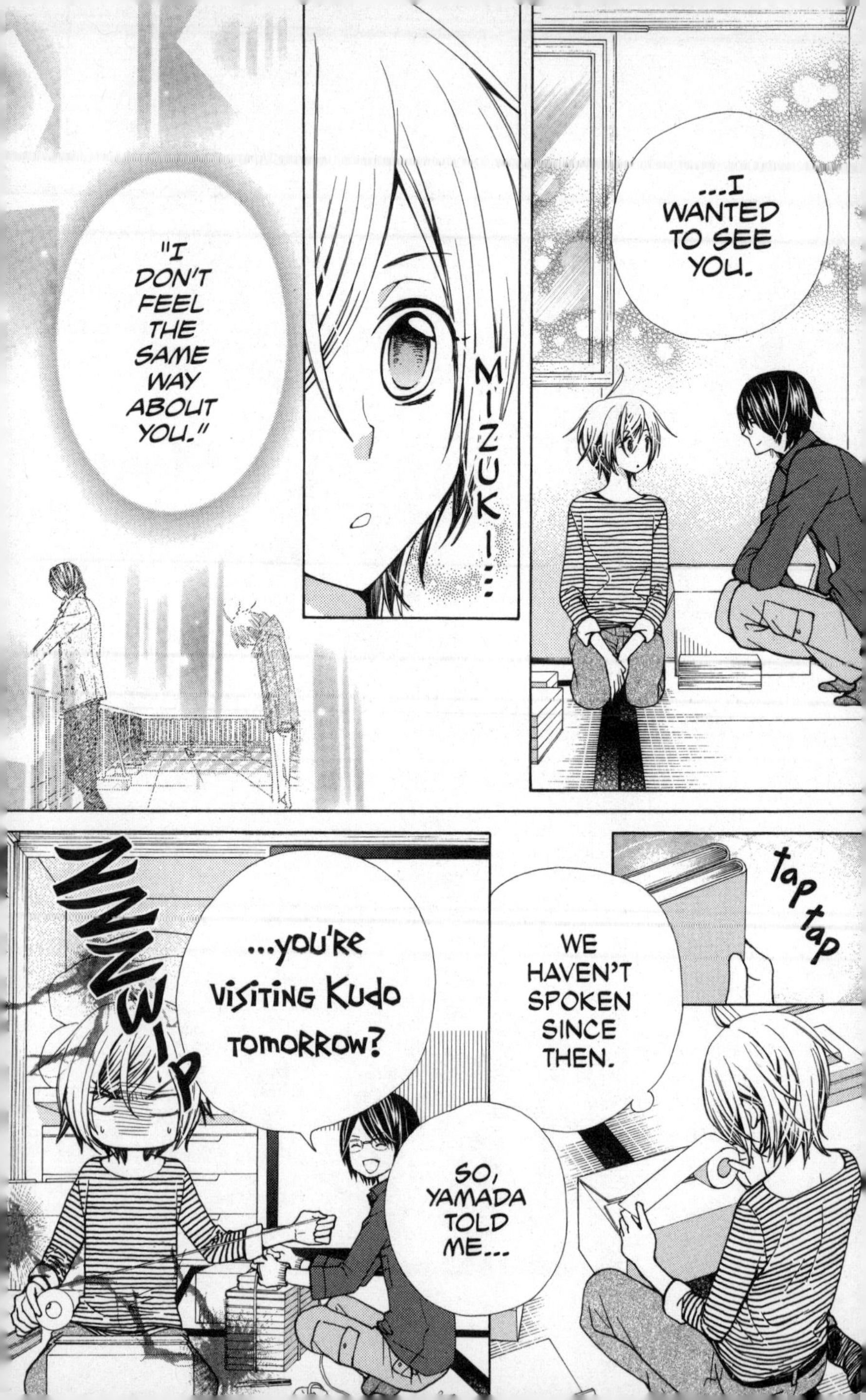
...I WANTED TO SEE YOU.
MIZUKI...!
"I DON'T FEEL THE SAME WAY ABOUT YOU."
tap tap
WE HAVEN'T SPOKEN SINCE THEN.
SO, YAMADA TOLD ME...
...you're visiting Kudo tomorrow?
NNNWIP

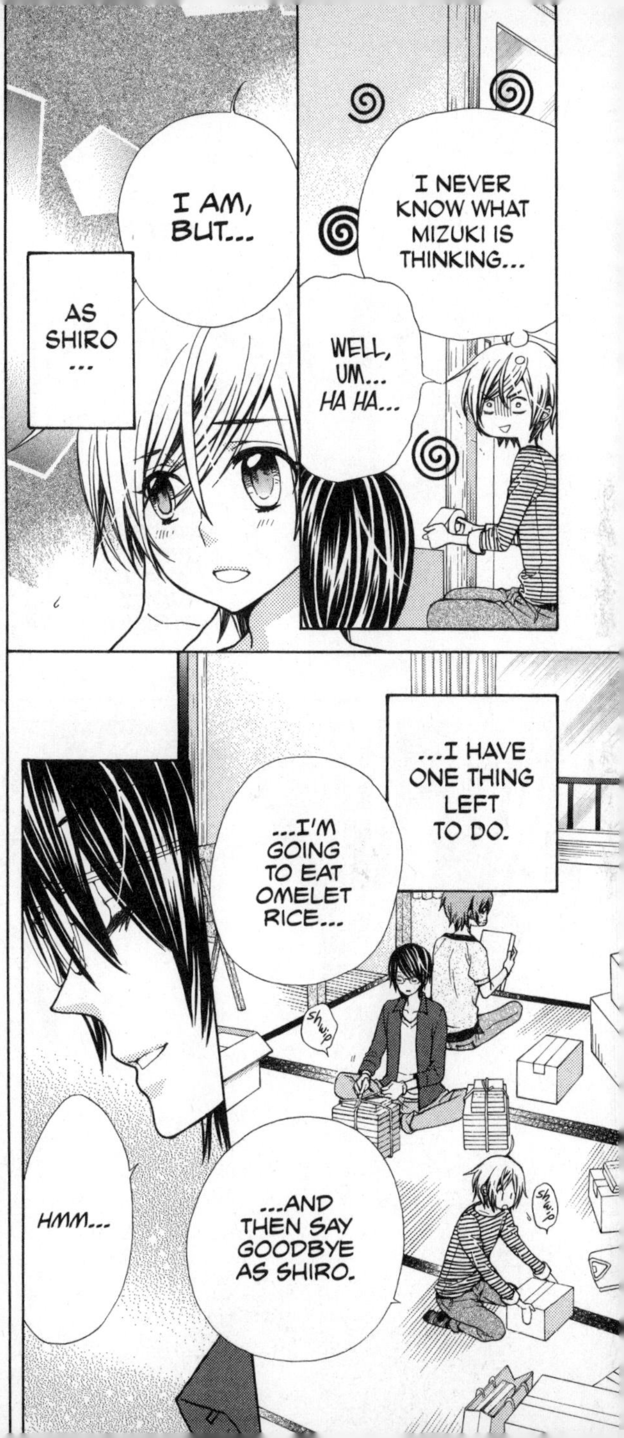
I NEVER KNOW WHAT MIZUKI IS THINKING...
WELL, UM... HA HA...
I AM, BUT...
AS SHIRO...
...I HAVE ONE THING LEFT TO DO.
...I'M GOING TO EAT OMELET RICE...
shwip
...AND THEN SAY GOODBYE AS SHIRO.
shwip
HMM...

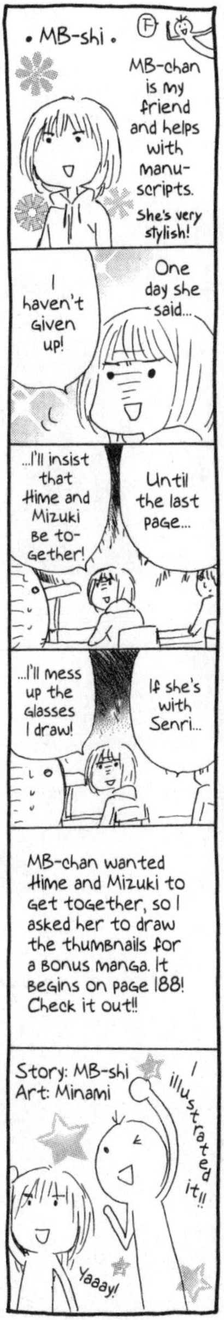
• MB-shi •
MB-chan is my friend and helps with manu-scripts.
She's very stylish!
One day she said...
I haven't given up!
Until the last page...
...I'll insist that Hime and Mizuki be to-gether!
If she's with Senri...
...I'll mess up the glasses I draw!
MB-chan wanted Hime and Mizuki to get together, so I asked her to draw the thumbnails for a bonus manga. It begins on page 188! Check it out!!
Story: MB-shi
Art: Minami
I illustrated it!!
Yaaay!

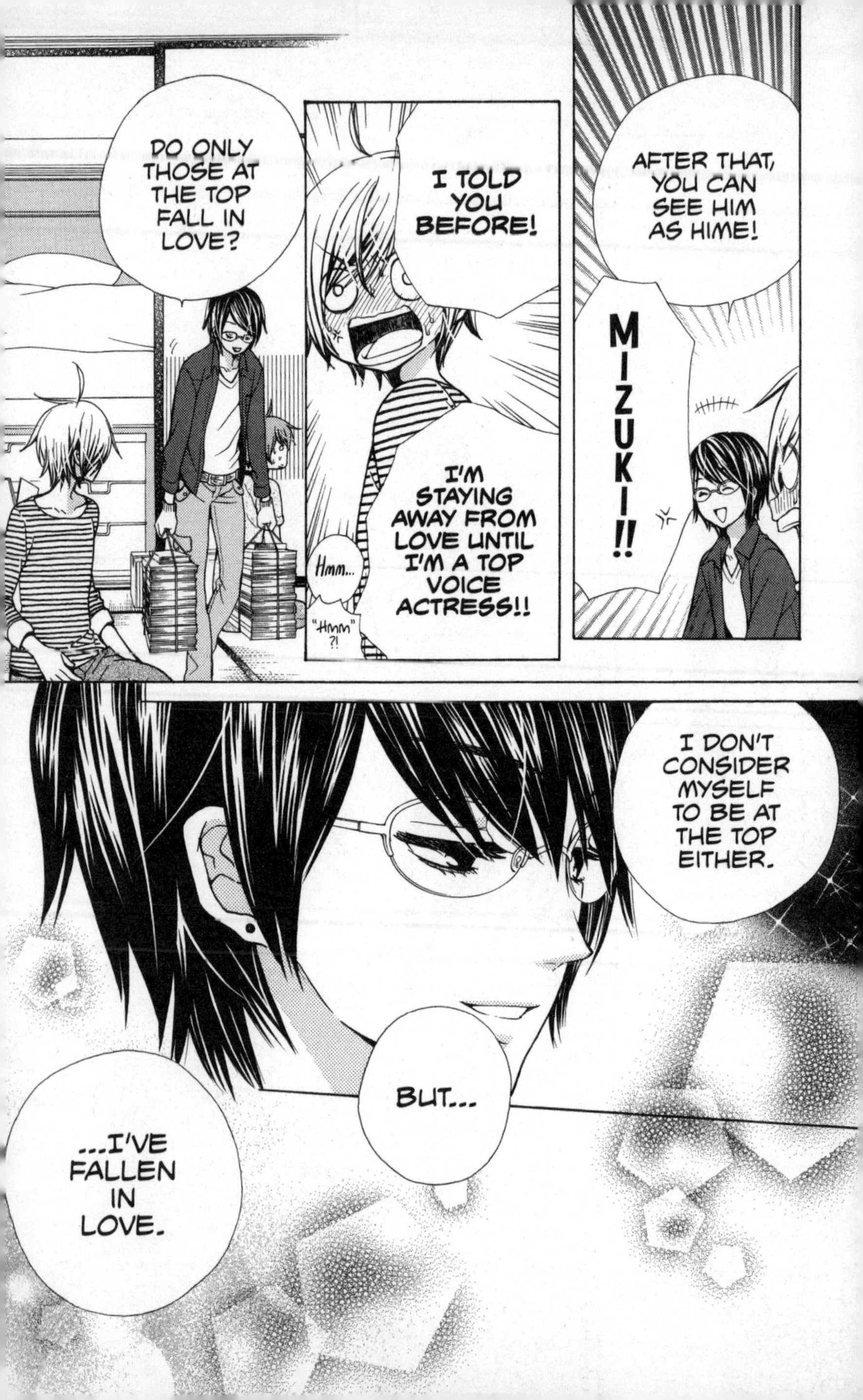
AFTER THAT, YOU CAN SEE HIM AS HIME!
MIZUKI!!
I TOLD YOU BEFORE!
I'M STAYING AWAY FROM LOVE UNTIL I'M A TOP VOICE ACTRESS!!
Hmm...
"Hmm" ?!
DO ONLY THOSE AT THE TOP FALL IN LOVE?
I DON'T CONSIDER MYSELF TO BE AT THE TOP EITHER.
BUT...
...I'VE FALLEN IN LOVE.

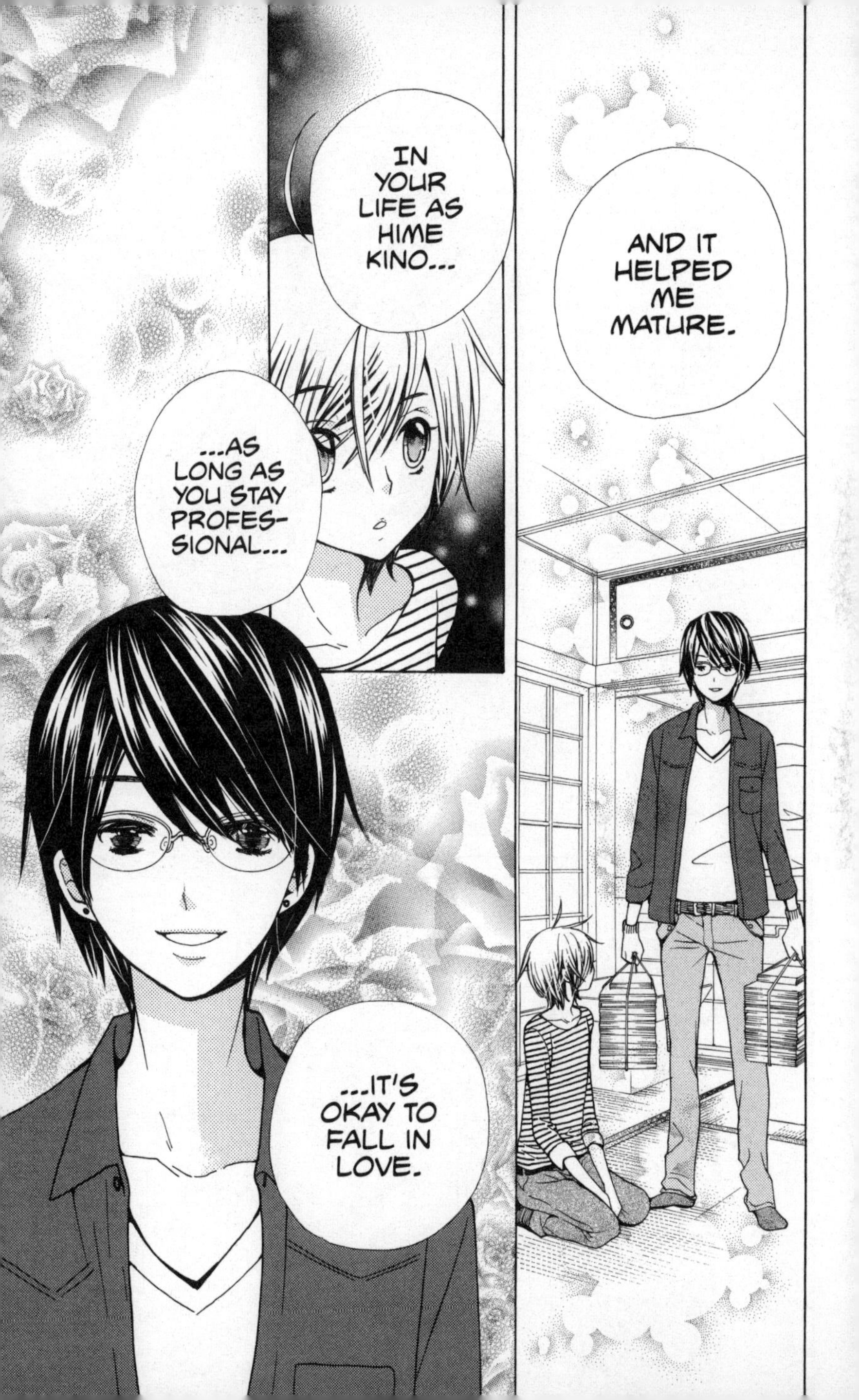
AND IT HELPED ME MATURE.
IN YOUR LIFE AS HIME KINO...
...AS LONG AS YOU STAY PROFES-SIONAL...
...IT'S OKAY TO FALL IN LOVE.

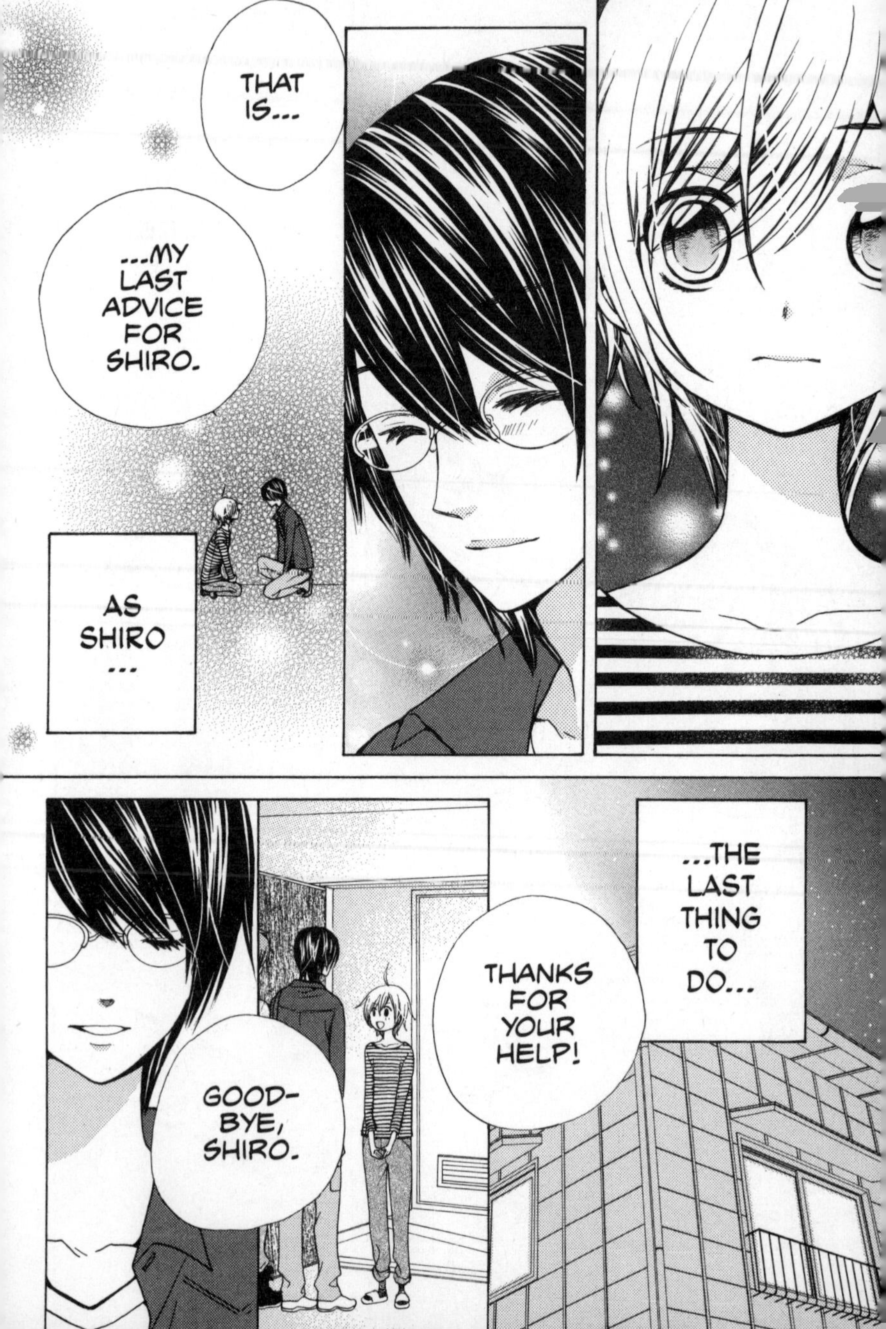
THAT IS...
...MY LAST ADVICE FOR SHIRO.
AS SHIRO...
...THE LAST THING TO DO...
THANKS FOR YOUR HELP!
GOOD-BYE, SHIRO.

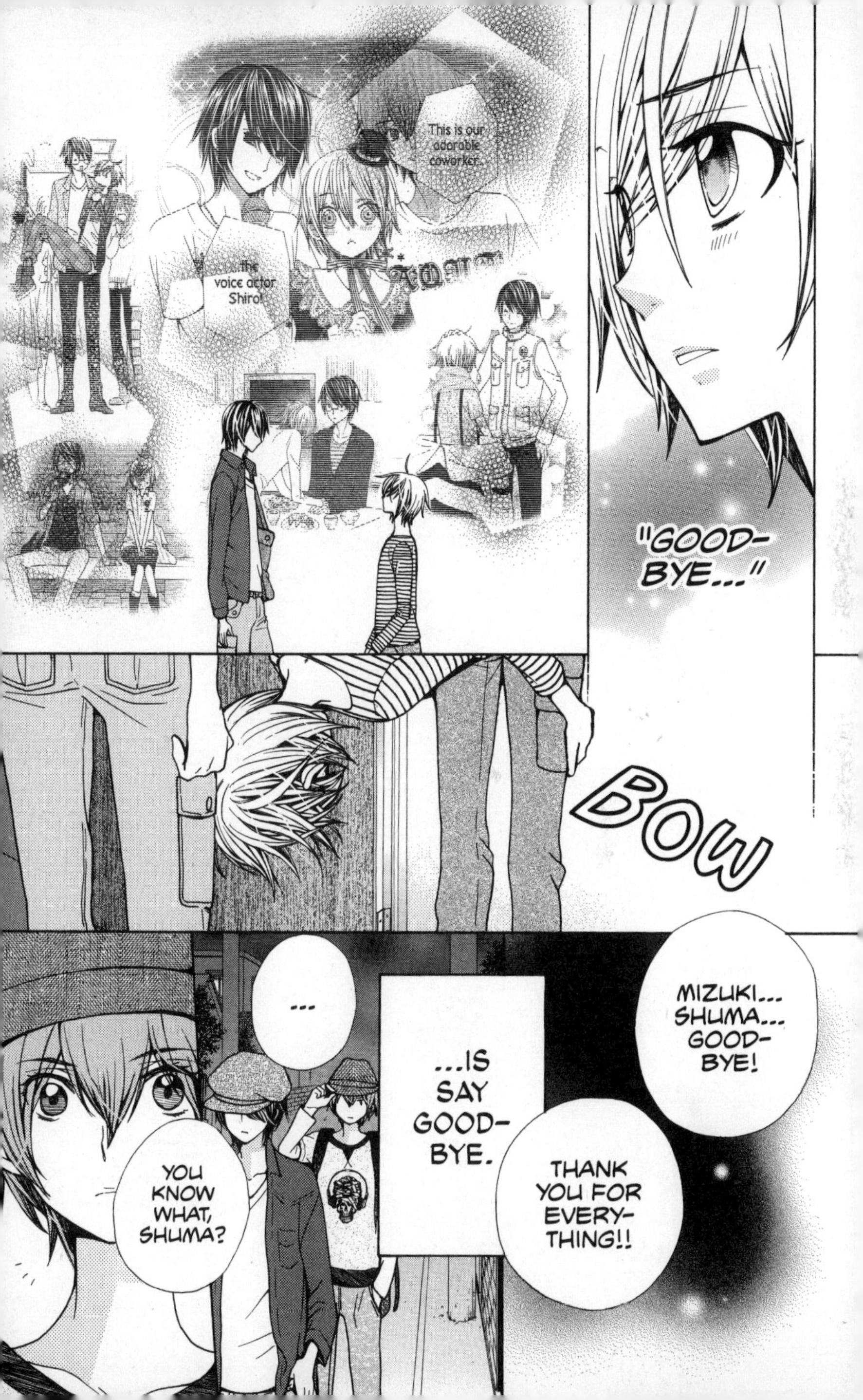
"GOOD-BYE..."
This is our adorable coworker...
the voice actor Shiro!
BOW
MIZUKI... SHUMA... GOOD-BYE!
THANK YOU FOR EVERY-THING!!
...IS SAY GOOD-BYE.
...
YOU KNOW WHAT, SHUMA?

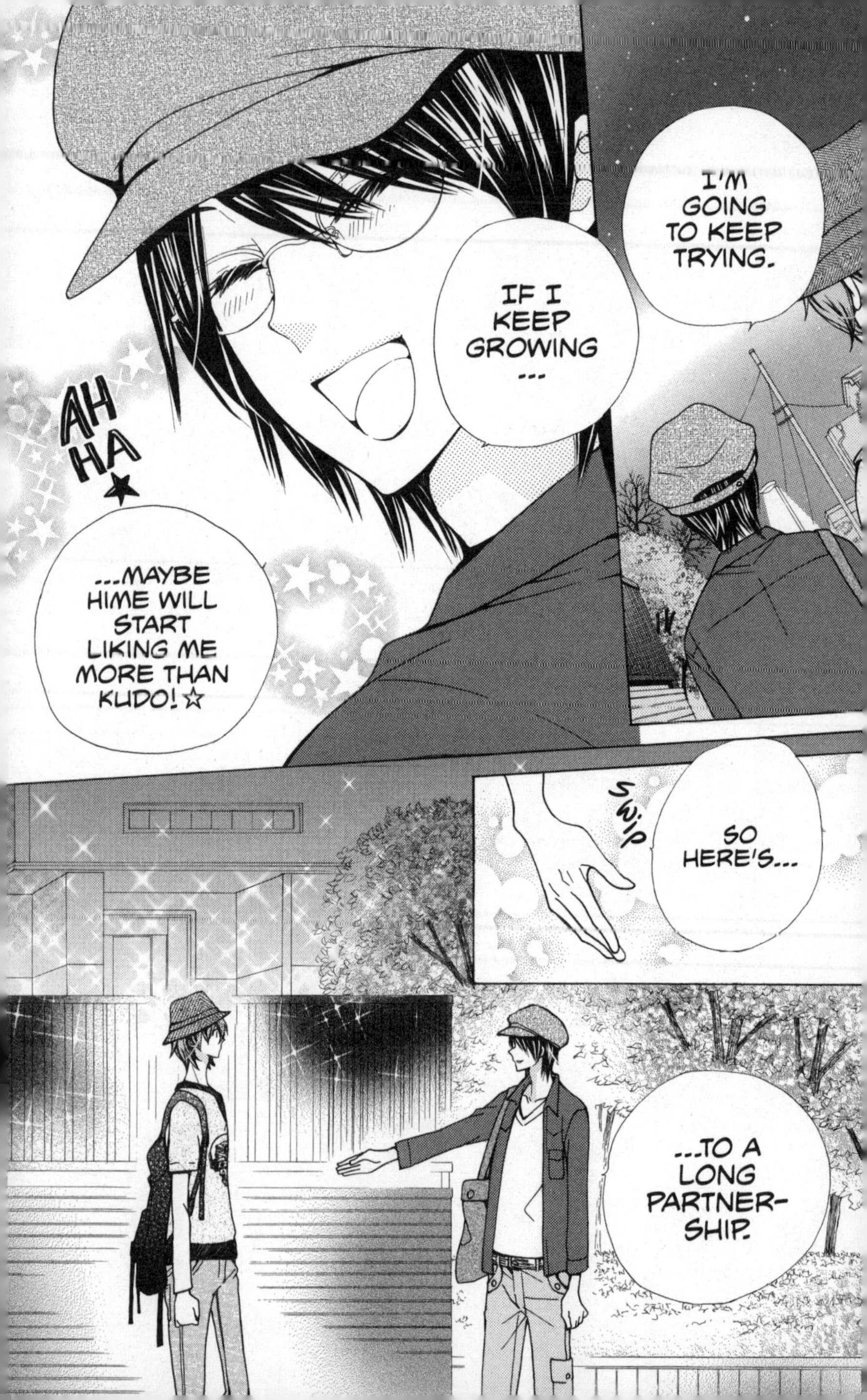
I'M GOING TO KEEP TRYING.
IF I KEEP GROWING ---
AH HA★
...MAYBE HIME WILL START LIKING ME MORE THAN KUDO!☆
SWIP
SO HERE'S...
...TO A LONG PARTNER-SHIP.

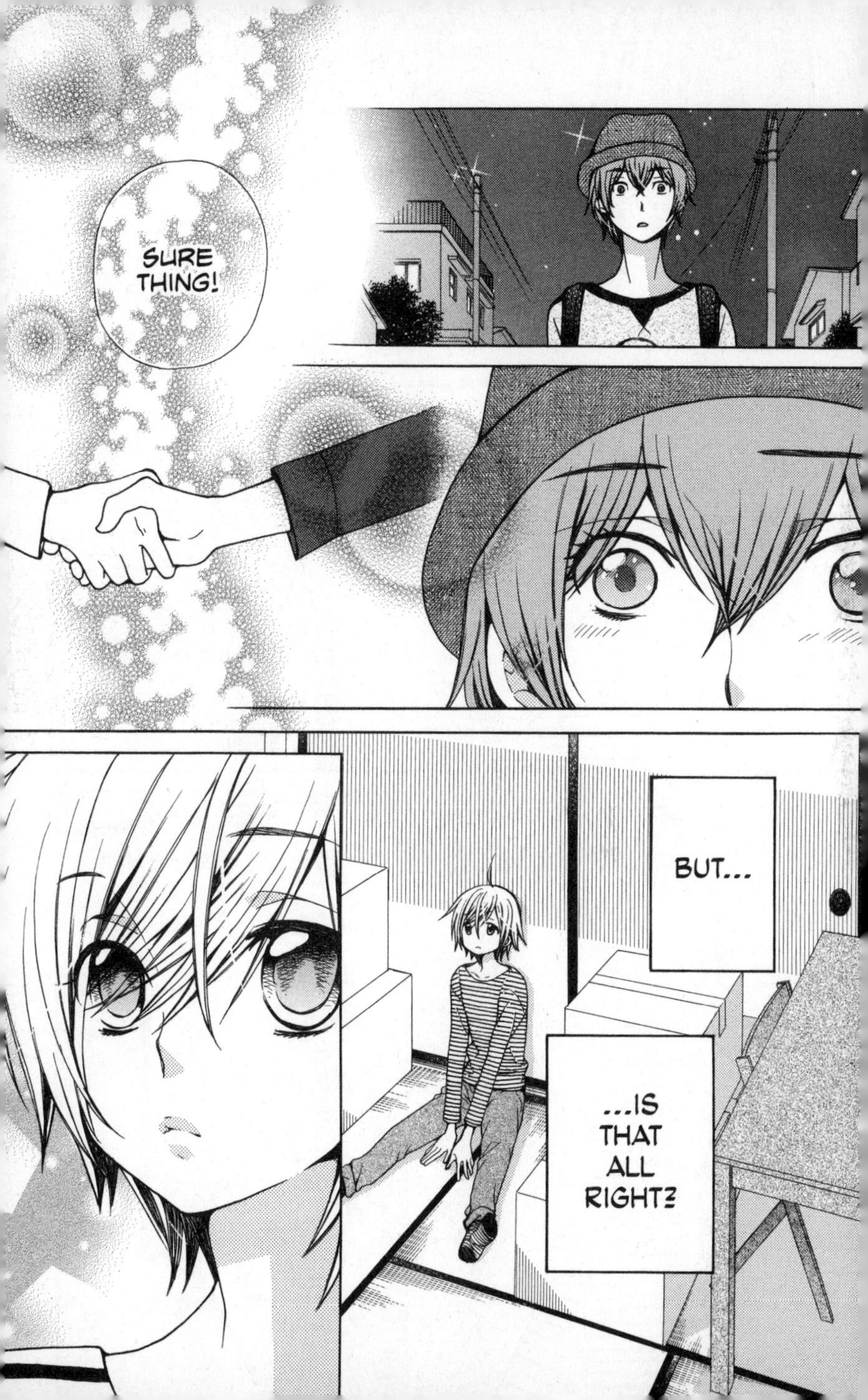
SURE THING!
BUT...
...IS THAT ALL RIGHT?

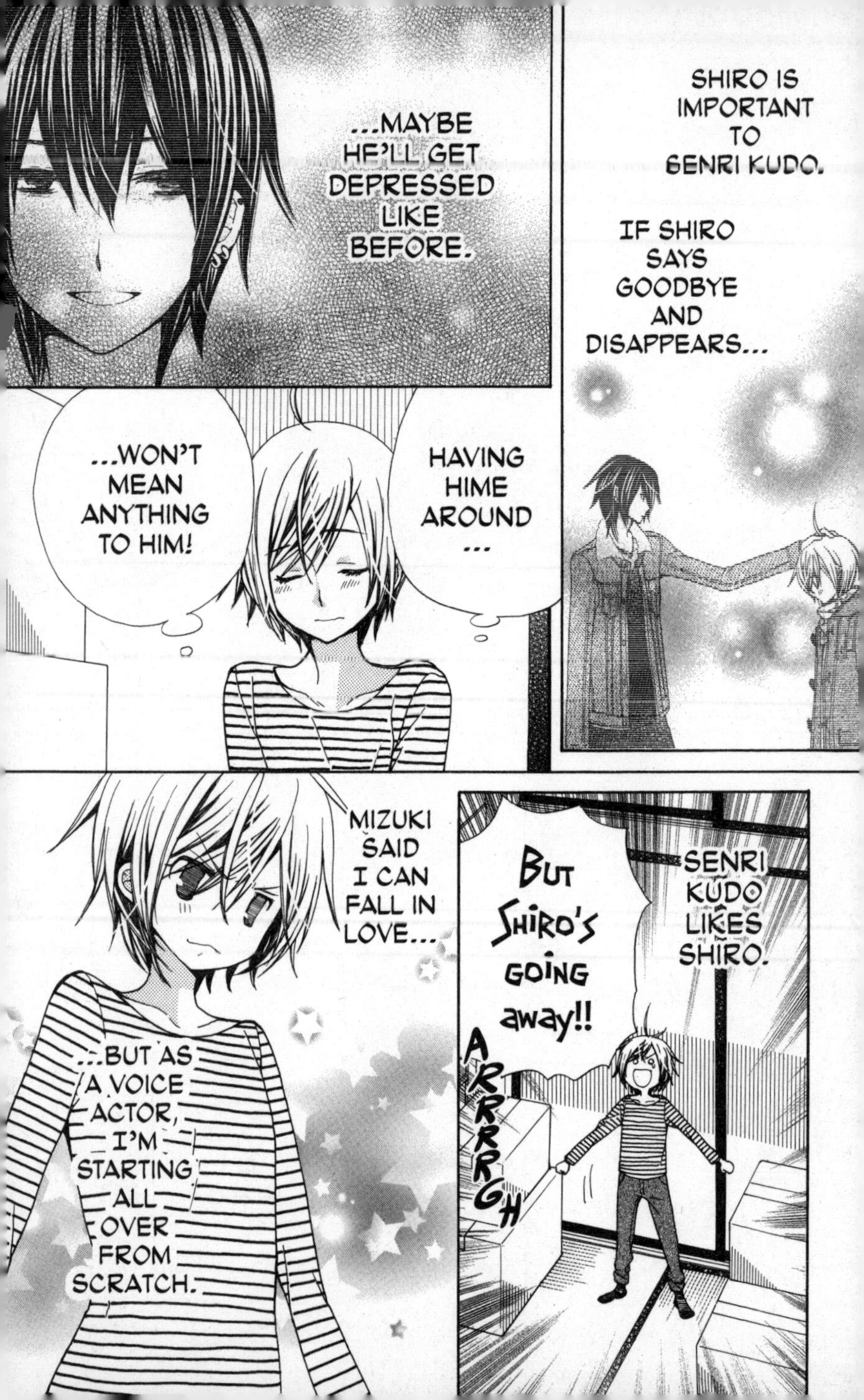
SHIRO IS IMPORTANT TO SENRI KUDO.
IF SHIRO SAYS GOODBYE AND DISAPPEARS...
...MAYBE HE'LL GET DEPRESSED LIKE BEFORE.
HAVING HIME AROUND...
...WON'T MEAN ANYTHING TO HIM!
SENRI KUDO LIKES SHIRO.
But Shiro's going away!!
ARRRRGH
MIZUKI SAID I CAN FALL IN LOVE...
...BUT AS A VOICE ACTOR, I'M STARTING ALL OVER FROM SCRATCH.

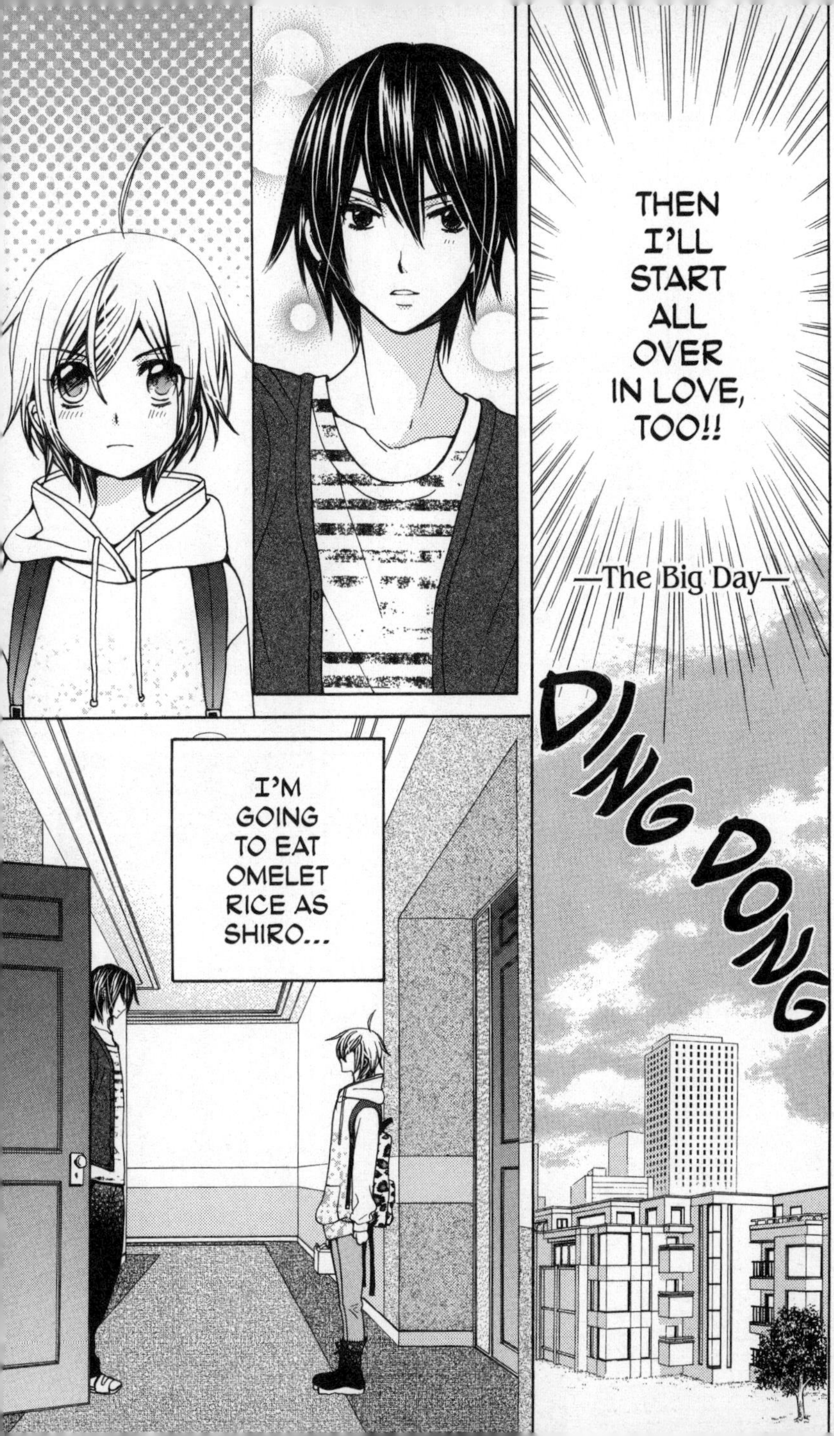
THEN I'LL START ALL OVER IN LOVE, TOO!!
—The Big Day—
DING DONG
I'M GOING TO EAT OMELET RICE AS SHIRO...

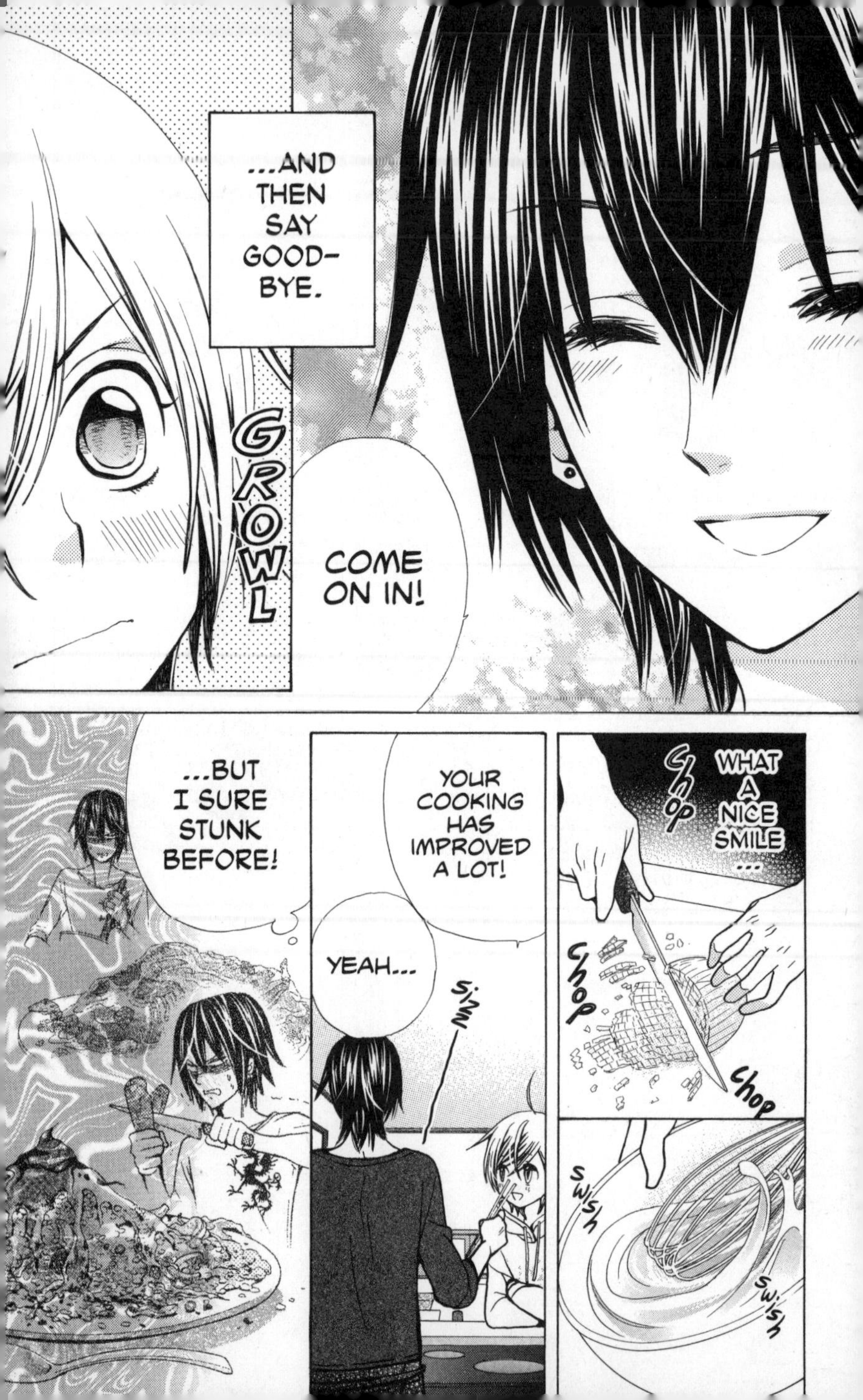
...AND THEN SAY GOOD-BYE.
COME ON IN!
GROWL
WHAT A NICE SMILE...
Chop
Chop
Chop
Swish
Swish
YOUR COOKING HAS IMPROVED A LOT!
YEAH...
SIZZ
...BUT I SURE STUNK BEFORE!

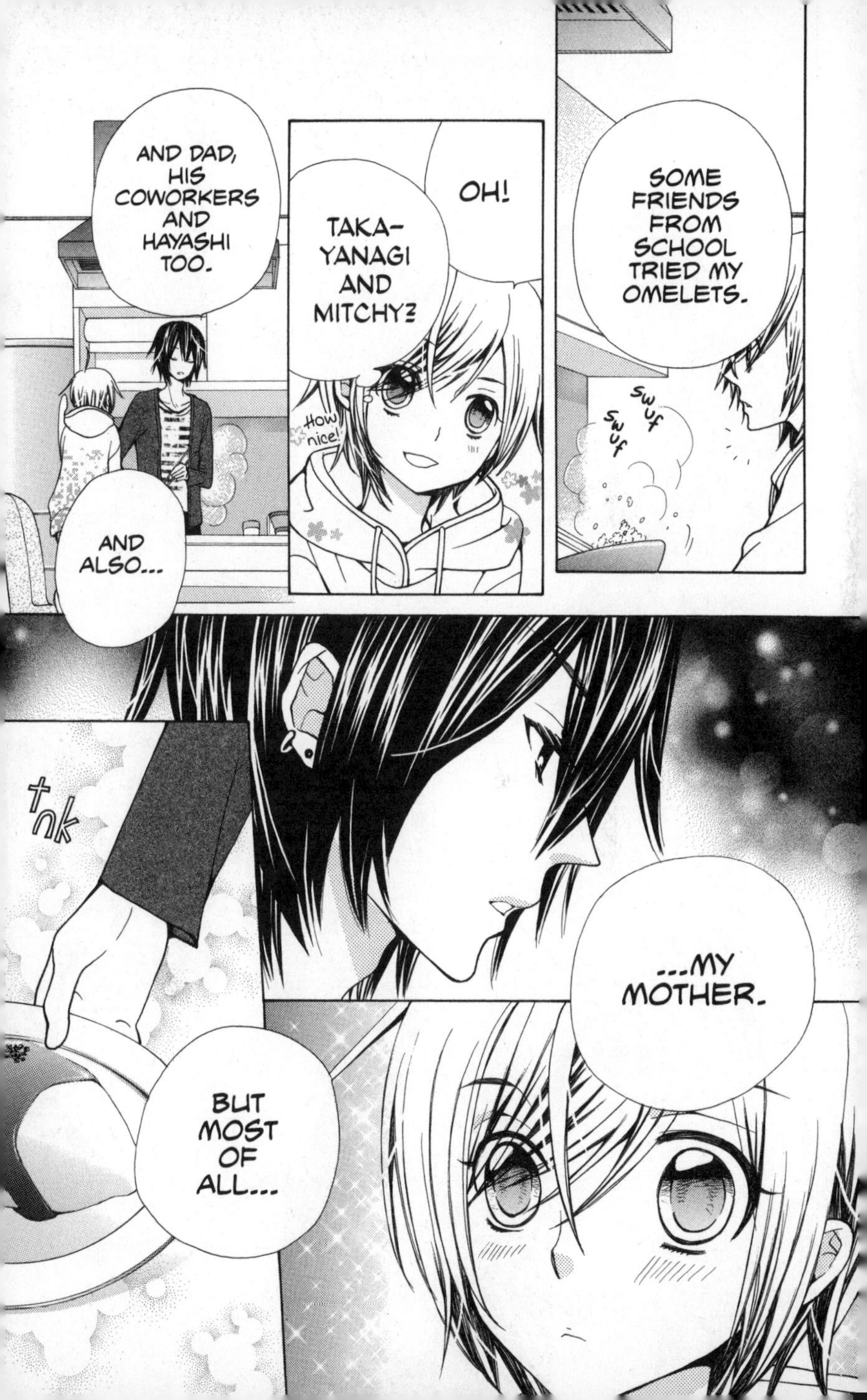
SOME FRIENDS FROM SCHOOL TRIED MY OMELETS.
SWUF SWUF
OH!
TAKA-YANAGI AND MITCHY?
How nice!
AND DAD, HIS COWORKERS AND HAYASHI TOO.
AND ALSO...
TNK
...MY MOTHER.
BUT MOST OF ALL...

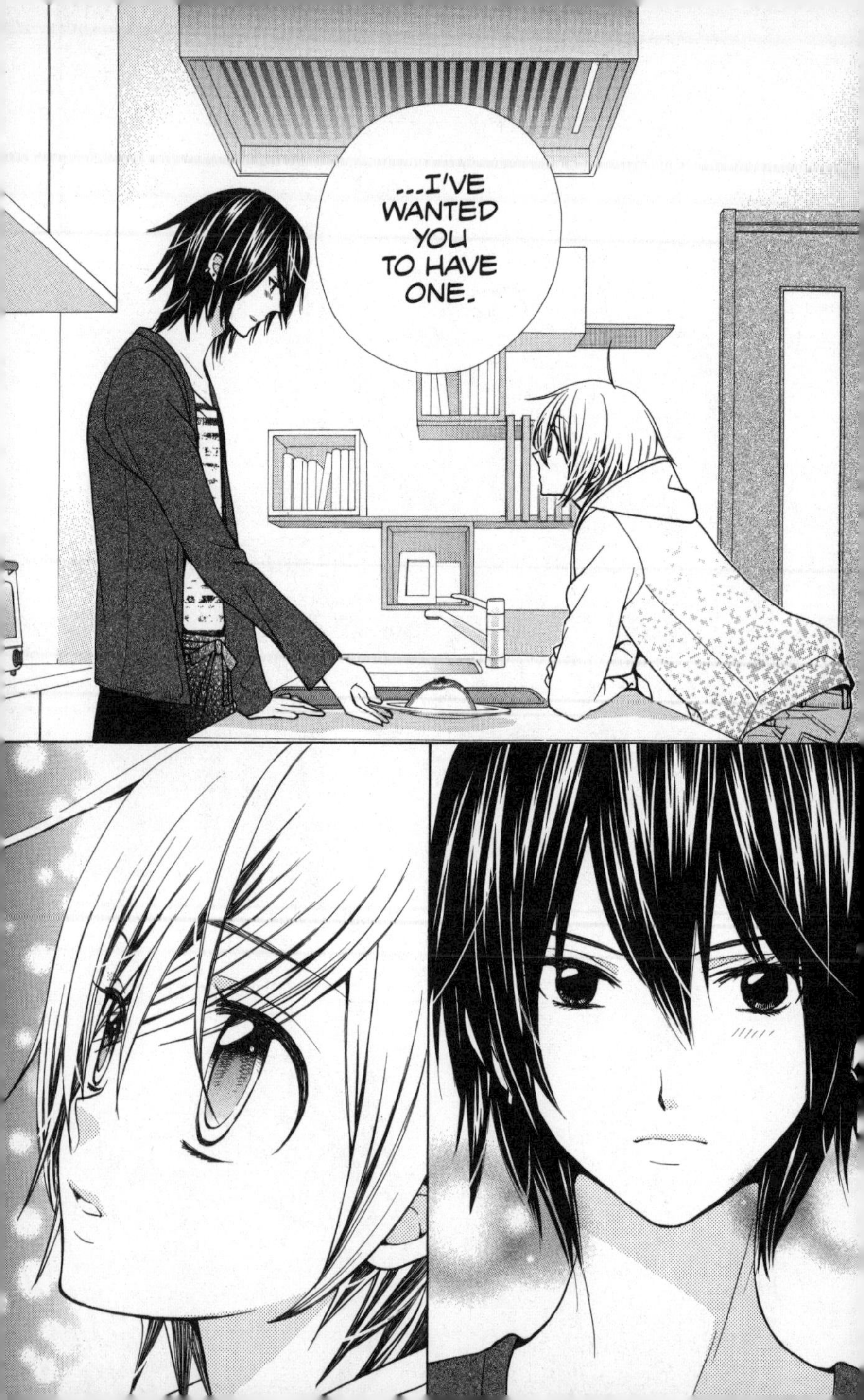
...I'VE WANTED YOU TO HAVE ONE.

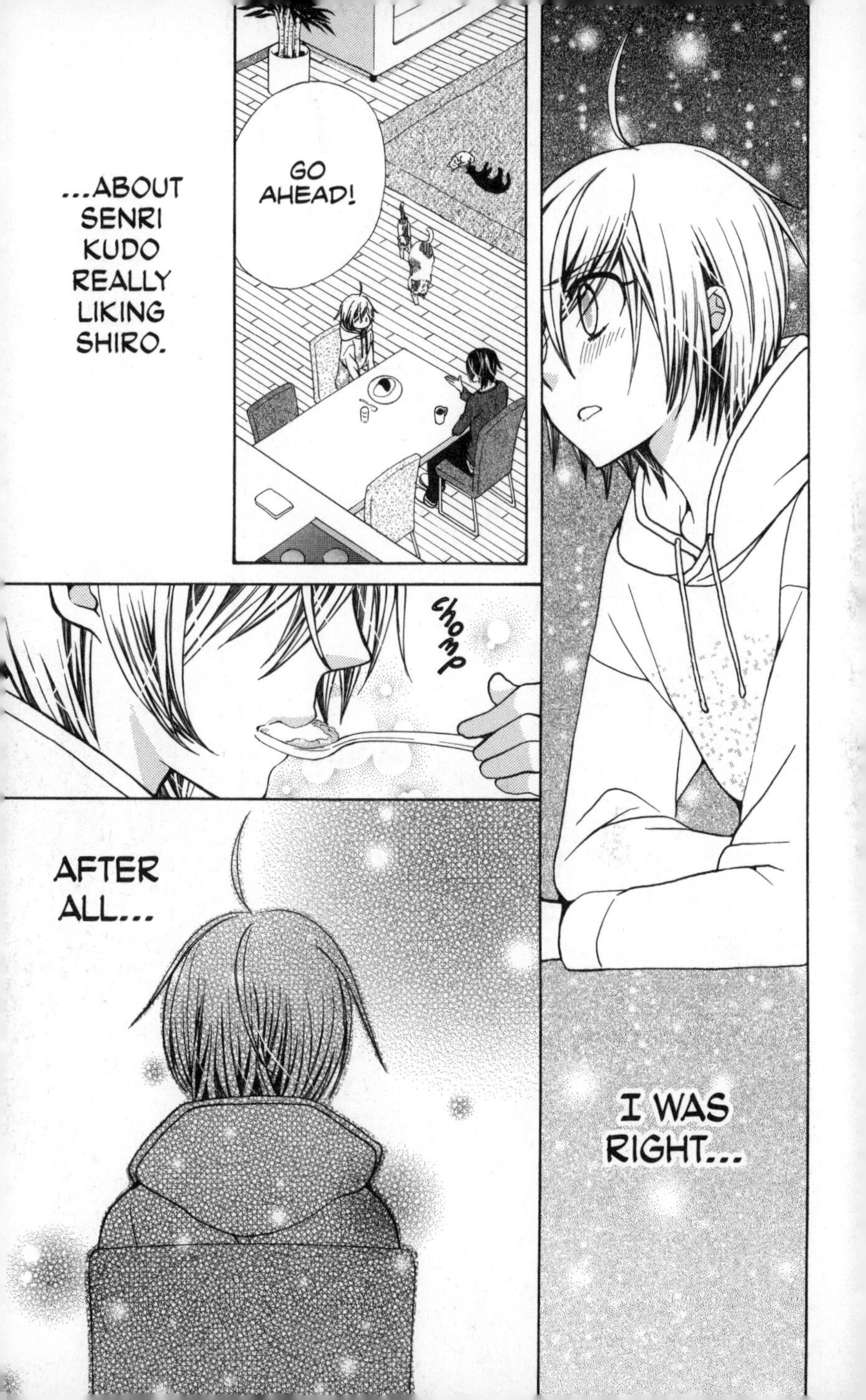
I WAS RIGHT...
GO AHEAD!
...ABOUT SENRI KUDO REALLY LIKING SHIRO.
chomp
AFTER ALL...

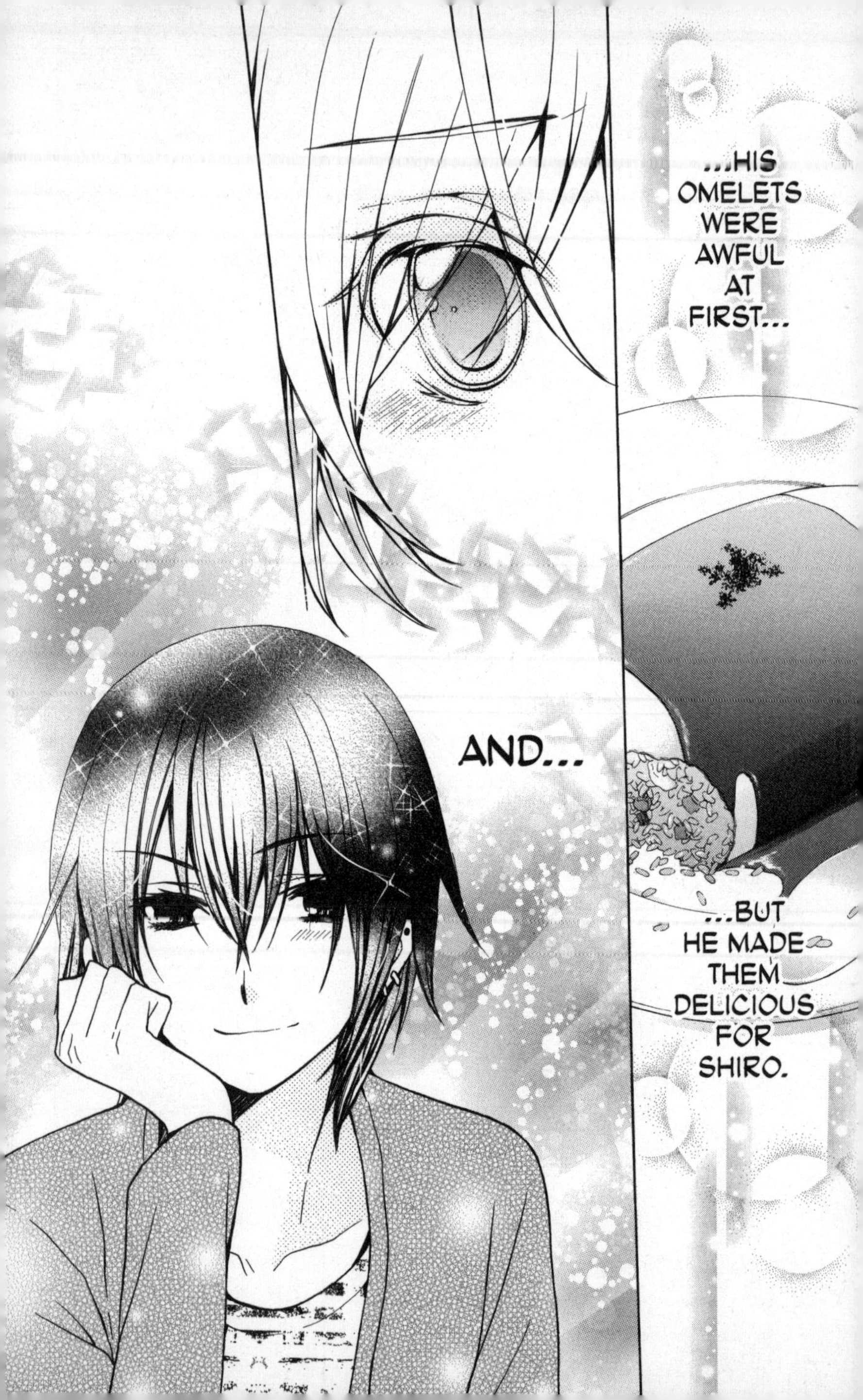
...HIS OMELETS WERE AWFUL AT FIRST...
...BUT HE MADE THEM DELICIOUS FOR SHIRO.
AND...

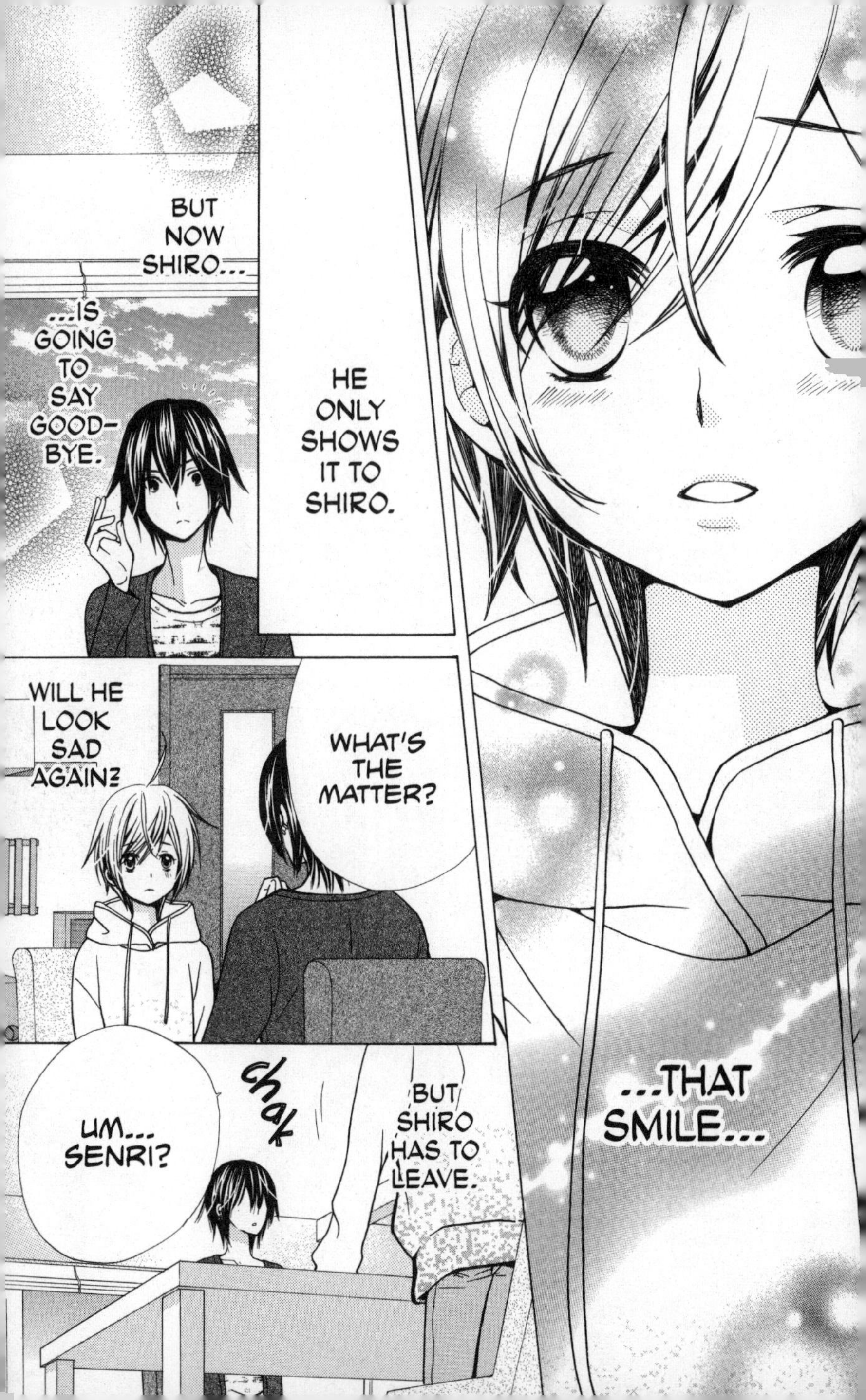
...THAT SMILE...
HE ONLY SHOWS IT TO SHIRO.
BUT NOW SHIRO...
...IS GOING TO SAY GOOD-BYE.
WHAT'S THE MATTER?
WILL HE LOOK SAD AGAIN?
BUT SHIRO HAS TO LEAVE.
chak
UM... SENRI?

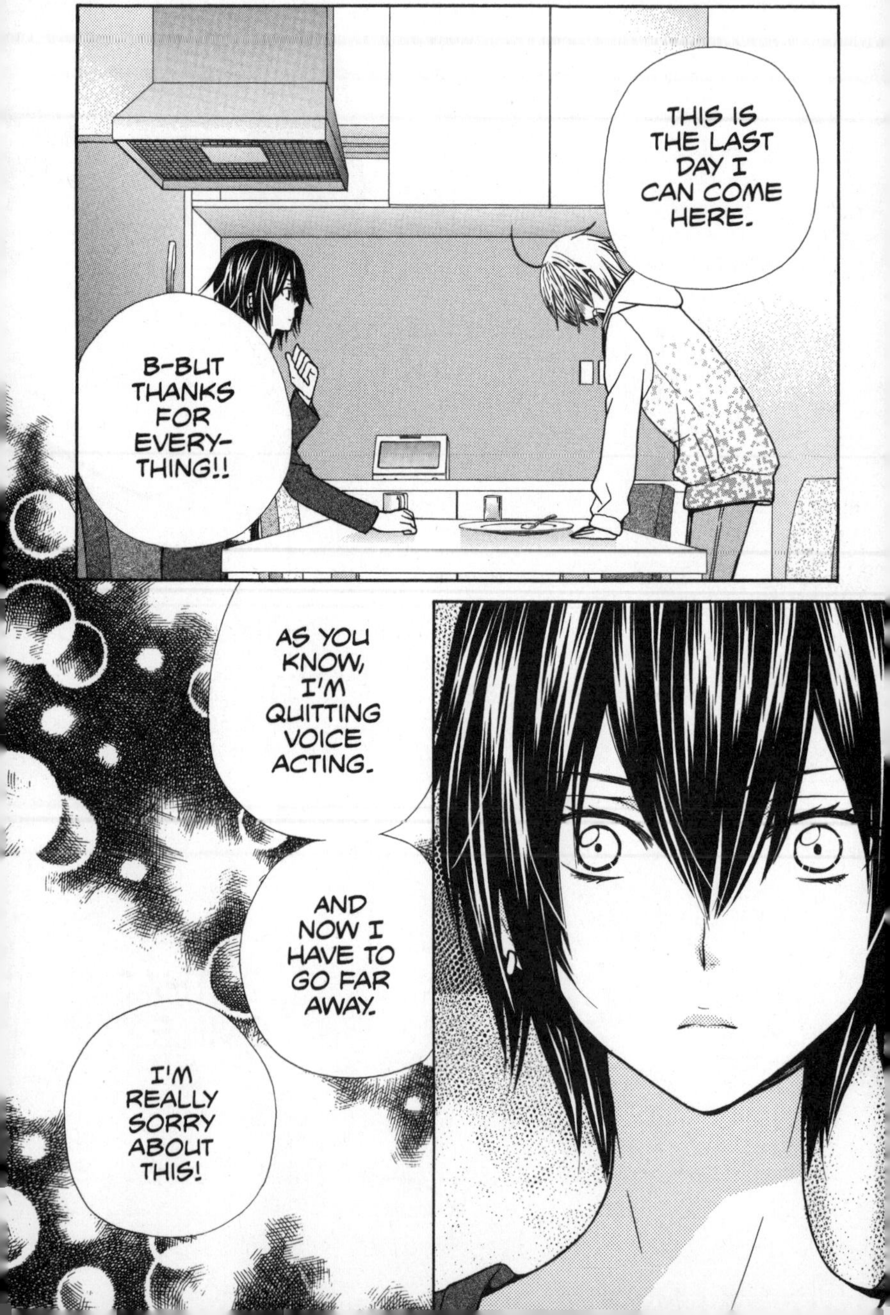
THIS IS THE LAST DAY I CAN COME HERE.
B-BUT THANKS FOR EVERY-THING!!
AS YOU KNOW, I'M QUITTING VOICE ACTING.
AND NOW I HAVE TO GO FAR AWAY.
I'M REALLY SORRY ABOUT THIS!

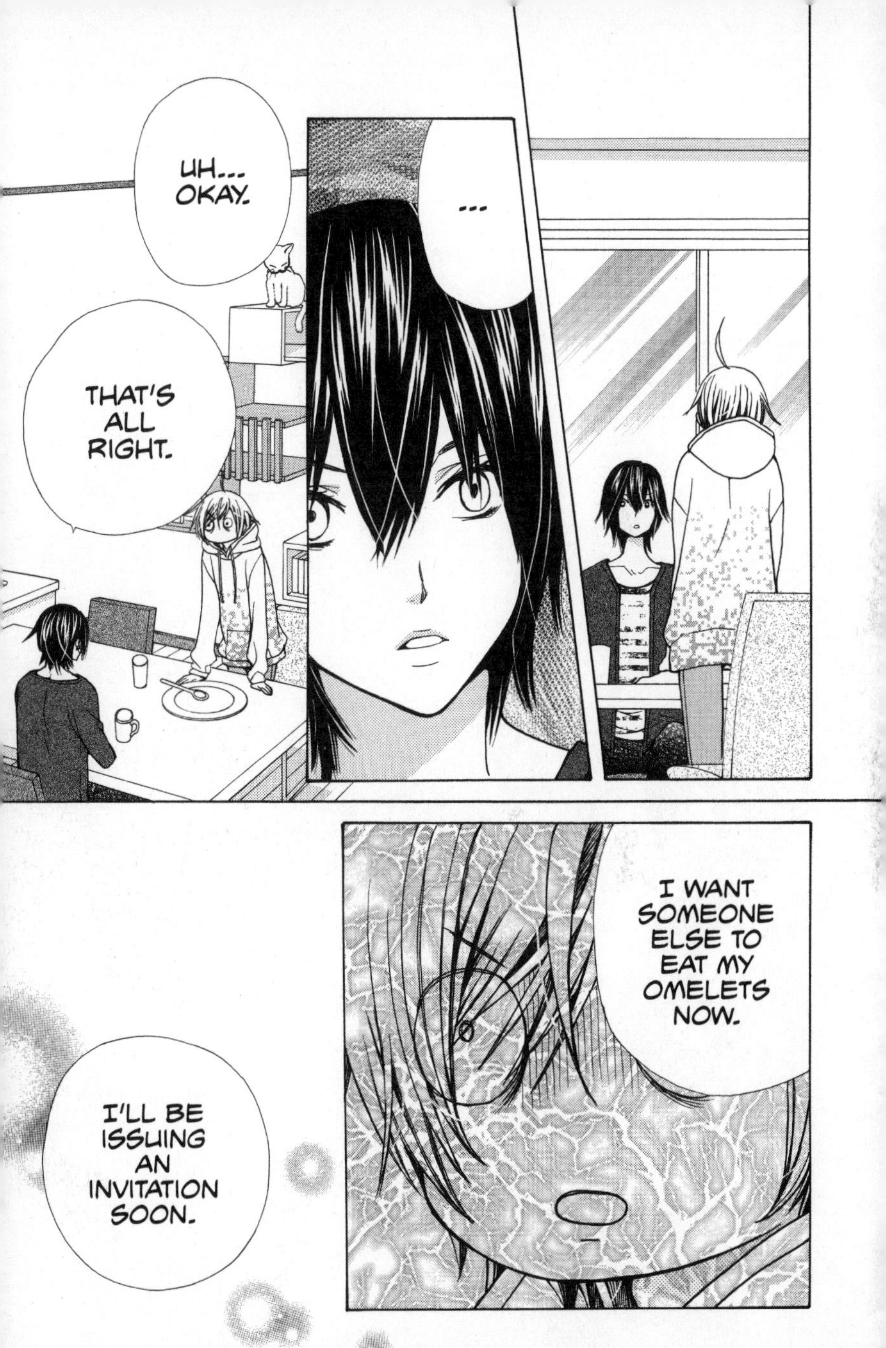
...
UH... OKAY.
THAT'S ALL RIGHT.
I WANT SOMEONE ELSE TO EAT MY OMELETS NOW.
I'LL BE ISSUING AN INVITATION SOON.

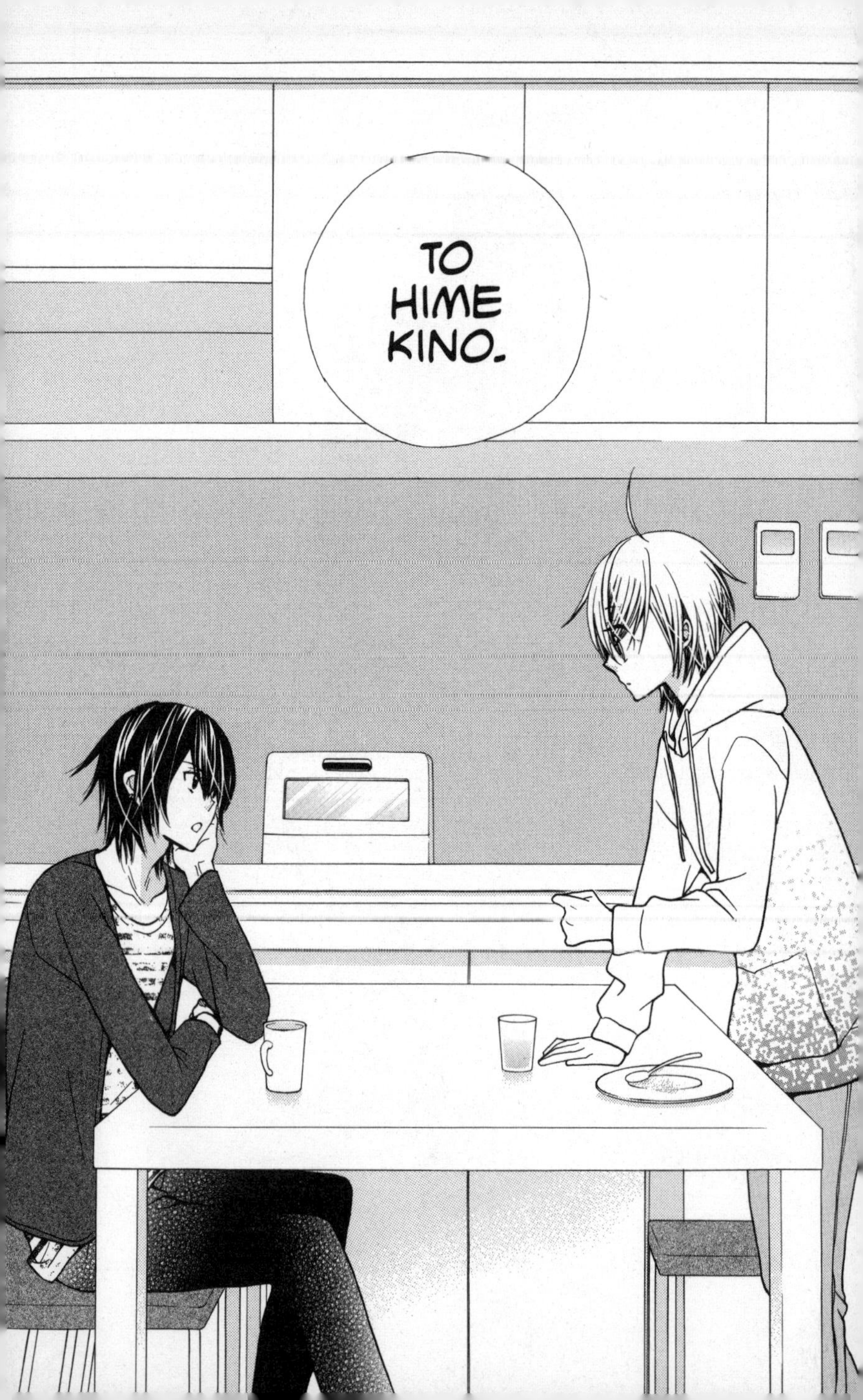
TO HIME KINO.

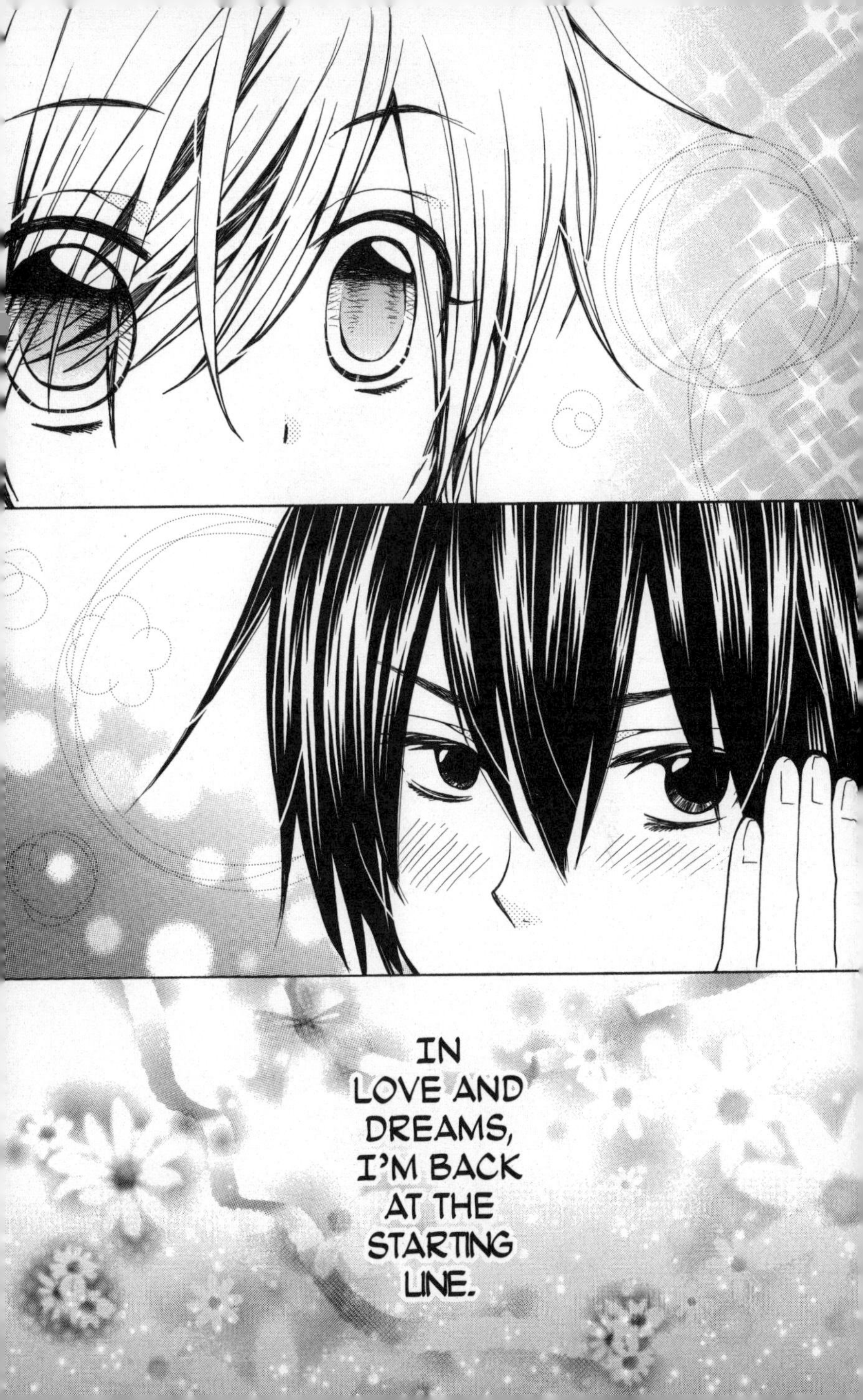
IN LOVE AND DREAMS, I'M BACK AT THE STARTING LINE.

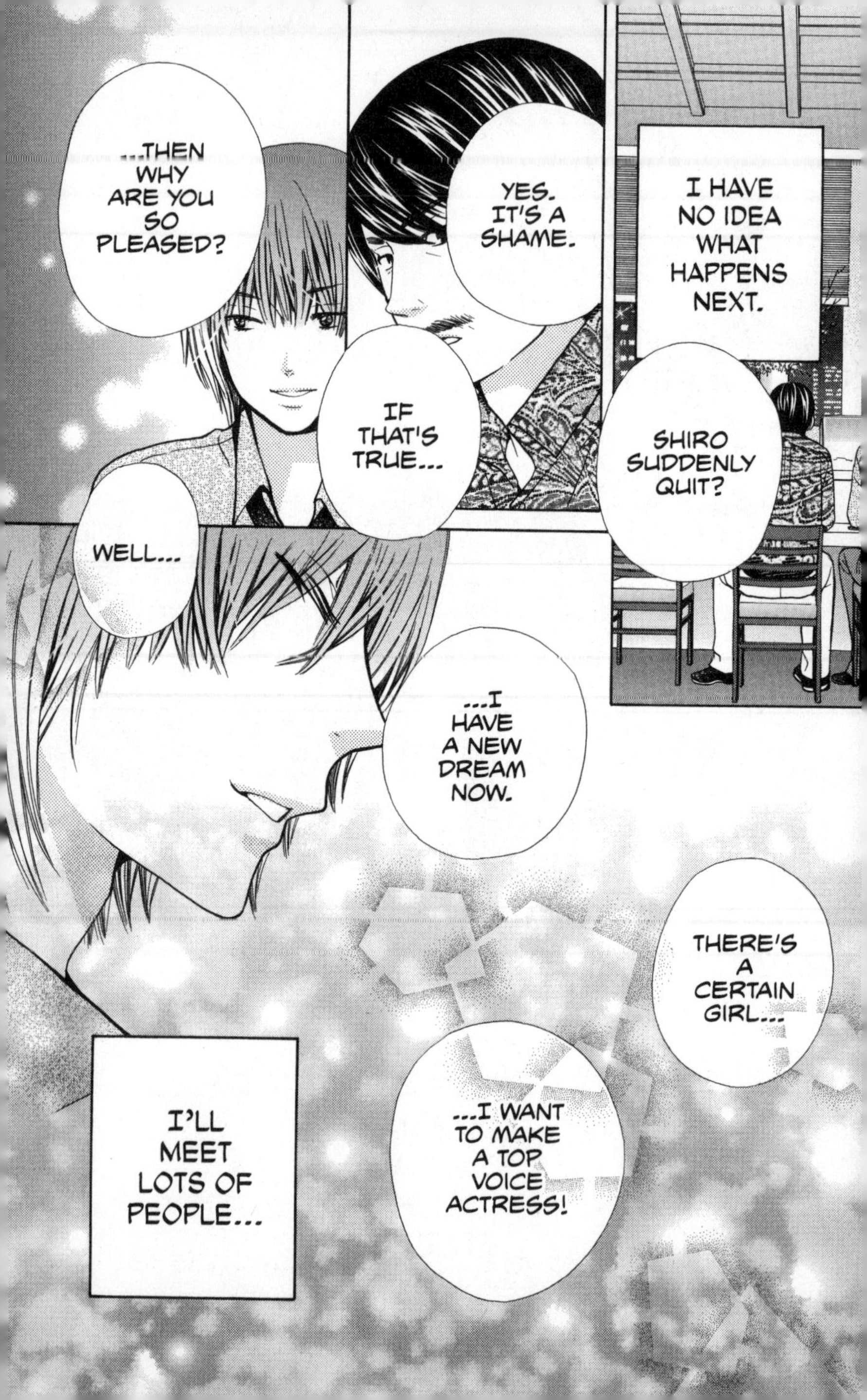

I HAVE NO IDEA WHAT HAPPENS NEXT.
SHIRO SUDDENLY QUIT?
YES. IT'S A SHAME.
IF THAT'S TRUE...
...THEN WHY ARE YOU SO PLEASED?
WELL...
...I HAVE A NEW DREAM NOW.
THERE'S A CERTAIN GIRL...
...I WANT TO MAKE A TOP VOICE ACTRESS!
I'LL MEET LOTS OF PEOPLE...

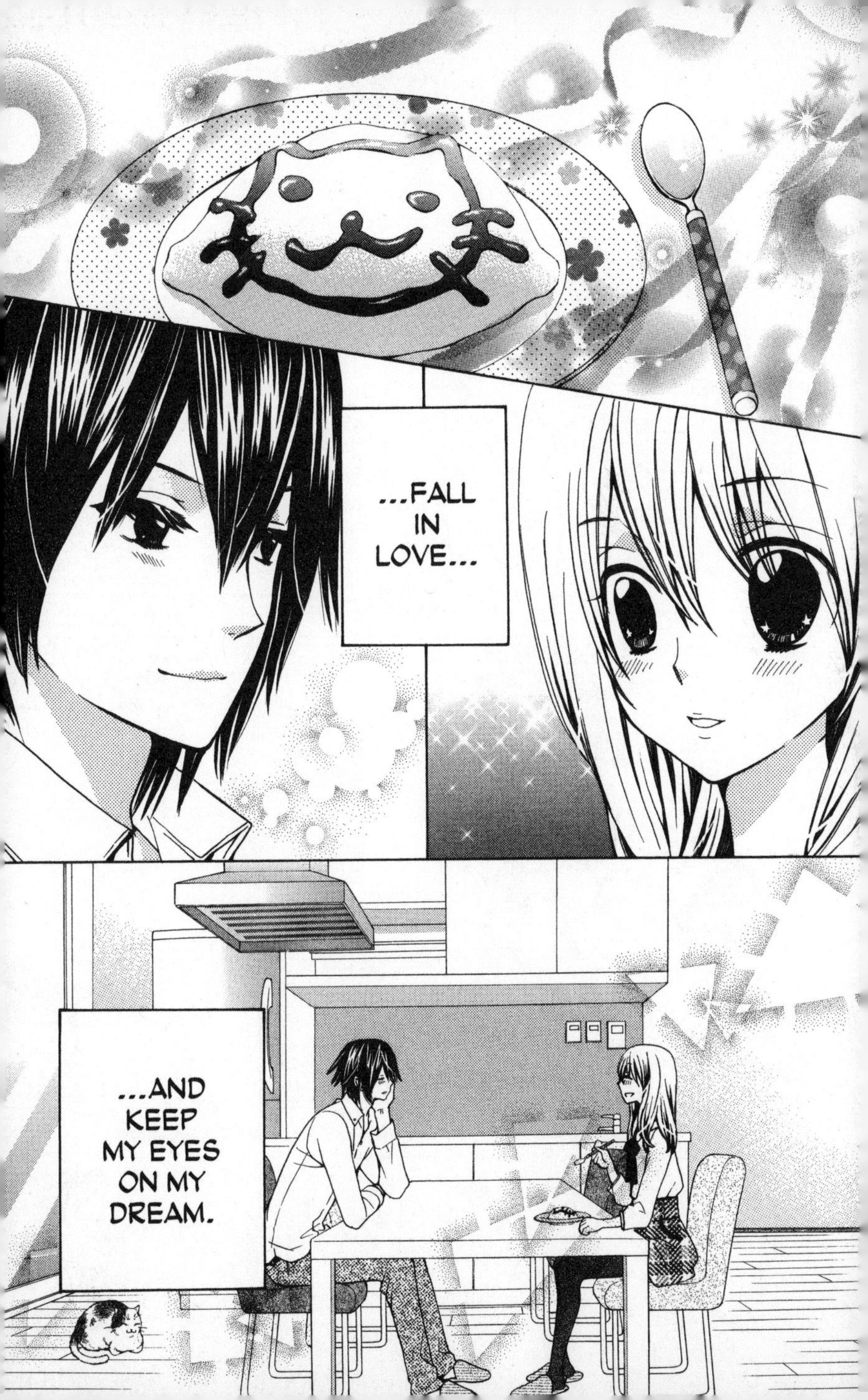
...FALL IN LOVE...
...AND KEEP MY EYES ON MY DREAM.

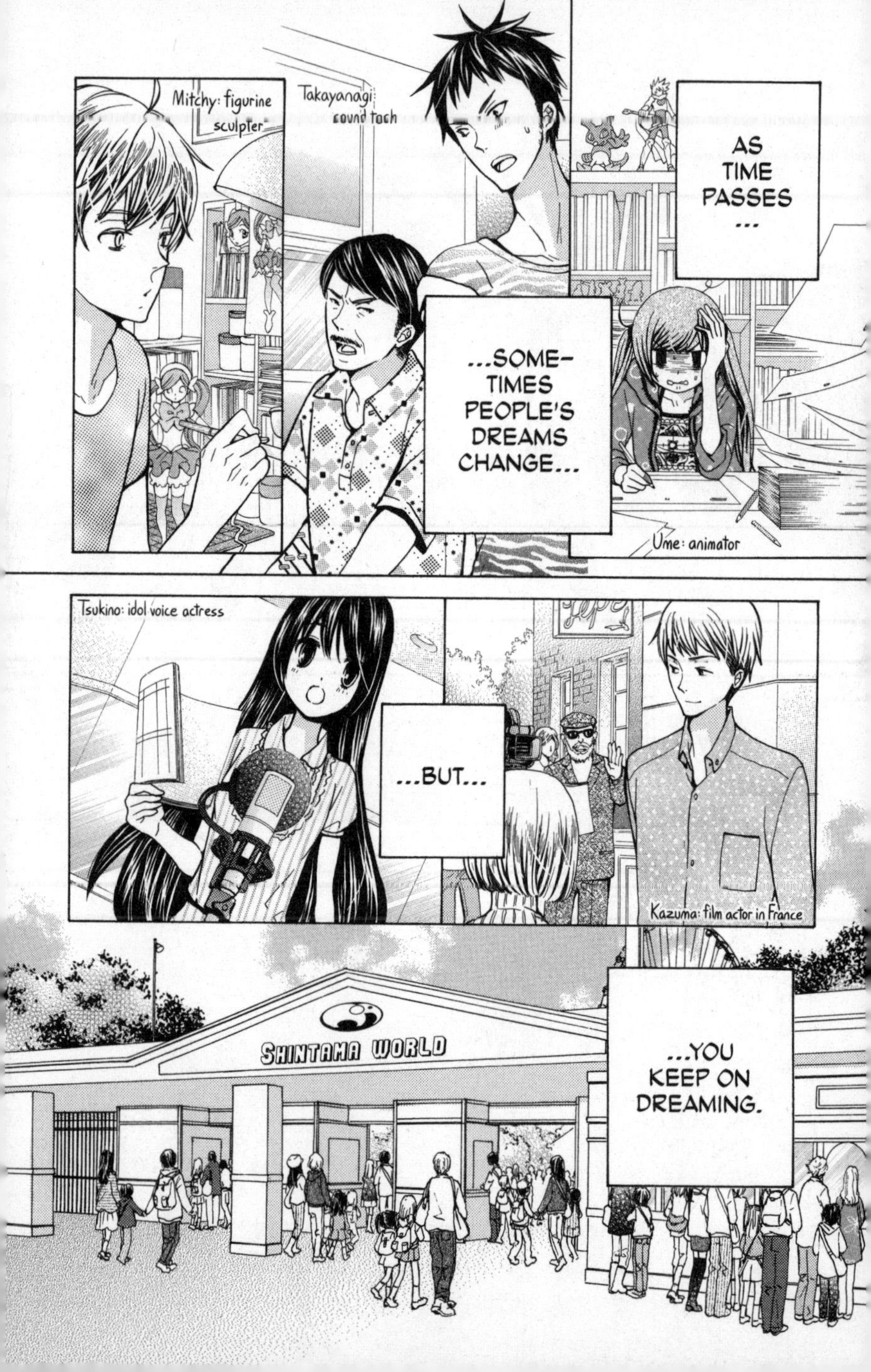
AS TIME PASSES...
Ume: animator
Takayanagi: sound tech
...SOME-TIMES PEOPLE'S DREAMS CHANGE...
Mitchy: figurine sculpter
Kazuma: film actor in France
...BUT...
Tsukino: idol voice actress
SHINTAMA WORLD
...YOU KEEP ON DREAMING.

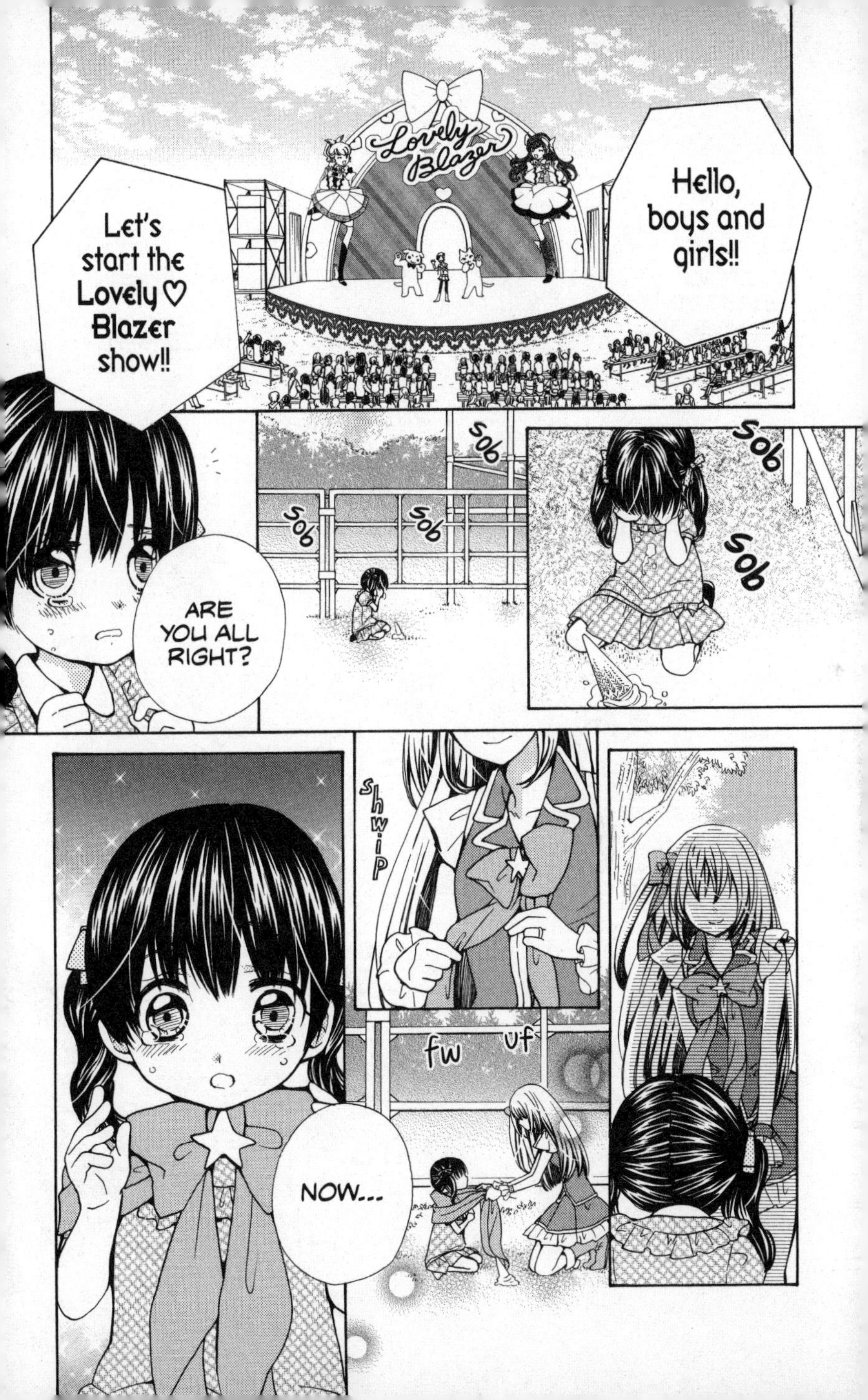
Lovely Blazer
Hello, boys and girls!!
Let's start the Lovely ♡ Blazer show!!
sob
sob
sob
sob
sob
ARE YOU ALL RIGHT?
shwip
fw uf
NOW...

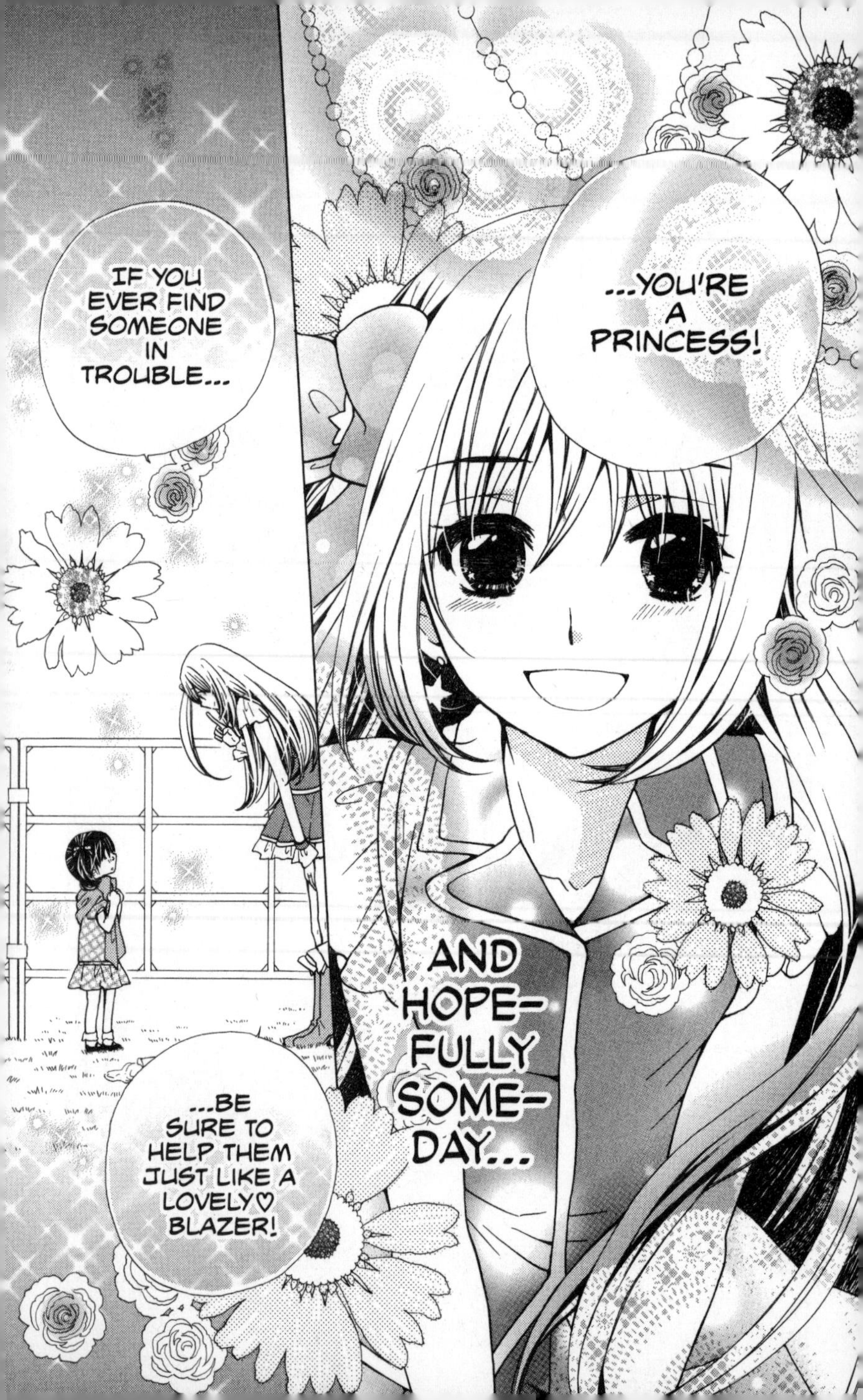
IF YOU EVER FIND SOMEONE IN TROUBLE...
...BE SURE TO HELP THEM JUST LIKE A LOVELY♡ BLAZER!
AND HOPE-FULLY SOME-DAY...
...YOU'RE A PRINCESS!

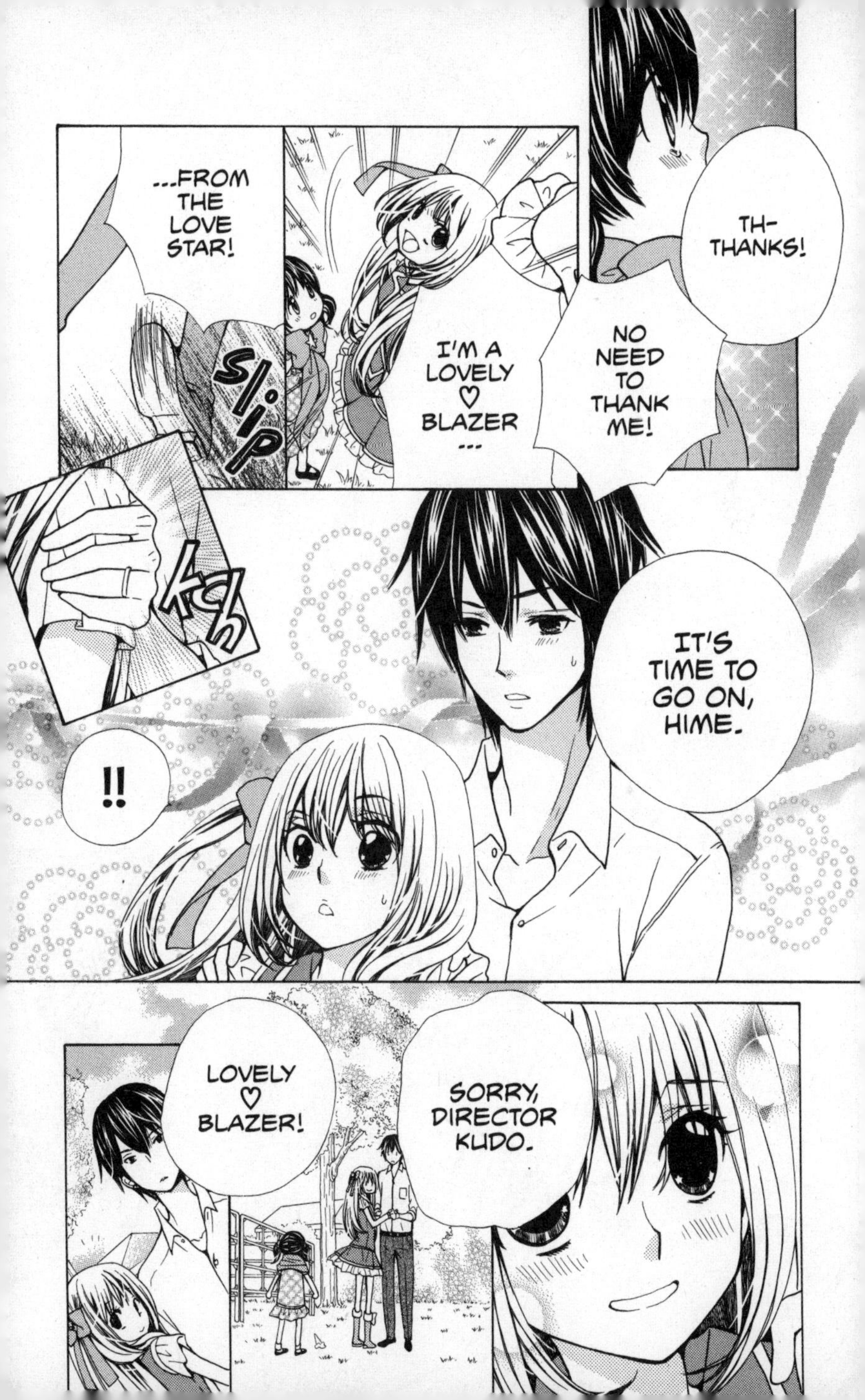
TH- THANKS!
NO NEED TO THANK ME!
I'M A LOVELY ♡ BLAZER ...
...FROM THE LOVE STAR!
slip
IT'S TIME TO GO ON, HIME.
kch
!!
SORRY, DIRECTOR KUDO.
LOVELY ♡ BLAZER!

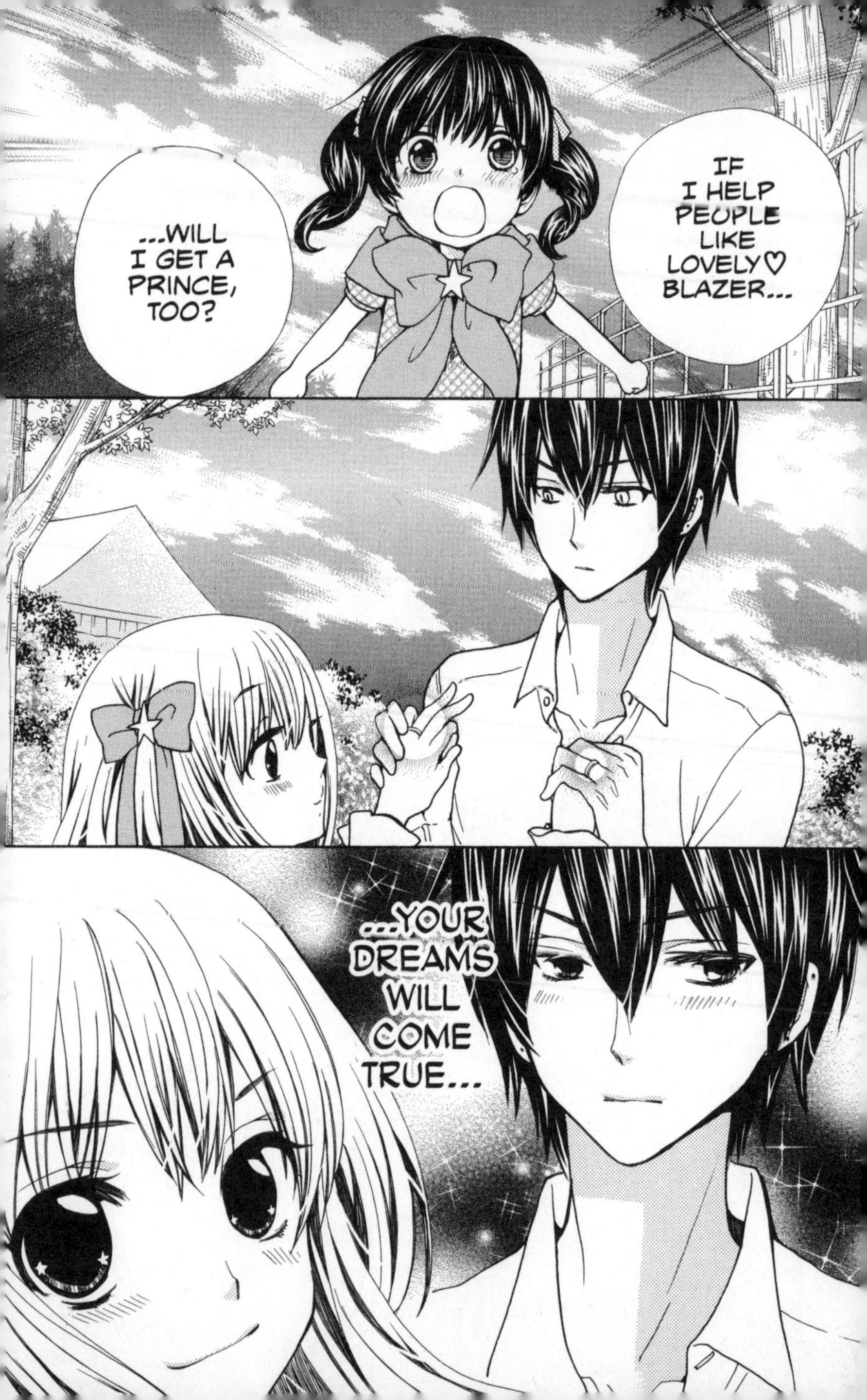
IF I HELP PEOPLE LIKE LOVELY♡ BLAZER...
...WILL I GET A PRINCE, TOO?
...YOUR DREAMS WILL COME TRUE...

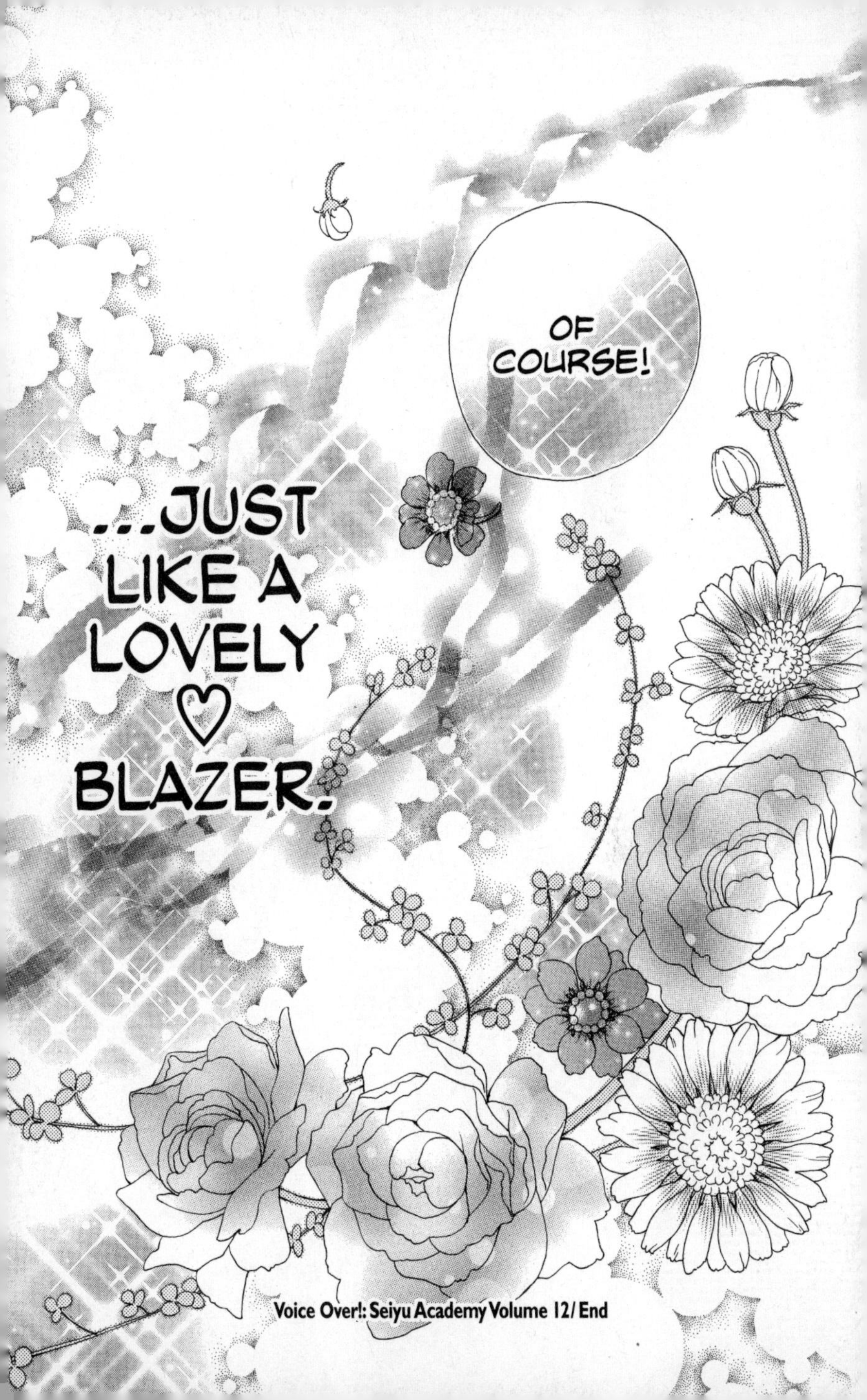
OF COURSE!
...JUST LIKE A LOVELY ♡ BLAZER.
Voice Over!: Seiyu Academy Volume 12/ End

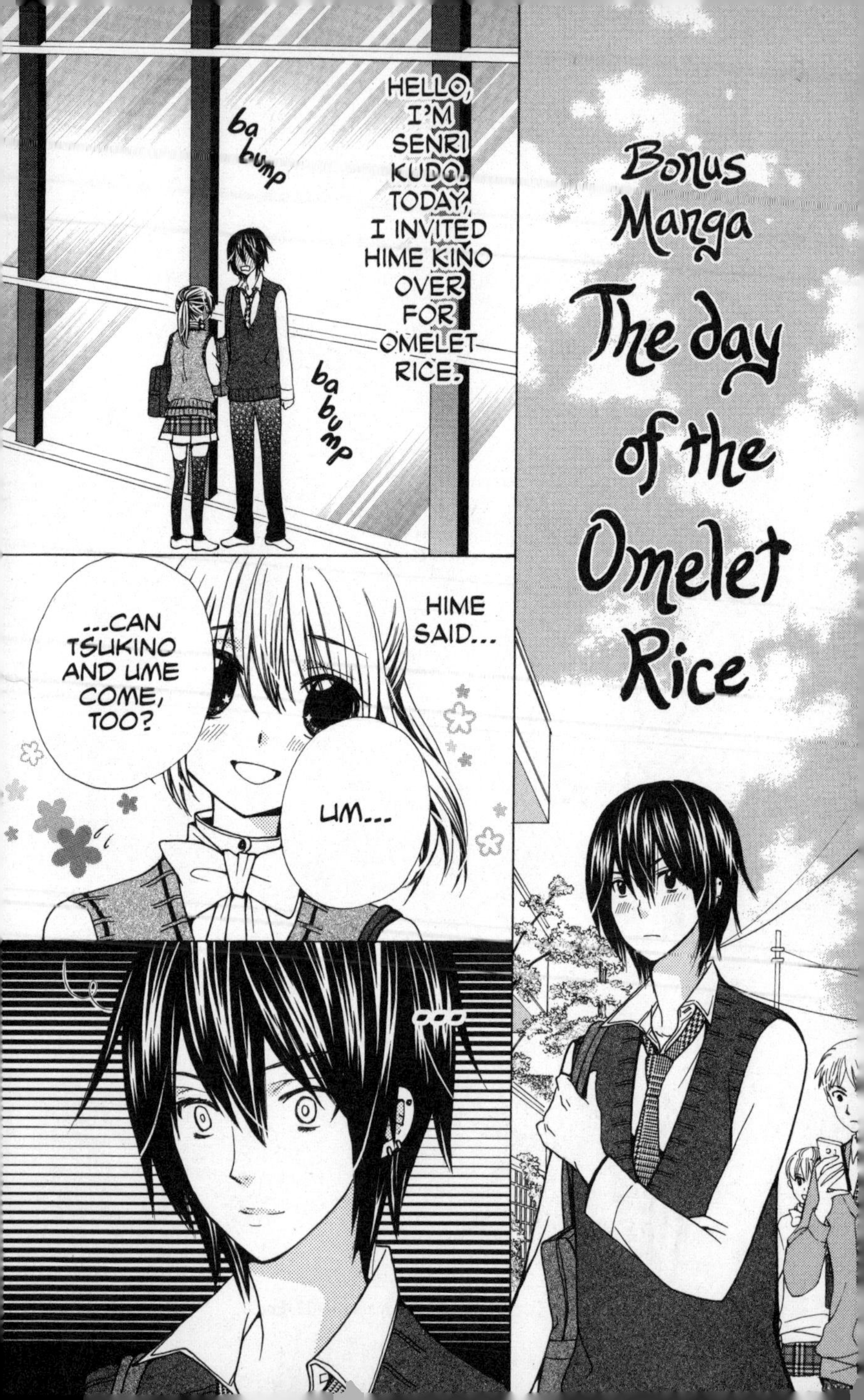
Bonus Manga
The day of the Omelet Rice
HELLO, I'M SENRI KUDO. TODAY, I INVITED HIME KINO OVER FOR OMELET RICE.
ba bump
ba bump
HIME SAID...
...CAN TSUKINO AND UME COME, TOO?
UM...
...

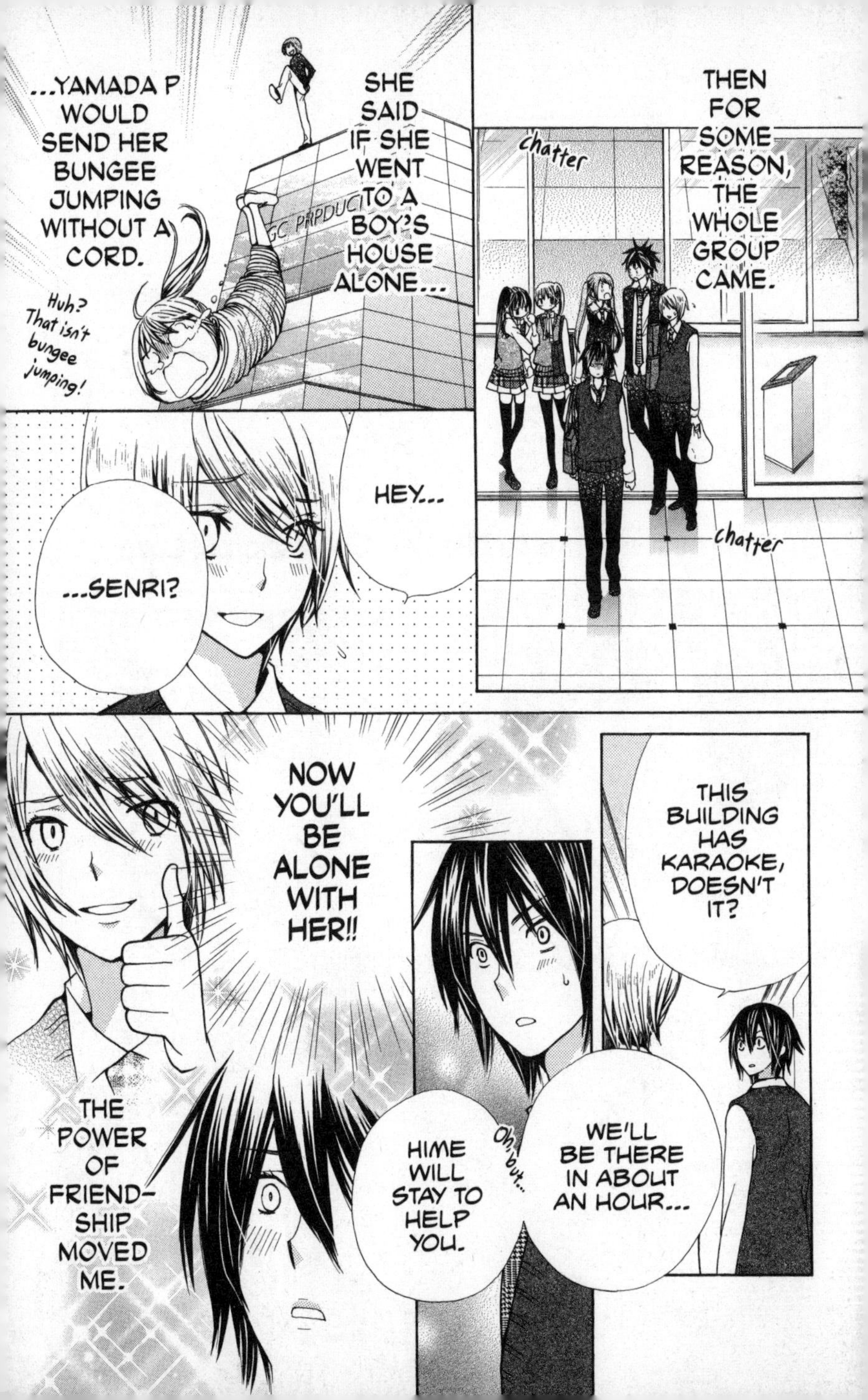
THEN FOR SOME REASON, THE WHOLE GROUP CAME.
Chatter
Chatter
SHE SAID IF SHE WENT TO A BOY'S HOUSE ALONE...
...YAMADA P WOULD SEND HER BUNGEE JUMPING WITHOUT A CORD.
Huh? That isn't bungee jumping!
HEY...
...SENRI?
THIS BUILDING HAS KARAOKE, DOESN'T IT?
WE'LL BE THERE IN ABOUT AN HOUR...
Oh, but...
HIME WILL STAY TO HELP YOU.
NOW YOU'LL BE ALONE WITH HER!!
THE POWER OF FRIEND-SHIP MOVED ME.

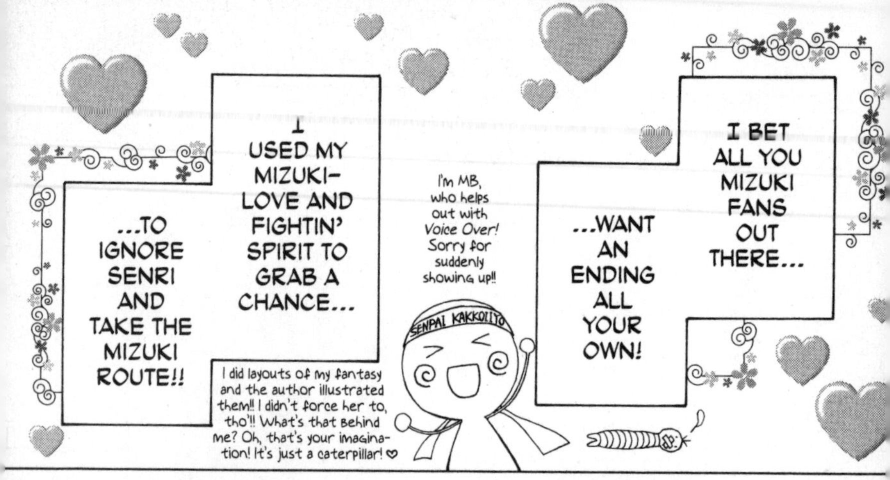
I BET ALL YOU MIZUKI FANS OUT THERE...
...WANT AN ENDING ALL YOUR OWN!
I'm MB, who helps out with Voice Over! Sorry for suddenly showing up!!
SENPAI KAKKOIIYO
I USED MY MIZUKI-LOVE AND FIGHTIN' SPIRIT TO GRAB A CHANCE...
...TO IGNORE SENRI AND TAKE THE MIZUKI ROUTE!!
I did layouts of my fantasy and the author illustrated them!! I didn't force her to, tho'!! What's that behind me? Oh, that's your imagination! It's just a caterpillar! ♡

Hime Responds to Mizuki's Confession of Love

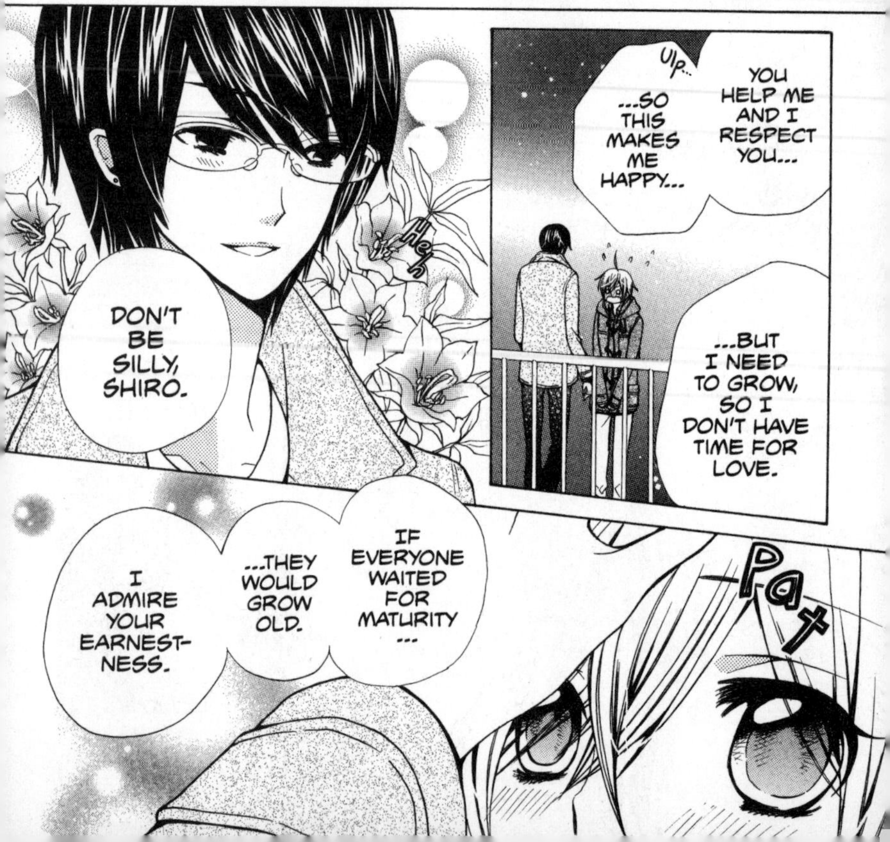
Ulp...
YOU HELP ME AND I RESPECT YOU...
...SO THIS MAKES ME HAPPY...
...BUT I NEED TO GROW, SO I DON'T HAVE TIME FOR LOVE.
Heh
DON'T BE SILLY, SHIRO.
Pat
IF EVERYONE WAITED FOR MATURITY...
...THEY WOULD GROW OLD.
I ADMIRE YOUR EARNESTNESS.

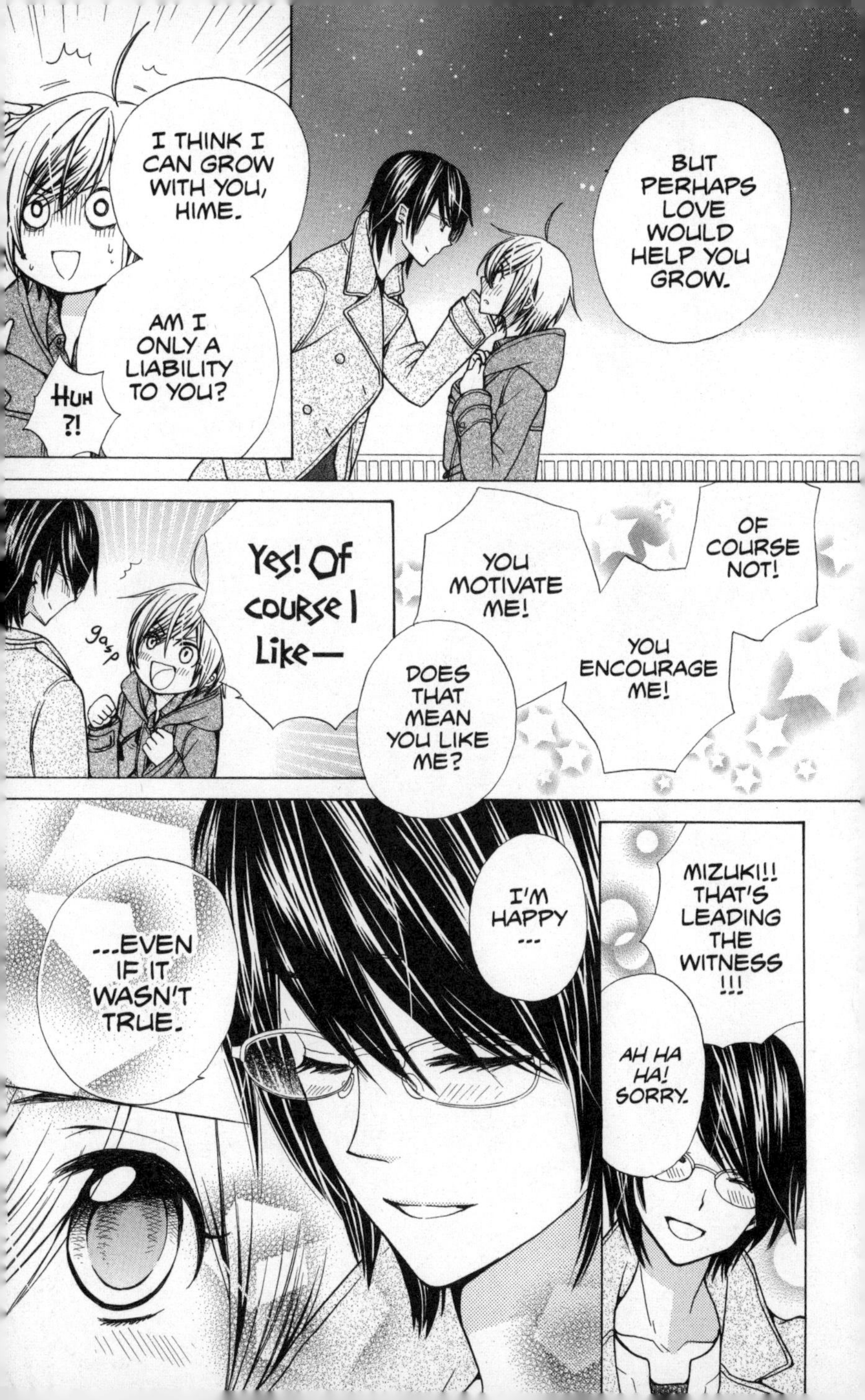
BUT PERHAPS LOVE WOULD HELP YOU GROW.
I THINK I CAN GROW WITH YOU, HIME.
AM I ONLY A LIABILITY TO YOU?
HUH ?!
OF COURSE NOT!
YOU MOTIVATE ME!
YOU ENCOURAGE ME!
DOES THAT MEAN YOU LIKE ME?
Yes! Of course I Like—
gasp
MIZUKI!!! THAT'S LEADING THE WITNESS !!!
AH HA HA! SORRY.
I'M HAPPY ...
...EVEN IF IT WASN'T TRUE.

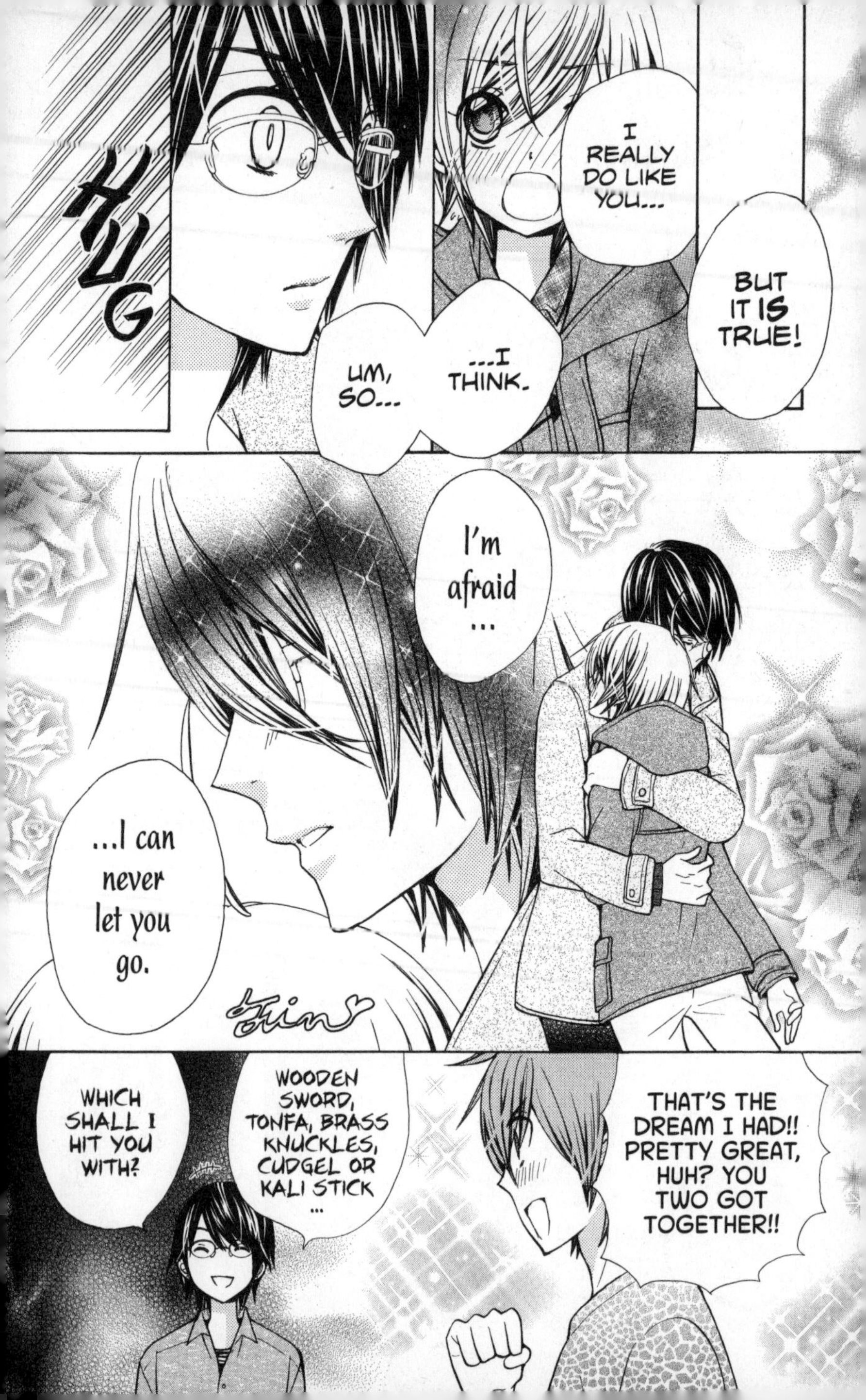
I REALLY DO LIKE YOU...
BUT IT IS TRUE!
...I THINK.
UM, SO...
HUG
I'm afraid...
...I can never let you go.
THAT'S THE DREAM I HAD!! PRETTY GREAT, HUH? YOU TWO GOT TOGETHER!!
WOODEN SWORD, TONFA, BRASS KNUCKLES, CUDGEL OR KALI STICK ...
WHICH SHALL I HIT YOU WITH?

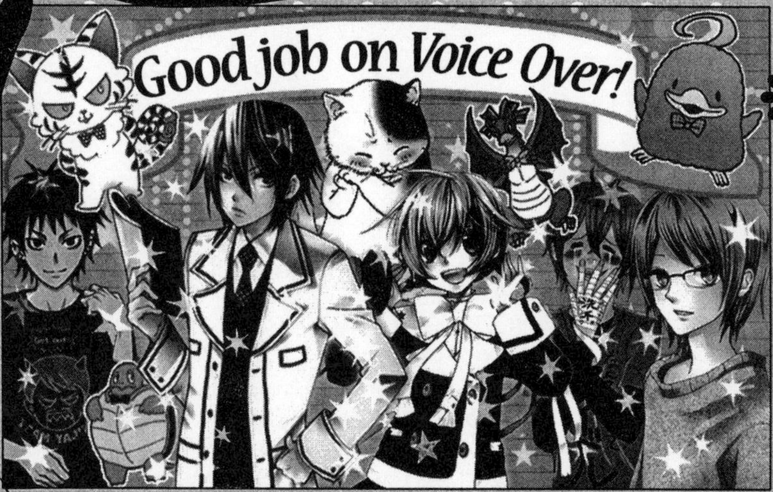
Good job on Voice Over!

↑ My assistants sent me this illustration while working on the end of *Voice Over!* I was so happy!! Thank you!!

Thank you for reading *Voice Over!* all this way!!!

- How was the bonus manga? MB-chan, who always helps me with stories about Mizuki, drew the thumbnails!! But then I added the concluding joke and ruined it...
- I really do owe it to everyone's help that I was able to continue all the way through 12 volumes. Thank you so very much!! I had a great time working on it!
- And now, much heartfelt thanks to everyone who read this far, everyone who helped with research, everyone who worked on the graphic novel, my editor, everyone who helped with composition, all my assistants, my friends and my family!!

♡ If you feel like it, lemme hear your thoughts! ♡

Maki Minami c/o Shojo Beat P.O. Box 77010
San Francisco, CA 94107

I wanna know what was wrong with me!

← What MB-chan had Mizuki say above.

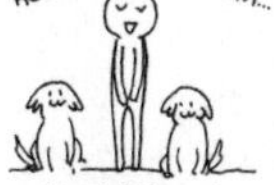
From the bottom...
...of my heart!

Maki Minami
南マキ

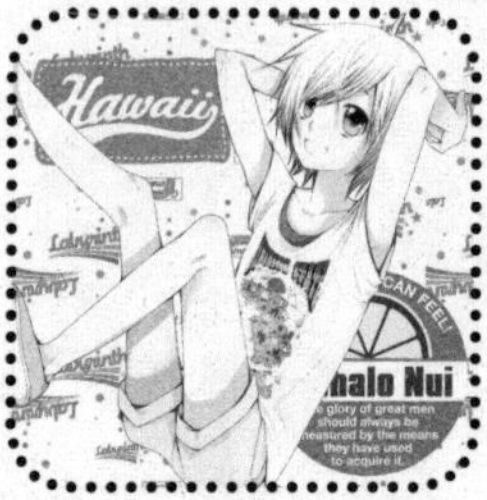
Hawaii

Maki Minami is from Saitama Prefecture in Japan. She debuted in 2001 with *Kanata no Ao* (Faraway Blue). Her other works include *Kimi wa Girlfriend* (You're My Girlfriend), *Mainichi ga Takaramono* (Every Day Is a Treasure), *Yuki Atataka* (Warm Winter) and *S•A*, which was published in English by VIZ Media.

VOICE OVER!
SEIYU ACADEMY
VOL. 12
Shojo Beat Edition

STORY AND ART BY
MAKI MINAMI

Special Thanks
81produce
Tokyo Animator College
Tokyo Animation College

English Translation & Adaptation/John Werry
Touch-up Art & Lettering/Sabrina Heep
Design/Yukiko Whitley
Editor/Pancha Diaz

SEIYU KA! by Maki Minami
© Maki Minami 2013
All rights reserved.
First published in Japan in 2013 by HAKUSENSHA, Inc., Tokyo.
English language translation rights arranged with
HAKUSENSHA, Inc., Tokyo.

Printed in the U.S.A.

Published by VIZ Media, LLC
P.O. Box 77010
San Francisco, CA 94107

10 9 8 7 6 5 4 3 2 1
First printing, August 2015

www.viz.com   www.shojobeat.com

Kyoko Mogami followed her true love Sho to Tokyo to support him while he made it big as an idol.
But he's casting her out now that he's famous enough! Kyoko won't suffer in silence—
she's going to get her sweet revenge by beating Sho in show biz!

Vol. 1 ISBN: 978-1-4215-4226-3

Vol. 2 ISBN: 978-1-4215-4227-0

Vol. 3 ISBN: 978-1-4215-4228-7

Only
$14.99
for each volume!
($16.99 in Canada)

Show biz is sweet...but revenge is sweeter!

Skip·Beat!

Story and Art by YOSHIKI NAKAMURA

In Stores Now!

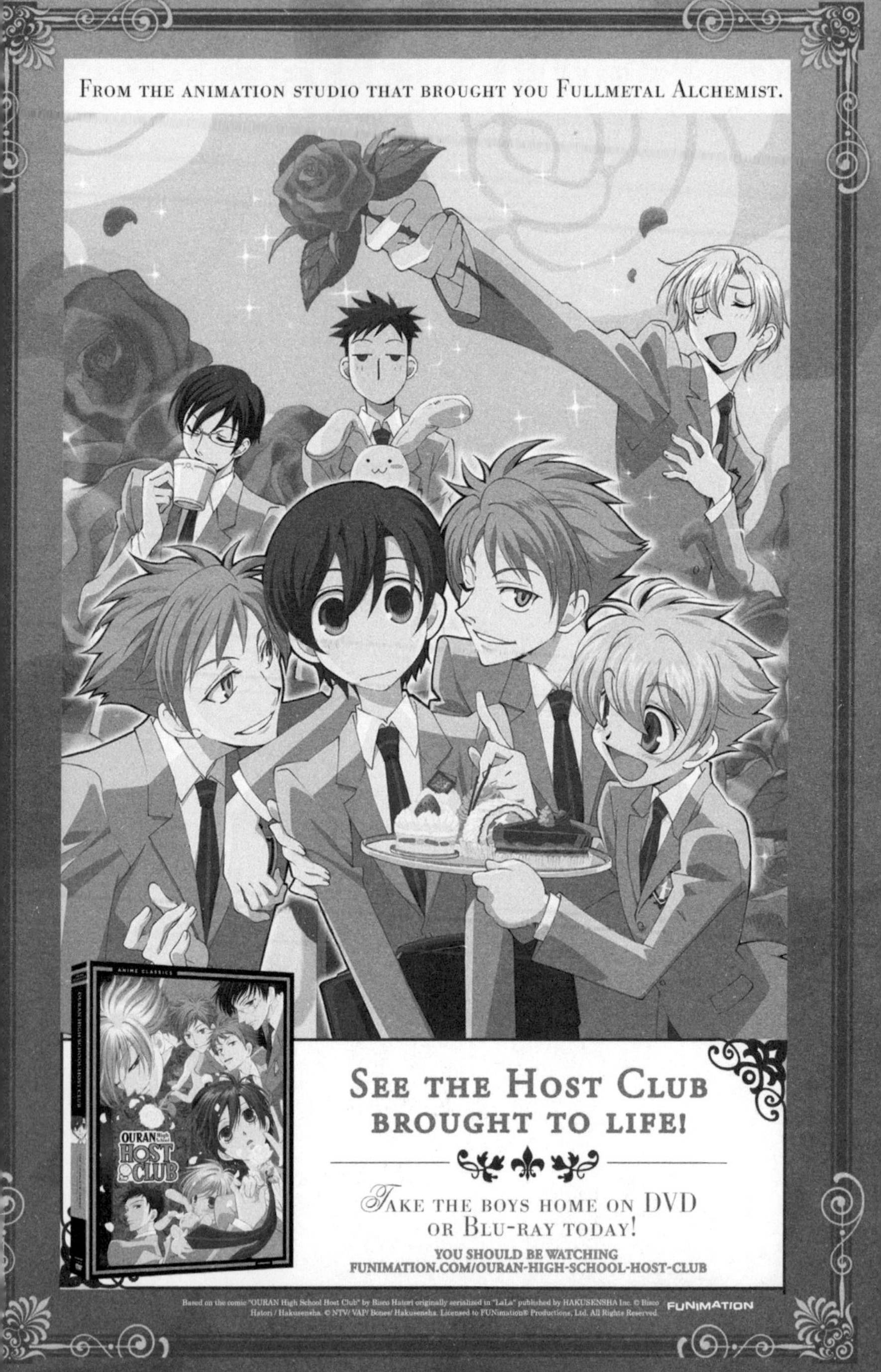
FROM THE ANIMATION STUDIO THAT BROUGHT YOU FULLMETAL ALCHEMIST.
SEE THE HOST CLUB
BROUGHT TO LIFE!
TAKE THE BOYS HOME ON DVD
OR BLU-RAY TODAY!
YOU SHOULD BE WATCHING
FUNIMATION.COM/OURAN-HIGH-SCHOOL-HOST-CLUB
Based on the comic "OURAN High School Host Club" by Bisco Hatori originally serialized in "LaLa" published by HAKUSENSHA Inc. © Bisco Hatori / Hakusensha. © NTV/ VAP/ Bones/ Hakusensha. Licensed to FUNimation® Productions, Ltd. All Rights Reserved.
FUNIMATION

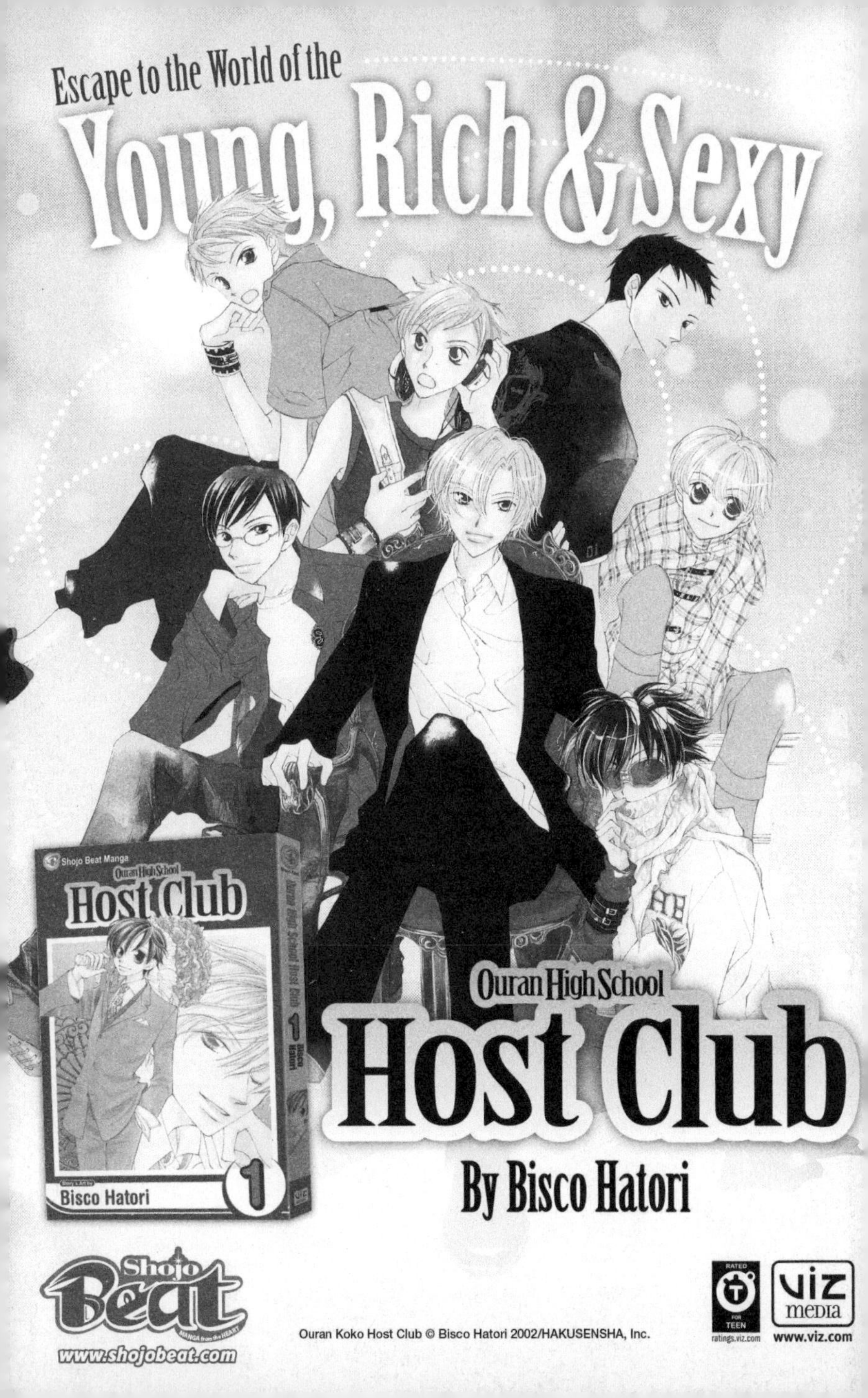

Escape to the World of the
Young, Rich & Sexy
Shojo Beat Manga
Ouran High School
Host Club
1
Bisco Hatori
Ouran High School
Host Club
By Bisco Hatori
Shojo Beat
www.shojobeat.com
Ouran Koko Host Club © Bisco Hatori 2002/HAKUSENSHA, Inc.
RATED
T
FOR TEEN
ratings.viz.com
VIZ media
www.viz.com

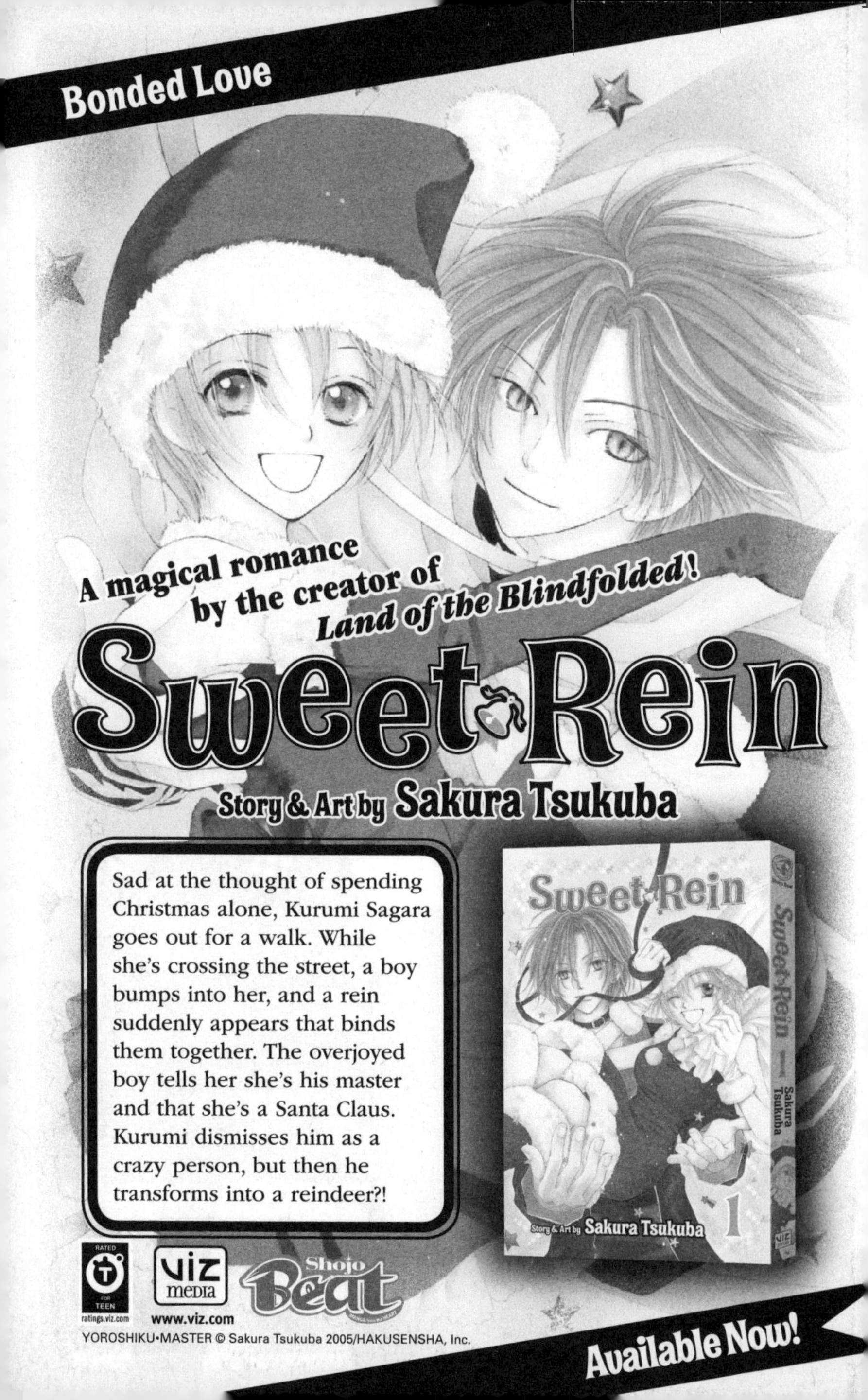
Bonded Love
A magical romance by the creator of Land of the Blindfolded!
Sweet Rein
Story & Art by Sakura Tsukuba
Sad at the thought of spending Christmas alone, Kurumi Sagara goes out for a walk. While she's crossing the street, a boy bumps into her, and a rein suddenly appears that binds them together. The overjoyed boy tells her she's his master and that she's a Santa Claus. Kurumi dismisses him as a crazy person, but then he transforms into a reindeer?!
Sweet Rein
Sweet Rein 1 Sakura Tsukuba
Story & Art by Sakura Tsukuba 1
RATED T FOR TEEN
ratings.viz.com
viz media
Shojo Beat
www.viz.com
YOROSHIKU•MASTER © Sakura Tsukuba 2005/HAKUSENSHA, Inc.
Available Now!

This is the last page.

In keeping with the original Japanese comic format, this book reads from right to left—so action, sound effects, and word balloons are completely reversed. This preserves the orientation of the original artwork—plus, it's fun! Check out the diagram shown here to get the hang of things, and then turn to the other side of the book to get started!

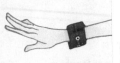

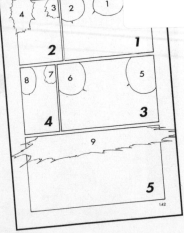